Confetti of Thoughts on Library & Information Studies

Essays in Honour of Prof. (Dr.) C. V. Rajan Pillai

Prof. (Dr.) C.V. Rajan Pillai

Family of Dr. C.V.R

tting : Dr. Rajan Pillai, Rajat (grandson), R. Sreekumari Amma (wife) , Sreyas (grandson)
Standing : Remya (daughter in law), Sreejesh (son), Rajesh (son), Raji (daughter in law)

Confetti of Thoughts on Library & Information Studies

Essays in Honour of Prof. (Dr.) C. V. Rajan Pillai

Edited by

S Humayoon Kabir

K G Sudhier

Worldwide Circulation through Authorspress Global Network
First Published 2010
by
Authorspress
E-35/103, Jawahar Park
Laxmi Nagar, Delhi-110 092
e-mail: authorspress@yahoo.com

Confetti of Thoughts on Library & Information Studies: Essays in Honour of Prof. (Dr.) C. V. Rajan Pillai

ISBN 978-81-7273-558-6

Printed in India at Tarun Offset, Delhi.

Prof. (Dr.) C.V. Rajan Pillai: Biographical Sketch

Birth: Born on 31st November 1941 in Karichal Village, Haripad, Alleppy District, Kerala. Son of the Sri. M.N. Padmanabha Pillai, (late) and Smt. L. Bhavani Amma.

Education: B.Sc.,B. Lib.Sc. (Kerala University), M.Lib.Sc. (Banaras Hindu University) and Ph.D (Kerala University).

Professional Experience: Served as Assistant, University of Kerala; Assistant Librarian, Kerala University Library, 1963-1978; Lecturer in LIS University of Kerala, 1978-1984; University Librarian CUSAT, 1984-1996; Prof and Head, DLIS Mahatma Gandhi University 1997-2005; Principal Investigator of UGC project, Modernisation of Cochin University Library; Visiting follow of U.G.C.; Research guide in LIS, University of Kerala, CUSAT and M.S. University, Tirunelveli, 5 Ph. Ds were awarded under his guidance.

Membership in Academic Bodies: Served as a member in Academic Council, Faculty of Arts, Board of Studies, Doctoral Committee of University of Kerala, Board of Studies and Doctoral Committee (Mangalore University), BoS (M.G. University, M.S University, Tirunelveli and Calicut University); Expert member in selection committees of UPSC, KPSC, and universities, Adjudicator and Chairman of Open Defense of Ph. D theses.

Publications: Authored one book, compiled two bibliographies and published 33 articles.

Membership in Professional Bodies: Life member of ILA, IASLIC, KLA, IATLIS and Editorial advisory board member of KELPRO Bulletin.

Family: Wife, Prof. R. Sreekumari Amma, Rtd. Principal, Maharaja's College, Ernakulam, Two sons: R. Rajesh and R. Sreejesh. (IT Professionals).

Prof. (Dr.) C. V. Rama Pillai
Biographical Sketch

[illegible]

Crawford Hall, Mysore-570 005
INDIA
Tel Work : +91 0821 2419666
Res : +91 0821 2419350
Fax : +91 0821 2419363
E mail : vc@uni mysore.ac.in

Prof. V G. TALAWAR
M A MLibSc Ph D
VICE CHANCELLOR

Foreword

It is my great pleasure to write Foreword to the Festschrift Volume being brought out in honour of Prof. C.V Rajan Pillai, former Professor and Head of the Department of Library and Information Science, Mahatma Gandhi University, Kottayam and Former University Librarian, Cochin University of Science and Technology.

Prof. Rajan Pillai as I know since nearly three decades, is a special personality in Library and Information science field who served in different capacities not only in Kerala University and Cochin University of Science and Technology but also in various other Universities in the country on different academic bodies. Prof. Pillai served as an expert member of selection committees of different Universities, institutions and other agencies including KPSC, Kerala and UPSC. He has authored one book and thirty-three articles and thereby strengthened information resources on library and information science. Number of students he taught, guided and nourished have blossomed today and are serving in various parts of the country and abroad. His contribution to the field of Library and Information Science as a teacher, as a librarian and as a member of various bodies is always appreciable.

Prof. Rajan Pillai richly deserves recognition for the service he has rendered for nearly four decades in the field of Library and Information Science, and I am indeed happy that a Festschrift is being brought out in his honour. This festschrift contains as many as 44 articles on different aspects of Library and Information Science, such as, bibliographic standards, metadata, ICT applications, open access and open source software, knowledge management, electronic resources and services, scientometrics, web 2.0 and so on. I am sure, this volume containing articles by well experienced senior professionals will be useful to young librarians and library and information science professionals and therefore will be a rich contribution to the body of Library and Information Science literature.

I wish good health, and long life and many more laurels to come to Prof. C.V Rajan Pillai. My best wishes are also due to family members of Prof. Rajan Pillai. I congratulate all those who have worked hard to bring out this piece of academic content.

Place: Mysore
Date : 16.01.2010

V.G. Talawar
Vice-chancellor

Preface

Prof. (Dr.) C.V. Rajan Pillai has been continuously emerging as a visionary leader in the profession of Library and Information Science for about a period of five decades. He is honoured very much in this profession by his writings, speeches and lectures. One of the goals of his research has been a better understanding of the process of Library and Information Science, creation from insight to proof. Being a good administrator, he contributed a lot to bring the library profession less hierarchical and more democratic. He advised always his students and professionals to develop a culture for respect of knowledge and scholarship. To reflect his contributions and achievements in the library field, his friends, students and colleagues suggested to publish a Festschrift Volume. It is our first and foremost duty and privilege to thank Prof. (Dr.) C.V. Rajan Pillai for accepting the suggestion to bring out this volume in his honour.

The book *Confetti of Thoughts on Library and Information Studies* presents an excellent collection of fortyfour research and expository articles on various facets of Library and Information Studies. The articles highlight current developments and trends in the field with uptodate data and subject coverage. The contributors, eminent library and information science professionals, are from different parts of India, spread over more than fourteen states. Institutional affiliation of authors, scatter among universities, university libraries, science and technology libraries, college libraries and research libraries. The articles included in this volume maintain a high academic standard.

The book commences with a foreword by Prof. (Dr.). V.G. Talawar, Vice-Chancellor, University of Mysore, a distinguished Professor of LIS and an eminent personality in the higher education field of this country. We express our humble thanks and gratitude to Prof. Talawar for writing the foreword to this volume in the midst of his busy schedule of programme.

The fortyfour articles presented in this volume are grouped under 11 thematic categories. They are : Management of Library and Information Centres, Knowledge Management, ICT Applications, Information Literacy and E- learning, Open Access and Open Source Software, Electronic Resources and Services, Scientometrics/Webometrics, Web 2.0, Meta data, Other topics and Prof. C.V. Rajan Pillai: Reminiscences and Impressions.

Under the first category, *Management of Library and Information Centres*, altogether there are five articles, which mainly focus on output analysis of university libraries, job involvement, job satisfaction, quality improvement and quality of work life and occupational stress. The second category *Knowledge Management* consists of four articles—two articles on knowledge management tools, KM and librarianship, and Web content management. Three articles are included under the category *Information Literacy and E-learning* which concentrate on the need for E-learning in Higher Education and Information Literacy programmes. There are three articles in the category *Open Access and Open Source Software* which deal with building digital libraries, institutional depository and open sources. In the next category *Electronic Resources and Services*, five articles are presented. Under *Scientometrics/Webometrics*, four articles are included which deal with scientometric ranking algorithms, authorship pattern, bibliometric study of doctoral dissertations and publication productivity. *Web 2.0* lists three articles. In the *Metadata* section, three papers are included—metadata standards, mapping of metadata standards and bibliographic standards. The articles which are not confined to the above grouping are separately listed under the category of *Other Topics*. There are three articles presented in this category.

The last section presents *Reminiscences and Impressions*. It begins with a brief summary of the interview by the editors with Dr. Pillai and that narrates how he 'looks back'. The reminiscences collected are from his Professor at BHU, Vice-Chancellor of CUSAT, where he served more than one decade, his guide for Ph. D research, a classmate, a friend and a student.

For this endeavour, we have contacted eminent library professionals and faculty numbers of the LIS schools from all over the country. To our surprise and beyond our expectation the response was overwhelming. That shows Prof. Pillai's popularity and respectful position he earned in the minds of his colleagues, friends and well wishers. The list of contributors marks the magnitude of response. The editors are grateful to all authors for promptly responding and contributing to this volume.

We also express our indebtedness to Authorspress, New Delhi for their willingness to execute this work and publish it in a meticulous manner.

No doubt, this book will be an asset to Library and Information Science education and research at different levels. It is hoped that the LIS professionals would accept this valuable publication whole heartedly.

Dr. S. Humayoon Kabir
Dr. K.G. Sudhier

Contents

Prof. (Dr.) C.V. Rajan Pillai: Biographical Sketch *v*

Foreword *vii*

Preface *ix*

1. A Confetti of Thoughts on Libraries 1
—*Achutsankar S. Nair*

I
Management of Library and Information Centres

2. Output Analysis of University Libraries in Kerala: A Comparison 13
—*K. P. Vijayakumar*
3. Job Involvement of Librarians Working in Arts and Science Colleges in Trichy, Tamil Nadu 31
—*V.Geetha and B.S. Swaroop Rani*
4. Job Satisfaction among Professional Librarians in the College Libraries in Kerala 39
—*T. Mohana Kumar*
5. Quality Improvement in Libraries in the Changing Landscape of Library Resources, Services and User's Perceptions 57
—*Ramesha*
6. Quality of Work Life and Occupational Stress among the Library Professionals in Kerala 69
—*K. P. Somanathan Nair* and *K. K. Reena*

II
Knowledge Management

7. Feasibility of Knowledge Management Tools in Academic Library Services 81
—Lalitha Aswath

8. Knowledge Management and the Profession of Librarianship 95
—Khaiser Muneebulla Khan

9. Web Content Management: A Case Study of E-books Access required by IISc Digital Library 107
—K. S. Chudamani and *H. C. Nagarathna*

10. Application of Knowledge Management Tools in Library and Information Centres 123
—M. Natarajan

III
ICT Applications

11. Information and Communication Technology (ICT) in Higher Education- A Conceptual Frame Work 135
— *N. Radhakrishnan* and *Sophia Johnson*

12. Libraries and Information Centres as Publishers of Scholarly Literature in the Electronic Era 143
—P. M. Noushad Ali and K. Mohammed Musthafa

IV
Information Literacy and E-learning

13. E Learning in Higher Education: Opportunities and Challenges in India 153
— *K. Anas*

14. Imparting Information Literacy: A Practical Approach 161
— *Indira Koneru*

15. Information Literacy Programmes in Research Libraries in Kerala: An Assessment 179
—*C. Jalaja Kumari* and *Mallinath Kumbar*

V

Open Access and Open Source Software

16. Open Access and Institutional Repositories: The New Scholarly Publishing Scenario 189
— *V. Gopakumar and A. K. Baradol*

17. Open Access resources in S & T Field with Special Reference to Engineering and Medicine 197
— *Susmita Chakraborty*

18. Open Licences and Radical Shift in Digital Content Distribution 213
—*V. Vimal Kumar* and *S. Chitra*

VI

Electronic Resources and Services

19. Availability and Use of Electronic Information Resources in the Arts and Science College Libraries in Kerala: A Case Study 227
— *V. Jalaja and A. Vijayakumar*

20. Electroic Journals: An Outlook 245
—*Khushpreet Singh*

21. Impact of Digital Information Culture on the Academic Libraries 253
—*Puttaraj A. Choukimath* and *Muttayya M. Koganuramath*

22. Mastering the Web Search—Tools, Techniques and Tips for Users 273
—*Fayaz Ahmad Lone*

23. Proliferation of Electronic Resources: A Conjectural Approach 291
– Dillip K. Swain and K. C. Panda

24. Digital Reference Service: An Overview 301
—V. S. Midhula Soman and *M. Varghese*

VII
Scientometrics/ Webometrics

25. Authorship Pattern and Collaborative Research in the Field of Hepatitis 317
—B. Ramesh Babu and *J. Ramakrishnan*

26. Bibliometric Analysis of Doctoral Dissertations in English Language and Literature 339
—R. Rajani and *S. Humayoon Kabir*

27. Publication Productivity of Physics Researchers of Indian Institute of Science: A Scientometric Study 351
—K. G. Sudhier

28. Visualising Academia: Contributions of Scientometric Ranking Algorithms to the Study of Universities in Karnataka 363
—K. Manjula and *K. S. Chudamani*

VIII
Web 2.0

29. 'Library One'—Forward from Library 2.0 and Further 379
—H. P. S. Kalra

30. Online Social Networks and their Impact on Information Communication 385
—Dineshan Koovakkai

31. Reaching Net Gen Students through Web 2.0: Challenges for University Libraries in India 397
—N. Nikesh and M. Ramina

IX
Meta Data

32. Metadata Standards for Cataloguing Indian Manuscripts: Some Reflections 411
—N. S. Harinarayana and *N. N. Prasad*

33. Mapping of Metadata Standards: Issues in Metadata Crosswalks 433
—V. Chandrakumar

34. Bibliographic Standards 443
—M. Parameswaran

X
Other Topics

35. Classification: A Universal Concept 455
M. P. Satija and *K. P. Singh*

36. Copyright in the Digital Environment: A State of the Art Report 471
—K. N. Prasad

37. Origin and Development of Library & Information Science Periodicals 489
—A. Gopikuttan and *P. R. Hima*

XI
Prof. C. V. Rajan Pillai: Reminiscences and Impressions

38. Prof. (Dr.) C. V. Rajan Pillai: A Towering Personality in Library and Information Science Profession 507
—Dr. S. Humayoon Kabir and Dr. K. G. Sudhier

39. Rajan Pillai : My Student at BHU 511
—Prof. P.N. Kaula

40. My Respects to Prof. C. V. Rajan Pillai: A Teacher Par Excellence 512
—*Prof. A.K. Baradol*

41. Prof. C. V. Rajan Pillai: A Rare and Good Friend 516
—*Prof. P. Leelakrishnan*

42. *Guruvandanam* 517
—*Dr. K. P. Somanathan Nair*

43. Dr. Rajan Pillai as the CUSAT Librarian 519
—*Prof. (Dr.) S. Balaraman*

44. Dr. Rajan Pillai as a Researcher 521
—*Prof. (Dr.) Puthusseri Ramachandran*

List of Contributors **522**

Index **527**

1

A Confetti of Thoughts on Libraries

—Achuthsankar S. Nair

Universal Digital Library

The process of education best takes place in an environment which is properly nourished with certain critical resources, both physical and virtual. Inspirational leadership, active peer-groups, institutional pride, cultural activities, teaching and learning resources are some examples. A library forms an essential component of this environment. The term knowledge repository is more appropriate in this context today. However, a traditional library is miles apart from what a knowledge repository should be. Further, it seems imminent that knowledge repository concept itself is poised for a major revolution. I was inspired by the youtube video of the lecture by Brewster Kahle, a champion of digital libraries.

Imagine how education will be transformed if all the knowledge resources ever created by humanity could be pooled, made searchable and available to every educational institution! When I say all knowledge resources ever created by humanity, I mean everything that starts with Sumerian clay tablets of Alexandria to this document that you are reading now. It is not restricted to text documents alone, as an educational technologist may compulsively point out, our intellectual resources are quite well distributed among images, movies, videos, songs, softwares, web pages and ephemeral blogs. Today technology is gearing up for the final phase of technological and economic feasibility of such a universal library. This universal library will have to digitally hold 320 lakhs of books, 7.5 crores of articles, 250 lakhs of songs, 50 crores of images, 5 lakh movies, 30 lakh videos, TV shows and short films, 50,000 softwares and 10000 crore web pages. This is estimated to require 50 Peta Bytes of Memory. A peta byte is 1000 Tera bytes or 1000,000 Giga Bytes (GB). We are already in moving from GB to TB era. Thus we are on the verge of the Penta Byte era.

The hope is also that we can hold the universal library in a mobile wan. Yes, the whole knowledge resources of humanity in a mobile wan! The cost is surprisingly affordable, if all the content is copyright free (most of which are and many will be under enormous pressure to be, in the digital library age). Digitisation of a book costs Rs 500 upwards, when done in huge volumes. Songs, cinema, web pages etc are already in digital format. The transformation hinted above is not merely going to be a collection and access providing exercise. But the dream being pursues is that every book will be crosslinked, cited, indexed, annotated and full-text searchable. Every video/song will likewise be tagged to enable text-based search. These are very important transformations in the offing. The texture of knowledge resources is going to be subtly different. This will have to be reflected in every facet of the process of education.

Democracy in Classification Systems: Towards Reader-Centric Libraries

Thinking of public tagging, I am reminded of the days when we were penalised for "damaging" the book with our written comments on it, which ranged from "For God's sake don't read this book" to "page 22-56 is all that is enough to pass Electrical Materials Examination". Time has now come, when the readers are invited to do exactly this on books, only that it is on soft copies. It is only a question of time before such reader-doodles get captured and become searchable. The possibility of public tagging is going to democratise the knowledge classification system, putting an end to archaic systems such as Dewey Decimal

Classification System. The libraries are undergoing the third wave of transformation. From the Book-centred to Librarian-Centred to Information-Service-centred to Reader-centred libraries. Public Tagging is only one of the aspects to reader centricity. A virtual bookshelf (much like what is there in Amazon.com) of all books read by every user with the tagging they contributed would perhaps be treasured by future libraries. Today we have no open trace of the results of the intercourse between books and the readers. In future, this will be present in the digital atmosphere of libraries. Imagine, wouldn't we be interested to know what the great scholar C. P. Ramaswamy Iyer (who was the founder Vice-chancellor of University of Travancore in 1937) read from the Travancore University Library and what were, at least, his telegraphic comments on the books he read? Our traditional libraries have failed to capture these. Before any modern software comes up to implement this seamlessly, our present libraries would do well to get its readers into the centre stage of the library through meetings, bulletins and notices which focus on the importance of readers as catalysts for other readers. The walls of the library should proudly display paintings of the great readers of the library. They should have awards for readers of the year and publish a compendium of their romance with books.

S. R. Ranganathan

I am not sure if any other discipline in universities in India can claim a colossal father figure as Library Science can. Prompted by a scholarly librarian, I read Prof S. R. Ranganathan's *Prolegomena to Library Classification (1937)*. I did not read much, only a page first. I had to close the book as my day was made. I understood that Ranganathan was not only a library professional, but a great motivating guru. A week before I read it, one of my dynamic research scholars, sought my audience to help her to overcome the pain and disappointment. Some original work that she did was found to be already published by someone else. I tried to console her saying that she can be assured that she is on the right track and thinking at the level of international researchers. I do not think I succeeded, but to my surprise, I found a recursive assurance from Prolegomena to Library Classification. In the opening pages, he talks about surprise idea, a sense of assurance and enjoyable journey. The second one struck me. I quote all the three verbatim. I would say this is wisdom for the knowledge era, packaged 75 years ago by a guru. This is the mantra for researchers attempting generation of new knowledge.

Surprise Idea: When one is engaged on a problem, the most useful ideas occur suddenly. They seem at once to cast a flood of light over murky tracts of half-formed thought and promise reward to further exploration. This has been my experience and it is doubtless shared by many others. These surprise-ideas present themselves as readymade wholes, coming at the oddest moments. They seldom come if they are sought land delight in choosing; moments when pen and paper cannot be used to impede their flight. They come and whisper in our ears as we lie sleepily in bed, or as we mechanically repeat a long-drawn-out hymn as part of the daily routine of worship. To sit at the study table with notebook and pen, with the intention of meditating on one's problem, invariably produces only sleep.

Sense of Assurance: There is one notable feature of these surprise-ideas; they always seem at first inspired. We think them quite original. But before long, there comes awakening, usually even before we have developed our first notes. Somebody else is found to have thought of the same thing before, and has expressed it all in some well-known work! One's feelings at this discovery are mixed. First, there is dismay at being deprived—nay, robbed—of well-deserved priority. Then there is relief that one is pared the labour of cudgelling one's brains over the subsequent pioneer work involved. Further, there is satisfaction in the thought that if other, cleverer, men have trodden this way before, the one is probably on the right path and not wandering hopelessly in the wilderness. A sense of assurance emerges.

Enjoyable joruney: Finally, one is buoyed up by the hope that if one continues long enough on the path, one will in the end have climbed the rests of the known and be looking forward into undiscovered terrain. Would that it were possible that in this book the distant peaks should be visible through the wreaths of mist! One can hope for no more than this; and yet one is conscious of a thoroughly enjoyable journey, which has recalled again and again the sentiment expressed by R. L. Stevenson, "To travel hopefully us a better thing than to arrive."

Do We need Library Fine or Fine Libraries?

The small library in Centre for Bioinformatics, University of Kerala, is a place for wild experimentation (there is no librarian to assist/resist!). In a house meeting of the centre where all the people in the centre, students, staff, teachers get together as a flash crowd, the idea of library fine was raised. In an effort to transform the traditional mindset, I commented that we must actually have fine for people not using the library. The pun did not vanish into thin air. It was expanded and made the "fine policy" of this library:

1. Re 1 per day for each day in which no book is issued to the member.
2. Re 10 per book on which they have not done public tagging.
3. Rs 100 per semester if no books have been recommended for purchase.
4. Rs 1,000 per semester if they never entered the library in each semester.

At least in small-membership libraries, there should be no fines for late return, readers should talk to each other in getting back books. It is a way to catalyse reading. These talks will possibly generate exchange of reading values. Anyway, in the age of automation, any action that will make people talk to each other will be of great value to humanity.

Oldest Library in Trivandrum

Many believe that the oldest modern library in Trivandrum is the Public Library which was founded by Maharaja Swathi Thirunal in 1829. In his book *Military Reminiscences,* Colonel Welsh who visited Trivandrum in 1825 refers to the studies of the young prince Swathi Thirunal (Col. James Welsh, "Military reminiscences extracted from a journal of nearly forty years active service in the East Indies", London, Smith, Elder & Co., 1830.).

This reference will make clear that Swathi Thirunal was a friend of books. Welsh says: "He read a chapter of Malcolm's Central India; the Governor-General's Persian letter on the capture of Rangoon; a passage in Sanskrit; another in Malayalam and seemed equally clever at each. He then took up a book of mathematics, selecting the forty-seventh proposition of Euclid, sketched the figure on a country-slate; but what astonished me most was his telling us in English that Geometry was derived from the Sanskrit which was 'Jawmeter,' to measure the earth, and that many of our mathematical terms were also derived from the same sources, such as hexagon, heptagon, octagon, decagon, dua-decagon, etc." This is a pointer to the possibility that Swathi Thirunal had at his disposal a library which had a collection of books ranging from history and literature to western science.

In a report on education in Travancore (*The Literary Gazette: A Weekly Journal of Literature, Science, and the Fine Arts* by John Mounteney Jephson, George Augustus Frederick Fitzclarence, 1840, p 705), Sir David Brewster mentions: "The Rajah had also established a magnetical and meteorological observatory, having being led to do so by becoming acquainted with a report on meteorology, published by the British Association [for the Advancement of Science]." No wonder that during the first year of his reign (1829) the public library in its early form was established in Trivandrum.

British Resident Col. Edward Cadogan, the grandson of Sir Hans Sloane, the founder of the British Museum, was the President of the Library and Swathi Thirunal was the Patron. The Library was managed by an Association known as Trivandrum Public Library Committee. Membership in those days was limited to only those persons invited to the Royal Durbar. In 1837, Swathi Thirunal granted Rs. 1000 to the Library based on a request from the Library Secretary Mr. Roberts (this is possibly Mr. J. Roberts, Master of the Free School, which later became the University College, Thiruvananthapuram).

In 1847 the Public Library Society was organised with a limited membership. Soon the Society was registered as a Joint Stock Company and became the Public Library Association, membership being open to all persons residing in Trivandrum who conformed to the rules. In 1889 the society entered into an agreement with Government according to which their entire assets were handed over to Government on condition that "Government would erect suitable buildings for a new Library for the benefit of the public and to that end, provide a well stocked and furnished reference Library and should undertake the maintenance of the same in a suitable manner under such regulations as may be best calculated to carry out the end in view." It was also agreed that the Government should erect a suitable building and "establish a free library to be handed over to the public in commemoration of the sixtieth year of Queen Victoria's reign." Accordingly the Government took over the management of the institution and it was treated as one of the minor Departments of the State. The British Resident continued to serve as the President of the Committee. From then on, the management of the institution rested with the Government until 1938, when it was transferred to the Travancore University (present Kerala University).

A new committee was constituted by Government with the Pro-Vice-Chancellor as the President and the University Librarian, the Secretary. The committee had full powers to manage the affairs of the institution and to approve all expenditure. But this transfer of the institution met with resentment and protests from the public and the newspapers published a number of articles against this order. In 1948 a resolution was unanimously passed by the Legislature resolving that the Government should take over the institution from the University and manage it as a separate department, as was done up to 1938. Accordingly the Government resumed the control of the institution in 1949 reconstituting the Committee with the Minister for Education as President, and the Librarian as Convener of the Committee.

There are remnants of libraries in two other institutions in Trivandrum that are worth investigating. One is the Observatory, the other being the Museum. The Museum Library is closed to public, but has a sizeable collection of rare books. It also seems to have been organised professionally as indicated by a catalogue printed by the Trivandrum Government Press in 1876. I wish that some book lover will research the history of modern libraries in Trivandrum.

Napier Museum

Library

CATALOGUE

TRAVANCORE GOVERNMENT PRESS—1876.

Gazing into the Crystal Ball: IT, BT and Future of Libraries

Perhaps to pull back my mind from its frequent excursions to history (I love to learn about early nineteenth century local history of Trivandrum), of late I have swung to the other side, and fantasize the future. Of course it is more creative and open the ended to talk about the future than history (and the farther the future, the safer the prognostics!). I am imagining how the University of Kerala would be in AD 2100. What comes to my mind first is that the University's Senate House premises will be like a forest with large number of trees. I guess that eco-issues will take the central role, carbon emission will be monitored for each institution, and the University too would be forced to do so (its funding and even existence will be based on careful management of environment). The Asan Square too might be a huge mangrove with the statue illuminated carefully, not to disturb the large number of birds in the mangrove. And the University library will also have thick trees all around and no air-conditioners will be there. It will be a heritage building and will be completely vacated. It will still be a library, but you will not see books, but only people, reading books downloaded on to electronic readers which have plastic pages (with digital display) that can be physically flipped, giving the feel of real books. There is no need for people to come to the library since all books would be open access and downloadable from the "supernet", anywhere. But the library would be the place where readers get together and share a passion for books. There will be reading spaces and readers club meeting rooms. All the books might be in a underground godown, created by digging the road between University college and the Senate House Campus in Palayam. Readers will make up the library, not books.

A bit more wild fantasy is regarding technology. We already see the infusion of Information Technology into Libraries. The twenty-first century is the century of bio-technology; will it have any impact in libraries? One cannot rule out. Bio-technologist already know how to manipulate the DNA to modify life forms. They can, in principle, modify the DNA to achieve printing in leaves (or even the skin, say of a zebra). Will libraries be gardens where people read from leaves? The present concern of books being not eco-friendly as they can be traced back to cutting down of trees, might be settled. A bit far-fetched, but not a bad thing if it can happen.

End Note

The draft of the above writing attracted two kinds of reactions. One an appreciation for the humanist thoughts. Another is criticism for the techno-centric fantasies. Here is a sample of the letter. Catherine Schloss, a library professional from University of Southern Mississippi (which seems to have lost some of its library collections to the hurricane *kathrina*) wrote to me thus: *This article is almost a direct reputal to my term paper for graduation in Library Science. The paper was entitled: Are Librarians Becoming Obsolete. Electronic Information that is readily available to all is a fantastic idea. I cannot dispute that. However, the human element is necessary. The profession of librarians has changed dramatically as it has made the shift towards an even more service oriented profession. In addition to this opinion, I have one more, and that is the old fashioned notion that nothing can take the place of an "old fashioned" book. There are many people out there (myself included) that would rather have the experience of holding the book in ones hands, feeling the pages as one turns to find out what happens next, the smell of paper and ink. The size of the book, the shape of the book. People like the (I reiterate..myself included) have an emotional connection that we can't find on a web screen. I would hate to think that there would be a future without this one simple pleasure. The electronic dissemination of information should be available to all....But by the same token, so should the book.*

Unknown to Catherine, I share the same feelings about books which I consider as a cultural entity and not a media of recording information. I feel the fragrance of the yellowed pages of old books right now. Shall I ever trade that for a CD ? No.

I

Management of Library and Information Centres

2

Output Analysis of University Libraries in Kerala: A Comparison

— K.P. Vijayakumar

This paper assesses the quantum of work involved in the different sections of university libraries in the five major universities in Kerala, viz., University of Kerala, Calicut University, Cochin University of Science & Technology, Mahatma Gandhi University and Kerala Agricultural University. The study reveals that the reference sections are used heavily because of the presence of textbook collection. No library was found to offer user education programme to its users. A common observation is that there is shortage of unskilled manpower in all the libraries selected for the study.

Introduction

The state of Kerala as a single physical entity came into existence only in 1956 by the amalgamation of the erstwhile principalities of Travancore, Kochi and the Malabar region which was part of the Madras Presidency. There are evidences that ancient rulers were keen on the establishment of educational institutions. During the age of the Cheras (A.D. 800-1102) more thrust was given to education. (Velu Pillai, 1940). The educational institutions attached to the temples were known as *Salais*. The *Salais* at Kandalur, Parthivasekharapuram, Tiruvalla and Muzhikulam were well known. It is obvious from early inscriptions that while the Kandalur and Parthivasekhara-puram were open only to the privileged few, the latter two admitted common students also and provided them with free boarding, lodging and tuition. (Sreedhara Menon, 2003).

The rulers of Travancore, Kochi and Malabar of the nineteenth and twentieth centuries had given high priority to education, and this paved the way for the establishment of a number of schools and colleges in the region. As a logical corollary of the expansion of higher education, the demand for a separate university arose, especially in Travancore. After a number of deliberations and consultations, the University of Travancore came into being in 1937 by a promulgation of the Maharaja of Travancore, Sri Chitira Tirunal Balarama Varma, as the sixteenth university to be set up in India. Soon after the formation of the university, the ten colleges, hitherto affiliated to the University of Madras, were shifted to the new university.

After the formation of the Kerala State in 1956, the University of Travancore was renamed as University of Kerala by the Kerala University Act, 1957 (Act 14 of 1957). The university with the entire state under its jurisdiction at that time had three campuses located in three different parts of the State at Trivandrum, Ernakulam and Calicut. In 1968, the university centre at Kozhikode became a full-fledged university covering the colleges and departments located in Kannur, Kozhikode, Palakkad and Thrissur districts of Kerala. Another university meant for science and technology, namely, Cochin University of Science and Technology, and a fourth one for agriculture and related disciplines located at Kochi and Thrissur respectively also came up in 1971. Again in 1983, the Mahatma Gandhi University was established at Kottayam. Two more universities – the Sree Sankaracharya University of Sanskrit, Kaladi, the place of birth of Sri Shankara and the Kannur University, Kannur—were established in 1993 and 1995 respectively. Thus, the number of universities, all of them of affiliating type, increased to seven in about a quarter century. Again in the present century came up the National University of Advanced Legal Studies (NUALS), Kochi (2005) and the Central University at Kasaragod (2008). Apart from the full-fledged state universities, two institutions of national importance, viz., National Institute of Technology, Kozhikode and Sree Chitira Tirunal Institute of Medical Sciences and Technology, Thiruvananthapuram also came up in the state (*Universities Handbook*, 2004). In the meanwhile, the number of colleges, both arts and science and professional, were also increasing year by year. Thus, at present, there are nine universities in the state. They are:

i. University of Kerala, Thiruvananthapuram (1937)
ii. University of Calicut, Tenhipalam, Malappuram (1968)
iii. Cochin University of Science and Technology, Kochi (1971)
iv. Kerala Agricultural University, Vellanikkara, Thrissur (1971)
v. Mahatma Gandhi University, Kottayam (1983)
vi. Sree Sankaracharya University of Sanskrit, Kaladi (1993)
vii. Kannur University, Kannur (1995)
viii. National University of Advanced Legal Studies (2005)
ix. Central University of Kerala, Kasaragod (2008)

Of these nine, the first five have got full-fledged university libraries, whereas the libraries of the last four universities are at the fledgling stage with skeletal staff. The first five university libraries have very strong central libraries and separate departmental libraries/constituent college libraries. Therefore, in order to study the utilisation of manpower, only these five universities are taken.

The Kerala University Library (KUL) system comprises the Central Library at Palayam, the Campus Library at Kariavattom, the departmental libraries attached to the teaching and research departments located at the city and Kariavattom campuses, the University Engineering College Library again at Kariavattom and the study centre libraries functioning at three locations within the area of jurisdiction of the university. The University of Calicut (CUL) and Mahatma Gandhi University (MGUL) also have central libraries, departmental libraries and study centre libraries and engineering college libraries. The Cochin University of Science and Technology (CUSATL) has got a central library, departmental libraries and Engineering College Library The Kerala Agricultural University (KAUL) has a central library and separate libraries for all the ten constituent colleges located at different parts of Kerala.

Quantum of Output in Different Sections

The main objective of this paper is to assess the quantum of work involved in the different sections of the libraries selected for the study. Since there can be variations in the volume of work in individual years, in order to have an objective analysis, the average output of the five libraries for the five years from 2001 – 02 to 2005 - 06 was taken. The data were collected by personal visit to all the five libraries and by verification of the records.

Acquisition

The Acquisition Section is concerned with the selection, ordering, receipt and accessioning of purchased as well as donated books (*UGC Report*, 1965). If the library accessions the bound volumes of periodicals and theses/dissertations also along with the books, then it is also carried out by the same section. In some libraries acquisition of electronic documents, especially CDs, also is vested with the Acquisition Section, but in some others this is attended to by the Information Technology Section. The volume of work involved in the Acquisition Section of different libraries is given in Table 1.

Table 1

Quantum of Work in the Acquisition Section

Routines	*Number*				
	KUL	*CUL*	*CUSATL*	*MGUL*	*KAUL*
Books selected	4,200	2,900	1,885	2,700	250
Books ordered	4,100	2,100	1,750	1,450	250
Books received	2,850	1,090	1,558	1,327	250
Gift books	628	82	152	213	70
Books on exchange	—	—	—	—	—
Books accessioned	3,352	1,172	1,426	1,162	320

Back volumes accessioned	1,051	—	114	700	2,000
Theses/dissertations accessioned	100	1,522	152	76	170
Reports accessioned	—	—	—	—	280
Non-book materials					
Audio	—	—	—	—	—
Video	—	—	—	—	—
CDs / DVDs	—	—	63	—	130

The Kerala University Library is found to select order and receive more books. CUL and MGUL seem to select a large number of books, but the number received by them is comparatively less. While KUL gets 69.51 per cent of the books ordered, the corresponding percentages are 51.9, 89.02, and 91.51 for CUL, CUSATL and MGUL. KAUL seems to get all the books ordered. They have purchased an unusually high number of back volumes in order to make their collection comprehensive. Only KAUL procures reports. CUSAT Library and KAU Library procure CDs/ DVDs through the Acquisition Section.

Average annual addition of documents

Since the procurement of books in a particular year may increase or decrease depending on the availability of funds, in addition to the number of books acquired not only in 2004-05, but the average addition in the last five years was also collected. Similarly, the average addition of bound volumes of periodicals, theses and dissertations and other materials was also collected. The average addition of different types of documents is given in Table 2.

Table 2
Average Annual Addition of Documents

Document	*KUL*	*CUL*	*CUSATL*	*MGUL*	*KAUL*
Books	2,670	1,335	1,312	1,138	798
Bound volume of periodicals	185	195	208	265	904
Theses/dissertations	140	103	66	84	48
Other documents	30	46	—	—	—
Total	3,025	1,679	1,586	1,487	1,750

In the case of annual addition also Kerala University occupies the first position followed by KAU and CUL. The high intake of bound volumes of periodicals accounts for the second position of KAUL.

Technical Processing

The Technical Section is charged with the classification, cataloguing and physical processing of documents (*UGC Report*, 1965). Though in some libraries, physical processing is done in the Acquisition Section, in all university libraries studied, this work is done in the Technical Section. As done in the case of Acquisition Section, here also, in addition to the statistics for 2004-05, the output for the previous four years was also collected in order to have the average output of the five years from 2000-01. This average output is presented in Table 3.

There is considerable difference in the number of documents accessioned in the year 2004-05 and the average number of documents processed. In the case of CUL, there appears to be a crash programme to finish of the backlog of classification and cataloguing during 2004-05. But KUL stands first in terms of output. The number of volumes processed there is almost double that of CUSATL, MGUL and KAUL. Only CUSATL attempts processing of non-book materials.

Table 3

Average Annual Volume of Work in the Technical Section

Type of documents	*Classification, Cataloguing and Physical processing*				
	KUL	*CUL*	*CUSATL*	*MGUL*	*KAUL*
Books	3,428	1,785	1,570	1,150	320
Bound volumes of periodicals	219	230	24 8	615	1,318
Reports	—	—	—	—	—
Theses/ Dissertations	179	235	107	85	162
Patents	—	—	—	—	—
Non-book materials	—	—	50	—	—
Others	—	—	—	—	—
Total	3,826	2,250	1,975	1,850	1,800

Maintenance

The maintenance Section is endowed with the responsibility of the maintenance of books and bound periodicals in the correct sequence on the shelves, the maintenance of gangway guides, the bay guides and the shelf guides in the stack room in order to facilitate open access, the daily replacement of books returned by the users from time to time during the day and preparation of books for repairs and binding week after week (*UGC Report*, 1965). Since there is no likelihood of any remarkable variation in the volume of work in the Maintenance Section from year to year, the statistical data pertaining to 2004-05 alone were taken. The annual output in each library is given Table 4.

It is a matter of common knowledge that the total book collection and membership of the library have a direct bearing on the volume of work in the Maintenance Section. This is true in the case of KUL, CUL and CUSATL, but the volume of work seems to be comparatively more in the MGUL. This may be due to the fact that there is no separate Reference Section and the Maintenance Section is in charge of the reference collection also. The KAUL also is more like a reference library and therefore output is high. In the KUL and CUL, user assistance is also indicated in the category of other jobs.

Table 4

Quantum of Annual Output in the Maintenance Section

Routines	*KUL*	*CUL*	*CUSATL*	*MGUL*	*KAUL*
No. of books replaced	323,000	23,800	32,500	102,000	19,600
No. of books rectified	153,000	62,500	25,500	60,000	14,000
No. of books bound	500	350	90	200	50
Other jobs					
User assistance	17,000	3,500	–	–	–

Circulation

The Circulation Section is mainly charged with the charging and discharging of documents (*UGC Report*, 1965). In addition, the registration of members, renewal, reservation, overdue charge collection, cancellation of membership and interlibrary loan are also attended to by this Section. A comparison of the volume of work in the five university libraries is presented in Table 5.

In the case of issue, return, renewal, reservation and all other routines in the Circulation Section of KUL is much ahead of other libraries. The annual issue of books is about six times that of CUL and MGUL and more than seven times that of CUSATL. The same proportion can be seen in the relationship of total operations also. This is mainly due to the location of the library in the heart of the city which is quite accessible to students of nearby colleges and graduate members, whereas all other libraries are located in the respective university campuses and, therefore, are primarily used by the students and teachers of the universities themselves. No library was found to offer interlibrary loan facility except KUL. Some government departments used to borrow books from KUL for their use.

Table 5
Annual Volume of Work in the Circulation Section

Routines	*Average output per year*				
	KUL	*CUL*	*CUSATL*	*MGUL*	*KAUL*
Issue	70,000	30,600	25,160	27,300	8,400
Return	167,500	30,000	25,000	27,200	8,400
Renewal	25,500	6,800	4,080	6,800	2,800
Reservation	3,400	3,900	1,700	3,500	—
Reminders	2,500	3,800	1,700	2,720	—
Interlibrary loan	600	—	—	—	—
Overdue receipts	74,800	6,800	7,200	12,250	850
Registration of members	8,500	2,040	2,800	1,700	600
Cancellation of membership	5,200	1,800	1,200	1,400	400
Issue of non-liability certificate	5,000	1,700	1,100	1,300	350
Total operations	463,000	87,440	69,940	84,170	21,800

Periodicals

The Periodical Section or Periodical Publications Section as Dr. S. R. Ranganathan refers to it, is concerned with the ordering, receipt, preparation and display of current periodicals, their cumulation and preparation for binding on the completion of the volume. (*UGC Report*, 1965)

Method of Procuring Periodicals

Libraries usually build up the periodicals collection either by subscription or gift or exchange. All the libraries get periodicals both by subscription and gift. The fact is that all the subject journals are subscribed to while quite a number of popular periodicals, except the more established ones, are received gratis. Only KAUL is found to get periodicals on exchange basis since the Kerala Agricultural University has its own periodical publication.

Method of Periodical Subscription

There is no uniform practice of getting periodicals in the library. While some libraries get all the periodicals, except popular periodicals, directly from the publishers, some libraries get all the periodicals through agent or agents. There is also the practice of resorting to both the methods. Only CUSAT Library does all the subscription directly. All others resort to the dual methods i.e. directly as well as through agents.

Periodicals received

While KUL has a current subscription of 364, the corresponding numbers are 162, 149, 344 and 193 for CUL, CUSATL, MGUL and KAUL.

Output in the Periodical Section

The peculiarity of periodical publications is that even though the number of titles is fixed they are received in instalments and, therefore, the work of receipt and display spans throughout the year. The number of issues received in a year depends on the frequency of periodicals. Therefore, the average number of issues of newspapers and periodicals received in a year and the number of reminders sent was taken and the details are given in Table 6.

Table 6
Workload in the Periodicals Section

Routine	*Quantity*				
	KUL	*CUL*	*CUSATL*	*MGUL*	*KAUL*
Receipt of issues of periodical in a year	12,388	7,356	4,387	8,322	4,259
Reminders sent in a year	450	250	300	260	200

The number of issues of newspaper and periodicals received in a year varies from 12,388 in the KUL to 4,259 in the KAUL. Similarly the number of reminders sent in a year range from 450 to 200. It appears that there is no relationship with the number of periodicals and newspapers subscribed to and the number the reminders sent.

Reference Section

The Reference Section has the responsibility of helping the students, teachers and research workers, in the choice of books and articles in periodicals appropriate to their interest at the moment (*UGC Report,* 1965). In the changing context of information, the Reference Service assumes greater significance and a wide variety of services are offered as offshoots of this service.

Observation of the working of the Reference Section of the university libraries shows that the section is used more by students for consulting textbooks and the main work is issue of textbooks kept as closed collections. The next most sought after items are guides for the preparation of UGC-CSIR NET Examination and question papers of various examinations. Reference queries do come, but mostly of ready reference nature. It has been found that the Reference Section routines are attended to by junior professionals in all libraries. The reference collection of all the universities contains pretty old materials, in the absence of constant combing operations. This problem is more acute in KUL where shelves are found to be tightly packed with subject reference books.

Strength of the Reference Collection

The strength of the reference collection has a direct bearing on the quality of the reference service rendered from the library. It is also related to the membership and users, finance and space available. The number of volumes available in the reference collection is given in Table 7.

Table 7

Strength of the Reference Collection

Name of the library	*No. of volumes in the reference collection(approximate)*
KUL	12,000
CUL	7,100
CUSATL	9,000
MGUL	3,900
KAUL	2,650

The Kerala University Library has the biggest reference collection with about 12,000 volumes followed by CUSATL. In the MGUL there is no separate Reference Section, but the collection forms part of the Maintenance Section. In all the university libraries there are textbook collections also forming part of reference collection. In KUL and CUL there is the practice of issuing textbooks for overnight use.

Average annual output of the Reference Section

The routines in the section include the attending of queries, reshelving of used documents, referral service and initiation of fresh man. The details of the workload in each library are given in Table 8.

Table 8
Annual Volume of Work in the Reference Section

Routines	*KUL*	*CUL*	*CUSATL*	*MGUL*	*KAUL*
Queries attended	17,500	4,800	1,500	3,900	1,500
Sources consulted	112,000	45,000	18,000	21,000	6,000
Referral service	6,000	3,000	900	—	4,000
Reshelving	90,000	45,000	15,000	19,500	6,000
Others					
Issue of textbooks	6,000	3,500	—	—	—

KUL tops the list of libraries in terms of the ready reference queries attended, the volumes consulted, reshelving and other services. In the referral service also, KUL is in the forefront with KAUL closely behind. It is revealed that most of the queries are related to the availability of specific sources in the Kerala Agricultural University Library system, i.e., in the constituent college libraries and research centres. As stated earlier, the majority of documents consulted are either textbooks or career guidance materials. No library offers facilities for direct telephone enquiry service which would have enhanced the use of the materials.

Documentation/Information

Documentation Section is charged with the preparation of documentation list and of the abstracts of the relevant articles in current periodicals having a bearing on the research work in progress in the university (*UGC Report,* 1965). But information services have assumed new dimensions in university libraries. These services now include Current Awareness Service, Selective Dissemination of Information, and preparation of digests, trend reports / state-of- the-art reports, critical reviews, Technical Enquiry Service and other data services (Seetharama, 1990). The documentation activities of the university libraries in Kerala are clear from Table 9.

Table 9
Annual Workload in the Documentation Section

Routines	*KUL*	*CUL*	*CUSATL*	*MGUL*	*KAUL*
Items indexed	1,200	—	—	—	—
Items abstracted	700	—		—	—
Bulletins/Notification issued	—	—	—	—	.
Bibliographies compiled	10	—	—	—	—
Reprint collection building	—	—	—	1,200	—
Other services					
E-mail alerts	—	—	20	—	—

Only KUL and MGUL have separate Documentation Sections. Of these two, only KUL does the routine indexing work, mainly to bring out the quarterly indexing periodical *Kerala Index*. CUL, CUSATL and KAUL do not have Documentation Sections. But CUSATL attempts e-mail alerts, though at a limited scale. The major work of the Documentation Section of MGUL is building up of a reprint collection – a collection of reprints requested by the users at the rate of about 1,200 items per year. It appears that documentation activities, in the true spirit, have not been taken up seriously by the university libraries in the state.

Information Technology

A separate section for giving services using IT gadgets started in 1980s because of the scarcity of computers, dearth of skilled staff in IT related operations and absence of LAN facilities. This practice is still continued though the factors that led to centralisation of computers and others equipment are no more tenable. The section is concerned with Internet search, CD-ROM search, online search, scanning of documents, etc. In the CUL, it is named as the Computer and Internet Section. As is the practice in the country, university libraries in Kerala also have separate IT Sections and the volume of work of each is given in Table 10.

Table 10
Annual Workload in the Information Technology Section

Routines	*KUL*	*CUL*	*CUSATL*	*MGUL**	*KAUL*
On-line search	1,500	3,500	6,000	1,500	4,500
CD-ROM search	1,200	–	4,500	1,500	1,500
Delegated Internet search	1,750	700	24,000	45,000	4,500
Infonet full text search	7,000	12,000	7,200	15,000	–
Printout (no. of pages)	12,000	8,000	3,000	210,000	3,000
File copying	4,500	7,500	1,500	15,000	1,800
Other services/issue of CDs of books / journals	–	–	1,800	–	–
Scanning	–	–	–	600	–

* MGUL has a combined Documentation and Information Technology Section.

It is clear that all the libraries offer Internet search facility, on line search facility, Infonet service, printout service, file copying facility, etc. All libraries except CUL provide CD-ROM search facility also. The use of these facilities is very high in the CUSATL and MGUL when compared to KUL and CUL which are more traditional in nature. The Internet and Infonet facilities are heavily used in MGUL and CUSATL. If the output of the searches is measured in terms of the number of pages of print- outs and files copied, MGUL is much ahead of CUSATL and others. In spite of this, there is no independent IT Section. The issue of books and journals in CD format is also undertaken by the IT Section in CUSATL. MGUL, on the other hand, undertakes scanning work also as a service to the users.

Other Sections

Ranganathan has dealt with Acquisition, Technical, Maintenance, Circulation, Periodical Publications, Reference and Documentations Sections in a university library. Owing to the extensive use of IT, the IT Section was also added in most of the Indian libraries subsequently. Besides the sections mentioned above, there are certain sections unique to each library developed depending on the peculiar circumstances prevailing in each set-up. They are the following:

Kerala Studies

The Kerala Studies Section consists of an Area Studies collection which is quite unique to Kerala University Library and is endowed with the responsibility of providing all types of documents, including rare ones, relating to Kerala to researchers for reference purpose. In addition to the books belonging to the area studies, the section accommodates the gift collection of Dr. K. M. George, noted Malayalam critic, and back issues of many old periodicals in Malayalam. On an average 35 users, mostly researchers, make use of the collection in this section. The routines in the Section are much akin to the Reference Section.

Research

The Research Section, peculiar to the Kerala University Library, accommodates the research scholars of Humanities and Social Sciences subjects. The section was started at a time when there were research guides in the affiliated colleges but the departments concerned may not be recognised as research centres of the university. With the introduction of the Faculty Improvement Programme (FIP) of UGC, the number of research guides increased and in the absence of adequate facilities in the colleges, the university library has become the most sought after centre in the university. Over the years, it has emerged as the biggest research centre under the university by virtue of the number of researchers. The section looks after the accommodation and information needs of the research scholars who have selected the university library as the centre of research. No other university library in the state provides this facility. The section offers facility for Junior and Senior Research Fellows (JRFs and SRFs) of the university, UGC JRFs, post- doctoral fellows, researchers under Faculty Improvement Programme (FIP). Taken together, the number of full-time research scholars at present comes to about 205. The number varies from period to period and year to year.

In addition, there are about 150 part-time research scholars also. It also houses the theses collection which comes to 3,000 and bound volumes of periodicals in Humanities and Social Sciences. All the jobs in the section appear to be non-professional in nature.

UN & World Bank

The depository collection of UN and World Bank constitutes the pride possession of the Kerala University Library. In the absence of a separate accession register and a catalogue of this collection, the number of books can only be approximated. The number of publications in this section comes to 12,000 including CD-ROMs. The number of visitors to this section per day is about 25.

Union Catalogue

The Union Catalogue Section is seen only in the Mahatma Gandhi University Library. The section is engaged in the compilation of a union catalogue of the documents of the university library, departmental and study centre libraries. The compilation work is almost over and the updating work is going on.

Table 11 summarises the routines and quantum of work in the sections unique to KUL and MGUL.

Table 11

Routines and Quantum of Work of Other Sections

Name of the Library	*Name of the Section*	*Routines*	*Quantum of Work (per year)*
		No. of visitors	11,000
		Queries attended	11,200
	Kerala Studies	Titles consulted	30,600
		Reshelving	30,600
		Referral Service	900
		Issue of facility certificate	100
		Seat allocation	100
		Maintenance of attendance register	350
		Issue of attendance certificate	2,500
		Issue of NOC	30

Kerala University Library	Research	Assistance related to the retrieval of theses	4,500
		Assistance related to back volumes of periodicals	9,500
		No. of visitors	1,400
		Reshelving	12,000
	U N and World Bank	No. of visitors	7,000
		No. volumes consulted	11,200
		Reshelving	11,000
M G University Library	Union Catalogue	Supervision of the preparation of the Union Catalogue of the Library System Outsourced	

Since each section is unique to the library, no comparison of the output is possible.

Conclusion

The Reference Sections are used heavily because of the presence of the textbook collections and books meant for career guidance and competitive examinations which at present are kept as part of them. No library was found to offer user education programmes in earnest. Only the Kerala University Library and the MG University Library are found to do some form of indexing and abstracting work. MGUL does the indexing of reprint collection but in the absence of a separate section, the manpower available is considered as part of the Information Technology Section. The non-conventional sections like Kerala Studies, Research and UN & World Bank – all of KUL — have the required staff. But the Union Catalogue Section of MGUL has two staff members though the work is being carried out by other agencies through outsourcing. A common observation is that there is shortage of unskilled manpower in all libraries, especially to work in different sections. It becomes clear that in the absence of skilled manpower, even the routine jobs are attended to by the professionals leading to the presence of more professional staff than required by the norm.

References

Seetharama, S. (1990). *Guidelines for planning of libraries and information Centres.* Calcutta: IASLIC, 148.

Sreedhara Menon, A. (2003). *History of the University of Kerala.* Vol.1. Thiruvanathapuram: Publications Division, University of Kerala, 3.

Universities Handbook. 30th ed. New Delhi: Association of Indian Universities, 2004; 1282.

University and College Libraries. Report of the Library Committee of the University Grants Commission. New Delhi: UGC, 1965; 71-72.

Velu Pillai, T. K. (1940). *Travancore State Manual.* Vol. III. Trivandrum: The Government of Travancore, 700.

3

Job Involvement of Librarians Working in Arts and Science Colleges in Trichy, Tamil Nadu

—Geetha, V. and B. S. Swaroop Rani

This paper attempts to study the level of job involvement among librarians working in arts and Science Colleges in Trichy. The data required for the study was collected through a questionnaire. The major findings of the study are age, experience, qualification and income have a significant relationship towards job involvement. The article concludes that involving people to make decisions will increase loyalty and job involvement.

Introduction

Human interaction is a need of man and a requisite for society. The maintenance of good customer relation brings efficient customers. Services are said to be major priorities of banks over the years for the promotion of their overall depth and growth. In fact, the government has to expand its geographical network and financial operations throughout the country along with the main object of providing better and efficient customer service in nationalised banks. It refers essentially to counter level interface with the customers. The major component of customer service is related to the involvement and the commitment of people rendering such services. The performance of employees depends upon their ability and willingness to interact. It has been achieved through a deep dependence and involvement with others.

The concept of job involvement attaches a large importance withit , because its important role is to provide the employee his needs and the best quality or working life. Job involvement has been described with reference to several items and conditions. For instance, central life interest, work rule involvement, ego-involvement, ego-involved performance, occupational involvement, morale and job satisfaction. The attitude towards overtime, the working hours and the adequacy of organisation information are significantly related to both organisational involvement and job status satisfaction.

Need

A librarian's involvement in job is one of the factors in human behaviour which judge the activities of the libraries. The tremendous pressures to satisfy the ever-changing demands of today's consumers, to meet the challenges of a global economy and to battle the onslaught of foreign competition have forced all countries to adopt a broad range of strategies to meet the competitive realities of the global marketplace.

Scope

The study was conducted among various Arts & Science College librarians in Trichy. The study intends to find the level of involvement of college librarians in their job. Hence, the study covers only librarians in academic institutions.

Objectives

The study began by framing the following objectives:

1. To study the socio-demographic characteristics of the college librarians.
2. To study the level of job involvement among college librarians.
3. To find out the extent of association or relationship between the selected socio-demographic variables with various dimensions of job involvement.

Methodology

The study adopted simple random sampling. A framed questionnaire was distributed to 66 college librarians in the Arts and Science Colleges. Of these 52 librarians were responded. Based on the collected data tabular columns have been drawn and interpretation is being presented.

Analysis and Interpretation

Age-wise Distribution of Respondents

Table 1
Distribution of Respondents Based on Age

Sl. No	*Age in Years*	*No. of Respondents*	*Percentage(%)*
1.	20–30	20	38.46
2.	31–40	18	34.62
3.	41–50	11	21.15
4.	51–60	03	5.77

The analysis (Table 1) shows that 38.46 per cent of the respondents are in the age group of 20-30 years, 34.62 per cent are in the age group of 31-40 years and 21.15 per cent are between 41 and 50 years 5.77 per cent of the respondents are in the age group of 51-60 years.

Qualification-wise distribution of respondents

Table 2
Distribution of Respondents Based on Educational Qualification

Sl. No	*Educational Qualification*	*No. of Respondents*	*Percentage(%)*
1.	P.G Degree	26	50.00
2.	Professional Degree	26	50.00

Table 2 indicates that 50 per cent of the respondents are PG holders and 50 per cent have M.Phil and Ph.D. degrees.

Income-wise distribution

Table 3 shows that 3.76 per cent are in the income group of below Rs. 5,000; 21.15 per cent are in the income group of Rs 5,001–8,000.

5.76 per cent and 17.30 per cent are in the income group of Rs.11, 000–14,000 and Rs. 14,001 and above.

Table 3

Distribution of Respondents Based on Income

Sl. No	*Income of the Respondents*	*No. of Respondents*	*Percentage (%)*
1.	Below 5000	16	3.76
2.	5001–8000	11	21.15
3.	8001–11000	13	25.00
4.	11,001–14000	3	5.76
5.	14,001 and above	9	17.30

Years of Experience

Table – 4

Distribution of Respondents Based on Year of Experience

Sl. No	*Years Experience*	*No. of Respondents*	*Percentage(%)*
1.	01–03 years	14	26.92
2.	04-07 years	13	25.00
3.	08–11 years	09	17.30
4.	12–15 years	08	15.38
5.	15 years and above	08	15.38

Table 4 shows that 26.92 per cent of the respondents have 1 to 3 years of experience. 25 per cent and 17.30 per cent of them have four to seven years and eight to 11 years of experience respectively; 15.38 per cent of the respondents have 12 to 15 years and above each.

Job Involvement

Table 5 shows that 48.07 per cent of the respondents perceive low job analysis and 51.93 per cent perceive high job analysis. 42.31 per cent of the respondents perceive low job interest and 57.69 per cent perceive high job interest. 46.15 per cent of the respondents perceive low job autonomy and 53.85 per cent perceive high job autonomy 38.46 per cent of the respondents perceive low job motivation and 61.54 per cent perceive high job motivation. 50 per cent of the respondents perceive low job commitment and 50 per cent perceive high job commitment.

Table 5

Distribution of Respondents Based on Various Dimension of Job Involvement

Sl. No	*Dimensions*	*No. of Respondents*	*Percentage(%)*
1.	Job analysis		
	Low	25	48.07
	High	27	51.93
2.	Job Interest		
	Low	22	42.31
	High	28	57.69
3.	Job autonomy		
	Low	24	46.15
	High	28	53.85
4.	Job motivation		
	Low	20	38.46
	High	32	61.54
5.	Job commitment		
	Low	26	50.00
	High	26	50.00
6.	Overall		
	Low	24	46.15
	High	28	53.85

Overall job involvement shows that 46.15 per cent of the respondents perceive low job involvement and 53.85 per cent perceive high job involvement.

Relationship between Ages of Respondents with Job Involvement

Table 6 shows that there is a significance relationship between age and job involvement.

Table 6

Chi Square-test to find out the Relationship between Ages of the Respondents with Job Involvement

Sl. No	*Age*	*Job Involvement*		*Statistical interface*
		Low (n:24)	*High (n:28)*	
1.	20–30 years (n=20)	8	12	$X^2 = 0.159$
2.	31–40 years (n=18)	8	10	df = 3
3.	41–50 years (n=11)	6	5	$P < 0.05$
4.	Above 50 years (n=3)	2	1	Significant

Relationship between Education with Job Involvement

Table 7

Chi Square-test to find out the Relationship between Educations of the Respondents with Job Involvement.

Sl. No	*Age*	*Job Involvement*		*Statistical interface*
		Low (n:24)	*High (n:28)*	
1.	P.G Degree (n=26)	14	10	$X^2 = 2.78$
2.	Professional Degree (n=26)	10	18	df = 1 $P < 0.05$ Significant

Table 7 shows that there is a significance relationship between education and job involvement.

Relationship between Experience with Job Involvement

Table 8

Chi-square Test to find out the Relationship between Experiences of the Respondents with Job Involvement.

Sl. No	*Age*	*Job Involvement*		*Statistical interface*
		Low (n:24)	*High (n:28)*	
1.	01–03 years (n=14)	8	6	$X^2 = 1.33$
2.	04–07 years (n=13)	5	8	df = 4
3.	08–11 years (n=9)	4	5	$P < 0.05$
4.	12–15 years (n=8)	3	5	Significant
5.	15 years & above (n=8)	4	4	

Table 8 shows that there is a significance relationship between experiences and job involvement.

Relationship between Income with Job Involvement

Table 9

Chi-square Test to find out the Relationship between Income of the Respondents with Job Involvement.

Sl. No	*Age*	*Job Involvement*		*Statistical interface*
		Low (n:24)	*High (n:28)*	
1.	Below 5000 (n=6)	8	8	$X^2 = 12.11$
2.	5001–8000 (n=11)	6	5	df = 4
3.	8001–11000 (n=13)	8	5	P > 0.05
4.	11001–14000 (n=3)	0	3	Not Significant
5.	14001 and above (n=9)	0	9	

Table 9 shows that there is a significance relationship between income and job involvement.

Conclusion

Much of the early research on job involvement provided mixed results and generated considerable confusion. Recently, a conceptual distinction has been proposed between job involvement, a function of how much the job satisfies one's salient needs, and work involvement, a generalised psychological identification with work. Several studies have provided moderate support for such a distinction. This study was designed to provide additional support for this conceptual differentiation by exploring with five dimensions. Job involvement is a function of the job's ability to satisfy salient needs, and the degree of work involvement that an individual brings to the work situation. Involving and empowering people to make decisions about their work increase loyalty and fastens librarianship. The continuous work processes depends on the work value people add.

References

Beverly, Lynch and Jo Ann Verdin. (1988). Job involvement and Librarians: A Replication. *Library Quarterly,* 157 (2).

Iffald, M.T and Muchinsk, P. M. (1995). Job involvement and Job performance: A meta analysis. *Psychological Bulletin,* 197.

Sibha, A. K. (2000). *Job involvement: a study of the bank employees.* New Delhi: Common Wealth Publishers.

Soal, F.E. (1997). Job Involvement: A Multivariate approach. *Journal of Applied Psychology,* 63.

4

Job Satisfaction among Professional Librarians in the College Libraries in Kerala

—T. Mohana Kumar

The paper discusses the importance of job satisfaction among professional librarians in the college libraries in Kerala. The author conducted a questionnaire survey of selected college libraries to carry out the work. A sample population of 269 professionally qualified college librarians was selected using stratified sampling method covering representation from all types of colleges. An attempt was also made to measure the present level of job satisfaction among professional librarians in the college libraries in Kerala. The significance of the difference between the mean scores of the level of satisfaction of different sub-groups was also tested. The major finding of the study was that the mean score of job satisfaction of librarians is 3.40. The result clearly reveals that the college librarians as a whole have an average level of satisfaction in their job. The authorities should pay more attention to increase the level of job satisfaction of the professional librarians.

Introduction

Manpower or human resources is the most vital resources in an ever-changing society. It constitutes an essential component for the functioning of any organisation and profession. Competent personnel can increase the quality of service. The performance of the personnel plays a vital role in the success and failure of an organisation. Libraries are no exception to this phenomenon. Modern management has been laying increasingly greater emphasis on the ability of the people in the organisation to achieve its goals and objectives. Managements are also concerned with utilising human resources to the optimum level and to make the organisation function more efficiently and effectively. In order to make the human resources more productive and effective they should be satisfied with their job or position. The paper discusses the job satisfaction among professional librarians in the college libraries in Kerala.

Job Satisfaction

Job satisfaction is of utmost significance from the standpoint of employee morale. On closer analysis, studies have revealed job satisfaction to be of great significance for the efficient functioning of an organisation. "Job satisfaction is a key element, which provides an insight into the psychology of work-disability as well as an innovative access to numerous management problems." (Garg, 1999). Job satisfaction is an integral component of the organisational climate and an important element in management employee's relationship. It may be described in terms of attitude towards the job like any other attitude it represents a complex assemblage of cognition (belief or knowledge), emotions (feelings, sentiments or evaluations) behaviours and tendencies (Raza and Gupta, 2000).

It is a complex of different attitudes possessed by an individual. These attitudes relate to several aspects of the job such as pay, status, designation, criteria for promotion, opportunity for advancement, job security, opportunity to use ideas, opportunity to enhance qualifications, opportunity to learn a job, steadiness of employment, supervision, co-workers, working conditions, cleanliness, working hours, ease at work, benefits, communication, recognition and allied factors. Weiss (2002) has argued that job satisfaction is an attitude but points out that researchers should clearly distinguish the objects of cognitive evaluation which are affect (emotion), beliefs and behaviours. This definition suggests that we form attitudes towards our jobs by taking into account our feelings, our beliefs, and our behaviors. As Tiffin and Mc Cormick (1971) point out, the satisfaction which an individual obtain in his job is largely the result of the extent to which different aspects of his work situations are relevant to his job related value systems. In addition to these job related factors, individual adjustment and group relationship outside the job also form major determinants of job satisfaction.

Harrel (1967), on the basis of numerous studies, classifies determinants of job satisfaction in three groups including personal factors, factors inherent in the job and factors controlled by the management. Personal factors relating to job satisfaction are sex, number of dependent, age, time of job, intelligence, education and personality. The job satisfaction factors inherent in the job itself relate to the nature of work, skill required, occupational status, geographical location and size of the organisation. The job satisfaction factors controlled by the management include security, pay, fringe benefits, opportunity for advancement, working conditions, co-workers, responsibility, supervision and downward flow of information.

According to Vaughn and Dunn (1974) job satisfaction is the feeling an employee has about his pay, his work, his promotion, opportunities, his co-workers, and his supervisors. An employee's feeling about each of these terms can be indexed; a numerical value can be assigned to each; and a great total can be computed. While discussing the job anxiety and job satisfaction among professional library employees Prasad (1994) points out that for successful functioning and performance of its manifold duties, libraries require personnel with a high degree of technical skills, intelligence, imagination, initiative, efficiency and understanding. They are, therefore, to be not only professionally qualified, competent and efficient but also to be lively, active, contended and well satisfied with their jobs. In short, Job satisfaction is a very important attribute which is frequently measured by organisations. The most common way of measurement is the use of rating scales where employees report their reactions to their jobs. Questions relate to rate of pay, work responsibilities, variety of tasks, promotional opportunities the work itself and co-workers. Some questioners ask yes or no questions while others ask to rate satisfaction on 1-5 scale (where 1 represents "not at all satisfied" and 5 represents "extremely satisfied").

Ten important aspects of job satisfaction are selected to measure the present level of job satisfaction of college librarians in Kerala. They are as follows:

Criteria of Job Satisfaction
1. Status
2. Your pay
3. Designation
4. Criteria for promotion
5. Library environment
6. Facilities (such as seating, toilet, resting etc.)
7. Working/ service conditions
8. Opportunities for steady work
9. Opportunities to take part in seminars/ conferences
10. Opportunities to enhance your qualifications

Objectives

i) To study the importance of job satisfaction of professional librarians.

ii) To measure the present level of job satisfaction of professional librarians in the college libraries in Kerala.

iii) To find out the significance of difference of job satisfaction between different criterions groups (Independent variables).

vi) To make suggestions for the improvement of the situation.

Methodology

The total population of the study is 392 professionally qualified librarians who are working in various college libraries in Kerala. A maximum sample of 68.62 per cent of the population (269 numbers) was selected by stratified sampling technique by representation from all types of colleges. The questionnaire method was applied to collect the data required for the study. The present level of job satisfaction of professional librarians in the college libraries in Kerala was measured using a scale developed for the purpose. The scale consists of ten items of Likert type on a five-point rating scale. Each item, therefore, contained five alternative responses such as Very Good, Good, Average, Poor,

Very Poor. It was a self-administering tool. The scoring was based on a five-point measurement. The items weighed a score of 5 for Very Good, 4 for Good, 3 for Average, 2 for Poor and 1 for Very Poor. The summated score of all the items provide the total score. The dependable variable of the study is Job satisfaction and the independent variables are the five criterion groups of the colleges and personal and professional characteristics of the librarians. The entire processing of data was done by using the computer software SPSS (Statistical Package for Social Sciences). The statistical techniques used for the analysis of data are the following:

1. Cross tables.
2. Descriptive statistics.
3. Z-test for comparing the mean scores of Job Satisfaction of two groups in the independent variables.
4. One-way ANOVA (F-test) was used for comparing the mean scores of more than two groups in the independent variables along with Scheffe test to identity the pairs of groups showing significant difference.

Analysis

The preliminary analysis of the data collected about the sample college libraries has been done in this part.

Sample College Libraries

The total sample selected for analysis consists of 269 college libraries, i.e., 68.62 per cent of the total population of 392 libraries where professional librarians are working. Out of 13 types of colleges selected, Arts and Science Colleges constitute the major section with 62.45 per cent (168) colleges. The others are Professional Colleges (37.55 per cent). There are 101 Professional Colleges selected for the study. Out of which 1 (0.37 per cent) Fine Arts College, 1 (0.37 per cent) Physical Education, 3 (1.12 percent) Law, 29 (10.78 per cent) Training, 33 (12.27 per cent) Engineering, 4 (1,49 percent) Agriculture, 6 (2.23 per cent) Medical, 5 (1.86 per cent) Dental, 4 (1.49 per cent) Pharmacy, 8 (2.97 percent) Nursing , 5 (1.86 per cent) Ayurveda and 2 (0.74 per cent) Homeo

Colleges in the sample. The distribution of libraries is presented in Table 1.

Table 1. Category-wise Distribution of Libraries

Sl. No	*Categories*	*No.*	*Percent*
1	Arts & science	168	62.45
2	Fine arts	1	0.37
3	Physical education	1	0.37
4	Law	3	1.12
5	Training	29	10.78
6	Engineering	33	12.27
7	Agriculture	4	1.49
8	Medical	6	2.23
9	Dental	5	1.86
10	Pharmacy	4	1.49
11	Nursing	8	2.97
12	Ayurveda	5	1.86
13	Homoeo	2	0.74
	Total	269	100.00

The distribution of the college libraries with regard to their characteristics is presented in Table 2.

Table 2. Characteristics-wise Distribution of College Libraries

Sl. No	*Characteristics*		*No.*	*Percent*
1	Academic type	Arts and science	168	62.45
		Professional	101	37.55
2	Location	Rural	158	58.74
		Urban	111	41.26
3	Management	Government	50	18.59
		Private	219	81.41
4	Financial nature	Aided	133	49.44
		Unaided	136	50.56
5	Research centre	Yes	52	19.33
		No	217	80.67

Academic type, location of the college, management status, financial nature and status as research centre of college libraries are the characteristics taken for analysis. The number and percentage wise distribution of the sub samples are also presented.

Job Satisfaction

Data collected on various important aspects of job satisfaction of college librarians are analysed and the result is presented in the Table 3.

Table 3. Mean Score of Satisfaction in Job/Position

Satisfaction	*Very good*	*Good*	*Average*	*Poor*	*Very poor*	*Mean Score*
1 Status	25.28	44.61	21.19	5.95	2.97	3.83
2 Your pay	13.38	36.80	29.74	15.99	4.09	3.39
3 Designation	24.16	34.20	29.00	8.55	4.09	3.65
4 Criteria for promotion	9.29	23.05	28.62	25.28	13.75	2.86
5 Library environment	25.28	32.34	32.71	6.69	2.97	3.70
6 Facilities (such as seating, toilet, resting etc.)	17.84	28.25	29.74	14.87	9.29	3.30
7 Working / service conditions	15.61	39.78	34.57	7.06	2.97	3.57
8 Opportunities for steady work	15.99	30.86	36.43	11.52	5.20	3.38
9 Opportunities to take part in seminars / conferences	11.52	20.45	39.03	19.70	9.29	3.04
10 Opportunities to enhance your qualifications	12.64	28.25	40.89	11.90	6.32	3.28
Average	17.10	31.86	32.19	12.75	6.10	3.40

Ten items are included in the scale to measure the level of job satisfaction of librarians. Out of the ten items in the scale, Status shows the highest score level of 3.83 followed by Library environment (3.70). The item which shows lowest score level is Criteria for promotion (2.86). Designation occupies the third position in the scale and has a score level of 3.65. The score level of other items are Satisfaction in working / service conditions(3.57), Satisfaction in their pay (3.39), Opportunity for steady work (3.38), Facilities (3.30), Opportunities to enhance their qualifications (3.28) and Opportunities to take part in seminars/ conferences (3.04). The analysis reveals that only four items show above 3.5 score level, i.e., above Average satisfaction (Item No.1. Status, 3. Designation 5. Library environment and 7. Working/ service conditions). The remaining six items except the fourth item (Criteria for promotion) show 3.04 to 3.39 range level. It is only an Average level of satisfaction. The fourth item Criteria for promotion has the score level of 2.86; it is below Average or above Poor. None of the items shows Good(4) or Very Good(5) level of satisfaction.

Percentage-wise distribution of librarians having satisfaction at different levels is also presented in the table.

1. In the criteria Status, one-fourth (25.28 per cent) of librarians have Very Good satisfaction, 44.61 percent have Good Satisfaction and 22.68 per cent have satisfaction at Average level. The total mean score level shows that Status is in an above Average level (Mean score-3.83).
2. As far as Pay is concerned only 13.38 per cent of librarians express Very Good satisfaction, 36.80 percent of librarians have Good satisfaction and 29.74 percent have Average satisfaction. The remaining shows Poor (15.99 per cent) and Very Poor (4.09 per cent) satisfaction (Mean score 3.39).
3. In the case of Designation nearly one-fourth of librarians (24.16 percent) answer Very Good satisfaction, 34.20 percent of librarians show Good satisfaction and 29.00 percent have Average satisfaction (Mean Score 3.65)
4. The criterion for promotion is the item in which very few (9.29 percent) librarians express Very Good satisfaction, 23.05 percent have Good satisfaction and 28.62 percent

have Average satisfaction. Others show very low level (Mean score 2.86).

5. Satisfaction with respect to Library environment, 25.28 percent of librarians show Very Good satisfaction, 32.34 percent of librarians show Good satisfaction and 32.71 percent have Average level of satisfaction (Mean score 3.70).

6. In the case of Facilities in the library 17.84 percent of librarians have Very Good satisfaction, 28.25 have Good satisfaction and 29.74 percent shows Average satisfaction and the remaining shows Poor (9.29 percent) and Very Poor (3.30) satisfaction (Mean score 3.30).

7. As far as Working / service conditions are concerned 15.61 percent of librarians answer that they are Very satisfied, 39.78 percent have satisfaction at Good level and 34.57 percent of librarians have satisfaction at an Average level. (Mean score 3.57).

8. In the item opportunities for steady work 15.99 percent of librarians express Very Good satisfaction, 30.86 percent have Good and 36.43 percent posses only Average satisfaction (Mean score 3.38).

9. Opportunities to take part in seminars/ conferences are concerned only few percent (11.52) of librarians have Very Good satisfaction, 20.45 percent have Good satisfaction and 39.03 percent have Average level of satisfaction (Mean score 3.04)

10. Last item in the scale is Opportunities to enhance qualifications. In this item also only few librarians (12.64 percent) express Very Good satisfaction, 28.25 percent of librarians show Good satisfaction and 40.89 percent shows satisfaction at an Average level. The remaining Librarians show Poor (6.32 percent) and Very Poor (3.28 percent) satisfaction (Mean Score 3.28).

The result of the analysis clearly reveals that the college librarians as a whole have an Average level of satisfaction in their job/ position (mean score 3.40). A diagrammatic representation of the mean scores of librarians' satisfaction in their job/ position is given below.

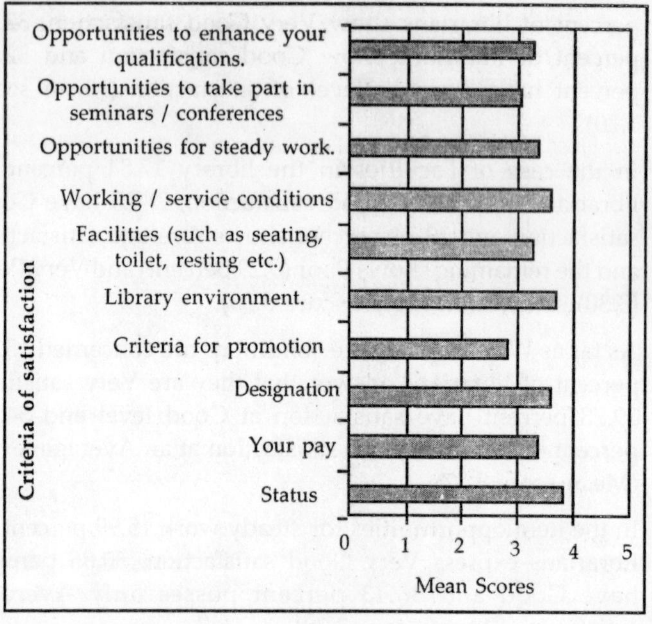

Figure 1 : Average Score of the Level of Satisfaction in Job/ Position

Estimation of Group Differences in Mean Scores of Job Satisfaction of Five Criterion Groups (Sub Samples) of the College.

In this part significance of difference between mean scores of the five groups on the basis of the following characteristics of the college - Academic type (Arts and Science and Professional), Location (Rural and Urban), Management status (Government and Private), Financial nature (Aided and Unaided) and status as University Research Centre (Yes or No) as presented in Table 4. The means and standard deviation of each group were also calculated. The difference in means of each relevant pairs of groups was subjected to statistical test of significance for difference between means for Independent Variables. Z-test was applied to compare the difference of the mean scores of two groups. Results of the comparisons of the mean scores of Job Satisfaction of relevant groups, Standard deviation, the Z-value and level of significance obtained for this comparison are presented.

Table 4. Mean Scores of Job Satisfaction of Five Criterion Groups and Z Value of the Comparison of Means

Sl. No	*Criterion Groups*	*Sub samples*	*Mean*	*SD*	*N*	*Z*	*Sig.*
1	Type of College	Arts & Science	3.41	0.92	168	0.01	0.992
		Professional	3.41	0.65	101		
		Total	3.40	0.83	269		
2	Location	Rural	3.47	0.82	158	1.34	0.180
		Urban	3.33	0.84	111		
		Total	3.40	0.83	269		
3	Management Status	Govt.	3.27	0.77	50	1.37	0.174
		Pvt.	3.44	0.84	219		
		Total	3.40	0.83	269		
4	Financial Nature	Aided	3.33	0.87	133	1.64	0.101
		Unaided	3.49	0.78	136		
		Total	3.40	0.83	269		
5	Status as Research Centre	Yes	3.65	0.92	52	2.15	0.032
		No	3.35	0.80	217		
		Total	3.40	0.83	269		

The result of the test reveals that out of the five criterion groups only the status as Research Centre shows a significant difference. The mean of status as Research Centre is 3.65 and the mean of not status as Research centre is 3.35. The difference is found to be 0.30. The Z value is 2.15. The level of significance is 0.032.

In all other groups, the significant level is above 0.050 level. Therefore no significant difference is found to exist in the sub-samples of these groups. It is found from the result of the test that the librarians working in Colleges as Research Centre exhibit high level of Satisfaction compared with librarians of Colleges not as a Research Centre.

Estimation of Group Differences in Mean Scores of Job Satisfaction with Independent Variables Relating to the Personal and Professional Status of Librarians

In this part eight independent variables relating to the personal and professional status of librarians are selected for statistical test to determine the group differences in the job satisfaction of librarians. The independent variables are as follows:

1. Sex
2. Age
3. Professional qualifications
4. Information technology course taken
5. Professional experience
6. Refresher / Orientation course taken
7. Computer training taken
8. Computer experience

Z-test was applied to compare the difference of the mean scores of two groups. To compare the mean scores of more than two groups F-test (one-way ANOVA) was applied. When the difference between the means was found statistically significant Scheffe test was applied to identify, which two pairs of means contributed to make the statistical difference.

The significance of the difference between the mean scores of Job satisfaction of five criterion groups was tested using Z-test. Mean and standard deviation of the groups, the Z-value obtained for this comparison and level of significance are presented in Table 5.

The result of the test reveals that out of five groups put to test, four groups show significant difference. They are professional qualifications, IT course taken, refresher course taken and computer training taken. IT course taken shows a high significant level. No significant difference is found to exist in the remaining group Sex. It is found from the test that job satisfaction is not very much affected by their gender. But female librarians possess a higher level of satisfaction than male librarians.

The significance of the difference between the mean scores of Job satisfaction of librarians categorised on the basis of Age, Professional experience and Computer experience were compared using F-test (One-way ANOVA). The data and results of the test are presented in Table 6.

Table 5.

Mean Scores of Job Satisfaction of Independent Variables Relating to the Personal and Professional Status of Librarians and Z-value of the Comparison of Means

Sl. No	*Independent Variables*	*Sub Samples*	*Mean*	*SD*	N	Z	*Sig.*
1	Sex	Male	3.33	0.74	162	1.79	0.073
		Female	3.53	0.95	107		
		Total	3.40	0.83	269		
2	Professional qualifications	BLISc	3.26	0.88	98	2.28	0.023
		Higher	3.50	0.79	171		
		Total	3.40	0.83	269		
3	IT course taken	Yes	3.69	0.83	107	4.49	0.000
		No	3.23	0.78	162		
		Total	3.40	0.83	269		
4	Refresher course taken	Yes	3.49	0.84	181	2.31	0.021
		No	3.25	0.79	88		
		Total	3.40	0.83	269		
5	Computer training taken	Yes	3.59	0.81	104	2.83	0.005
		No	3.30	0.83	165		
		Total	3.40	0.83	269		

The result of the F-test given in Table 6 shows that out of three variables in the scale only Computer experience shows a significant difference. No significant difference is found to exist in the variables Age and Professional experience; its significance level is above 0.05.

Since the difference in the mean scores of Job satisfaction was significant in Computer experience as revealed from the F-test at 0.05 level, Scheffe test was applied to identity the pair of groups showing the significant difference. The data and the results of the comparison are presented in Table 7.

The result of the Scheffe test shows that the pairs of groups showing significant difference are No and 5-6; and No and 6+.

Table 6.

Mean Scores of Satisfaction of Librarians of Different Groups Based on Age, Professional Experience and Computer Experience, and the F-value of the Comparison

Sl. No	*Independent Variables*	*Sub-samples*	*Mean*	*SD*	*N*	*Z*	*Sig.*
1	Age	<=30	3.48	0.83	33	2.28	0.080
		31-40	3.45	0.76	69		
		41-50	3.29	0.89	126		
		50+	3.66	0.73	41		
		Total	3.40	0.83	269		
2	Professional Experience	<=5	3.39	0.74	63	1.02	0.396
		6-10	3.33	0.94	38		
		11-15	3.32	0.89	53		
		16-20	3.38	0.87	55		
		20+	3.60	0.75	60		
		Total	3.40	0.83	269		
3	Computer Experience	No	3.10	0.86	54	5.30	0.000
		1-2	3.29	0.94	37		
		3-4	3.27	0.78	55		
		5-6	3.60	0.80	56		
		6+	3.68	0.70	67		
		Total	3.40	0.83	269		

Findings and Suggestions

It is found that only four items in the scale (Status, Designation, Library environment and Working conditions) show above 3.5 score level, i.e., above average satisfaction. The remaining six items except Criteria for promotion show a 3.04 to 3.39 range level (Average level). Criteria for promotion has the lowest score level of 2.86. It is below average. None of the items shows Good (4) or Very Good (5) level of satisfaction. The college librarians as a whole have an average level of satisfaction. The mean satisfaction score is 3.40.

Table 7.

Linear Combination of Groups of Means of Job Satisfaction of Librarians by Computer Experience Using Scheffe Test

Sl. No	*Independent Variables*	*Computer Experience*	*No*	*Subset for alpha = 0.05* 1	2	3
1	Satisfaction	No	54	3.10		
		3-4	55	3.27	3.27	
		1-2	37	3.29	3.29	
		5-6	56		3.60	
		6+	67		3.68	
		Sig.		0.83	0.16	

Thirteen independent variables are selected and put to statistical test to compare the significance of difference in the job satisfaction of professional librarians categorised on the basis of different characteristics of the college library, personal and professional status of librarians. It is found from the result of the test that a significant difference of job satisfaction is found to exist between six out of thirteen independent variables selected for the study. They are Status as Research Centre, Professional qualifications, IT course taken, Refresher course taken, Computer training taken, Computer experience. The following suggestions are made to raise the level of satisfaction of college librarians.

1. Criteria for promotion has the lowest score level in the scale. Experts are of the opinion that promotion is an

effective tool for building employee morale. As Yoder et al (1958) observed, it provides an incentive to initiative, enterprise and ambition, minimises discontent and unrest, attracts capable individuals, necessitates logical training of advancement, forms an effective reward for loyalty and cooperation, long service, etc. This demands sound promotion policies involving a suitable combination of merit and seniority.

2. Provide better status, designation and scale of pay to professionals, which will lead to better satisfaction and results in better utilisation of manpower.
3. The librarian should have a congenial environment that will provide him with the necessary stimulus and encouragement to apply himself to his work creatively.
4. The professional staff should be provided with all possible opportunities to update their knowledge and enhance their qualifications for developing their individual competencies because development provides greater satisfaction for the professional.
5. All practising librarians should spend at least two weeks every year updating their knowledge.
6. Facilities for continuing education should be recognised as an essential part of manpower development programme in the library and information field.
7. For better utilisation of the existing staff, studies on job satisfaction should be conducted from time to time in college libraries in Kerala.

Conclusion

From the discussion of job satisfaction and the analysis it is evident that job satisfaction is of great significance for the fullest exploitation of professional library manpower. Among the factors pay, promotion and opportunity for advancement are considered as significant sources of job satisfaction, although its significance varies in terms of the labour market, economic conditions and allied factors. Lakhanpal (1968), writing on job evaluation, asserts: "if the library administration wants that the employees should consider their work to be enjoyable and interesting, it must bring their salaries to an equitable level. A sound salary structure evolved after a careful job classification will increase job satisfaction." The professional also has a stake in development, for he acquires a greater sense of worth, dignity and well-being as he becomes more valuable to society. He will receive a greater share of the material gains that result from his increased productivity. These two factors give him a sense of satisfaction in the achievement of personal and social goals. It follows that a more highly developed professional will also cause fewer problems and will have greater job satisfaction. So, authorities should take special interest to ensure the satisfaction of their employees in order to utilise and develop the manpower resources.

References

Garg, B. S. (1999). Determinants of job satisfaction of librarians: A multivariate analysis. *Journal of Library and Information Science*, 24 (2), 108-109.

Harrell, T. W. (1967). *Industrial psychology*. New Delhi: Oxford & IBH Publishing Co., 260-274.

Lakhanpal, S. K. (1968). Job classification and evaluation the basis for equitable salary administration in libraries. *Indian Literature*, 24 (1), 5.

Prasad, H. N. (1994). Job anxiety and job satisfaction among professional library employees: A study. *Annals of Library Science and Documentation*, 41 (2), 41-54.

Raza, Masoom and Gupta, Anita. (2000). Job satisfaction and job anxiety among library professional employees working in Delhi University Library system. *IASLIC Bulletin*, 45 (3), 129.

Tiffin, J. and Mc Cormick, E. J. (1971). *Industrial Psychology*. New Delhi: Prentice-Hall of India, 354.

Vaughn, William J, and Dunn, J. D. (1974). A Study of job satisfaction in six university libraries. *College and Research Libraries*, 35(3), 163-177.

Yoder, D., Heneman, H.D., Turnbull, J.G. and Stones, C.H. (1958) *Handbook of personnel management and labour relations*. New York: McGraw-Hill Book Co., 9:5

Weiss, H.M. (2002). Deconstructing job satisfaction: Separating evaluations, beliefs and affective experiences. *Human Resources Management Review*, 12, 173-194. Available at:http://www.en.wilkipedia.org/wilki/job_satisfaction (Accessed on 12 December 2009).

5

Quality Improvement in Libraries in the Changing Landscape of Library Resources, Services and User's Perceptions

—Ramesha

The method of Total Quality Management (TQM) represents a new age in the in the management of an organisation. TQM is a management method that libraries can benefit from it in several ways. The paper discusses the quality improvement in libraries in the changed ICT environment. The concept and meaning of quality and library services are explained. The application of TQM in library and Information services, the Quality Management System (QMS) and strategies applied in the academic library system are discussed. The new role of LIS professionals in the changing environment is also mentioned.

Introduction

The library is unique in society in that it not only identifies, selects, acquire, organises, stores, retrieves and preserves information, it also subsidises access, protects intellectual freedom, and provides direct assistance and instruction to its users.

In the contemporary context there is a need to reshape the vision of libraries and information centres by adopting new, concepts and principles to guide the library management especially with reference to what is going on in the higher education, R& D and Science and Technology (S &T) activities at the global level. Certain ways of thinking about the strategies of developing viable library activities for present century seem to be still bound by or limited to the strategies followed here-to-before a few decades ago. The quest for information has been expanded significantly and it is, now, coupled with a desire for swift and better services. Our perspectives and service programmes must reflect this context. Libraries and information centres need to, among other tasks, provide all users with the information seeking skills needed not only to be productive learners but also to be lifelong learners and efficient contributors to social, cultural and academic endeavours no matter where they eventually work or live.

Quality is the way that a service fulfils the user's expectations, and in that way it could help the user to reach a complete satisfaction. The concept of quality is something the user must say; therefore it is worthless that a librarian qualifies high its own service. If a service doesn't satisfy a user's need, he might say that the service was good although he hasn't found what he was looking for; in this case we didn't reach our goal that is, to get a totally good opinion from the user.

Quality service is the process by which a user satisfies a specific requirement. The user desires high quality service in order to obtain his requirements. The librarian desires to satisfy the user's need of information, so he would come back again soon. The quality of service is the way in which the user satisfies his requirements, knowing that the service has fulfilled his expectations. Provide a quality service we need to system. The system is a group of processes that work together in order to get a specific goal. A system needs resources to generate a service.

Quality and Library Services: Concept, Meaning and Definitions

In order to critically analyse and examine the applications of quality concept to Library and Information Services, it is essential in the first place to understand the various related concepts.

Quality

Quality is often used synonymously with excellence. However, for proper quality management, defining quality and its measurement are essential. Quality has been defined variedly in different contexts. There is wide range of definitions or approaches to quality, describing the relative nature of the concept in the context of higher education. Some of the definitions are discussed here.

Green and Harvey identified five different approaches to quality in higher education. These are, quality:

- in terms of exceptional (high standards);
- in terms of consistency;
- as fitness for purpose (meeting stated purposes);
- as value for money; and
- as transformative (transformation of the participant).

Nunan and Calvert point out that the term quality defies any definition which will be universally accepted. When it is linked to performance, quality implies evaluation for comparative purposes; 'measures' of quality involve norms and standards, and judgements of quality are assisted through use of norm or criterion referenced indicators. Where measurement focuses on the student as a product of education, quality is seen as 'value-based' by the process of education. When the emphasis is management of quality, attention focuses on strategies for achieving or improving quality.

Garvin (1988) identified five approaches to define quality:

- Transcendent approach (quality always exists)
- Product-based approach (products meeting high quality standards)
- User-based approach (quality to meet user's requirements)
- Manufacturing-based approach
- Value-based approach.

In the context of Information Systems, quality pertains to:

- Performance of the system,
- Quality and quantity of the document store,
- Quality of information products judged in terms of defined norms or criteria,

— User satisfaction in terms of value for money spent (cost-benefit) and value for information content (cost-effectiveness). Therefore, the Quality Management Strategies should integrate these various approaches for achieving improved Quality Information Services.

The performance of the Information System mainly relates to:

— Accuracy of the services;

— Adequacy of and need-based services;

— Timeliness of the services.

The term 'quality', according to various glossaries, means one of the following: fitness for purpose, fitness for use, conformity to requirements and absence of defects. The standard ISO 11620 defines quality of libraries as "totality of features and characteristics of a product or service that bear on the library's ability to satisfy stated or implied needs" (ISO 11620, 1998). Over recent years one can observe an increasing interest and different approaches to quality in libraries and information services, especially in a management area. A common factor of several concepts and approaches to quality is the focus on user expectations and needs. In the TQM context, "the quality of service is defined by the customer's perception of both the quality of the product and the service providing it"(Barnard 1994). Academic libraries should fulfil their own strategic plans and also goals of the higher education system. They "like other service institutions have to show that they are using given resources for the right purpose and in the best way, that they are providing high quality services" (Poll and Boekhorst, 1996).

A high quality of library performance is crucial for each academic library to survive. Wide online access to information makes teachers and students demand the highest quality library services. It is the quality of library services that decides on the perception of the library within its parent institution and the society. Comparable quality measures (which refer not only to library services but to all aspects of library performance) are of vital importance for efficient and effective library management. A library needs both to satisfy its users and to prove to its funding bodies that it is worth investment. Moreover, in India the NAAC in the process of the assessment of higher education institutions takes the quality of library services into account.

Application TQM in Library and Information Services

In recent years the academic libraries stood against the fast improvement of technology, with low budget and with more requirements for responsibility. Because of these, new strategies of renewal have been developed at a quick pace. A first step which is necessary for a library is to define which approach in the procedure of change is more appropriate for itself, considering the size, the environments and the conditions of functions of the library.

The method of TQM (Quality Management System) represents a new age in the management of an organisation. Its elements, such as participating management, the personnel training and the responsible service of customers, are views that libraries are already driven by. As a result of this, the libraries are up to improving these principles which already have been valued positively by them and put them partially in practice. Many libraries have embarked on plans for implementing quality-related philosophies such as TQM. It is well-known that TQM is a management method that libraries can benefit from it in several ways.

The Quality Management System (QMS) and Libraries

The objective of the quality management system of academic libraries is to create a user-oriented library. The approach centres on four specific variables:

- The organisational structure
- Process management and key result areas
- The introduction of continuous improvement groups, as a means by which to involve the staff in the quality management process
- Certification and self-evaluation

But the combination of organisational changes and the use of information technology to develop new processes are, of themselves, insufficient—if not reinforced by strong leadership of the library management team and a change in outlook by the library staff—to successfully implement all the services and products on offer to the user.

Consequently, a series of strategies should be developed, with the user uppermost in mind. Some of good the strategies are as follow:

1) Identification of users, their characteristics, their documentary or informational needs, their expectations, etc. The process of analysis and definition is followed by a period of direct consultation with the users and other members of the organization who are familiar with their needs.
2) Standards of service achievable by the library, known to users and updated on a regular basis. These represent the operational objectives of the library, expressed in terms of its commitments to users.
3) Training and development of interdisciplinary work teams and the creation of continuous improvement groups, essential elements in the process to establish modern management practices in the library system and to develop open organisational structures which are truly dynamic, flexible and multifunctional.
4) Strong leadership of the library management team; by that is meant the exercise of authority based on delegation and the promotion of user-oriented initiatives and teamwork.
5) Feedback is a two-way process (users/work teams), the results of which should be made immediately available to all the members of the library staff.
6) Official recognition and recompense for those individuals who best apply the standards of service in their work and who achieve user-oriented improvements.

Best Practices and Quality Library and Information Services

Globalisation and ICT have had impact on the functioning of libraries and information centres. The developments in IT and ICT more particularly advent of Internet and WWW have changed the users' expectation from the libraries in many ways. The ways to build collection and services to the end users' vary from the recent past practices. To meet the end-users demands effectively and efficiently, the academic libraries need to identify and adopt good practices and benchmarks. Thus, preparing guidelines in a standardised way based on the best practices employed by libraries is significant which will ultimately enhance the value-based services of academic libraries. Though, it is institutional accreditation that the NAAC does, the assessment of a library, a vital sub-unit, is a key step that integrates itself with the overall evaluation. A library is the fulcrum of support for the entire range of academic activities on an educational campus. In today's high-tech learning environment, the library as a learning resource is taking up increasingly more academic space and time in the life of a learner. In times ahead, this will be even more so. The NAAC has identified the set of best practices in Library and Information Services, with the help experts and a few case presentations from few selected libraries of the accredited universities and colleges. The NAAC, really an eye opener for the management as well as librarians to understand better in situations apply the best practices accordingly for quality library and information services.

In the LIS context, a practice qualifies to a best practice if it results in high value impact on information use. The most effective way to ensure continuous improvement is to focus on the basic processes by adopting appropriate changes. In general, the use of technology and innovative ideas lead to evolve best practices in library and information environment. In academic libraries, best practice bench marking involves various factors like quality and quantity of users, focus of the institutions, pedagogy of teaching and learning, academic and research programmes delivered, etc. Adaptation and adoption of best practice have to go with institutional environment.

Quality Collection v/s. Quality Services

Collection development and quality services are interrelated in right dissemination of right information to the right user in a right personal way. A well-defined and appropriate collection development policy would greatly help in designing information products and quality services to the users. Collecting, evaluating, organising, seeking of alternatives and leveraging the information resources is the foremost activity of any academic library in establishing an appropriate and need based information system at the affiliated colleges. The philosophy of collection development lies on meeting the information needs of the community. A library rich in terms of its collection in meeting the exact needs of its user population is always recognised to be a centre of excellence in learning. Collection of an academic library has to reflect vision, mission, scope and the community of the academic institution in its size, diversion, content and the quality.

Collection development has to go with periodic changes of the academic and research activities prevailing in the institution. The collection should maintain up-to-datedness, authoritativeness, cost effectiveness and quality of the content, and also to meet standards in physical, electronic forms of the documents. The library would develop a collection of open sources as to the need of its clientele in addition to the procured and budgetary sources. The methods of procuring books and other documents have to pave the way for active participation of all the stakeholders with less process time.

Use of IT in Quality Improvement

The impact of Information Technology (IT) is enormous and global in its magnitude. IT has become an integral part of all aspects of the library. It has profoundly affected library operations, information resources, services, and staff skills requirements and users expectations. It has virtually unlimited potential for variety of useful applications in libraries as it significantly contributes to improved quality, increased productivity, more efficient operations, better resource sharing and more effective services to the users. The proper exploitation of new technologies in libraries is no longer a matter of choice but a matter of survival in an era of rapidly changing technology and global knowledge society. Today, the success of a modern library is increasingly dependent on the most effective utilisation and strategic management of new technologies in libraries. It is believed that the versatility and power of information technology which include accommodation of increase workload, achievement of greater efficiency in improving existing services, ability for generation of new services, facilitating cooperation and in providing for an integrated approach without regard to format, location or medium through which it is served, which can light heartedly be called "one stop informaticn shopping," can stand in good stead in the quest for quality and productivity in information services and products.

Role of the LIS Professionals in the Changing Environment

LIS professionals, they know the new role and responsibilities in the changing networked, liberalise, globalise environment. Here I would like to emphasize that the Information and Communication Technologies (ICT) offer you a lot of opportunities to redefine how information and associated instruction are communicated to users. As information systems increase in complexity and new resources like digital resources or electronic resources continue to spring up, librarians are becoming indispensable counsellors in the electronic environment. They are called upon to assist users in identifying evaluating sources, and to serve as true advisors and teachers rather than as custodians of collections.

Today's educational milieu enables the librarians and the users to work together, wherever each may be located; physical proximity is no longer essential. It is equally unnecessary for the librarian to reside only in the library building; he or she can become as "distributed" as modern electronic information, and work with the faculty and students in their own spaces.

Changing technologies and formats are also recasting the roles of librarians who collect, organise, and conserve information resources. Electronic collections will require new procedures for selecting and cataloguing, and librarians will confront critical new preservation and archiving challenges. Some tasks associated with print publications will disappear, allowing more time to be redirected to the instructional aspects of the librarian's changing role.

Conclusion

Effective, high quality undergraduate library services successfully support the undergraduate programmes of the institution. To facilitate academic success, library services to undergraduates must provide access to a broad range of information resources. Referencc and referral services, orientation activities, and instruction sessions that teach students the critical thinking skills necessary for using library resources are basic services provided by undergraduate library personnel. Varied and innovative undergraduate teaching programmes include teaching by personal contact and through the preparation and use of instructional materials in various formats, formal group instruction and informal, unstructured contacts with students. Undergraduate library services provide a laboratory for students to acquire information literacy skills: identification of needed information, effective and ethical use of intellectual and physical resources, and knowledge of when to ask for help as well as the confidence to do so. Undergraduate library services provide a gateway to all future library inquiry, not only preparing students for graduate work and research but also teaching them to use information sources as citizens, as consumers, as professionals, and for recreational purposes.

The universities and colleges are in a state of transformation. In the future, it will be less place-dependent and more distributed than the present academy. The student body will be more diverse, and learning more student-centered. Approaches to teaching and learning are also changing, both in the traditional classroom and through distance/online education. New models are emerging in which students combine conventional classroom experience with a range of learning experiences independent of time and location.

For all these reasons, the library of the future will continue to emphasize selecting, accessing, and subsidising information resources. Of equal importance will be teaching students and faculty to identify, locate, and evaluate information, wherever individuals or resources may reside. Librarians will assist faculty and students as they teach and learn, whether locally or at a distance.

References

Altman, E. and Hernon, P. (1998). Service quality and customer satisfaction do matter. *American Libraries,* 53-54.

Barnard, S. B. (1994). Total quality management: customer-centered models for libraries. In: *Total Quality Management in Libraries. A Sourcebook,* Englewood. 1-4.

_______________ (1998) Total Quality Management. In: *Encyclopedia of Library and Information Science*. 61, 311-325.

Derfert-Wolf, L. and Bednarek-Michalska B. *Eds*. (2000). Quality management in academic libraries. International conference held in Bydgoszcz - Gniew, 10-13 September 2000. In: *EBIB Conference Proceedings* Available at: http://ebib.oss.wroc.pl/matkonf/atr/indexen.html, (Accessed on 9.October 2009).

Gorny, M, Jazdon A. (1997). The Implementation of Information Technology Projects in Polish Research and Academic Libraries in the early 1990s. Questions of Scope and Effectiveness. *Library Management*, 18 (6), 280-285.

Hernon, P., Nitecki D., Altman, E. (1999). Service quality and customer satisfaction; an assessment and future directions. *Journal of Academic Librarianship*, 25 (1), 9-17.

ISO 11620 (1998), ISO 11620: 1998/AD1: 2003. *Information and Documentation.* Library performance indicators.

Meera, B M. (1998). Performance measurement: a criteria for quality improvement in library and information services. *Library Science with a Slant to Documentation and Information Studies.* 35(3), 149-156.

Mowat, I. R. M. (1996). Ensuring quality staff in a modern university library. In: *Library Management and Information Technology*. Proceedings of the seminar held in Vilnius, Lithuania, 27-33.

Nitecki, D. (1996). Changing the concept and measure of service quality in academic libraries. *Journal of Academic Librarianship*, 22 (3), 181-190.

Osman, Z., Goon, C. A., Aris, W. H. W. (1998). Quality services: policies and practices in Malaysia. *Library Management*,19 (7), 426 - 433.

Peter Rophy (1993) Quality Management: a University approach. *Aslib Information* 21(6), .246-248.

Poll, R., te Boekhorst, P. (1996). *Measuring quality : international guidelines for performance measurement in academic libraries.* IFLA Publications 76. München.

Pritchard, S. M. (1996), Determining quality in academic libraries - Perspectives on Quality in Libraries. *Library Trends*, 44 (3); 572-594.

Quality management in academic libraries. International conference held in Bydgoszcz, Gniew, 10-13 September 2000. *EBIB Conference Proceedings*, Polish Librarian Association, Available at:http://ebib.oss.wroc.pl/matkonf/atr/buzdyg_abs.html, (Accessed on 12 September, 2008).

Revill, D. (200). Looking a back in Anger. *Ariadne*,18 ; 4-6. Available at http://www.ariadne.ac.uk/issue18/revill/ (Accessed on 11September 2008).

Total Quality Management in Libraries. A Sourcebook, Englewood, 100-121.

Winkworth, I. (2001). Innovative United Kingdom approaches to measuring service quality. *Library Trends*, 49 (4), 718-732.

Webster, Duane E. (1977). Choices tacing academic libraries in allocating scarce resources. In. *Library Building: Critical Challenges for the future*. Ed. Sul H. Lee, Ann Arbor, Mich.,: Persian Press, 75-87.

6

Quality of Work Life and Occupational Stress among the Library Professionals in Kerala

—K. P. Somanathan Nair and K. K. Reena

This paper describes a study on Quality of Work Life and Occupational Stress among the library professionals in Kerala. The tools used for the study are Quality of Work Life Scale for Library Professionals (QWLSLP) and Occupational Stress Inventory for Library Professionals (OSILP). The results revealed that Quality of Work Life among library professionals in Kerala are not very high and library professionals in Kerala do not experience stress in their occupation. The Quality of Work Life and Occupational Stress are found to be negatively correlated.

Introduction

In a volatile and insecure environment workers are forced to cope up with more frequent changes in their tasks. A blending succession of frequent transfer, retrenchment, product changes, reorganisations, and changes in the organisation of work etc., enforce new roles and relationships, which will have a direct impact on jobs and staff. The advancements in new technologies also made the problem a little more complex.

In this age of global economic recession the job security of the professionals are also at peril. The speed of the busy life; cultural, economic and political changes in the society; ever changing roles and role ambiguity of the individuals, etc., are causing to precipitate a strange disease to human beings – the stress. Stress has become common and very frequent when and wherever there is human involvement. It has also become one of the most serious occupational health hazards of the time. Stress at work and the stressful transactions are characterised in all organisational settings. The factors that lead to stress at the workplace are categorised mainly into four by Summers, *et al.*, (1994): Personal characteristics, Organisational characteristics – structural, Organisational characteristics - procedural, and Role characteristics.

A person who enjoys the work and derives satisfaction alone can perform in the best perfect manner. The fulfilment of personal needs and goals leads to satisfaction, well being and happiness. But how far and how long can the individual be satisfied in the profession, which is full of work-related stress and strain? For this reason, one needs to be sensitive to factors related to performance, recognition, work content, responsibility, promotion and pay, organisational policies, working conditions, etc.

The Quality of Work depends on the Quality of Work Life. It has been clear that one can accomplish his mission and provide the level of service the public demands only if we recruit and retain the best and the brightest and provide them with a work environment that supports them in getting their jobs done. The phrase "Quality of Work Life" (QWL) has come in use recently to evoke a broad range of working conditions and the related aspirations and expectations of the employees. The QWL can be described as the subjectively perceived satisfaction in one's different aspects of work life as reported by the individual. It is an index of what people find interesting and satisfying at their work. The Quality of Work Life is a concern not only to improve life at work, but also life outside work. Hence it encompasses a vide variety of programmes and techniques that have been developed to endeavour to reconcile the twin goals of an individual and the organisation, i.e., the Quality of Life and Organisational Growth. The Quality of Work Life has, therefore become a key area of consideration now-a-days.

The stress situation vitiates adverse effects in the running of an organisation. It creates unpleasant situations in the employer-employee relationships and staff-clientele relations may deteriorate, inaccuracies may develop in the work and so on. The serious effects of job stress could include employee absenteeism and burnouts, which may increase the workload of the fellow workers. The stress management has got enough significance in improving the quality of work life.

In the changing environment of modern technological advancements, the traditional concept of the library profession is being subjected to rapid changes. The advent of computer, Internet technology, etc., has added new dimensions to the roles and responsibilities of the profession. The user's demands are also changing according to the new developments in the information scenario. Consequently, the librarians are now better known as Information Professionals and their role is to collect, organise and disseminate information to the users to cater to their complex needs.

The present study attempts to measure the extent of Quality of Work Life (QWL) and the amount of Job Satisfaction the library professionals derive, and to identify the stressors that accelerate the Stress (OS) and burnout in the profession.

Objectives

The study has been designed to attain the following objectives.

i) To find out the extent and levels of 'Quality of Work Life' and 'Occupational Stress' among the Library Professionals in Kerala.

ii) To compare the 'Quality of Work Life' among the Library Professionals in Kerala (taken in pairs) categorised on the basis of select independent variables.

iii) To compare the level of 'Occupational Stress' among the Library Professionals in Kerala (taken in pairs) categorised on the basis of select independent variables.

iv) To estimate the relationship between the 'Quality of Work Life' of Library Professionals in Kerala and each of the select independent variables.

v) To estimate the relationship between the 'Occupational Stress' of Library Professionals in Kerala and each of the select independent variables.

vi) To study the extent of association between 'Quality of Work Life' and 'Occupational Stress' among the Library Professionals in Kerala.

Methodology

The target population of the investigation consists of library professionals in the state of Kerala, having at least a graduation in Library and Information Science as the minimum professional qualification.

Gender, Age, Marital status, Number of children, Educational background, Job title category, Professional experience, Primary functional area, Salary range, Involvement in IT applications, Number of supervisors, Work schedule, Type of library, Size of library, and Type of management are chosen as the independent variables for the study.

The study was carried out on a representative sample of 300 Library Professionals in Kerala, drawn from institutions like universities, colleges and other organisations. Stratified random sampling technique was employed for the selection of the sample. Due representation was given to the factors like age, sex, job category, qualification, experience, type of the library etc. while selecting the sample.

The following two tools were specifically constructed and standardised by the investigators for the purpose of the study.

i) Quality of Work Life Scale for Library Professionals (QWLSLP)

ii) Occupational Stress Inventory for Library Professionals (OSILP)

The scales were framed on Likert type of five-point scoring, i.e. SA (Strongly Agree), A (Agree), NAD (Neither Agree Nor Disagree), D (Disagree) and SD (Strongly Disagree).

Data were collected from the sample of library professionals through questionnaires containing three parts: 1) General Data Sheet to collect data on independent variables 2) Quality of Work Life Scale for Library Professionals (QWLSLP) and (3) Occupational Stress Inventory for Library Professionals (OSILP)

Analysis of Data

The collected data were analysed using appropriate statistical techniques, such as:

i) Percentage analysis

ii) Pearson's Product Moment Coefficient of Correlation
iii) Test of significance of difference between Means.
iv) One-way ANOVA
v) Scheffe' test of multiple comparison.
vi) Chi-square test of independence.

Findings

The major findings of the study are as follows:

Extent and Level of Quality of Work Life among the Library Professionals

The percentage of library professionals having high level of QWL is significantly high. The population value of the percentage lies between 70 and 80 at 95 per cent confidence level. However librarians with the highest level of QWL are only 5 to 11 percentage at 95 per cent confidence level. Further, the magnitude of the mean value of QWL suggests that the QWL experienced by the librarians in Kerala are not very high.

Extent and Level of Occupational Stress among the Library Professionals

The percentage of librarians having high level of Occupational Stress is zero. The magnitude of the mean score of OS is 118.89 in the sample with a standard deviation of 14.39. This shows that the library professionals working in different types of libraries do not experience any stress in their occupation.

Group Differences in Mean QWL Scores

On investigating group difference in mean QWL scores it was found that significant difference existed between supervisory librarians and non-supervisory librarians at 0.01 level of significance. The mean scores of the two categories shows that supervisory librarians have greater QWL than non-supervisory librarians. Meanwhile, no significant difference was noticed among the groups of librarians categorised on the basis of characteristics: Gender, Age, Marital status, Number of children, Educational background, Professional experience, Primary functional area, Salary, Involvement in IT applications, Number of supervisors, Work schedule, Type of library, Size of library, Type of management.

Group Differences in Mean OS Scores

All the respondents in the sample experienced only low stress in their occupation. Therefore it was concluded that the librarians in Kerala did not have occupational stress at all. Hence comparisons of the mean OS scores of relevant sub samples became irrelevant in the context of the study.

Association between QWL and Independent Variables

Association between QWL and select independent variables were studied using Chi-square test of independence. The results are:

1) Significant association was found to exist between QWL and three independent variables: Size of library in terms of number of books (0.05 level), Professional experience (0.01 level) and Job title category (0.05 level).
2) QWL was found not related significantly with the following variables: Gender, Age, Marital status, Number of children, Educational background, Primary functional area, Salary, Involvement in IT applications, Number of supervisors, Work schedule, Type of library, Size of library in terms of journal titles, Size of library in terms of number of staff, Type of management.

Association between OS and Independent Variables

1) A significant association was found to exist between OS and three independent variables: Size of library in terms of number of staff (0.05 level), Age (0.01 level), Involvement in IT application (0.05 level).
2) The occupational Stress of the library professionals in Kerala was found not related significantly with the following independent variables: Gender, Marital status, Number of children, Educational background, Job title category, Profesional experience, Primary functional area, Salary, Number of supervisors, Work schedule, Type of library, Size of library in terms of number of books, Size

of library in terms of number of journal titles, Type of management.

Association between QWL and OS

Relationship between QWL and OS was studied using the Chi-square test and Pearson's Coefficient of Correlation. The Chi-square value showed that the variables were significantly related at 0.01 level. However the degree of association is not high since the value of C-coefficient is only 0.3434. The Coefficient of Correlation shows that the variables are negatively correlated. The correlation is significant at 0.01 level with a value of – 0.377.

Conclusion

The main aim of the study was an indepth examination of the relationship of Quality of Work Life and Occupational Stress of librarians with the independent variables. Based on the findings evolved from the investigation, the following suggestions have been made for implementation.

i) To improve the Quality of Work Life of the librarians in Kerala, Work Assessment Committees may be constituted in the organisaions, headed by a qualified professional. The Committee shall meet frequently and assess the performance and appreciate the sincere efforts made by the professionals.

ii) The librarians may be given due participation while framing policies in the organisation they serve, which will give them a feeling of part of the whole. This will help them to contribute to the achievement of the institution's goals.

iii) Professionals at entry cadres and junior level librarians may be given on-the-job training to make the job and the service more qualitative and useful. Also efforts may be made to find out the skills and talents and the area of interest of the professionals and tap it for the improvement of one's own welfare and that of the organisation, which may improve the work efficiency.

iv) In the current scenario, the librarians are not identified with their position in the organisation they serve and in the society they live. To solve the identity crisis, their present designations as Librarian, Catalogue Assistant, Reference Librarian, Archivist etc. may be changed to Scientist, Jr. Scientist, Sr. Scientist, Information Scientist, etc.

v) There shall be chances and open forums for professionals to have better exchange of their professional matters and discuss their problems to improve their service quality and to make themselves satisfied in their job. Quality circles are small informal units of professionals formed in the organisation for meeting the professionals at frequent intervals. The professionals shall meet at short intervals in their work place to discuss their professional matters, which will help them to make radical changes in their services and may also help to find remedies in the crisis they confront in their day- to-day professional life. This may improve the quality of work life of the individuals.

vi) The fringe benefits given to the library staff may be enhanced. The employees shall be provided with canteen, crèche, recreation and entertainment, health facilities, etc., in their workplace.

vii) The librarians may be made very friendly with usages of modern information gadgets like Internet and computer technologies. They shall be imparted proper training and orientation to equip themselves to rise up to meet the current requirements.

viii) QWL and OS of librarians are found significantly and negatively correlated. So reducing the levels of stress is one of the best ways to enhance QWL. Hence it is suggested that, on the basis of the outcome of the study, effective stress management programmes may be adopted in libraries in Kerala to maintain the stress at reasonable and acceptable levels.

References

Ahmad, S. and Mehta, P. (1997). Role stress, Quality of Work Life and alienation. In D. M. Pestonjee and U. Pareek (Eds.), *Studies in organisational role stress and coping*. Jaipur: Rawat Publications.

Anastasi, Anne (1990). *Psychological testing*. Ed.6. New York: Macmillan Publishing Co.

Awasthi, Neeru (2002). Stress and burnout among library professionals in the universities and colleges of Punjab, Haryana and Chandigarh, Unpublished Ph.D Thesis.

Balu, V. (2001). Improving Quality of Work Life – The need for dynamic H.R.D. practices. In Bhatia, B. S. and Batra, G. S. (Eds.) *Human Resource Development.* New Delhi: Deep and Deep Publications.

Biswas, S. K. (1993). Quality of Work Life - What is it? *The Indian Journal of Labour Economics*, 36 (4), 759-764.

Bohlander (2000). Quality of Work Life. *In Principles and techniques of personnel management/ human resource management.* New Delhi: Deep and Deep Publications.

Bunz, *et.al.* (1974). Quality of Working Life: Social indicators for job satisfaction and employment opportunities, In *Bonn: Bundesministrarium fur arbeit und sozialordnugg,* 267.

Cronbach, Lee J. (1984). *Essentials of Psychological testing,* Ed. 4. New York: Harper and Row Publishers.

Edwards, Allen L. (1969). *Techniques of attitude scale construction.* Bombay: Vakils, Feffer and Simons .

Ferguson, G. A. (1976). *Statistical Analysis in Psychology and Education.* Ed. 4. Tokyo: McGraw-Hill.

Golembiewski, Robert T. *et.al.* (1998). Estimates of burnout in Public Agencies: Worldwide, how many employees have which degrees of burnout, and with what consequences? *Public Administration Review,* 58.

Goswami, P. R. and Gaur, R. C. (1998). *The profession of librarianship:* Hopes and despair. *ILA Bulletin*, 34(1-2), 1-7.

Hudson, Mary Pelzer (1999). Conflict and stress in times of change. *Library Management*, 20(1), 35-38.

Jain, Sangeetha (1991). *Quality of Work Life.* Delhi: Deep and Deep Publications.

Julit Nawe (1995). Work-related Stress among the library and information workforce. *Library Review,* 44 (6), 30-37.

Kaya, Ebru (1995), Job satisfaction of the librarians in the developing countries, 61st IFLA General Conference Proceedings, August, 20-25.

Lowe, Graham S. (2000). *The Quality of Work: A people-centred agenda.* Oxford: Oxford University Press.

Pestonjee, D. M. (1999). *Stress and coping: The Indian experience.* Ed. 2. New Delhi: Sage Publications.

Raza, M. Masoom and Gupta, Anita (2000). Job satisfaction and job anxiety among library professional employees working in Delhi University library system. *IASLIC Bulletin,* 45(3), 129-134.

Sornam, S and Sudha, S. (2003). Occupational role stress on women librarians: A study. *SRELS Journal of Information Management*, 40(2), 147-156.

Summers, T.T *et al.* (1994). A field study of some antecedents and consequences of felt Job Stress. In R.Candall and P.L.Perrewe (Eds.), *Occupational Stress: A Handbook.* Washington D.C: Taylor& Francis, 113-127.

Togia, Aspasia (2005). Measurement of burnout and the Influence of Background Characteristics in Greek Academic Librarians. *Library Management*, 26(3), 130-138.

Topper, Elisa F. (2008). Job satisfaction in libraries: Love it or leave it. *New Library World*, 109(5/6), 287-290.

II
Knowledge Management

7

Feasibility of Knowledge Management Tools in Academic Library Services

—Lalitha Aswath

The evolution of information and knowledge has impacted on all organisations, including academic libraries. Knowledge Management has drawn the attention of LIS professionals for past decade. Knowledge management in the beginning was a feature of the corporate sector; it has been soon realised to play a role in academic libraries too. This paper discusses the various components of knowledge management process, identifies Intranet as one of the tools of KM, its contents, resources required and advantages as a tool for KM. The study explores the feasibility of services offered through Intranet in University libraries.

Introduction

This is an era of information and knowledge explosion. The unprecedented growth of knowledge and information has impacted on all organisations including libraries. The libraries are the repositories of knowledge and form an integral part of education. Libraries have long history, beginning with chained and closed access libraries of earlier times to present day digital and virtual libraries that use the latest technology for providing information through various services. The success of LICs depends upon their ability to utilise information/ knowledge of its staff to serve the user community. The ICT has played a significant role in this dynamics which has not only made access across the globe easier, but has facilitated integration of thought process, synergy in working methods and places, team learning and enhancing organisational transparency. Accordingly librarians have also changed their work as custodians of information resources in the library to information providers, navigators, Cybrarians who are busy in satisfying the information requirements of their clients. To provide relevant and value added services to user community and libraries must strive to provide right information at the right time with a right expense of financial and human resources.

Academic Libraries

Academic libraries are information centres established in support of the mission of their parent institutions to generate Knowledge, equip people with knowledge in order to serve the society and advance the well being of mankind.

The primary objective of academic institutions of higher education is advancement of learning and acquisition of knowledge. Academic libraries are part of the university and its organisational culture. Whatever affects universities has an impact on their libraries too. As a result the role of university libraries is changing to provide the competitive advantage for the university.

And today librarians are connected to a vast ocean of network-based services. Academic libraries are the nerve centres of academic institutions need to support teaching, research and other academic programs.

Changing Role of Universities

Universities are faced with a challenge to create and disseminate knowledge to society. Traditionally, universities have been the sites of knowledge production, storage, dissemination and authorisation (Reid, 2000). Universities and other higher education institutions face similar challenges that many non-profit and for-profit organisations face. The challenges are financial, increasing public demand, accountability, rapidly evolving technologies, changing role of staff, diverse student demographics, competing values and a rapidly changing world (Naidoo, 2000).

Universities need to share information and knowledge among the academic community within and outside the institution. Knowledge management has become a key issue in the universities due to changes in knowledge culture. Universities are not isolated entities but exist as a part of society. They engage in teaching, research and community services. Therefore, knowledge created in university through research and teaching should be relevant to the society, and promoting knowledge as a major factor of business of the University and higher education institutions.

Knowledge Management

Knowledge has been identified as a key resource in all organisations whether non-profit making for-profit making. Organisations are beginning to realise that there is a vast and largely untapped asset diffused around in the organisation, i.e., knowledge. This realisation led to the changed role of Academic libraries to provide competitive advantage for the parent universities.

Knowledge and management of knowledge are regarded as increasingly important features of an organisational survival. Application of knowledge resources successfully helps the organisation to deliver creative products and services. Knowledge management has been hyped since late the 1990's, first in the business sector and then in the higher education, and to library management. The need for embracing knowledge management in academic libraries is mainly due to a combined impact of library budget shortfall and higher user expectation and staff user ratio (Dimattia, 1997). A survey conducted by Branin (2003) on collection management over the last 50 years has depicted an evolutionary path from collection development to collection management and now to knowledge management.

Need for KM in Libraries

The exponential growth in human knowledge in a variety of formats has led libraries to develop their resources, access and share strategies from print to electronic and digital resources.

Due to budget shortfalls in libraries, limited technological access, poor staffing and space, libraries have to carefully analyse the needs of their users and seek co-operative acquisitions plans to meet the needs of users.

In fact, the lion's share of the library budget is allocated to its staff and acquisition and cataloguing of library materials. Effective use of staff (HR) and improvement of efficiency and effectiveness of technical services operations are the real focus of knowledge management in academic libraries.

The goal is to make full use of the knowledge existing in the organisation to increase the operational efficiency and productivity.

Components of KM

The knowledge management environment centred round three components:

1. People – Technology experts
Knowledge professionals
Knowledge managers
2. Process - Creation, capturing, storing, sharing, application, and
3. Technology - Hardware and software packages
(Robertson and Brun, 2005)

1. *People:* All members of an organisation are the focus of the KM; they are the creators as well as users of knowledge assets (both explicit and tacit). They act as target groups, they are involved in creation, sharing and use of generated knowledge with in the organisation and outside – knowledge is associated with human cognition. The primary requirement in KM is knowledge sharing culture. The people associated with knowledge management are of three types:
   - *Technology experts:* Technology experts are those concerned with design and development of tools and services for knowledge discovery. They build applications, databases, networks that allow the

organisation to do its work with accuracy, reliability and speed (Kim, Seonghee, 2000).

— *Knowledge professionals:* They are the individuals in the organisation who have the skills, training and know-how to organise information/knowledge into systems and structures that facilitate effective use of knowledge resources. LIS professionals have long been working as information managers and they differ from knowledge managers as information managers are concerned with public domain knowledge, while knowledge managers are oriented towards institutional implicit/tacit knowledge.

— *Knowledge managers:* They are the groups of people, who focus on the achievement of organisational goals. Identify present needs and problems, initiate practical and manageable activities to achieve set goals.

Most important feature of knowledge management is motivation of staff to contribute and share their knowledge (not an easy task). A large portion of the knowledge in any organisation is tacit, embedded with in individual experience, judgements and intuition (Ahmed, Lim, & Loh, 2002). Some staff may have difficulty in expression and communication. Some staff may not want to share their knowledge for the fear that once their knowledge is shared, they might no longer be valued/ indispensable. Some staff may not share their knowledge for free, as there are free riders who take others knowledge for granted but never share their own (Susarla,Liu, & Whinston, 2003).

2. *Process:* THe knowledge management process consists of several stages:

— *Environment creation* – People working in the organisation have to change their mindset to share their tacit knowledge, nurture it, and learn more about the system, users of the system identify and integrate people and process and technology.

— *Knowledge creation* – Knowledge in public domain is

explicit and published. In a personal domain it is tacit. Knowledge is human capital. Identifying new knowledge and creating new knowledge and adding value and vision to the new knowledge and its application is the essence of KM

— *Knowledge organisation* – The traditional and the current KM oriented organisation have a common orientation i.e. establishing semantic relationships, providing syntax, hyper linking, etc., (Data gathering, classification knowledge database creation content mapping...etc. (Library professionals have expertise).

— *Knowledge sharing* — In KM knowledge sharing deals with creating a value for the intangible assets (HR/ Tacit Knowledge).

— *Knowledge synthesis* – The intrinsic value of knowledge created lies in its application in an appropriate situation. Application may be started from top-down or bottom up and even in the middle. Each strategy has its own merits and risks.

3. *Technologies:* They are the gadgets (hardware and software) required to interconnect individuals – i.e., Intranet. And technologies needed for processing, storing and retrieval with in and out side – Internet and a variety of KM solution software packages are available from vendors. We are making use of existing technology to store and retrieve knowledge for promoting knowledge management in library operations. Open source technology and software are ideal, but require high level of programming skills to utilise. On the contrary, majority of the libraries/librarians have Microsoft Office Suite installed on their work stations. MS Word is good for creating operational procedures and other documentations related to library operations. MS Excel is good for keeping statistics and creating charts at departmental/section level. Ms Access can store data for retrieval with customised queries, and can also be converted to web pages (Static/dynamic), facilitate retrieval. And most of the staff members are familiar with

MS Word and Excel. In addition, web portals, online help desk, virtual reference desk, etc.

Significance of KM in AL

KM is defined by Gartner Group (2000) as a discipline that promotes as integrated approach to identifying, capturing, evaluating, retrieving and sharing all the in formation assets of organisation. Balcombe (1999) defines knowledge management as systematically capturing, sharing, using and creating knowledge to add value to the organisation. It also refers to effectively identifying, acquiring, developing, resolving, using, storing and sharing knowledge, to create an approach for transforming tacit knowledge into explicit knowledge (Shanhong, 2000).

For the purpose of this paper and in the light of above mentioned definitions, KM may be defined as a process of identification, capturing, storing and exploiting knowledge (both tacit and explicit).

To determine the value of Intranet as a KM tool at university libraries in Karnataka, small survey has been conducted to know their understanding of KM. Their understanding of KM is "a process of identifying, acquiring, organising and sharing of information packages among the user groups."

Intranet as a KM tool

Intranets have emerged as one of the most effective ways of sharing information and knowledge in most of the organisations. They act as circulation system for supporting the flow of information. Therefore it is necessary here to mention the importance of Intranet as a KM tool.

Blackmore (1997) described an Intranet as 'a means of exploiting Internet Technologies within organisation based computer environment to aid the progression towards the seamless navigation of both internet based and in-house generated learning materials.

Curry and Stancich (2000) have defined Intranet as a private computing network, internal to an organisation, allowing access only to authorised users.

Yen and Chou (2001) have defined it as a private computer network based on the data communication standards and technologies of the public Internet.

Based on the above definitions an Intranet can be defined as a network that uses Intranet concepts and technologies within the organisation in order to be accessed and shared by user groups and employees. And such knowledge is stored electronically and access is usually controlled by password. To persuade people to share knowledge, they have to be motivated and provided with the necessary tools. If given the right tools and guidance, the individual will be able to make the knowledge sharing process as efficient as possible. Intranets have emerged as one of today's most effective ways of sharing information and knowledge in organisations.

Resources Required by KM

KM is a useful resource. Qualified and dedicated personnel are required for a successful KM effort, as is supporting technology. One of the resources required for a successful KM effort is personnel. KM requires not only knowledgeable employees, but also specialised knowledge workers. A KM worker requires varying depths of knowledge in particular areas (Skyrme, 1998):

- *Technical skills* – information (resources) management, information technology skills.
- *Business knowledge* – industry, markets, customers, competitors, and general business context.
- *Interpersonal skills* – networking, listening, interpreting, challenging, teamwork, communications.
- *Management skills* – motivating, coaching, facilitating, influencing.
- *Company/organisation knowledge* – knowledge of procedures and culture.
- *Personal characteristics* – integrity, confidence, openness, trust, supportive, honesty, willingness to learn.

Advantages of Intranet

1. *Consistency:* Knowledge existing on intranet can be viewed by all always as long as the network is online.
2. *Interactivity:* One can create discussion groups, and other two way communication tools.
3. *Inexpensive Updating:* One can easily and inexpensively update online publications. This can be done as frequently as necessary.
4. *User-friendly Interface:* Intranet application uses an interface that is conducive to point and click navigation. Users can easily get to the information they need and it is easy to learn.
5. *Centralisation:* Users can access information from a central database at any time and in number of geographical locations.
6. *Simplicity*: It can be created and maintained with a minimum of programming expertise.
7. *Flexibility:* Provides one access point to the organisations database from all corners of the organisation, as if it is available in one's own office.
8. *Faster and Improved services:* Intranet improves the way in which services are rendered easily and quickly.
9. *Accuracy and timeliness:* Information and data are as accurate as supplied by people and will not change between requests and barring technical problems, messages will be delivered on time.
10. *Reduces Paperwork:* Intranet is closer to a paperless working environment, because the more the intranet progresses the less paper will be used.
11. *Currency:* The Intranet contains the most current information, knowledge: in a format that can be searched, they are the major steps in the transition towards paperless workplace.

Contents of an Intranet

The content of an Intranet is the engine that drives the Intranet as a KM tool. To be a value to an organisation it must be up-to-date and of interest to employees. The content of the intranet depends on the needs of the employees and therefore differ from organisation to organisation. An Intranet should have minimum features like discussion forums and bulletin boards, which are excellent media for knowledge sharing. Robinon (1999, p.96) stressed that Intranets should be always fresh and up-to-date, and concentrates on sharing best practices and the "how was it done factor". Jussilainen (1999, p.13) opined that all the information on the intranet must be up-to-date and valid. Many authors have stressed that the following information should be available on the intranet like news concerning staff, directories containing details of personnel; annual budget of the organisation, reports , agreements, policies, forms, management information , discussion forums, bulletin boards and electronic documents (Magazines and books) etc., which can assist in sharing of knowledge. Availability of such information can save time; it improves the productivity and provides opportunity to share with the rest of the colleagues.

Based on the foregoing information a survey has been conducted in state of Karnataka in the south and Jammu and Kashmir in the north. In Karnataka there are nine general universities, of which six have been selected for the study purpose (Bangalore University, Bangalore; Gulbarga University, Gulbarga; Karnatak University, Dharwad; Kuvempu University, Shivamoga; Mangalore University, Mangalore; University of Mysore, Mysore). Three universities—Kannada University at Hampi, Tumkur University at Tumkur and Karnataka State Women's University at Bijapur—have not been considered as they are still in their infancy.

The survey conducted to identify the availability and usage of intranet as a KM tool in selected university libraries in Karnataka yielded a mixed response. Generally Librarians are satisfied with work they are doing. But the content of the intranet in all the libraries was very limited and are not systematically developed. None of the libraries surveyed complied with minimum requirements for an intranet specified by Robinon and Jussilainen. The only service common in all eight libraries with intranet facility was e-journal service. It was learnt during the telephone interviews that the contents of these intranets are not updated regularly and that resulted in less frequent visits to intranet by staff/ users. Based on the analysis of the content, frequency of updates and telephone interviews with the library staff and users, it can be said that the potential of intranet as a KM tool has not been fully utilised. Knowledge management requires a holistic and multidisciplinary approach to management process and an understanding of the dimensions of knowledge/ information work.

Table 1: Services through Intranet

KM - services	*Intranet services in UL*	
	Yes	*No*
Directory service	1	5
Staff news	1	5
Budget information	0	6
Reports	1	5
Agreements	0	6
Policies	0	6
Management information	1	5
E-Journals	6	0
Forms	1	5
Training material	0	6
Discussion groups	0	6
BBS	1	5
Archive	1	5
OPAC	3	3

As such, Intranet has a great potential usage for many purposes and in many ways. It can be used for communication support, provision of nascent information to internal staff, as an interactive platform. But the libraries under survey have shown that they have not been properly equipped to establish/ use intranet as one of the KM tools.

Though they are some success stories of KM in corporate sectors and research laboratories coming under CSIR, ICMR, and ICAR, KM is still in its infancy in other university/academic libraries. Little effort has been devoted to the study of how to improve library operations through Knowledge Management. KM becomes inevitable in Academic libraries because of three reasons:

1. Budget cut is a primary driving force for implementation of KM.
2. Students, faculty and University administration have greater expectation of academic libraries.
3. And they have sensed the threat of being marginalised by internet-based information services and level of computer literacy of library users (both students and daculty).

So the challenge of Km is to determine what information within the organisation qualifies as 'Valuable'. All information is not knowledge and all knowledge is not valuable, significance of KM lies in identification of valuable knowledge, which is ever changing and is always complementing to the existing system.

Conclusion

Though knowledge management so far a corporate feature, the environment in which the academic libraries operate is changing. Academic libraries have not yet been fully realised the potential of knowledge management. It is not individualistic but teamwork. They have the knowledge of Information organisation along with certain amount of expertise in ICT application too. But, they are poor in integration of work and individual skills. This is very essential as knowledge is considered as serviceable good and insures continued viability of libraries in the ever changing environment.

References

Ahmed, P. K., Lim, K. K., and Loh, A.Y.E. (2002). *Learning through knowledge management*. Oxford: Butterworth-heineman.

Balcanbe.J. (1999). Getting out of Box: the role of the information professional in Knowledge management. *The Law Librarian,* 31(2), 91-94.

Blackmore (1997). The development of an Intranet within college of further and higher education. *ASLIB Proceedings,* 49 (3), 67-72.

Branin, J. J (2003). Knowledge Management on Academic Libraries: Building the knowledge bank at the Ohio State University. *Journal of Library Administration,* 39(4), 41-56.

Curry, A and Stancich , L (2000). The Intranet: an intrinsic component of strategic information management. *International Journal of Information Management,* 20, 249-68.

DiMattia, S and Oder, N (1997). Knowledge Management: Hope, Hype or Harbinger? *Library Journal,* 122 (15),33-35.

GarternerGroup: Knowledge Management .Available at: www.stevedenning.com/what is knowledge management.html

Jussilainen, M. (1999). Intranet as a tool for knowledge management: the case of the Council of State in Finland, *International Online Information Meeting,* 23 (2),111-16.

Kim, Seonghee (2000). The roles of knowledge professionals for knowledge Management. *INSPEL,* 34 (1),1-8

Naidoo, V. (2002). *Organisational culture and sub-culture influences on the implementation and outcomes of aspects on internal quality assurance initiates.*

Reid, I.C (2000). The Web and the Universities. Available at: http//:ausweb.scu.edu/aw2k/papers/reid/ . (Accessed on 6 April 2008).

Robertson, Shaunagh and Brun, Caroline De (2005). Developing the Knowledge Management environment. NLH Knowledge Management. Specialist Library. Available at: http://www.library.nhs.uk/knowledgemanagemet/viewResource.aspx? (Accessed on 5 July 2005)

Robinson, H. (1999). The development of an intranet as a knowledge management tool, *The Law Librarian,* 30 (2), 95-7.

Shanhong, T. (2000). Knowledge management in libraries in the 21st. century, 66th IFLA Council and General Conference, Jerusalem, Israel. Available at: http://ifla.inist.fr/IV/ifla66/

Skyrme, D. (1998). Knowledge management – a fad or a ticket to ride? Available at: www.skyrme.com/pubs/iis0298.htm

Susarla, A., Liu, D, and Whinston, A. B. (2003). Peer-to-Peer Enterprise knowledge Management. In *Handbook on Knowledgement*. Pt.2: Knowledge Directories, Berlin: Springer, 129-139.

Yen, D.C and Chou, D.C (2001). Intranets for organisational Innovation. *Information Management and computer Security*, 9 (2). 80-87.

8

Knowledge Management and the Profession of Librarianship

— Khaisar Muneebulla Khan

This paper gives an outline of the concept of Information Management, Knowledge Management and the profession of librarianship. It defines knowledge management and its objectives, type and principles. The process, techniques and tools of knowledge management are also stated. The benefits of knowledge management particularly in an organisation has been discussed. The knowledge management activities that can be carried out by library and information science professionals are mentioned. Finally, it concludes with reminding the LIS professionals to equip themselves with latest techniques, methods and skills of knowledge management in successfully mastering the profession of librarianship in the 21st century.

Introduction

Librarianship is the art and science of putting into practice the theory of library and information science (LIS). LIS is the science that deals with collection, organisation and dissemination of information – knowledge – to readers or knowledge seekers. The concept of knowledge management is as old as the library itself, though the terminology is new. Previously this activity was so simple to perform. However, with the emergence of interdisciplinary and multidisciplinary knowledge it is not possible to accomplish this activity manually. In the process of retrieving and disseminating the knowledge at certain places the manual techniques fail to satisfy the demands of seekers. Information technology can do this job effectively and efficiently. Hence, the knowledge manager must be on expert in the field i.e. Library and Information Technology.

Application of management principles in the acquisition, control, dissemination and use of Information is called information management. The term information management is used in several fields. In computer science it is used as a synonym for information technology or as identical to data management. In business of management studies it has similar connotations to technology management.

In the field of library and information science it is identified with the emerging market for information workers (managers) whose perception of information embraces data organisational intelligence, information technology for handing these different sources. Compared with other areas in the context of library and information science, It is more widely concerned with information resources management for the information user and information retrieval issues.

Definitions

Knowledge management has been defined as "A discipline that promotes an integrated approach to identifying, capturing, retrieving, sharing and evaluating enterprises information assets." These information assets may include databases, documents, policies and procedures as well as the unrecorded, tacit expertise and experience resident in individual workers." According to Davenport, the KM process is about acquisition, creation, packaging and application or reuse of knowledge. The KM process includes terms and terminology such as:

1. *Tacit Knowledge:* It includes the individual employee's expertise, memories, values and beliefs, view points and values.
2. *Explicit Knowledge:* It is the process of communication from one place to another in a systematic way through documents and is more formal and codified.

3. *Corporate Memory:* It is connection of know-how of an organisation. This know how relates to problem solving, project experiences, and human resource management.
4. *Intellectual Assets/Knowledge Assets/ Capital*: Similar terms, which comprise knowledge assets regarding products, technologies and market that a business owns.
5. *Information Economics:* is a study of the clear value of information to an organisation.
6. *Data Mining:* is the exploration and analysis of automatic and semiautomatic means of large quantities of data in order to discover meaningful patterns and rules.
7. *Knowledge Presentation:* is the process of describing and presenting, a usable way of knowledge that is known by a person.
8. *Knowledge Mapping:* is finding existing knowledge in an organisation and creating a detailed picture of skills. Maps can be simple directories of names to search online databases of human expertise, research materials and pre-recorded information.
9. *Concept Mapping:* is the visual summary of ideas or topics and these ideas and topics are related to each other.
10. *Knowledge Engineer:* is a person responsible for acquiring knowledge and developing data and rules for expert systems.

Objectives

The objectives of KM is generally discussed and stated in the literature as follows:

1. Knowledge management ensures an effective and efficient development of new knowledge and improvement of existing knowledge with a view to the strategy of the organisation and the individual objectives of the employee. It ensures a specific distribution of new knowledge to other departments and transfer of knowledge to new employee through knowledge transfer process.

2. It ensures an effective securing of knowledge, and makes each accessible to the whole organisation. Further, it ensures the effective and efficient combination of the best knowledge available within an organisation or its network. However, in terms of knowledge, further the following objectives can be also considered.

3. Knowledge management keep the contents of knowledge bearers abreast with latest development in the changing circumstances and helps the application of best knowledge. It makes location of knowledge to bearers at optimum level in the context of service process.

4. Improve the form of knowledge bearers in the relation to the users and the expected use of it; apply knowledge in the best form. Adapt the availability of knowledge to the time that the knowledge is needed, apply knowledge when required.

5. Knowledge management creates knowledge repositories, which store both knowledge and information, often in documentary form. A common feature is added value through categorisation, It improves knowledge access, or to provide access to knowledge or to facilitate its transfer among individuals; here the emphasis is on connectivity, access and transfer, and technologies such as video-conferencing systems, document scanning and sharing tools and telecommunications networks are central to this objective.

6. Knowledge management enhances the knowledge environment so that environment is useful to more effective knowledge creation, transfer and use. This involves tackling organisational norms and values. It manages knowledge as an asset, and recognises the value of knowledge to an organisation. Assets, such as technologies that are sold under licence or have potential value, customer database and detailed parts catalogues are typical of companies intangible assets to which value can be assigned.

Types and Principles of Knowledge Management

The knowledge can be divided into two categories;

a) Explicit

b) Implicit or tacit knowledge

a) *Explicit Knowledge.* Explicit knowledge is the traditional form of knowledge and is available in documented form. It is formal, systematic and easily disseminated or communicated as and when required. It can also freely and easily shared amongst the users. Realising the value of this knowledge, the librarians and information professionals have already been engaged in the collection, organisation and dissemination of it. A library is a place where knowledge is managed.

b) *Implicit Knowledge.* Implicit knowledge is available with the individuals. It is a personal knowledge based on the individual experience. It is a personal asset. Such knowledge is vanishing with the person. It is also known as tacit knowledge. It is something not easily visible, expressible.

Thomas H. Davenport has pointed out very explicitly principles which are self explanatory by themselves, that is, it is expensive, It requires knowledge managers, knowledge management benefits more from maps than models more from markets than from hierarchies. Sharing and using knowledge are both often natural and unnatural acts, Knowledge management means improving knowledge work processes, Knowledge access is only the beginning. It never ends.

Four Pillars of Knowledge Management

ICT and Connectivity

Participation in a knowledge society in the era of the information economy is based on connectivity to modern ICTs. The backbone of a knowledge society is therefore a well-developed, well-maintained and affordable information infrastructure that allows access to, and manipulation of the digital economy. The skills and knowledge of people living in a society are clearly of central importance to its development as a knowledge-based economy and society. The stock is built up over time mainly through investment in education (public and private expenditure on education and training). A knowledge-based society framework is therefore concerned with education and training inputs, both formal and informal, as well as outputs in terms of the resulting skills and abilities of the population.

Usable Content

Access to, and accessibility of information to enable participation in the digital economy, alone are not enough. The information available should be affordable, available, timely, relevant, readily assimilated, and in a language users can understand. There is a critical mass of useful information needed to be available on the Internet before people will use the Internet on a regular basis.

Infrastructure and Deliverability

A dematerialised economy without a physical infrastructure is of little use as it is the combination of the materialised and dematerialised infrastructure which creates economic value. This new digital or "dematerialised" economy is under-pinned by a "materialised" and top-heavy infrastructure comprising airports, railways, roads, trucks, warehouses and physical addresses of people.

Human Intellectual Capability

The development of human capital represents on of the most important factors that facilitate development and economic growth. Of relevance here is the concern expressed by Freeman and Soete (1997) that, if developing countries do not invest more in education and specifically in R &D, they will be excluded from the triadic knowledge and innovation networks, which are mainly concentrated in North America, Europe and Asia. A knowledge society needs people who can create as well as utilise knowledge to ensure not only sustainability, but also prosperity.

Process of Knowledge Management

The process of knowledge management requires creation, capturing, organisation; accession and dissemination are the activities to be performed for the management of knowledge. However these activities should be undertaken carefully so that the right knowledge be captured and disseminated to the right users at right time to take right decisions and in the right situation. Knowledge management consists of the following steps:

a) Create a new knowledge from all fields. Identify the individuals and capture the knowledge what they posses and convert it into explicit form. All knowledge may not have an importance for the organisations or an enterprise. Therefore while identifying the individuals and capturing the knowledge from them care should be taken not to capture unwanted knowledge.

b) Organise the useful knowledge systematically and scientifically so that it can be retrieved easily and that which is needed relevant and useful. Knowledge management identifies the ways and means by which the organised knowledge can be disseminated to proper requests.

c) Knowledge management is one of the ways for the development of the nation as a whole. Society is made up of the different organisations such as social, governmental, economical, educational, cultural and industrial. All such organisations should perform the task of knowledge management. For creation of new knowledge the organisation has to identify the expertise, working with that organisation.

d) To motivate this expertise, the activities such as seminars, workshops, symposiums, conference must be organised. On these platforms the individuals share their views, ideas and experiences. From the platform of such intellectual activities, new implicit knowledge creates. The organisation can convert the individual assets of knowledge into explicit one to transmit to the knowledge seekers.

Techniques and Tools of Knowledge Management

Organisation retrieval or search of knowledge is the key step of knowledge management. To carry out these functions successfully and effectively certain techniques such as classification, cataloguing, etc., have to be used. Besides these techniques some other techniques are also in existence. Among those indexing, abstracting has for a long time drawn the attention of the experts of knowledge management. Verities of indexing techniques have been developing so far organising and retrieving the knowledge. Pre coordinate, post co-ordinate, automatic indexing, citation are the prominent indexing techniques using for the knowledge organisation and retrieval.

The understanding and knowledge of technological tools is essential for the informational professional to practice his profession of librarianship. Though technology is not the do-all and end-all of knowledge management, it offers powerful tools. for the same. The technologies that enable knowledge management are:

a) Internet, intranet and extranet
b) Data mining.
c) Data warehousing.
d) Artificial intelligence (AI) and expert systems.
e) Push and pull technologies.
f) Electronic publishing.
g) DBMS.
h) Groupware

a) *Internet, Intranet and Extranet.* The internet provides a strong collaborative platform of knowledge management. Intranets and Extranets help to efficient document transfer, exchange, conversations and discussions.

b) *Data Mining.* Data mining finds correlation within data without human intervention of effort It uses artificial intelligence tools, neural networks and fuzzy logic in which data is automatically analysed and explored.

c) *Data Warehousing.* Data warehousing is a subject oriented integrated, time-variant, non-volatile collection of data in support of management's decision-making process. It stores the information required for decision making in an organisation.

d) *Artificial Intelligence (AI) and Expert System.* Artificial intelligence and expert systems add value to knowledge management. They make knowledge management functions like search, information retrieval and filtering very fast and easy.

e) *Push and Pull Technologies.* Push and pull technologies are useful for the librarians to make their searches more efficient and more effective they help in sending the right information to the right reader at the right time. Pull technology provides tools for navigation like directories, search engine or web browsers. They locate and deliver information very fast. Push technology alerts the searcher to information and information sources. Email and voice mail are two examples of push technology. Thus push technology helps in information capture, whereas pull technology helps in navigation.

f) *Electronic Publishing.* Electronic publishing the material and providing hyperlinks for the same helps in sharing knowledge. The blogs published intranet or Internet help in publishing experience and thoughts of the persons and thus help in knowledge management.

g) *DBMS.* It is a set of software programs that controls the organisation, storage, management, and retrieval from a database. They are categorised according to their data structures or types. It is a set of prewritten programs that are used to store, update and retrieve a Database. The DBMS accepts requests for data from the application program and instructs the operating system to transfer the appropriate data. When a DBMS is used, information systems can be changed much more easily as the organisation's information requirements change. New categories of data can be added to the database without disruption to the existing system.

h) *Groupware.* Groupware helps knowledge workers share their expertise. This is a hypertext system having e-mail, computer conferencing and shared screen editing. It allows user to use bulletin board going to the file the user can add own notes.

Knowledge Management Activities

Some of the KM activities that can be carried out by the practitioners of the profession of liberationship are:

a) The developments in satellite technology and information technology, teleconferencing has been made possible. Online virtual conferencing programs can be arranged on a particular topic so that tacit knowledge of the experts may be tapped. Expert-user network can be established so that the users can get in direct touch with the experts through the network whenever required.

b) Libraries and information centers, knowledge centres which have good internet facilities can locate websites which exclusively deal with a particular topic and encourage users to discussion forums, chats, talks, etc. Such involvement of the users will help them in getting information and knowledge, sometimes information and the relevant knowledge that may not be available in books or other documents or even if available may not be accessible.

c) Opinion surveys on the topics of interest to the organisation and user groups may be conducted this can be done more importantly in the absence of expert user network by professional librarians.

d) Conducting seminars, workshops, etc and arranging UGC and educational programs on TV will help in sharing and use of knowledge. Further, special lectures by eminent persons and experts in different fields may be arranged in Library and Information Centres to share and disseminate information and knowledge.

e) A skill database of the employee's knowledge in an organisation. Besides, professional librarians with their sound knowledge about knowledge organisation and information retrieval can join hands with computer scientists and subject experts in designing and creating expert systems knowledge-based systems, etc.

The Benefits of Knowledge Management

The benefits of knowledge management are manifold. In today's information driven economy, the organisations have to tap most of the opportunities and drive the maximum value from intellectuals rather than from physical assets. To get the maximum value from the organisation's assets, knowledge must be shared since it serves as the foundation for collaboration. Knowledge management should:

a) Foster innovation by encouraging the free flow ideas and thoughts.

b) Improve user service by streamlining response time of information generated at the library.

c) Generate resources by getting how products and services to foster the user demand for creditable information.

d) Recognise the resourceful research investigators and reward them with enhanced knowledge supply and value their queries for additional and valuable information.

e) Streamline service operations and reduce costs by eliminating redundant or unnecessary processes.

f) A creative approach to knowledge management would result in improved efficiency higher productivity and increased resources mobilisation in any organisation.

Conclusion

Information management basically deals with information present in the documents while knowledge management deals not only with the information content of documents but also with the knowledge present in the employee's brain. Also, in information management, coded information becomes knowledge for the future use but in knowledge management, coded knowledge becomes information for future knowledge base. Information management and knowledge management have different challenges but then they are primarily intended to provide quality information and knowledge to users and decision makers.

Library and information science professionals working in different fields in a way act as knowledge managers but then, the LIS practitioners can be the best knowledge managers too. This is because they are dealing with knowledge on a day-to-day basis in order to satisfy the complex and ever-growing needs of information/knowledge seekers. Library and information science professionals are acting as information officers, Information specialists, information analysts, information marketers, information auditors, information evaluators, system and network managers, information mappers, and information technological experts, and also the knowledge manager. This will be bestowing a series of responsibilities and challenges on the profession of librarianship for their successful performance management and to give further value and status to the profession of librarianship.

References

Babu, Ramesh B (2003). *Information Management: Trends and Issues*. New Delhi: Researcho Book Centre, 154-163.

Davenport, T.H. The Future of Knowledge Management Available at: http://www._Cio.com/archieve 01096-devenpor content.Html.

Khan, Khaiser Muneebulla and Nair, Ravichandra (2009). Marketing of Information Product and Services; Library Professional In the proceedings of 10th Annual National conference of MANLIBNET, KIIT University, Bhubaneswar on Organisational Excellence in Business and Management Libraries: Current trends and future directions Jan 22-24, 2009.

Khode, Subash and Singh, Umersh Kumar. (2006). Knowledge Management. *ILA Bulletin*, 42 (1), 6-8.

Misra, Rabinarayana. (2005). *Web based for Knowledge Management is LIS professions in India for 2010*. Kolkata: IASLIC, 178-80.

Rowley, Jennifer. (1999). What is knowledge Management?. *Library Management*,20 (8), 416-419.

Sahoo, K. K. (2004). *Information Management with I T Application*. Ludhian: Medallion Press, 38-52.

Sirurmath, Somagayya S. (2003). *Information Management; Trends and Issues*, New Delhi: Research co Book Centre, 154-163.

Soo-guan Khoo, C. (2008). *Competencies for new era Librarians and information professions*. Division of Information Studies, N T University, Singapore.

9

Web Content Management: A Case Study of E-books Access Acquired by IISc Digital Library

—K. S. Chudamani and H. C. Nagarathna

Digital libraries have to use all modern network and server's technologies in order to supply service of a high quality. This paper discusses the process of managing a web content management project in an efficient and effective manner, giving digital library strategies, best practices, and techniques for implementing e-books to research students of the Indian Institute of Science (IISc), Bengaluru. Digital library is an enterprise open-source CMS (Content Management System) and development framework with functionality for web publishing, intranets, e-commerce, extranets, and web portals. After describing the benefits of e-books the authors describe the content management process for acquiring e-books at IISc.

Introduction

The main goal of digital library initiative is to provide scientific users with new opportunities for the development of science and technology oriental applications services. It covers implementation of standard services as well as multimedia and meta-computing applications.

The term 'e-book' represents content, which is made available digitally and electronically. E-book publishers' respective combination of hardware and software components undoubtedly impacts e-book consumers' selection of content and usage patterns of the content. Web content management is a cooperative for the creation of next-generation e-resources for reading digital publications. The software and accompanying format are for books, periodicals, newspapers, business documents, and other similar types of publications – most any type of content best presented in a page-based manner. This has enormous potential for long-term access to electronic records and other digital objects. Originally, whose design as a *multi-media* reader for e-books became a E-Content Delivery System, which allows them to create online virtual libraries, and distribute ebooks to those libraries. It also gives those libraries an instantaneous web presence and the ability to lend ebooks to their patrons.

New virtual library creation, which is branded and managed independently by the library administrator is possible. The patrons of the libraries get a very compelling ebook experience with the ability to read the ebook online using a richly featured Open ebook (OEB) Reader - allowing seamless searching and reading concurrently across multiple ebooks. In addition, patrons are able to checkout ebooks and download the ebook to their PC for offline reading with the Adobe ebook Reader. The Adobe ebook Reader allows the patron to read the book for a period designated by the library administrator - thus forcing an automatic check-in of the book. During this offline checkout period, the fair use of the ebook is enforceable with the use of Digital Rights Management technology.

The patron experiences a state of the art digital library, with the ability to do full-text searches, preview books and checkout books for online or offline use. Additionally, each patron has a virtual bookshelf that allows him or her to see any books they have checked out and the duration of those checkouts.

Benefits of E-books

The advantages of e-books are:

- Easy access to content.
- On-demand availability (accessible anytime from anywhere).
- Capabilities to search within a book and across a collection of books.

- Links to other resources, including dictionaries and thesauri.
- No risk of loss, damage, theft, or misplacement; no physical space requirements.
- No device requirements for access to the content.
- Accessibility to content using standard web browsers.
- Customisable search interfaces.
- Ease in transportability.

Publishers' Digital Library Access at IISc

Library websites are easy to navigate, so users can find their way quickly to e-resources. Working with publishers web contents is the core of the e-searching of e-library.

Fig. 1 shows web content and web link. It is only a fraction of the Web-OPAC op links offered through the introductory e-resources image of IISc at www.library.iisc.ernet.in.

The library offers services such as Reference Services, Referral Service, User Guidance Service, Circulation Service including Inter-Library Loan and Document Delivery Service, Weekly display of recent additions of periodicals and books including E-mail distribution of these lists to users on our mailing list, Bibliographic Service, Xerox Service, etc. The library has been using the LIBSYS as an Integrated Library Management software package with all the modules for the library housekeeping operations. The library Online Catalogue database has more than 1.50 lakh records of books (Bibliographic Information) and information about 1,72,000 back volumes of periodicals. "E-book" represents content that is available digitally and electronically. E-book publishers' respective combination of hardware and software components undoubtedly impacts e-book consumers' selection of content and usage patterns of the content.

Several steps in the traditional content management process require manual work, which are more efficient. One area is telling the system how to assemble content components into pages. Publishing content onto a page usually requires several steps:

- Professional and vibrant design
- Simple to use navigation
- Secure Administration Intranet
- Integrated Content Management Modules
- News Display System
- Quote Display System
- Email Newsletter System
- Workshop & Seminar System

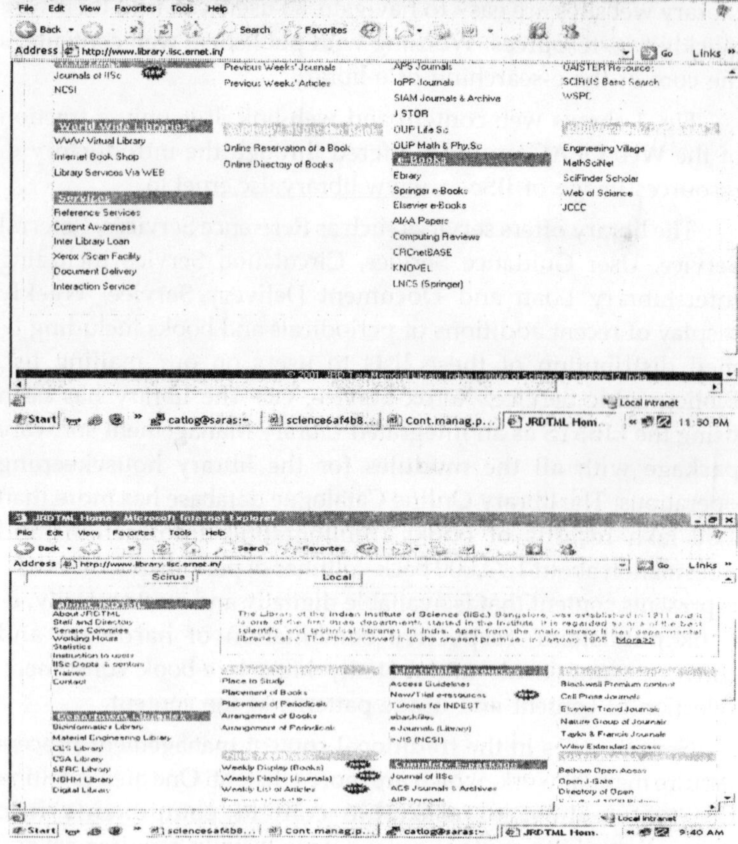

Figure 1: JRD Tata Memorial Library home pages 1 and 2

Now, it is worthwhile to proceed with the navigation. Initially, the Ebrary site is chosen for starting the search because of some noted advantages of the same as shown below. In the starting page, there is a 'getting started' guide. Then, comes the search window, which displays several subject areas for selection for searching a keyword. If the user is sophisticated, he is able to pinpoint his search. Otherwise, he can just carry on as in google. Finally, the system responds that it does not have anything on the given term/s.

Then, if we move on to springer, after having learnt some lessons from ebrary, one may wish to go to the advanced search. IN this, if the user selects a title search, gives the same title, there is an immediate result, indicating that there are no hits.

The next publisher chosen is engineering netbase. It is one of the most talked about e-resource. It has a special feature, which is noticeable, i.e., it displays pages where the term occurs in different books and chapters. The user can go ahead with his exploration chapter by chapter of different books. Instead, he may proceed for a Google search. Why people choose Google search is the question. The answer as perceived by the authors is it a one shot search, which displays books, journal articles, web pages, etc.

Instead, if a librarian is approached, he may directly search woldcat or Library of Congress and provide much more details about the book as these two catalogs are well known and provide detailed information on the book and also enable further search for additional books.

In this article, we use the term e-book publishers to represent the combination of hardware and software components which undoubtedly impact e-book consumers' selection of content and usage patterns of the content. It is, for example, a different matter to read something on one's PC or laptop surrounded, perhaps, by neatly organised piles of paper representing the user's accompanying active cognitive engagements, as opposed to reading material that can be carried in, say, one's purse without the intellectual annex that a desk represents (Gladwell (2002).

There are a few major benefits to this kind of system over a conventional CMS:

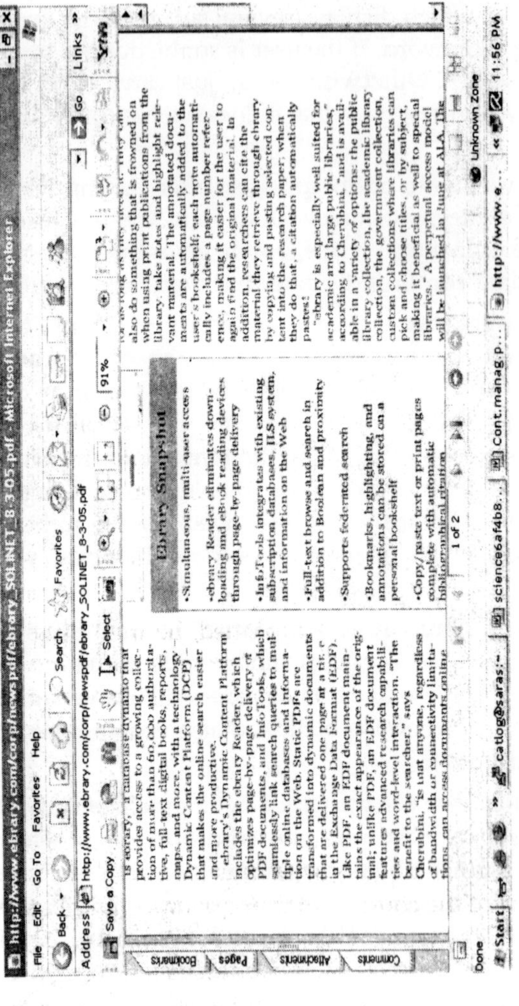

Figure 2 : Ebrary Snapshot

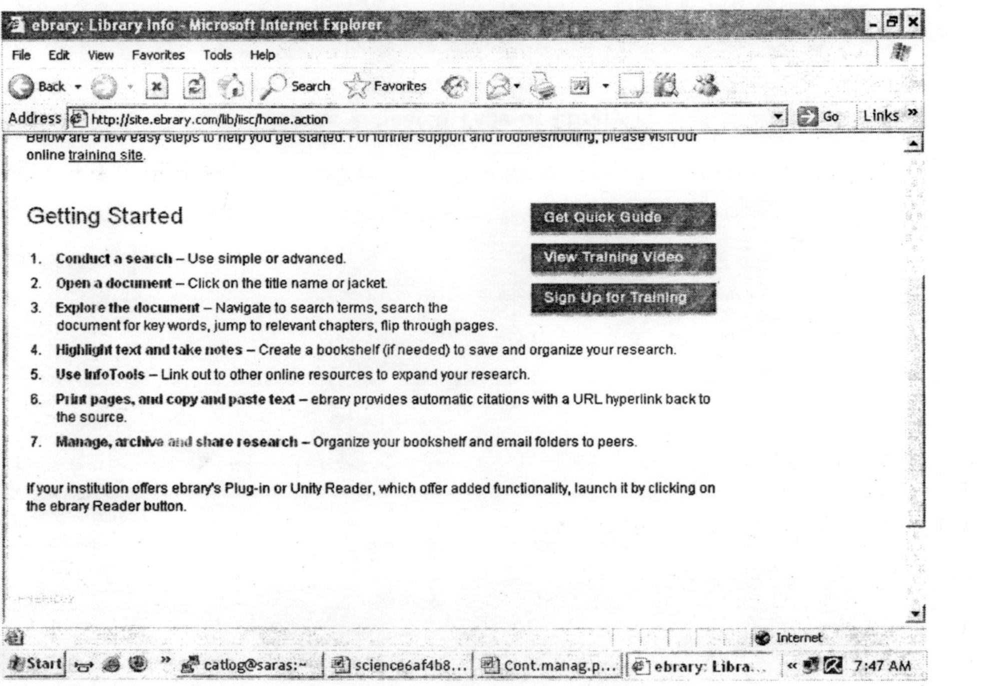

Figure 3: The Starting Page of Ebrary

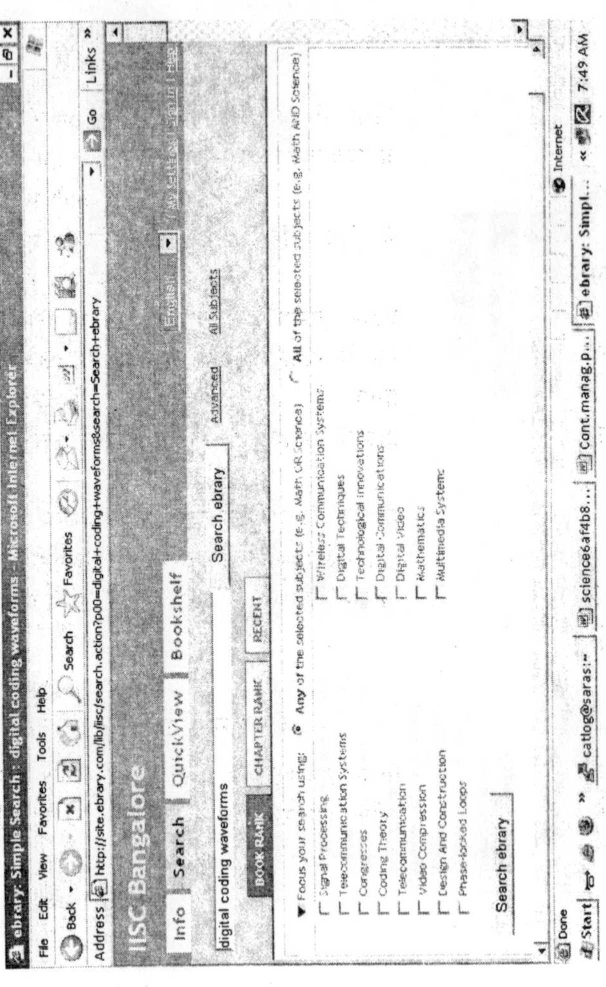

Figure 4: Search Page of Ebrary

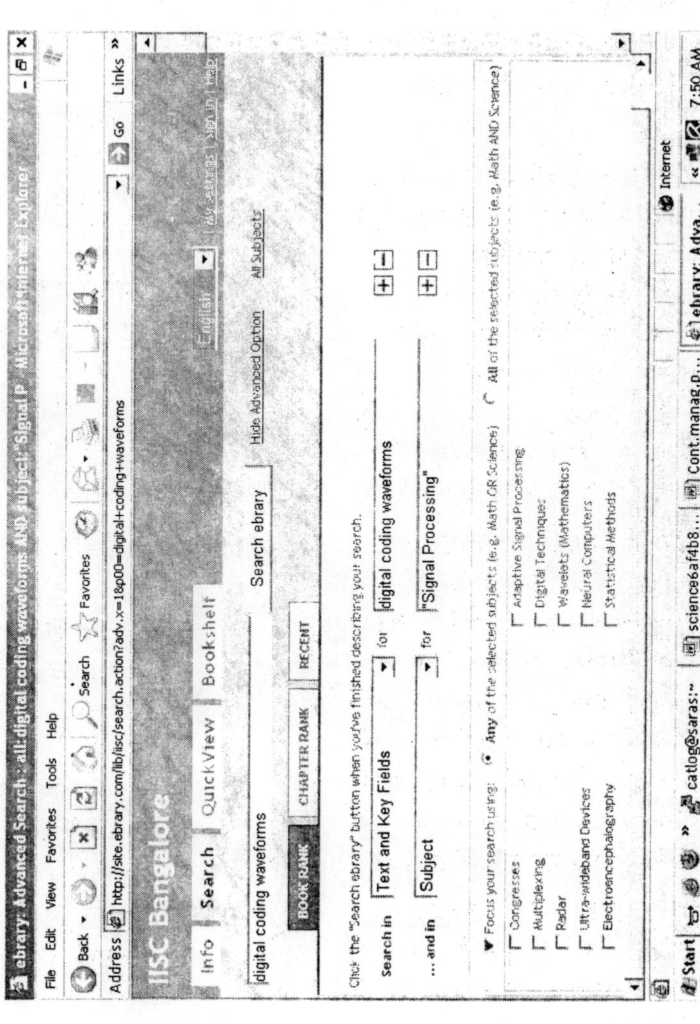

Figure 5: Searching Sbrary Using More than One Subject Area

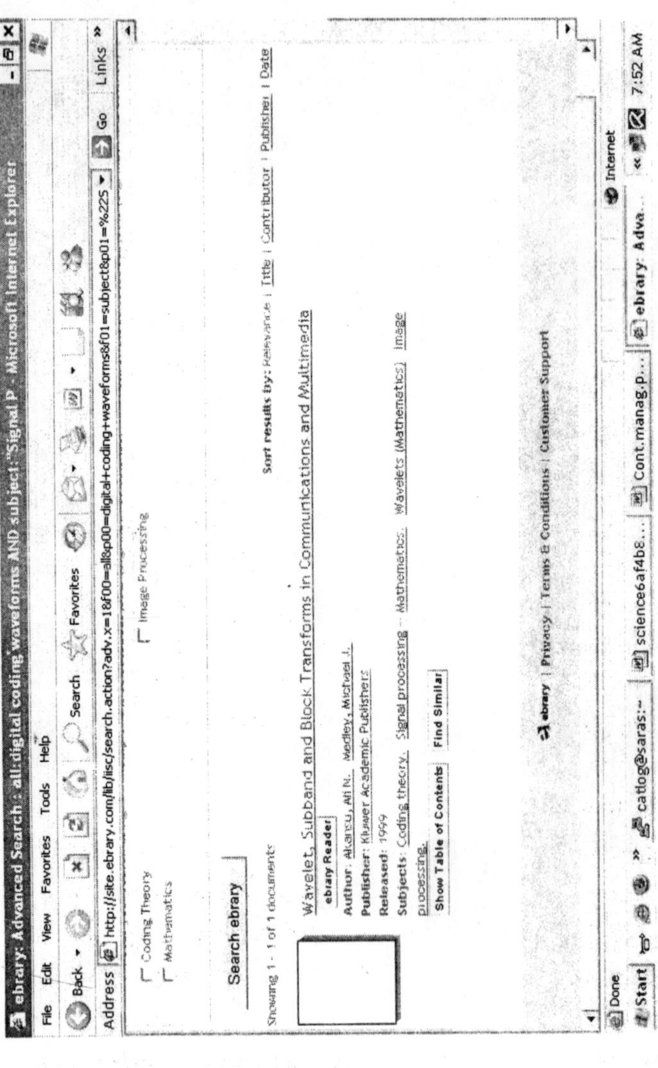

Figire 6: Display of Bibliographic Details of the Book Matching Selection.

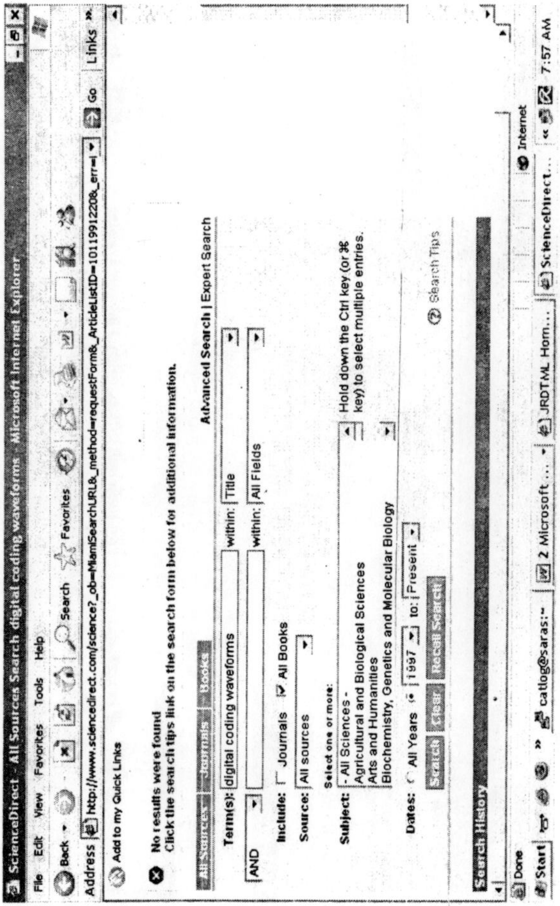

Figure 7: Searching Science Direct Using Advanced Search

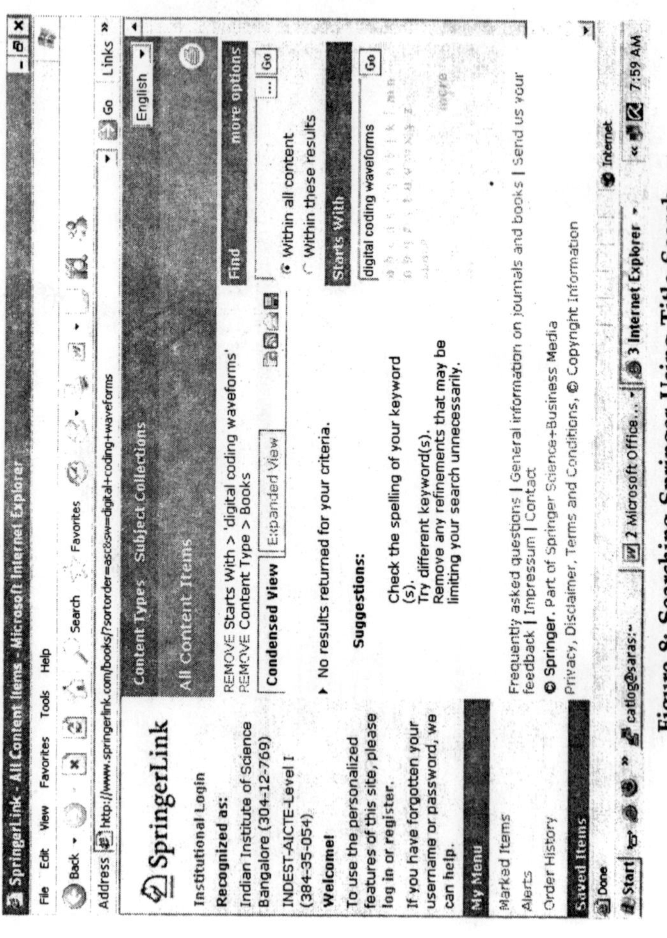

Figure 8: Searching Springer Using Title Search

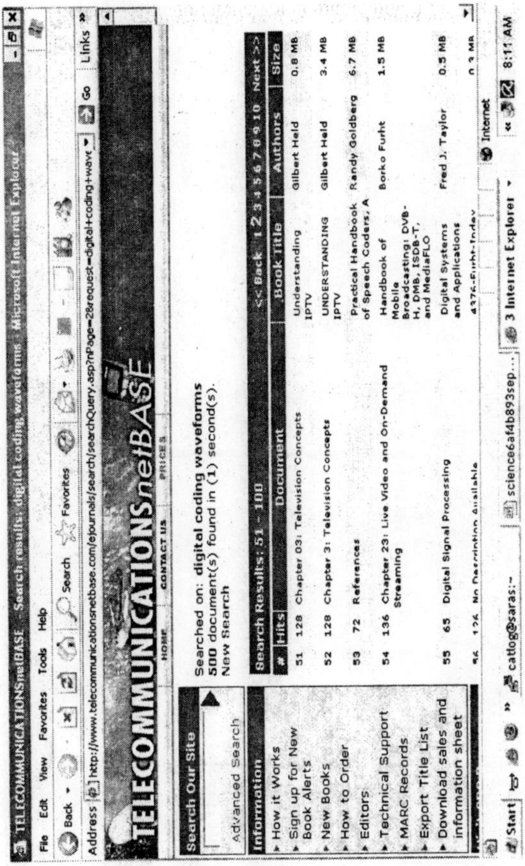

Figure 9: Searching Engnetbase for "Digital Coding Waveforms"

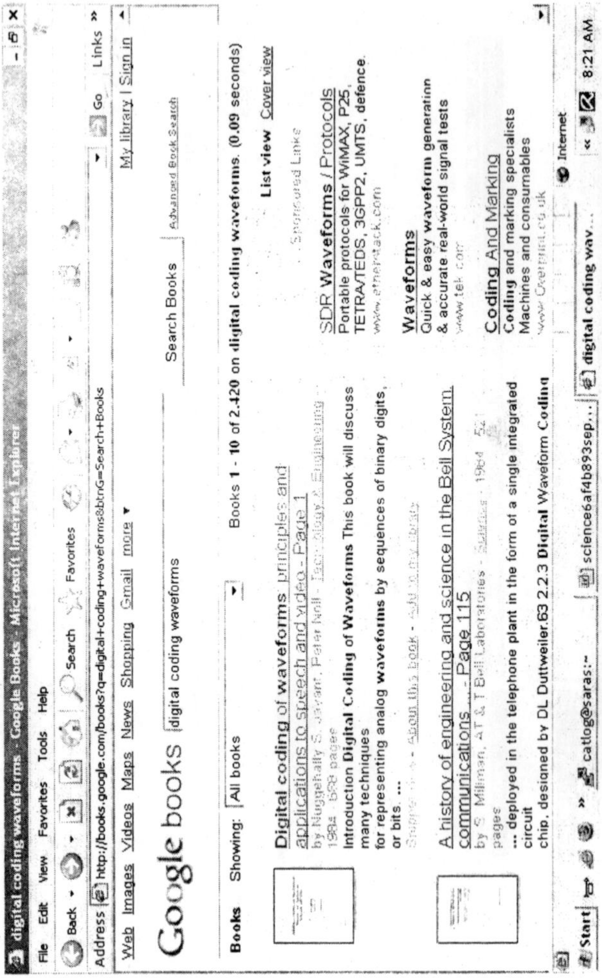

Figure 10: Searching Google Book Search

Brief Record (Library of Congress Online Catalog) - Session timeout in 4:48 - Microsoft Internet Explorer

File Edit View Favorites Tools Help

Address http://catalog.loc.gov/cgi-bin/Pwebrecon.cgi?DB=local&Search_Arg=digital+coding+waveforms&Search_Code=TKEY%5E Go Links »

Brief Record | Subjects/Content | Full Record | MARC Tags

Digital coding of waveforms : principles and applications to speech and...

Relevance:
LC Control No.: 83022170
LCCN Permalink: http://lccn.loc.gov/83022170
Type of Material: Book (Print, Microform, Electronic, etc.)
Personal Name: Jayant, Nuggehally S., 1946-
Main Title: Digital coding of waveforms : principles and applications to speech and video / N.S. Jayant, Peter Noll.
Published/Created: Englewood Cliffs, N.J. : Prentice-Hall, c1984.
Description: xvi, 688 p. : ill. ; 25 cm.
ISBN: 0132119137

CALL NUMBER: TK5102.5 .J39 1984
Copy 2
-- Request in: Jefferson or Adams Building Reading Rooms
-- Status: Not Charged

CALL NUMBER: TK5102.5 .J39 1984

Session timeout in: 4:48 Internet

Start catlog@saras:~ Brief Record (Libr... 12:41 AM

Figure 11: Searching LOC

- Pages are automatically updated with links to new, relevant content
- Users can search the site using an interface that allows them to create their own rules, with more precise results than free-text search
- People without web design and development skills can publish websites using concepts they understand instead of having to learn how to create web pages

Conclusion

E-book searching from various publishers' web page is rather an arduous task. It enables continuous learning of searching each home page following different set of criteria and obtaining a varied set of results. The user has to sift and weigh the output to reach a conclusion about the need and availability. They have their own advantages and disadvantages as described above

References

Gladwell, Malcom (2002) The Social Life of Paper: looking for method in the mess. Available at: http://www.ariadne.ac.uk/issue33/netlibrary/Yorker. (Accessed on 25 March 2002.

http://site.ebrary.com/lib/iisc/home.action

http://www.library.iisc.ernet.in/iisccrcnetbase.aspx

http://www.springerlink.com/books/

10

Application of Knowledge Management Tools in Library and Information Centres

— M. Natarajan

Knowledge management (KM) has generated much interest in recent years and become the latest buzz in each and every organisation, from business to Government. The arrival of information society and the move toward the knowledge–based economy highlighted the importance of tacit knowledge and the need to manage knowledge resources. The definitions of KM are discussed with the technologies that will enhance knowledge by generation, codification and transfer are discussed. Various technologies that support the capturing, storing, access and analyse data are discussed. Tools like e-mail, collaboration tools, web technology, knowledge warehouses, enterprise resource planning are considered for the libraries to enhance the library management activities and services to the users either from local or from remote. The role played by knowledge repositories is emphasised with the systems and tools that support and contribute to KM are listed in the article. Application KM tools to libraries are described in detail and concluded that library science professionals must extend their relationships with other staff in the organisation and take it as challenge to implement KM activities by having the resources internally and also from external links.

Introduction

Knowledge and innovation plays an important role in the development of society. The transformation from an agrarian society to the information society has largely been brought about as a result of accumulation of knowledge through the centuries. Knowledge by its very nature depends on other knowledge to build on. Knowledge creation is, in fact, a process of value addition to previous knowledge through innovation (Duffy, 1999;

Narayanan, 2001). The key to economic success is always linked to the advances in knowledge creation and the ability of a nation in translating knowledge into products and services. It has been now recognised as the driver of productivity and economic growth, leading to a new focus on the role of information, technology and learning in economic performance. Knowledge creates knowledge and in the process brings competitive advantage and leads to wealth creation. Davenport and Prusak (1998) stated: "Knowledge is a fluid mix of framed experience, values, contextual information, and expert insight that provides a framework for evaluating and incorporating new experiences and information. It originates and is applied in the minds of knower. In organisations, it often becomes embedded not only in documents or repositories but also in organisational routines, processes, practices and norms."

Knowledge embodied in books and journals does not necessarily translate into useful and usable knowledge unless it is read, manipulated and communicated from one person to another. Knowledge in the form of skills and competencies can only be transferred from one person to another through interaction. Information management on the other hand deals with knowledge that can be captured, processed and managed. The knowledge management (KM) activities comprise the construction of information management systems, artificial intelligence, data mining and other enabling technologies. The core KM activities encompass assessing, changing and improving human individual skills and/or behaviour. It is a complex set of dynamic skills and know-how that is constantly changing. This article deals with the techniques and tools that are available for using the KM in general and implications of the tools are reviewed in library and information centres.

Definitions of KM

Colleges, universities, and their libraries are social organisations where workers transform resources for use by consumers through the functions of teaching, research, and service. The pace of change increases and people change jobs more frequently, information and knowledge that used to be concentrated in one person or process increasingly is being held by multifunctional teams with limited lifespans, operating with rapidly changing systems and environments.

Knowledge management (KM) may be defined as the set of processes that create and share knowledge across an organisation to optimise the use of judgement in the attainment of mission and goals. There are two types of KM. They are:

Explicit knowledge: It is the visible knowledge available in the form of letters, reports, memos, literatures, etc. Explicit knowledge can be embedded in objects, rules, systems, methods, etc.

Tacit knowledge: It is highly invisible and confined in the mind of a person. It is hard to formalise and therefore, difficult to communicate to others. A master craftsman after years of experience develops a wealth of expertise 'at his fingertips'. But he is often unable to articulate the scientific or technical principle behind what he knows. Transformation of knowledge from tacit to explicit form increases its usability and visibility. Capturing the expert's tacit knowledge that resides within him in the form of know-how and insights is a very difficult and challenging task.

A few other ways to define KM are,

- Capturing, storing, retrieving and distributing tangible knowledge assets such as copyrights patents and licenses.
- Gathering, organising and disseminating intangible knowledge, such as professional know how and expertise, individual insight and experience, creative solutions and the like, brands, technology.
- Creating an interactive learning environment where people readily transfer and share what they know, internalise it and apply it to create new knowledge.

Technologies for KM

KM tools are technologies, broadly defined, which enhance and enable knowledge generation, codification (know how), and transfer (Ruggles, 1997b). Typically, they are designed to ease the burden of work and to allow resources to be applied efficiently to the tasks for which they are most suited. It is important to note that information management tools are a subset of KM tools. Information management tools allow organisations to generate, access, store, and analyse data, usually in the form of facts and figures. Knowledge tools can help us create, see, and share the paintings. Various technologies support the capturing, storing, sharing and use of information, know-how and insights within and across communities of people and organisations with similar interests and needs to create knowledge. Where KM is concerned, technology is a necessity, in order to expand access to valuable information and codified knowledge on a timely basis. Many technology options are available for KM: knowledge representation, document management, data mining, data warehousing, knowledge bases, expert systems, artificial intelligence, enterprise resource planning, and legacy systems, decision support, groupware, the Internet, intranets, network computing, e-mail, web conferencing and multimedia. By integrating the various technologies into hardware, software, network and services, a network knowledge infrastructure is created that facilitates and supports KM (Seng, 2002).

Technology plays an important role in KM, and it facilitates the process of transmitting and exchanging information. It can be used to manage uncertainty and complexity, where information is more factual and a high degree of interaction is not required. Technology enables individuals to coordinate the logistics of face-to-face meetings. It can also be used to catalogue expertise of organisational members and as a result facilitating access to the right people and enhancing knowledge sharing. Computer-mediated communication such as electronic mail or computer-conferences can help to maintain continuity and connection between conversations, especially for those in different locations (Marwik, 2001). Collaboration tools enable a company's professionals to work together and work virtually regardless of the geographical location. Web technology allows organisations to build Web and knowledge portals that can handle substantial amount of information and made it accessible to users anywhere anytime (Al-Hawamdeh, 2002).

KM Tools

Typical KM tools include knowledge warehouses and enterprise resource planning (ERP) systems. KM tools facilitate human resource management, supply-chain management and customer relationship management, ultimately leading to better and faster decision making. KM starts with the individual and moves through an organisation. Every individual uses KM tools, including personal memory, date books, notebooks, file cabinets, email archives, calendars, post-it notes, bulletin boards, newsletters, journals, and restaurant napkins. KM begins when an organisation enables individuals to link their personal knowledge management systems with organisational knowledge management systems.

KM tools only work when individuals see direct benefits in linking their personal knowledge management systems with organisational knowledge management systems. If development workers believe that the chores of contributing to an organisational knowledge management program benefit only their bosses, and not themselves or the communities with which they work, they may decide the best way to take advantage of the value of their individual knowledge is to use it for personal or local advantage. This results in serious knowledge deficits for the wider organisation. KM tools go beyond electronic or paper-based data repositories. They include communities of practice as through which people create personally meaningful knowledge networks. Development organisations need to encourage development workers to take advantage of communities of practice by enabling, encouraging and rewarding them to join professional and special interest groups. The major KM tools are:

- Email and synchronous interaction tools
- Collaboration tools for community-building and networking; shared documents; conversations
- Document or knowledge repositories
- Tools for knowledge capture, distillation and presentation
- E-learning tools and applications
- Staff and expertise directories; Yellow pages
- Calendars (personal, group and corporate); personal portals

E-mail is basically used for communication within and outside library for users, publishers (contacts for acquisition, reminders, invoice, exhibits, etc.) and for library services like answering reference queries. Collaborative tools are library networks and human networks with local, regional, national and international level. Knowledge repositories store different types of explicit information which can be accessed and shared among the users locally and from outside also. Portals act as a very useful tool for anyone who is interested to know about the availability of the resources, collection details, OPAC, FAQs, contact with library professionals, subject specific responses, etc.

Some of the systems and tools that contribute to knowledge management (Kari and others, 2006) are listed in Table 1.

Lawrence Prusak (1997) outlines six environmental issues that are forcing organisations to focus on knowledge.

1. An accelerating world means rapid knowledge decay and the need to create new knowledge more quickly. Knowledge must be managed consciously if workers are to learn fast enough for an organisation to remain competitive.
2. Products such as selective dissemination of information services, offer knowledge as part of the product. Such knowledge must be current if it is to contribute to the product's value.
3. Globalisation is creating distributed systems of production and as more teaching and research takes place away from the campus and as libraries outsource more scholarly information and services, more effort must be made to ensure needed access to, and sharing of, knowledge.
4. Turnover is increasing throughout academia. Knowledge that used to be embedded in one person for a career now leaves as individuals change jobs with greater frequency. The coming retirement of large numbers of academics who began careers in the 1960s will create a knowledge deficit situation in academia.
5. Virtual operations require more embedded knowledge to work effectively.
6. Knowledge begets knowledge. As systems become more knowledgeable and interactive, new opportunities to use new knowledge proactively are generated.

In sum, knowledge is a key asset of any organisation, one that now can be added to the classic assets of facilities, labour and capital. Through KM, libraries have an opportunity to collaborate with other units to increase both their effectiveness and that of higher education.

Applications of KM Tools

In an organisation for knowledge management, few core activities for implementing KM systems that move from personal to organisational knowledge management have been identified,

Table 1: KM Tools

Portal	*Bibliography Tools*	*Identity Management*
Grants management	Tagging enabled organization of online information	nline community workspace
Experts databases	Concept or mind mapping	Social networking
ePortfolio	Learning object repository	Instant messaging
KEEP toolkit	Accreditation management	Chat
Curriculum Management	Advisement	Email / listserves
Graduation planner	Calendar	Web conferencing tools
Constituentdatabases	Blogs	Online presentation tools
Grassroots mobilisation networks	Podcasts	Off-line presentation tools
Management Information systems	Wiki	On-line multimedia authoring tools
IT governance	Threaded discussion board	Reporting & dashboard tools
Enterprise transactional systems	Competency tracking	Search engines
Course management	Tags / Labels / Keywords	Recommendation engines
Content management	Helpdesk-style knowledge engine	Video analysis tools

which are from the selection of tools and processes. Participants need opportunities to learn about KM tools and processes employed elsewhere. They need opportunities to see KM at work, whether it be through workshops, personal visits, case studies, guest speakers, journals or websites. Once people have seen the tools and processes available, they need opportunities to develop a consensus on the tools and processes that can work across the organisation and / or within their personal working contexts. Fundamentally, KM requires use of communication media.

KM stages like generation, codification, refinement and transmission of knowledge is applied directly in libraries for creation, i.e., acquisition of documents, accessibility to resources in e-environment; for codification - the adaptation of different types of cataloguing systems, creation of metadata; for refinement – queries from the users are refined for searching from the databases and from other sources like interlibrary loan, intranet, library networks, human resources, etc.; and finally the transmission of knowledge applies in library directly with the users from the reference desk, library counter, documents of different types from print to electronic, databases, data warehouses, library web pages, links from other sources, etc. People are typically socialised to use whatever is the traditional tool for storing or accessing information, and when something new comes along it can be hard for people to adapt and adopt. Technology alone cannot make people into better knowledge managers. KM means asking people to devote their scarce time to codifying their newly acquired knowledge and transmitting it to others. People need to have personal and organisational incentives and they need to be able to access training to use new tools (Richardson, 2001).

Independently, librarians have developed and applied many KM principles in the provision of academic library services. Reference, cataloguing, and other library services are designed to encourage the use of scholarly information and thus increase the amount of academic knowledge used in higher education. Questions in a reference interview and the points of access in a catalogue both are intended to reinforce the ways that scholars work to create new academic knowledge. However, libraries have done little to use organisational information to create knowledge that can be used to improve the functionality of library and higher education processes. In many ways, KM incorporates principles that academic librarians have developed and used with scholarly information for many years. It then applies these principles and others to organisational information in ways that create new knowledge to improve organisational effectiveness (Marshall, 1997).

Organisations can create knowledge repositories composed of explicit knowledge that has been documented and organised for access. Often these are called data warehouses or data malls. Frequently, they resemble libraries or archives in some respects. The knowledge is collected and organised in some symbolic form, such as a catalogue or a bibliography. Authorised users may access the knowledge. External knowledge repositories also can be used to achieve organisational objectives. Knowledge is embedded in products and services. Academic libraries focus on delivering scholarly information and support services in print, electronic and sometimes recorded, media exclusively (Townley, 2001).

Conclusion

Knowledge management as a concept is very attractive and too many organisations are trendy and nice to be associated with. For the majority of those interested in KM, the key drivers are organisational efficiency, maximising organisation's potential, competitive advantage, building a learning organisation and managing intellectual capital. Organisations wanting to implement KM have to grabble with issues such as strategy, technology, organisational culture and knowledge organisation. But despite all these issues, companies / organisations / institutions worldwide in both the private and public sector have shown keen interest in KM, judging from the amount of money expected to be committed for KM in the next few years. KM does present several significant professional issues to librarians. Perhaps the most profound is in the area of proactivity and confidentiality. KM can be incorporated into many library operations to improve effectiveness. In addition, it offers the opportunity to expand the role of libraries in the academic community and to result in strengthened relationships with related units, inside and outside the university. As a social phenomenon, KM is both similar to and different from academic libraries. Librarians and KM workers must address several issues before they can work together effectively, but the opportunities suggested by their collaboration are great.

References

Al-Hawamdeh, S. (2002). Knowledge management: re-thinking information management and facing the challenge of managing tacit knowledge. *Information Research,* 8(1), paper no. 143 Available at http://InformationR.net/ir/8-1/paper143.html.

Davenport, T.H. and Prusak, L. (1998). *Working knowledge: how organisations manage what they know.* Boston, MA: Harvard Business School Press.

Duffy, J. (1999). *Harvesting experience: reaping the benefits of knowledge.* Kansas: ARMA International.

Kari, Branjord et al. (2006). Knowledge management: what is it? Why do you need to know? How do you support? Annual Meeting of Educause Learning Initiative, 30-31 Jan 2006 held at San Diego, California.

Prusak, Laurence. (1997). Introduction to Knowledge in Organisations. *Knowledge in Organisations,* Ed. Laurence Prusak. Boston: Butterworth, ix-xv.

Marshall, Lucy (1997). Facilitating Knowledge Management and Knowledge Sharing: *New Opportunities for Information Professionals. Online*; 21 (Sept/Oct), 92-98.

Marwick, D. (2001). Knowledge management technology. *IBM Systems Journal*; 40(4), 814-830. Available at:

http://researchweb.watson.ibm.com/journal/sj/404/marwick.html (Accessed on 19th September 2009)

Narayanan, V. K. (2001). *Managing technology and innovation for competitive advantage.* Englewood Cliffs, NJ: Prentice Hall.

Richardson, Don (2001). The practical reality of knowledge management within development initiatives. Presented in the Workshop (2nd) for the International Fund for Agricultural Development's Electronic Networking for Rural Asia / Pacific Projects (ENRAP) during 6-9 Feb 2001 at Singapore.

Ruggles, R.L. (1997b). Knowledge tools: using technology to manage knowledge better. Cambridge, MA: Cap Gemini Ernst & Young, Center for Business Innovation. Available at: http://www.cbi.cgey.com/pub/docs/KnowledgeTools.PDF (Accessed on 1st September 2001).

Seng, C V et al. (2002). The contributions of knowledge management to workplace learning. *Journal of Workplace Learning,* 14 (4), 138-147.

Townley, Charles T. (2001). Knowledge Management and Academic Libraries. *College & Research Libraries*; 17 (4), 44-55.

III

ICT Applications

11

Information and Communication Technology in Higher Education: A Conceptual Framework

—N. Radhakrishnan and Sophia Johnson

Information Communication Technology (ICT) is gaining more popular in the 21st century. With the convergence of information technology and communication, the term, ICT, has been significantly drawing attention in everyday life. Educational institutions have started to experience the necessity to include the ICT programme in their curriculum. ICT programmes play important role in organisations especially in higher educational institutions. This paper stresses on the necessity and use of 'Information and Communication Technology (ICT) programme' in the education system where it has slowly been adopted.

Introduction

Information age emerged in late twentieth century with the use of computers and internet, and the ways to access and manage information. But the twenty-first century has bloomed with an advanced version of "Information Technology" and "Communication Technology" termed as *Information and Communication Technology (ICT)*. Despite the use of computers and Internet it is necessary to be sufficiently fluent with ICT, and exposure to technology does not automatically lead to increased ability to use it whereas a measure of success today is how well one can evaluate, manage and communicate all forms of information within a technological environment. These are identified as Information and Communication Technology (ICT) skills (ETS, 2007).

To cope up with this digital age it is inevitable to be ICT illiterate (Hillberg, 2008). Nowadays students start to use the computers and laptops to access Internet, e-mail, messaging and so on. Even high school students find it difficult to spend a day without laptops, Internet and social networking.

ICT is an effective tool for communication between teachers and students where it replaces the traditional method of teacher-centred and whole-class instruction, and helps to save time adopting the virtual online synchronous method of teaching. *Blackboard*, a web-based course management system, is an effective tool of ICT where students can access syllabi, course, related materials, assignments, assessments, and communication tools provided by instructors from any computer with internet access. Blackboard helps in classroom presentation for students at the graduation and postgraduation level, where each student has to attend virtual lecture, followed by group project exercise with the aid of audio/video conferencing, etc. Teachers and faculty realise the necessity of "educational re-designing" to implement ICT knowledge and skills.

Internet Technology

Students in higher education used to take up research/projects through web, searching journal and newspaper articles, completing assignments online and preparing presentations on a regular basis. Therefore it is necessary to guide the students on how to find and use the information effectively and wisely. It is equally important for the teachers to be fluent and skilled with the technological tools. Jager and Lokman (1999) presented a paper at the European Conference on Educational Research the functions of ICT: 1) as an assigning tool to make assignments, collect data and conduct research (2) as a medium for teaching and learning, and (3) as a tool for organisation and management in education. *Special Insight* reports (2007) stated that most of the opinion based studies investigating ICT impact on student performance, such as 'e-learning Nordic study', which was published in 2006 and gave a position picture with teachers being convinced that students relate the performance and basic skills (calculation, reading and writing) as well as educational achievements.

Over the past few years, use of Internet among the school students has increased dramatically. In the United States the

Internet access, Information Literacy (IL) and ICT availability are at a higher rate. IL applies in the digital learning environment and becomes very common in US and UK. Higher educational institutions in the Middle East have introduced 'information literacy' as a core competency. Faculty and librarians work together to frame IL (Information Literacy) models. But it is now known as the era of 'information and communication technology' where emphasis is made on the technology and how to use the information and communication with the help of human ware. Students must be confident in using email, browsing the web, conducting online searches, evaluating and citing sources, using spreadsheets and presentation, creating web pages, using databases, familiarity with social networking tools using web 2.0 such as blogging, podcasting, etc., during the ICT programme. Beyond classroom, ICT literacy is essential so as to be productive citizens in a knowledge-driven society and employers expect their employees to have such skills. As a result, higher education sectors are beginning to require them as competencies for graduation (ETS, 2006).

Educational institutions spend huge sum of money on library resources and services to gain access to the concepts and ideas of others which enable them to answer questions, solve problems, learn new things, and explore entertainment opportunities. Yet college students ignore the library resources and rely solely on commercial search engines such as Google and Yahoo for academic research (Hilberg , 2008). According to ETS report many students lack the critical thinking skills to perform the kinds of information management and research tasks necessary for academic success.

Experience in Higher Education

Most of the universities have established centres for ICT. There are a few schools of library science renamed as school of Information and Communication Technology (Singapore.) Case studies conducted in the Middle East have shown that many private colleges and universities still continue to conduct the traditional orientation programmes to students and faculty. Several factors have contributed to the lack of the use of technology and integration by the teachers and / authorities: (a) Faculties are excluded from the discussion of instructional technology, (b) Faculties are not well prepared to use the computers and internet in their teaching, (c) Faculties leave the courses not knowing how to create or implement the technologies, (d) Insufficient planning, (e) No proper funding, (g) Lack of infrastructure, (h) Students do not show interest in learning opportunities (Jager and Lokman, 1999). Some of the colleges and universities which are being run by the government have been conducting information literacy programmes which are embedded into the curriculum on a credit basis. They have also appointed information literacy instructors are either faculty members or qualified librarians. Recently, many metropolitan and hi-tech educational institutions have realised the necessity of applying and integrating technology into teaching and learning. A pictorial diagram is given below.

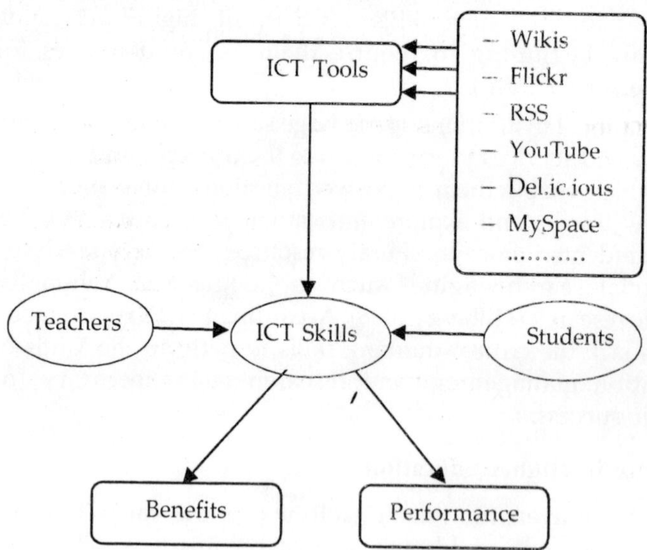

Emerging Technology Tools

Enhancing the learning environment with latest technology skills, e.g., wikis, social networking tools are the prime and significant role of teachers and librarians in the twenty-first century. Dana Hanson-Baldauf (2008) described some ICT tools or technologies required for application: (a) Communication technologies such as - blogs, electronic mail (e-mail), instant messaging (IM), live chats, threaded discussion forums, videoconferencing, voice-over IP (e.g. Skype, Gizmo), virtual conference (e.g.Hitchikr, EdTech talk), and wiki (b) Production and design technologies including digital camera, digital imaging tools (Adobe Photoshop), digital video production tools, GIS (Geographic Information Systems), electronic or interactive whiteboards (eg.SmartBoards), podcasts, portable media player (MP3, iPOD), presentation tools (MS PowerPoint), streamed video, and web design tools (e.g. DreamWeaver, FrontPage). (c) Virtual modelling technologies - animated narrative vignette (ANV), computer simulation, and online gaming. (d) File sharing technologies - audio file sharing tools (e.g. LimeWire, Morpheus), peer-to-peer (e.g. BitTorrent), photo file sharing tools (eg. Flickr, Zoto), RSS feeds, and videofile sharing tools (e.g.,YouTube, MetCafe). (e) Social networking technologies - social book marking (e.g. Del.ic.ious, Blinklist), social networks (e.g. MySpace, Facebook, Friendster), and virtual social networks (e.g. Teen Second life).

Infrastructure

An effective ICT infrastructure establishment is necessary in order to minimise disruption in communication channels (Katzy and Stung, 2001). A set-up of virtual lab with hardware & software, basic components can be Microsoft products such as the exchange servers Windows NT server and Outlook exchange to monitor and store data files.

In order to provide online synchronous video and audio conferencing, equipments like web cameras, microphones and speakers to react to problems, bridge culture location gap between counterparts. Other media-rich communication channels such as electronic whiteboard and high resolution video projectors can be installed and connected via a 100 mega-bytes and above the high speed of LAN network. Converging technologies like VoIP hardware and software systems will further enhance the communication capability of virtual lab.

It is necessary to analyse the activities to be carried out, teaching styles, and the number of students involved to ensure the setting up of labs and workshops for demonstration, evaluation including research and discussions both individually and in groups. However, a lab of 83-99 metre square is generally adequate for a class of 24-30 students. For ICT resource or display area, a bay of around 10-15 metre square should be adequate.

ICT Scenario in UAE

UAE press release (2007) stated that the UAE Ministry of Education, Abu Dhabi Education Council, Dubai Education Council and British Council are collaborating on the project aimed at supporting the introduction and effective use of Information and Communications Technology (ICT) in schools. Workshops were organised in collaboration with UK educational consultants to train the teachers about ICT tools for education, including e Languages and Global Gateway, a website managed by the Briish Council which is designed to create educational partnerships between schools and colleges across the world. In April, 2009 the Minister of Higher Education has signed an agreement between ICT development fund and Advanced Network for Education and Research linking to 28 universities, colleges, public sector schools in UAE, and later to be extended to other research institutions. It facilitates the research collaboration by providing access to databases and super computers. It is also used for teaching through rich multimedia content and high–definition videoconferencing. Advanced network applications will include inter-library access, grid computing, Voice over Internet Protocol (VoIP) and e-learning.

Ager and Kendall (2003) developed a project involving 700 children in an educational set-up at the foundation stage learning in Northamptonshire, UK, investing GBP 1000,000 in the first phase. According to them, a best resourced ICT set up should have computers to student ratio of 1: 15.

The UAE Government has sanctioned an amount of Dhs60m for internet network for academic and research institutions which will provide at a higher speed than commercial services.

Impact of ICT

ICT has different impact on different age groups. For the children aged 7-11, just having technology in the school is enough to make an impact, while for older students it is more about how ICT is used by teachers and learners and it has a different impact in different subjects as well. Students will work independently, be more creative so as to perform better than non-ICT users. ICT can enhance attainment in subjects like English Language, Mathematics, Science and Technology. The benefits of ICT on learning and learners show wider improvement in innovation, concentration, creativity, independent learning, critical thinking, collaboration and global awareness. ICT can benefit academically strong and weak students as well as students with special needs. It also helps the students to be better citizens of society as a whole. Moreover, it offers advantages such as: time saving, the facility to handle large quantities of data, automated operations etc.

Conclusion

ICT literacy has to be introduced in schools, colleges and universities to make the students in acquiring fluency in technology. In some of the universities, curriculum revision has occurred with new subjects absolutely requiring the use of computers such as CAD, design graphics, GIS and media production. Accordingly the syllabus pattern, areas of teaching have to be updated to suit the needs of employability and skills are further to be used effectively. Exposure to technology may not only help students to develop their knowledge within the area of ICT but to be successful in careers, employment and business areas. In order to train the students with ICT skills, it is necessary for teachers to be aware of ICT tools and skills (Fluck, 2003). In future, teachers will make even more use of ICT for professional activities including lesson planning and preparation of teaching materials, recording student assessment, and other administrative tasks (Jones, 2003). Students may also be motivated to take up small and large level research projects focusing on ICT tools. It is also necessary to evaluate the learning process and teaching practices so as to find out the ways and means of improving learning methods with ICT applications. Research findings revealed that ICT has its own impacts on e-mature schools and with e-confident teachers.

References

Ager, Rachel and Kendall, Mike (2003). Getting it right from the start: a case study of the development of a foundation stage learning and ICT strategy in Northamptonshire, UK.; *Australian Computer Society*. Paper presented at the IFIP working group conference.

Bauer, J. and Kenton, J. (2005).Toward technology integration in the schools: why it isn't happening. *Journal of Technology and Teacher Education*,13 (4),519-546.

Educational Testing Service (2006) College students fall short in demonstrating the ICT literacy skills necessary for success in college and the workspace. Available at: http;//www.ets.org

_____________ ICT literacy: equipping students to succeed in an environment-rich, technology-based society. An issue paper from ETS.

Fluck, Andrew E. (2003).Why isn't ICT as effective as it ought to be in school education? *Australian Computer Society*. Paper was presented at IFIP working groups.

Hanson-Baldauf, Dana (2009).The information and communication technology competencies of students enrolled in school library media certification programs. *Library & Information Science Research*,31,3-11

Hilberg, J Scott. (2008). Undergraduate fluency with Information and Communication Technology: Perceptions and Reality. *Communications of the ACM*.(October 16-18) Retrieved Sept.20, 2009 from ACM Digital Library.

Hoffman, M.E. and D.R Vance (2005), "Computer literacy: what students know and from whom they learned it," *SIGCSE'05*, February 23-27, 2005, St.Louis, Missouri.

Jager, A. K. and Lokman, A H (1999). Impacts of ICT in education: the role of the teacher and teacher training, Paper presented at the European Conference on Educational Research

Jones, Anthony J, (2003) ICT and future teachers: are we preparing for e-learning? *Australian Computer Society*. Paper presented at IFIP working groups.

Katz, I (2002). Beyond technical competence: literacy in information and communication technology. *Educational Technology*, 45(6), 44-47.

Katz, I.R. and Macklin, Alexius. Information and communication technology (ICT) literacy: integration and assessment in Higher Education. *Systemics, Cybernetics and Informatics*, 5 (4), 50-55.

_____________ Williamson, D. M; Nadelman, H.I.; Kirsch, I., Almond, R. G., Cooper, P.L., Redman, M.L. & Zapata-Rivera, D. (2004). Assessing information and communication technology literacy for higher education. Paper presented at *IAEA*, Philadelphia, P A.

Katzy, Bernhard R.; Stung, Gordon (2001).Information infrastructure for virtual projects requirements specification from a communication perspectives. 7th International Conference on concurrent enterprising 27-29 June 2001. Bremen.

12

Libraries and Information Centres as Publishers of Scholarly Literature in the Electronic Era

—P. M. Naushad Ali and K. Mohammed Musthafa

Electronic publishing is a modern method of dissemination of scholarly information. The term 'electronic publishing' is defined by various authors in different ways. Library as the centre of knowledge can play a successful role as publisher in electronic era. This paper gives details about the steps involved in e-publishing, various modes of electronic publishing, prerequisites and constraints of electronic publishing.

Introduction

The recent developments in information and communication technology have changed the mode of publishing scholarly information. The conventional channels of communication like print journals and books have been transitioned to electronic counterparts and further more to interactive information sources such as Web 2.0 and Web 3.0. The widespread popularity of Blogs, Facebook, Twitter, Social Networking and open software for Electronic Publishing have made the publishing more dynamic and vibrant.

Due to this accelerated growth of internet based publishing techniques, dissemination of information has become easier than ever. Once publishing was the monopoly of publishers where the research results may have to wait for long to be published. Electronic publishing is a new concept in the world which implies that the information technology has been used for generating, processing and disseminating the information to its users. The ultimate goal of electronic publishing is to provide fast and easy access to the information contained in the objective publications with simple powerful and retrieval capabilities (Annadurai, 2006).

Electronic Publishing: Definitions

F.W. Lancaster (1995) defines "Electronic publishing is a publication process where the manuscripts are submitted in electronic format, edited, printed, and even distributed to readers (users) in electronic form by employing computer and telecommunication technology."

Encarta Online Dictionary defines as "publishing on computer network or disk: the production of documents in computer-readable form for distribution over a computer network or in other formats such as CD-ROMs."

Wikipedia describe the "Electronic publishing or e-publishing includes the digital publication of e-books and electronic articles, and the development of digital libraries and catalogues. Electronic publishing has become common in scientific publishing where it has been argued that peer-reviewed paper scientific journals are in the process of being replaced by electronic publishing."

According to John Unsworth (1995) "electronic publishing refers to the dissemination of information, whether text-only or multimedia, via the internet or through some hybrid of local media and networked archives. Networked electronic publishing can be the basis for producing these other media, and indeed for producing print."

Libraries and Information Centres as Publishers

Karla Hahn, Director of the Office of Scholarly Communication for the ARL, expressed his view in an interview that libraries could assume a role and responsibility further up the research chain and participate in the scholarly communication taking place during the research process itself rather that, as presently, "sitting at the end of the line"(Byne 2008). It implies that it is the time for libraries and information centres to actively play their role in research and development activities. As the modern technology provide enough freedom and opportunity for libraries to fill the gap between the publisher and the end user and libraries are considered as the centre point of knowledge and information in any university or research institute, they can play this role as publisher very easily.

By stepping into the publishing arena, libraries can help level the playing field. The centrality of the library in the academy enables it to act as a primary catalyst for change in the scholarly communication domain. Libraries understand the culture of scholarship, and are strategically well positioned to approach publishing from a service perspective. A great deal of scholarship, particularly in the humanities, now goes unpublished because conventional publishing models make it unprofitable to publish this material. But academic libraries, by using innovative publishing models and strategic partnerships, can rectify these inequities by offering models and services that address unmet publishing needs inside the academy.

Librarians are known for their skills in acquiring, organising, preserving, and providing access to information. Now they are in the process of expanding their services to include the complete lifecycle of the content, which will be a critical function for twenty-first-century libraries.

Steps involved in Electronic Publishing

Step 1. Preparing Manuscripts: means the production of scholarly literature in machine readable form which can be distributed in digital format among the users.

Step 2. Editing: is the process of selecting and preparing language, images, sound, video, or film through processes of correction, condensation, organisation, and other modifications in various media.

Step 3. Organising: is the act of rearranging elements following one or more rules. The libraries can arrange the content of e-publication according to their pre-laid set of rules for this purpose.

Step 4. Production of E-Publications: libraries can use modern reproduction methods for the production of e-publications. These are one-time costly so that the parent organisation/ institutions do not want to invest frequently on it.

Step 5. Recording: the literature organised and produced by the library in electronic form should be kept in computers or in any other digital storage media such as CD-ROM and DVD.

Step 6. Marketing: it is considered a 'social and managerial process by which individuals and groups obtain what they need and want through creating and exchanging products and values with others.'

Step 7. Dissemination: for the distribution of electronically produced scholarly literature, libraries can use the method of online delivery through internet or broadcast networks using exclusive IP addresses or offline in CD-ROMs or DVDs.

Mode of Electronic Publishing

The following are the generally accepted mode of electronic publishing.

E-Books: An electronic book has an electronic text and that text is represented to the reader visually. Using e-publishing languages on internet like SGML (Standard Generalised Markup Language) and HTML (Hyper Text Markup Language) they can be represented and published attractively with multimedia effects.

E- Journals: E-journal is a periodical available online or in CD-ROM format. In an e-journal, all the routines of publishing from the initial stages of paper submission to publishing and distribution including accessing can be performed using electronic media.

Examples

1. *Oxford University Press Journals.* http://www.oxford journals.org
2. *IEEE Journals.* http://ieee.org/web/publications/journmag/ index.html

Electronic Database: e-database is an organised collection of data/ information and records of documents organised in machine readable form that can be accessed by a computer for retrieving the required information. It can be in two types such as reference databases and source database. Reference database includes only bibliographic reference on a subject. Source database contains source data, full text of original source or publication materials prepared specifically for electronic description.

Examples for online databases

1. *Business Library Electronic Databases.* http:// www.lib.berkeley.edu/BUSI/databases_A-Z.html
2. *European Commission Taxation and Customs Union E-*

databases. http://ec.europa.eu/taxation_customs/common/databases/index_en.html

Electronic Magazine: *E-zine* is the abbreviation for electronic magazine. A periodical publication that is stored on a file server and that may be distributed or accessed via a computer network. It is also called Web-zine.

Example

Electronic Products and Technology, Canada (http://www.ept.ca/)

E-Thesis and Dissertations (ETD): An ETD is a document that explains the research or scholarship of a graduate student. It provides a technologically advanced medium for expressing ideas. ETD is prepared using nearly any word processor or document preparation systems, incorporating relative multimedia objects, without the requirement to submit multiple copies.

Examples:

1. California Institute of Technology Theses Project. http://library.caltech.edu/etd
2. *Networked Digital Library of Theses and Dissertation (NDLTD)* http://www.ndltd.org.

New media

Podcast: A podcast is a series of digital media files (either audio or video) that are released episodically and downloaded through web syndication. The mode of delivery differentiates podcasts from other ways of accessing media files over the Internet, such as simple download or streamed webcasts: special client software applications known as *podcatchers* (e.g., iTunes, Zune, Juice, and Winamp) are used to automatically identify and download new files in a series when they are released, by accessing a centrally-maintained web feed that lists all files associated with the series. New files are thus downloaded automatically and stored locally on the user's computer or other device for offline use, giving simpler access to episodic content.

Support System Software or Collaborative software (also referred to as groupware or workgroup support systems): is software designed to help people involved in a common task achieve their goals. Collaborative software is the basis for computer supported cooperative work. Such software systems as email, calendaring, text chat, wiki, and bookmarking belong to this category. It has been suggested that Metcalfe's law – the more people who use something, the more valuable it becomes – applies to such software. The more general term social software applies to systems used outside the workplace, for example, online dating services and social networks like Friendster, Twitter and Facebook.

Prerequisites of Electronic Publishing

Kist (1989) enumerates the following supporting technologies for Electronic Publishing:

- Low cost computer facilities.
- Machine readable text (which can be processed by computer)
- Powerful and user-friendly software for desktop computer.
- High speed mass storage device incapacity and reliability.
- Low cost and dependable communication network to link between users and computer.
- Availability of reliable and inexpensive PC

Constraints of Electronic Publishing

Even though it is an easy process to publish electronically there are some inherent constraints too, like Gulati (1999) rightly noted:

- Electronic publishing includes high initial cost to publishers.
- The non-capability of hardware, due to absence of common standard and usage of different retrieval software by different publisher.
- Need strong infrastructure of computer and communication network.
- For developing country and any under-developed country electronic publishing is fruitless technology.
- Need training for the subscribers and readers.
- Need multiplying license/charges.

E-Publishing Trends in India

A study conducted by Chennupati K. Ramaiah (2006) reveals that 35 per cent of Indian publishers are engaged in e-publishing with a further 20 per cent of Indian publishers likely to start e-publishing in the next three years. Following the IT boom in India, many publishing companies set up branches and started publishing electronically in India. There is also a number of e-publishing service providers (such as Tata Infomedia, Mumbai; Dx Technologies, Pune; eMacmillan, Bangalore; Creative Graphics, New Delhi; Mizpaz Publishing Services Pvt Ltd, Chennai) that are involved in the production of e-publications and offer e-publishing-related services (such as data capture, online copy-editing, disk conversion, book production, graphic design, content writing, translation, indexing, web publishing, website development, website maintenance, interactive e-learning content, animation, interactive games, e-book conversion, etc.) to the rest of the world, particularly to the developed countries. This is in case of conventional book publishing industry in India. On the other hand many library and information centres have paced into the field of e-publishing.

THe National Institute of Science Communication and Information Resources (NISCAIR), New Delhi, many IITs and IIMs have electronic publications. The Indian National Science Academy (INSA), New Delhi have initiated an e-journal project in the year 2000-01 with the objective of producing electronic version of Indian journals thereby supporting research activities by providing all time access to the full text scientific information globally (Munshi, 2006). ICFAI University, Hyderabad has been publishing more than 50 scholarly journals and magazine since 2007 electronically along with their print form.

Conclusion

Electronic Publishing has become one of the common methods of information dissemination today. As it reduces the cost of scholarly journals and time lag, researchers are keener to accept e-publications. Now the publishers are concentrating in standardisation for e-publishing. Carnell University Library has successfully developed EPubS, an open source software system designed to enable the organisation, presentation, and delivery of scholarly journals, monographs, conference proceedings, and other common and evolving means of academic discourse.

If the libraries undertake the publishing of scholarly literature as part of their services, it will further interpret the basic law of library science, save the time of user and right information to the right user at right time.

References

Annadurai, P. (2006). Electronic publishing and its utilisation among research scholars of arts and science colleges in Erode: A Case Study. *In* Anandan, C, Gangatharan, M. *Digital Libraries from Technology to Culture*. New Delhi: Kanishka Publishers, 94-98.

Bhattacharya, Partha and Siddiqui, A. M. (2004). Developments in E-Publishing: An Overview. *IASLIC Bulletin*, 49 (4), 236-248.

Carnell University Library Digital Publishing System (DPubS). Available at: http://dpubs.org/about.html.

Clarke, Roger (1997). Electronic publishing: A specialised form of electronic commerce. Available at: www.rogerclarke.com/EC/Bled97.html (Accessed on 13 November 2009).

Dash, Smrutirekha and Panda, K.C. (2006). E-Publishing: A Challenge for the contemporary libraries. *In* Anandan, C., Gangatharan, M. *op.cit.*, 125-131.

Encarta Online Dictionary. Available at: http://uk.encarta.msn.com/encnet/features/dictionary/DictionaryResults.aspx?lextype=3&search=electronic%20publishing. (Accessed on 13 November 2009).

Gulati, A (1999). Implication of E-Publishing on Library and Information Centres. *Annals of Library Science and Documentation*, 46 (4), 121-125.

Hahn, Karla interviewed by Gerry Bayne, (2008). Publishing Services: An Emerging Role for Research Libraries. *EDUCAUSE Review, 43 (6).*

John Unsworth (1995). An Electronic Publishing FAQ. Available at: http://knowledgeway.org/living/publishing/unsworth.html (Accessed on 03 November 2009).

Kist, Joost (1989). *Electronic Publishing*. New Delhi: Institute of Book Publishing. 11-131.

Lancaster, F. W. (1995). The evolution of electronic publishing. *Library Trend,* 43 (4), 518-527.

Munshi, Usha Mujoo (2006). E-Publishing: A new publishing paradigm for enhanced scholarly communication. *Proceedings of ICDL* 2006. 395-408.

Ramaiah, Chennupati K (2006). Electronic publishing Trends in India. *The Journal for the serials Community,* 19 (2), 142-155.

Thapa, Neelam et al. (2002). E-Publishing: Beginning of a new era of E-Journals. *IASLIC Bulletin,* 47 (4), 216-221

Wikipedia. Available at: http://en.wikipedia.org/wiki Electronic publishing. (Accessed on 13 November 2009).

www.icfaiuniversity.in

www.insa.ac.in

IV

Information Literacy and E-Learning

13

E-learning in Higher Education: Opportunities and Challenges in India

—K. Anas

E-learning technologies have promised great advancement in today's learning and teaching scenario. The academia welcomed these cutting-edge technologies wholeheartedly in their daily academic practice. Though, as far as the Indian situation is concerned, there are many challenges faced by our higher education institutions while deploying e-learning technologies but many government and private institutions have experimented these technologies in their daily practice. As compared with other developed and developing nations our breakthrough in this direction is still in its infancy. There are many possibilities in deploying the modern technologies in the learning process. It is high time that the present educational system tries to incorporate these educational technologies in their regular practice in teaching and learning. This article spells out the possibilities and challenges of e-learning technologies in teaching and learning process in higher education.

Introduction

The invention of information and communication technologies (ICTs), Internet and the web have drastically changed the way we do business, govern and learn. This advancement in technology has persuaded peoples' attitude to some extent in dealing the things in their daily life. Perhaps higher education is one of the most influenced areas of technological development. The developed countries have already implemented the technologies in their teaching and learning process. They are offering various programmes through the e-learning mode. Developing countries like India has also started deploying the available technologies in the teaching and learning process but still they are lagging behind as compared to Western countries. There are many reasons for this as cultural, infrastructural, financial, lack of awareness and training, etc.

The mainstream academia and training professionals are examining the possibilities of implementing e-learning and ICTs in their daily practice with full zeal. Most of the multinational companies and other corporate institutions prefer e-learning system to provide further training to their employees. There are plenty of researches carried out in this field about the deployment of e-learning and its effectiveness in the traditional classroom system. A majority of these studies conclude that there is not much difference between the traditional face-to-face learning and e-learning (Alavi et al, 1997; Hiltz, 1993; Naidu, 2003).

The e-learning phenomenon is being felt throughout the world. As a result organisations such as the Commonwealth of Learning (COL) are emerging to help developing nations to improve access to quality web-based education and training. Web-based courses are being offered in universities in developing countries and regions as varied as India, Sri Lanka, Africa and South America. For example, in India, web-based courses in engineering and business are being jointly offered by strategic alliances between 'Education To Home' (http://education.eth.net) and several well-established universities (Aggarwal, 2000).

E-learning

The discipline of computing is definitely influencing and reshaping almost every aspect of our life, including education. One decade ago, the web was not critical to education. However, nowadays, it has become an integral part of the learning process. A huge number of educational institutes have some form of online courses. This number is increasing tremendously. The quality of an online course depends heavily on the learning material's content and the tools including images, sound, video, animation, etc., are used to accompany the explanation of that learning material (Shata 2001).

E-learning is a general term covering many different approaches that have in common use of information and communication technologies. Experts have defined e-learning in different ways; we can define e-learning in a simple way like the systematic use of networked information and communication technology in teaching and learning process. The use of the term e-learning is growing rapidly. It is also frequently being used interchangeably with terms such as computer-based training, networked learning, online learning, web-based learning, virtual learning, collaborative learning and flexible learning. Despite their unique attributes, each of these terms fundamentally refers to educational processes that utilise information and communications technology to mediate asynchronous as well as synchronous learning and teaching activities (Naidu, 2003).

Barajas (2002) clearly states the advantages of e-learning environment in his article as e-learning makes way for new modes of learning that bring education into one's home, breaking the traditional structure of educational institutions as well as their delivery methodologies. The virtual campuses have begun to develop, not only within distance learning institutions, but paradoxically within those institutions in which regular personal contact with students is the basis of their organisational, professional culture, and classroom-based curricula. New paradigms of learning, new teacher roles and functions, and new didactic methodologies begin to form as a result of e-leaning programmes. It is obvious, then, that we have entered a period in which educational institutions and learners must adapt the course management, and teaching and learning methodologies to the needs of these emerging forms.

Aggarwal (2000) very clearly states in his study that a growing segment of working, self-motivated students want to acquire skills that they feel are useful, and also want to able to choose how they will learn those skills. Convenience is becoming increasingly important, and there is growing demand for the twenty-first century education, that is:

- independent of time and space
- oriented towards goals and outcomes
- centred in the student/learner

— geared to active, hands-on learning, and

— able to accommodate differences in skills and language

There are many e-learning components and technologies available, which can be utilised for the day-to-day teaching and learning exercise. The major components of digital learning elements are images, charts, formula, presentation, e-mail, quizzes, multimedia, videoconferencing, teleconferencing, online chat, bulletin board online counselling and digital library.

Characteristics of E-learning

The e-learning milieu provides an integrated teaching and learning environment. Learning materials and other learning supports are organised in such a way that learners would feel at ease and find it convenient to access the learning materials, mentor and other learning components around the clock. The major features of e-learning environment are mentioned below:

— Systematic and well organised academic environment.

— Standardised multimedia integrated courseware and facilitate its reuse.

— This allows learners to choose learning content and tools appropriate to their varying interest, need and skill levels.

— Categorised and structured system of recording academic interactions and also make it re-usable for learning resources.

— The 24/7 accessibility makes it convenient to learner to access the learning components as they wish.

— It facilitates more interactive and collaborative ambience among the learners and mentors.

— This helps to link and integrate the university community.

— This helps to generate academic report and provide storage facility.

— This eliminates the geographical barriers and opens a broader learning opportunity.

Opportunities

Advances in ICTs, Internet and the web are making it possible to access higher educational programmes from a remote place. The existing traditional face-to-face teaching and learning system cannot accommodate all the people, and e-learning would be more worthwhile to encompass all of them and to fulfil their lifelong learning ambition. Traditional academic exercises like lecture note preparation and delivery, student participation, peer-to-peer discussion, peer-to-mentor discussion, instant message, feedback and assessment can be done more effectively with a reusable way in e-learning environment.

E-learning can be implemented in different levels of education from K-12 to higher education and also in distance education. These technologies can be implemented fully or partially. As far as the Indian scenario is concerned, a majority of the higher educational institutions are using some of the e-learning technologies in their daily teaching and learning exercises. But the states of affairs in European countries are different as they are offering various courses by utilising full-fledged e-learning technologies. There should be some pre-requisites such as necessary hardware and software, proper planning, thorough design, training facility, etc., to utilise these technologies in higher education.

The entire classroom-based face-to-face learning process can be replicated by using e-learning and web technologies for instance, preparation of online lecture notes, delivery of online lecture, design of courseware, online discussion forum, online assignment, online assessment, etc. Students can review, comment on and further clarify the learning materials. These technologies in turn would help mentors as well as students to share and exchange their thoughts and learning experiences. Students would be able to access the learning platform anytime and anywhere. Besides, they can discuss the assignments and homeworks with their peer. Mentors can post syllabus and course related material to the students.

Many institutions are providing a link to the library collection. This would help the students to access library materials instantly. A majority of the libraries are proffering web OPAC and digital library services by which students can access the entire library collection. The digital collections and online resources can be incorporated into the learning process. The students and mentors would be able to utilise the online reference desk to get quick services.

Challenges

There are many pedagogical, technical, administrative, cognitive, legal, training, assessment and support staff challenges which arise when the classroom-based teaching blends with the e-learning technologies. One cannot establish the e-learning environment within one night. This requires a strategic and systematic view. It is a complex process for a conventional institution of higher learning to come fully and successfully into the field of e-learning. There are many methodological and pedagogical precautions to be taken, besides organisational and logistic ones. These are deep and delicate issues, for they are strongly ingrained within the institutional life, experience and tradition—these are purely cultural issues (Barajas 2002).

Finance is one of the most important challenges in the process of e-learning implementation in traditional classroom-based system. This can be resolved to some extent by researching and utilising the freeware and shareware e-learning technologies. And also the institute has to plan the application of e-learning technologies in their traditional classroom system in different phases. The version and cost of hardware and software are constantly changing, and at the same time educational institutions in developing countries like India are facing the shrinking budget crisis. Therefore it is very imperative to consult with experts prior to acquireing these technologies.

A majority of the teachers are not aware about the new innovations taking place in the teaching and learning process. This is another limiting factor in applying technologies in their daily teaching exercises. Some teachers can learn about these new technologies independently but others might need formal a training programme. It is the duty of the institute or higher authority to arrange training programme for teachers to enhance their awareness about new educational technologies and provide hands on training. Only introducing training programme will not resolve the problem at present. The prevailing culture and attitude among the academia need to be changed by practising the creation and development of plans to integrate technology into the traditional classrooms.

Conclusion

The process of applying e-learning technologies in teaching and learning process is advancing at a pace that nobody could foresee its future course. This phenomenon is shifting the entire trend of modern approaches of teaching and learning. The technology-enabled learning process provides more focus on learners that would be a learner-centred learning system. Moreover the learner would be self-motivated and self-sufficient in e-learning. This is the high time for the academia to think about the possibilities of these technologies in their day-to-day academic exercise. In the past the student was totally dependent upon the teacher and books but today many sources of information and learning tools are available. Now it is the duty of mentors to motivate and train students on how to explore and make use of the new tools and sources. The technologies can help to develop the skills of the twenty-first century – the skill of the digital era – abilities to think creatively, communicate, produce and improve the basic skills (CEO, 2001). It is very clear that the task of the teacher is transforming from simple classroom-based teaching to make students capable to think over, find the answer from the sources, analyse and synthesis the located answer, and so on.

There would be many impediments encountered while implementing these learning technologies in face-to-face teaching and learning process like lack of awareness, lack of fund and infrastructure, etc. The academia have to give serious thought to these issues and try to resolve them. They have to approach these setbacks with a confident attitude towards the use of technologies in their usual practice. Though some initiations are going on towards the digital learning in our country yet we are still lagging behind. The former president of India, Dr. A.P.J. Abdul Kalam, has foreseen our country in 2020 with widespread use of digital learning. The academia have to change their outlook and try to become familiar with all these revolutionary technologies to make this as a reality. It is necessary that the institute has to provide unconditional support to incorporate new technologies into their traditional teaching environment.

References

Aggarwal, A. (2000). *Web-based learning and teaching technologies: opportunities and challenges*. London: Idea Group Publishing.

Alavi, M., Yoo, Y and Vogel, D. (1997). Using information technology to add value to management education. *Academy of Management Journal*, 40 (6), 1310-1333.

Barajas, M. (2002). Restructuring higher education institutions in Europe: The case of virtual learning environments. *Interactive Educational Multimedia*, 5, 1-28.

CEO Forum on Educational and Technology (2001). Key building blocks for student achievement in the 21st century: Assessment, alignment, accountability, access, analysis. Washington D.C., CEO Forum. Available at: www.ceoforum.org/reports.cfm.

Hiltz, R.S. (1993). *The virtual classroom: Learning without limits via computer networks.* Norwood, NJ: Ablex Publishing Corporation.

Naidu, S. (2003). *E-learning: A guidebook of principles, procedures and practices.* New Delhi: The Commonwealth of Learning.

Kannan, S., Bharadwaj, R.S. and Ravinder, D. (2004). E-education in modern era: in *Road map to new generation of libraries using emerging technologies*. Ahmedabad, INFLIBNET centre, 438-442.

Shata, O. (2001). A critique of Stephen Downs' article, Learning objects: A Middle East perspective. *International Review of Research in Open and Distance Learning,* 2 (1), 24.

14

Imparting Information Literacy: A Practical Approach

—Indira Koneru

Technological advances benefited users with the high speed information processing, storage and dissemination tools; but left us in a perplexed 'World of Information'. Information, available from multiple directions, in multiple formats and media, via multiple access paths and multiple providers, mystifies its users. Information literacy enables an individual: to identify his or her information need in terms of quantity, quality, format and extent, to access and assess information retrieved, to use it ethically and effectively to meet the need or problem at hand.

Having realised Information literacy as the thriving literacy of the information-intensive society, LIS practitioners need to design and develop instructional programmes to impart Information literacy. Information literacy instructions should aim at creating opportunities for self-directed and independent learning, wherein students can engage in using a wide variety of information sources to construct knowledge, expand their knowledgebase, ask informed questions, and sharpen their critical thinking. This paper focuses on 'How to impart Information Literacy instructions', along with 'The Why of Information Literacy'.

Introduction

Information Literacy has evolved from bibliographic instruction, library instruction, user education and other information skills-focused programmes to the current concept of information literacy. Precursors of information literacy, as an integral part of reference services aimed at making the users better informed of library resources and services for enhancing their information use. On the other hand, information literacy is fundamentally associated with the information seeking process and critical thinking and evaluating skills.

As instructors, LIS professionals have been assisting users in 'how to search through and use the library collections of the printed world'. This inherent quality prompted the academic librarians to initiate Information Literacy (IL) movement, so as to make learners information literate. "To be information literate, a person must be able to recognise when information is needed and have the ability to locate, evaluate, and use effectively the needed information" (ALA, 1989). Information literacy equips one with the skills necessary for filtering and discarding the information that is of poor quality.

Information Literacy

Information Competency, Information Skills, 21st Century Skills, Digital Literacy, Media Literacy, Information Fluency, are the variant phrases used for Information Literacy.

Paul Zurkowski (1974) coined the term Information Literacy and defined it as "being able to find what is known or knowable on any subject". He also described information literate as:

"People trained in the application of information resources to their work can be called information literates. They have learned techniques and skills for utilising the wide range of information tools as well as primary sources in molding information solutions to their problems."

Information literacy, a process-oriented approach to information is the amalgam of information fluency and technology fluency. Information fluency is the ability to understand the nature of information, its varying formats, sources of information, information retrieval tools; whereas technology fluency is the skills required to harness Information and Communication Technologies (ICT) and their associated search tools to search and retrieve information over the Web. Information fluency starts with 'information seeking' and ends with making users "wise information consumers" (UNESCO, 2007).

Various definitions of information literacy are available in the literature. Boekhorst (2003[1]) summarises the various definitions and descriptions of information literacy:

- *The ICT concept:* information literacy refers to the competence to use ICT to retrieve and disseminate information;
- *The information (re)sources concept:* information literacy refers to the competence to find and use information independently or with the aid of intermediaries; and
- *The information process concept:* information literacy refers to the process of recognising information need, retrieving, evaluation, using and disseminating information to acquire or extend knowledge. This concept includes both the ICT and information (re)sources concept and persons are considered as information systems that retrieve, evaluate, process and disseminate information to make decisions to survive, for self-actualisation and development.

Information literacy is "knowing when and why you need information, where to find it, and how to evaluate, use and communicate it in an ethical manner" (Chartered Institute of Library and Information Professionals, 2004).

CILIP further adds, the skills implied by this definition require an understanding of:

- the resources available;
- how to find information;
- the need to evaluate results;
- how to work with or exploit results;
- ethics and responsibility of use;
- how to communicate or share findings; and
- how to manage findings.

Information literacy is an intellectual capability that enables one to acquire the needed technological skills and information researching skills, paving the way for lifelong learning. Lifelong learning entails one to be on the learning curve and to befit with the current developments and changing scenarios, local, national and global. The Alexandria Proclamation adopted by the High Level Colloquium on Information Literacy for Lifelong Learning (2005) proclaims, "Information literacy and lifelong learning are the beacons of the Information Society. Information Literacy at the core of lifelong learning empowers people in all walks of life to seek, evaluate, use and create information effectively to achieve their personal, social, occupational and educational goals."

Information literacy and lifelong learning are interrelated concepts. Both these concepts are "self-motivated and self-directed, they do not require the mediation of an outside individual, organisation or other kind of helper, beyond the learner him/herself, although advice and assistance can be helpful" (Horton, 2008).

In succinct, information literacy is the information researching process that identifies and evaluates the requisite information resources and harnesses the ICT tools for searching and retrieving relevant and usable information resources.

Significance of Information Literacy

If the ability to read, write and do basic arithmetic is considered as literacy the ability to acquire and use the finest information is considered as information literacy. It is information literacy that equips one with the ability to find the best information among the myriad of sources and apply it to make wise decisions. Information literacy enables one to develop 'higher order thinking' required to understand, apply, analyse, evaluate and synthesize information.

Though technological advances benefited us with the high speed information processing, storage and dissemination tools, yet it left us in the information tsunami. "No other change in our society has offered greater challenges than the emergence of the Information Age. Information is expanding at an unprecedented rate, and enormously rapid strides are being made in the technology for storing, organising, and accessing the ever growing tidal wave of information" (ALA, 1989).

Information available in multitudes, multiple forms, formats and media, via multiple access routes, paths and multiple providers mystify us. The current technological advances put forth a bewildering amount of information, that too in different formats and media. Computer, digitalised holdings are seen as a solution to the problem of an exploding information base, but the problems of judgement of data, and useful and useable access remain (Kuhlthau, 1996). Information literacy, a thriving literacy of the information-intensive societies builds the required competency among us to cope with the 'Multi' nature of information.

Increasing attention to information literacy is partly the result of information overload, especially related to the growth of digital information, which has even caused a new ailment called as 'Information Fatigue Syndrome' (IFS) (Wilson, 2001) and partly because of the new focus on student learning in a lifelong learning context (Virkus, 2003).

The Australian Library and Information Association's (ALIA, 2001) *Statement on Information Literacy for all Australians* outlines the importance of information literacy in workplace learning, lifelong learning and participative citizenship as: Information literacy is a prerequisite for:

- participative citizenship
- social inclusion
- the creation of new knowledge
- personal, vocational, corporate and organisational empowerment
- learning for life

ALIA statement connects information literacy with personal empowerment, participative citizenship, social inclusion and lifelong learning. Information literacy is vital to create information literates, who are equipped with a critical understanding of quality information and skills required for its effective use. Information literates and/or informed citizens manage and cope with the ongoing S (Social), T (Technological), E (Economic) and P(Political) challenges and improve the capabilities of social inclusion.

Not only locating the relevant information but also judging its quality is essential for learner's academic excellence. "An 'educated' graduate will no longer be defined as one who has absorbed certain body of factual information, but as one who knows how to find, evaluate, and apply needed information" (Abid, 2004). An information literate graduate is desired to develop the ability to identify his or her information need in terms of quantity, quality, format and extent, accesses and assesses information retrieved, uses it ethically and effectively to meet the need or problem at hand.

UNESCO's IFAP (Information for All Programme, 2006) emphasizes the need to equip the people with skills for accessing and using information as:

"Information literacy enhances the pursuit of knowledge by equipping individuals with the skills and abilities for critical reception, assessment and use of information in their professional and personal lives."

IFAP (2006) accentuates, "Everybody should have the opportunity to acquire the Information Literacy skills in order to understand, participate actively in, and benefit fully from the emerging knowledge societies." So, we the LIS practitioners need to develop such information literacy instructional programmes that provide learners with ample scope to engage in learning activities and acquire skills required.

Information literacy instructional programmes need to impart the conceptual and procedural knowledge about what is the nature of information, its various forms and formats; where to look for and how to approach and access the information sources; how to evaluate and use the information retrieved; and how to synthesize new information.

Imparting Information Literacy

A student who is 'information illiterate' will have fewer opportunities to cope with the current information age, when compared to 'information literate'. So, information literacy instructions should enhance learners' knowledge and skills necessary for information researching, using technology and its associated tools and resources. Information literacy instructional programmes should also aim at creating opportunities for self-directed and independent learning, wherein students are engaged in using a wide variety of information sources to construct knowledge, expand their knowledgebase, ask informed questions and sharpen their critical thinking.

But, how to impart IL instructions is the question that resonates in LIS practitioner's mind. We all know, information literacy aims at equipping library users or learners with the range of skills required for effective handling and wise consumption of information (*see* Figure 1: SCONUL Seven Pillars).

Figure 1: SCONUL Seven Pillars of Information Literacy

As library and information services are need-based, we need to take into consideration the user groups, their information needs and level of understanding for deciding on what (content) to impart and how to impart. Say for instance, school library users may not require advanced skills as that of college and university libraries.

At the basic level, information literacy skills enable a learner to locate and access the skills. And the progression to advance skills improves learner ability to understand and use effectively. The Society of College, National and University Libraries (SCONUL, 1999) Seven Pillars Model of Information Literacy (*see* Figure 1) advocates the progression from basic skills to advanced skills.

Recognising information need; distinguishing ways of addressing gap; constructing strategies for locating and accessing sources of information constitute the basic skills, which bring a novice or beginner to a competent position. The advanced skills: comparing and evaluating; organising, applying and communicating; synthesizing and creating new information makes the learner proficient.

We ought to design such information literacy programmes that enable a new member of a library to transform into an expert by passing through the phases, advanced beginner though competent to proficient. Passing through all these stages equips a student/library user with the needed expertise to take informed decisions and generate new knowledge. Similarly, in a university library the user groups can be freshman, junior or senior graduates, research scholars, faculty, etc. New entrants may require basic skills and seniors might have reached the level of competent or proficient.

Additionally, the Information Literacy Standards of several national and international LIS professional bodies provide a a comprehensive framework to impart information literacy and assess the learning outcomes.

The Association of College and Research Libraries (ACRL), the Big Six expounded by Eisenberg and Berkowitz, are the standards and models from the United States, whereas the Society of College, National, and University Libraries (SCONUL) 7 Pillars model is from the United Kingdom and the ANZIIL standards are by the Australian and New Zealand Institute for Information Literacy and Empowering 8 is from South Asia. All these standards provide LIS professionals with general (not subject-specific) guidelines for imparting Information Literacy, instructions, because the learning outcomes of information literacy programmes are necessarily generic. The method and mode of imparting IL instructions should be decided in the planning stage itself, taking into consideration the financial resources available.

Methods of Imparting Information Literacy

Method of instruction implies 'the form or procedure planned for imparting instructions'. Information literacy instructions can be extra curricular in the form of 'formal instructions by library staff', i.e., stand-alone programmes that are general in nature, or curricular, i.e., subject-specific/curriculum-integrated.

Generic vs. Specific

Information literacy programmes can be generic or specific. Whether it be a generic or specific programme, an information literacy programme should create a constructive path for independent and lifelong learning. And the learning outcomes should be in line with the standards and goals set for the programme. We can use the information literacy standards set by an LIS professional body, say, for example, Information Literacy Competency Standards for Higher Education of the Association of College and Research Libraries (ACRL, 2000). Information Literacy Competency Standards for Higher Education provides us with a framework not only for setting standards and goals but also the performance indicators and desired learning outcomes required to assess the information literate individual/student (*see* Table 1).

For developing further understanding of performance indicators and their respective learning outcomes that identify a student as information literate, consult the source document (ACRL, 2000).

Information literacy skills, generic or specific can be "related to the total information acquisition, filtering, interpretation, production, communication and legal and ethical process irrespective of the technical or media form. In addition, information literacy can be viewed laterally in the different areas of information: literacy skills relating to different areas of science, to statistics, finance, advertising, politics, religions etc." (Kauhanen-Simanainen, 2005). Imparting subject-specific skills necessitates designing 'curriculum-integrated' information literacy programmes.

Curriculum-integrated Information Literacy Instructions

Curriculum-integrated instructions imply "Information Literacy skills are made an integral part of the course, which are relevant to their course curriculum." Embedding information literacy in the curricula provides learners with the opportunities to experience, reflect and apply learning in the novel contexts.

Table 1: Information Literacy Competency Standards for Higher Education

S. No.	*Standard*	*Performance Indicators*
1.	The information literate student determines the nature and extent of the information needed.	The information literate student: 1. defines and articulates the need for information. 2. identifies a variety of types and formats of potential sources for information. 3. considers the costs and benefits of acquiring the needed information. 4. reevaluates the nature and extent of the information need.
2.	The information literate student accesses needed information effectively and efficiently.	The information literate student: 5. selects the most appropriate investigative methods or information retrieval systems for accessing the needed information. 6. constructs and implements effectively designed search strategies. 7. retrieves information online or in person using a variety of methods. 8. refines the search strategy if necessary. 9. extracts, records, and manages the information and its sources.

(Contd...)

(Contd...)

3.	The information literate student evaluates information and its sources critically and incorporates selected information into his or her knowledge base and value system.	The information literate student: 10. summarizes the main ideas to be extracted from the information gathered. 11. articulates and applies initial criteria for evaluating both the information and its sources. 12. synthesizes main ideas to construct new concepts. 13. compares new knowledge with prior knowledge to determine the value added, contradictions, or other unique characteristics of the information. 14. determines whether the new knowledge has an impact on the individual's value system and takes steps to reconcile differences. 15. validates understanding and interpretation of the information through discourse with other individuals, subject-area experts, and/or practitioners. 16. determines whether the initial query should be revised.
4.	The information literate student, individually or as a member of a group, uses information effectively to accomplish a specific purpose.	The information literate student: 17. applies new and prior information to the planning & creation of a particular product or performance. 18. revises the development process for the product or performance.

(Contd...)

(Contd...)

	19. communicates the product or performance effectively to others.
5. The information literate student understands many of the economic, legal, and social issues surrounding the use of information and accesses and usesinformation ethically and legally.	The information literate student: 20. understands many of the ethical, legal and socio-economic issues surrounding information and information technology. 21. follows laws, regulations, institutional policies, and etiquette related to the access and use of information resources. 22. acknowledges the use of information sources in communicating the product or performance.

Source: Association of College and Research Libraries

"Through the creation, with faculty, of curriculum-integrated programs, librarians should actively contribute to the student's learning processes in their search to enhance or develop the skills, knowledge and values needed to become lifelong learners" (IFLA, 2006).

Supporting the integration of information literacy skills training into the core curriculum has become an important consideration of libraries. However, integrating IL instructions into curriculum in turn necessitates "collaboration between the faculty, curriculum designers and content developers and library and information professionals." This collaboration is necessary not only for 'curriculum alignment' but also to develop 'assessment' strategies and instruments in the context of a specific discipline.

Curriculum alignment is a collaborative effort required to maintain consistency between curriculum goals, learning objectives and outcomes, content, instructional strategies and learning activities, assessment and evaluation of information literacy skills in line with course goals (ANZIIL Standards, 2004). In addition to assessing basic information literacy skills, curriculum-based assessment is significant, as information literacy manifests itself in the specific understanding of the knowledge creation, scholarly activity, and publication processes found in those disciplines (ACRL, 2000).

Having decided the method of imparting information literacy, the choice about the mode of imparting IL instructions should be made, taking into consideration the resources available for successful implementation of information literacy programmes.

Mode of Imparting Information Literacy

In general, the modes of instruction may range from face-to-face courses to online tutorials through formal class settings, one-on-one or small group sessions, audio-visual presentation, self-learning packages (CD/DVD). However, online tutorials or Web-based information literacy programmes gained momentum, as Web technologies has the potential to reach out to the learners scattered across the globe. Moreover, empirical studies proved that students who use technology as a tool may become better at managing information, communicating and presenting ideas (Kent and Hall, 2001).

Before opting for technology-enabled information literacy initiatives, we need to ascertain whether institution's information infrastructure ensures uninterrupted and incessant access to information literacy modules and also whether students have access to technologies or not. If the institution has sound information infrastructure and technological tools are at the students' disposal, then we can think of Web-based programmes, as it inherently supports 24X7 access to information literacy programmes.

The mode of Web-based instructions can be (i) a stand-alone Web tutorial, (ii) a Web-based, for-credit information literacy course, (iii) Information literacy instruction that is integrated into the course content of an online academic course (Johnstone and Krauth, 2002). However, an information portal with a well-conceived user interface is a prerequisite to deliver Web-based information literacy modules. Instead, we can use Learning Management Systems (LMS) with in-built user interface, administrator interface and instructor interface. LMS facilitates content management; structuring learning activities, both individual and collaborative; developing assessment instruments; supporting online collaboration; above all to build a 'learning community'. For designing and developing effective information literacy programmes using an LMS demands integrating pedagogical theories and principles. Designing pedagogically-sound information literacy programmes creates 'student-centred' learning environments. Student-centred learning environments encourage students to inquire, think critically, and engage actively in reflective, constructive and problem-solving learning activities.

Pedagogically Sound Design

Etymologically, pedagogy means 'to lead the child'. Pedagogy, the art and science of teaching, focuses more on the 'activity of learning' than only on 'teaching of content'. It emphasizes on 'Activity of Learning', not on 'Activity of Teaching'. Providing learners with an active, collaborative and effective learning experience is the central concern of pedagogy.

Pedagogically sound learning design ensures consistency between the curriculum we frame, the instructional strategies and learning activities we integrate, the learning environment we provide, and the assessment criteria we adopt.

ACRL instructional section suggests the following tips on the pedagogy of Web tutorials:

1. *Outline the objectives and outcomes* clearly to establish purpose and realistic expectations;
2. *Provide a clearly defined structure* that:
   a) reflects the objectives of the tutorial; and
   b) allows for both linear and nonlinear learning, so students can review sections and/or select the pathways that best meet their needs.
3. *Include interactive exercises* such as with simulations, manipulation of objects, interactive quizzes, or the direct application of principles. These will encourage problem solving by students and allow them to:
   a) practice/respond to what is taught;
   b) self-assess their learning;
   c) engage in "deep learning" (understanding the meaning) rather than "surface learning" (memorisation and regurgitation); and
   d) receive feedback.
4. *Give attention to the concepts* behind the mechanics so that information skills are applicable to other search interfaces.
5. *Incorporate contemporary language and topics*, be as succinct as possible, and do not be afraid to entertain. This will:
   a) establish relevance to students' lives;
   b) not overwhelm them with verbiage; and
   c) help to keep their interest.
6. *Provide a way to contact a librarian;*
7. *When the tutorial is used, try to make it course-related* by encouraging faculty to link Web-based instruction to a course assignment. This will provide additional hands-on experiences using information resources in various formats within the context of an actual assignment, further reinforcing the tutorial's teachings and relevance.

So, we need to: (i) formulate such learning objectives that highlight expected student performance; (ii) provide well-structured content that facilitates easy navigation and access; (iii) develop active and interactive learning activities that engage learners in deep and self-evaluative learning; (iv) provide clarity with regard to concepts and also procedures involved; (v) try to develop lucid and stimulating content with real-life cases/ scenarios; (vi) encourage participants to interact with us for needed support, guidance and feedback on progress; and (vii) collaborate with the faculty to integrate information literacy in course curricula. With regard to content, we need not rely only on text; use a variety of media, such as PowePoint with narration, podcasts, screencasts, video and Web2.0 tools (http:// www.go2web20.net/). Above all, 'learner orientation' is vital to start Web-enable information literacy programmes on the right foot.

As learners are not that comfortable with the Web-based learning, orientation should provide information: about the prerequisites to register for an online programme; on the use of LMS (how to login, access and navigate) with requisite links to technical support and academic support at prime position on the user interface; elements of course and course schedule; amount of time to be spent on their course and deadlines (we can use LCMS in-built calendar for inserting dates for deadlines and reminders for upcoming events); anticipated outcomes and level of participation (interaction, collaboration and communication) expected, along with the assessment criteria and grading strategy.

Conclusion and Suggestions

"How to locate, evaluate and use information effectively?" for personal and professional needs is a challenge for an individual sailing in the information flood. Here arises the need for information literacy. In addition to understanding the technology relevance to finding information, information literacy focuses on "how to utilise those incredibly diverse and powerful technologies efficiently and effectively to search for, retrieve, organise, analyse, evaluate information and then use it for specific decision-making and problem-solving ends (Horton, 2008)". information literacy moulds individuals into self-directed, self-reliant and informed citizens.

Acknowledging the significance of information literacy as a thriving and driving force in the information society, libraries and LIS professionals need to play a pivotal role to foster information literacy by integrating it into their information services and collaborating with the faculty. Additionally, academic institutions need ιo develop strategies to ensure the inclusion of information literacy in the curricula at all levels.

Methods and modes of imparting information literacy instruction depend on and vary with the availability of resources both physical and human with the library and within the academic institution. Technological advances enabled us to design and develop Information literacy programmes in multiple modes, using multiple media. Among the various modes, Web-based programmes offer flexible options for both the students (for 24X7 access) and information literacy instructors (for updating, maintaining, redesigning, if necessary). However, designing pedagogically sound learning modules necessitates us to research on and to integrate appropriate instructional design theories and principles.

References

Indira, Koneru. (2008). *A study of information literacy skills of BRAOU learners: designing an integrated information portal.* PhD Thesis, GRADE, Dr. BR Ambedkar Open University, Hyderabad.

Pelz, Bill (2004). Three principles of effective online pedagogy. *JALN*, 8 (3). Available online: http://www.sloan-c.org/publications/jaln/v8n3/pdf/v8n3_pelz.pdf (Accessed on 21 October 2009)

End Notes

Abid, Abdelaziz. (2004). *Information literacy for lifelong learning.* World Library and Information Congress: 70th IFLA General Conference and Council, 22-27 August 2004, Buenos Aires.

ACRL (2000). *Information literacy competency standards for higher education.* Available t: http://www.ala.org/ala/mgrps/divs/acrl/standards/standards.pdf (Accessed on 19 October 2009)

ACRL (2004). Tips for developing effective Web-based library instruction. Available at http://www.ala.org/ala/acrl/aboutacrl/acrlsections/instruction/homepage.htm (Accessed on 29 July 2005)

ALIA, (2001). *Australian Library and Information Association Statement on information literacy for all Australians* Available at: http://www.alia.org.au/policies/information.literacy.html (Accessed on 25 August 2006)

American Library Association (1989). *Presidential Committee on Information Literacy, Final Report.* Chicago: ALA. Available at: http://www.ala.org/acrl/nili/ilit1st.html (Accessed on 9 Dec. 2005)

Boekhost, A.K. (2003). Becoming information literate in the Netherlands. *Library Review,* 52(7), 298-301.

Bundy, Alan (ed.) (2004). *Australian and New Zealand information literacy framework principles, standards and practice,* 2nd ed. Adelaide: Australian and New Zealand Institute for Information Literacy. Available at: http://www.anziil.org/index.htm (Accessed on 22September 2006).

Horton, Forest Woody (2008). *Understanding information literacy: a primer.* Paris: UNESCO.

IFLA (2006). *Guidelines on information literacy for lifelong learning.* Hague: IFLA.

Johnstone, Sally M. and Krauth, Barbara (2002). *Information literacy and the distance learner.* Whitepaper prepared for UNESCO, the U. S.. National Commission on Libraries and Information Science and the National Forum on Information Literacy. Available at: http://www.nc'is.gov/libinter/infolitconf&meet/papers/johnstone-fullpaper.pdf (Accessed on 10 June 2006)

Kauhanen-Simanainen Anne (2005). Collaborative information literacy by government. *IFLA Journal,* 31 (2), 183-187. Available at: http://ifla.sagepub.com (Accessed on November 12, 2007)

Kent Allen and Carolyn M. Hall (Ed.) (2001). *Encyclopedia of library and information science.* New York: Marcel Dekker, Inc.

Kuhlthau, Carol (Ed.). 1996. *The virtual school library: Gateway to the information superhighway.* Englewood, CO: Libraries Unlimited.:

Longworth Elizabeth (ed.) (2006). UNESCO : Information for All Programme (IFAP) Report 2004/2005, Paris: UNESCO. Available at: www.unesco.org/publications (Accessed on 6 August 2006)

SCONUL (1999). *Information skills in higher education: a SCONUL position paper.* London: SCONUL. Available at: http://www.sconul.ac.uk/groups/information_literacy/papers/outcomes.pdf (Accessed on 19 October 2009).

UNESCO (2007). *Development of information literacy through school libraries in South-east Asian countries.* Bangkok: UNESCO Bangkok.

_______________ (2005). *Alexandria proclamation on information literacy and lifelong learning.* Available at: http://www.ifla.org/III/wsis/High-level-Colloquium.pdf (Accessed on 7 March 2006)

Virkus, S. (2003). Information literacy in Europe: a literature review. *Information Research, 8(4), paper no. 159* Available at: http://informationr.net/ir/8-4/paper159.html (Accesed on 22 May 2005)

Wilson, L. A. (2001). Information literacy: fluency across and beyond the university. In B. I. Dewey (Ed.), *Library user education: powerful learning, powerful partnership.* Lanham, MD: Scarecrow Press.

15

Information Literacy Programmes in Research Libraries in Kerala: An Assessment

—C. Jalaja Kumari and Mallinath Kumbar

The purpose of this paper is to investigate the status of information literacy programmes in the libraries of R&D institutions in Kerala. Information literacy instruction programmes for researchers can be challenging to develop. Now, a wide range of information sources are available to the researchers in various forms. The availability of information does not necessarily mean actual use. Some of the available resources may not be utilised at all because the users are unaware of the availability of such resources, they do not know how to access them, or they do not know what the resources offer. How to penetrate into vast universe of information and access the required information pin-pointedly is a pertinent question here. All this calls for continued information literacy programme.

Introduction

The production of information is increasing day by day, as users are unable to tap its resources effectively. In this age of information technology, information storage and retrieval system have undergone rapid changes. The complexities of information handling systems necessitate the need for instructing the users on how to utilise the suitable tools require for accessing information.

In order to instruct the user community how to access the myriad information sources available, the library has to reassess and restructure traditional instructional methods. Nowadays, to meet the challenges posed by electronic information sources, it is not an easy task. Without intelligent and systematic guidance and subsequent use of all available sources, a library remains passive. A library can be said to be effective and efficient only when its resources are used to the maximum extent possible. The only solution for this is information literacy.

Information Literacy

'Information literacy' is defined as "the ability to recognise the need for information and to identify, locate, access, evaluate and effectively use the information to address and help resolve personal, job related, or broader social issues and problems."[1] or It is "about people's ability to operate effectively in an information society." It involves an appreciation of the need for information, to attain skills to locate, organise, evaluate information, and have effective use of information to solve problems, make decisions, create new knowledge and to supply information to others. Information literacy goes beyond simply acquiring the skills to use information tools and to find information resources. It includes lifelong learning and professional development, and the ability to interact in the information society.

Information literacy requires an awareness of the way in which information systems work, of the dynamic link between a particular information need, and the sources and channels required to satisfy that need.

Information literacy includes concepts such as the attributes of information (including relevance, currency, timeliness, consistency), evaluation of information sources (for credibility, currency, reliability), economic characteristics of information (expandable, shareable, diffusive), information value and cost effectiveness, the ability to define information requirements effectively, information overload and filtering.

Importance of Information Literacy

Information literacy is increasingly important in the contemporary environment of rapid technological change and proliferating information resources. Because of the escalating complexity of this environment, individuals are faced with diverse, abundant information choices in different walks of life. Information is available through various sources and increasingly, information comes to individuals in unfiltered formats, raising questions about its authenticity, validity and reliability. In addition, information is available through multiple media, including graphical, aural and textual, and these pose new challenges for individuals in evaluating and understanding it. The uncertain quality and expanding quantity of information pose large challenges for society.

Information literacy enables learners to master the content and extend their investigations, become more self-directed, and assume greater control over their own learning. An information literate individual is able to:

- Determine the extent of information needed.
- Plan a systematic and comprehensive search of the literature.
- Use advanced search techniques to find the most relevant information.
- Access the needed information effectively and efficiently.
- Evaluate information and its sources critically.
- Incorporate selected information into one's knowledge base.
- Use information effectively to accomplish a specific purpose.
- Understand the economic, legal, and social issues surrounding the use of information, and access and use information ethically and legally.

Need for Information Literacy in Research Institutions

There are many reasons that cater to the needs of IL programmes in research libraries as literature explosion, research on complex and interdisciplinary areas, the application of new technology in information retrieval, etc., have made the information handling process a complex one. Researchers create information and knowledge by utilising information, their own and others', and by producing new information. They require access to huge amounts and variety of information sources in order to accomplish their work. An active research scientist is constantly on the alert for scientific or technical information relevant to his ongoing research, while at the same time rapidly disseminating information about his own work.

Researchers are no longer interested in using traditional methods for literature search. Today, information is increasingly being published in electronic forms, and Internet has become the richest sources of global information, and no researcher can update himself without having access to electronic/Internet sources. Many researchers in Kerala are either not aware or do not have proper training to make optimum utility of these latest technological developments. Information literacy allows the researcher to cope by giving him the skills to know when we need information and where to locate it effectively. IL includes skills to use modern technologies to use modern library as a gateway to information.

Components of Information Literacy

Various components or important elements of IL are:

Library literacy

Library literacy requires the ability to use a library's collection and its services.

Information and Communication Technology (ICT) Literacy

This means literacy in using digital technology, communication tools, and/or network to access, manage, integrate, evaluate and create information in order to function in a knowledge society. ICT literacy is actually made up of several literacies such as, computer literacy, internet literacy, network literacy, digital literacy.

Computer Literacy

Computer literacy means taking control of your computer and not letting it control you. Otherwise, computer literacy requires a technological know-how to manipulate computer hardware and software.

Internet Literacy

Internet literacy aims to literate individuals use Internet for acquiring information needed for different purpose, because nowadays, library often is not a first place people choose to obtain information. The first place is the internet.

Network Literacy

Network literacy may be defined as "the ability to identify, access and use electronic information from the network."

Digital Literacy

The means "the ability to understand and use information in multiple formats from wide variety of sources when it is presented via computers."

Each of these literacies requires some level of critical thinking. But compared with computer literacy, information literacy goes beyond merely having access to and knowledge of how to use the technology, because technology alone does not guarantee quality learning experiences. And compared with library literacy, information literacy is more than searching through an online catalogue or other reference materials because information literacy is not a technique, but a goal for learners.

Status of IL Programmes in Research Libraries in Kerala

This survey tied to assess nature and type of user induction/ orientation / training activities and status of IL programmes conducted in the libraries of 20 research institutions in Kerala. The sample population consists of libraries attached to the following research institutions. The Central Coir Research Institute (CCRI) Alappuzha, Central Institute of Fisheries Technology (CIFT) Kochi, Central Marine Fisheries Research Institute(CMFRI), Kochi, Central Plantation Crops Research Institute (CPCRI), Kayamkulam, Central Tuber Crops Research Institute, (CTCRI) Trivandrum, Centre for Earth Science Studies (CESS), Trivandrum, Centre for Development of Advanced Computing (C-DAC), Trivandrum, Fluid Control Research Institute, (FCRI), Palakkad, Indian Institute of Spices Research (IISR), Kozhikode, Rajiv Gandhi Centre for Biotechnology (RGCB), Trivandrum, National Institute of Interdisciplinary Research In Science and Technology (NIIST) (formerly RRL) Pappanamcode, Trivandrum, Sri Chitra Tirunal Institute for Medical Science and Technology, Biomedical Wing (SCTMIST, BMT), Trivandrum, Liquid Propulsion Satellite Centre (LPSC), Valiyamala, Trivandrum, National Institute of Oceanography (NIO), Kochi, Rubber Research Institute of India (RRII), Kottayam, Vikram Sarabhai

Space Centre (VSSC), Trivandrum, Centre for Water Resources Development and Management (CWRDM), Kozhikode, Kerala Forest Research Institute (KFRI), Thrissur, Regional Cancer Centre (RCC), Trivandrum, and Indian Rare Earths Ltd. (IRE) Research Centre, Kollam.

User Study

Information literacy programmes are intended to address the promotion of general information literacy skills applicable to all library users and to promote the information skills required by specific target groups. Understanding the information needs of library users and their information seeking behaviour is necessary to plan and implement user-oriented information literacy programmes. The users' profiles are felt as an important aspect in the process of information services in a successful information centre. It is nothing but the interest of the users in different types of information in their day-to-day requirement.

Out of the 20 sample libraries only eight (40%) libraries are maintaining user profiles. Information about the user such as his/ her name, department/ section, area of specialisation/ subject of interest, etc. are recorded in the user profile. For providing the information services in a fruitful manner to the users, it is very essential to undertake user-need assessment periodically. User-need assessment is undertaken by 18 (90%) libraries and the periodicity of the same varies from library to library. When 22.22 per cent (4/18) libraries undertake user-need assessment yearly, 16.67 per cent (3/18) of the libraries conduct more than once a year and in 61.11 per cent (11/18) libraries it is irregular.

Out of the 20 research libraries selected for the study, 16 (80%) are conducting IL programmes very actively. Most (7/16) of the sample libraries conduct awareness programmes to their users either at the time of joining or when a new product or service is introduced in the library. In five libraries the frequency of IL programme is irregular and four libraries conduct twice in a year. Various methods adopted by the libraries are described in the following sections.

Initiation

Initiation to the new user means to acquaint the fresh users with the rudiments of the library and to help them to overcome the difficulties when they begin to make use of the library. Out of 16 sample libraries, two (12.5%) research libraries follow this method. Centre for Water Resources Development and Management (CWRDM), Kozhikode is following initiation in an informal way.

Orientation

It is intending the new user to the general techniques of library usages and services available in the library and in particular, to the organisation, services and layouts of the library. Orientation method is adopted by 2 (12.5%) libraries.

Instruction/seminars

Conducting classes and tutorials using lecture and demonstration with the help of audio-visual aids for teaching the essential concepts of information searching and evaluation in the area of interest to the user group. Among 16 research libraries four (25%) conduct literacy programmes by using this method. Demonstration of library software and databases is a common practice in Central Marine Fisheries Research Institute (CMFRI), Kochi.

Circulars/ Handouts

Four libraries (25%) use circulars/ handouts to support IL programmes. Circulation of user manuals for digital/ online services is done by CMFRI library.

Hands on Training

Hands on training in computers to find out information from web resources is followed by four (25%) libraries. For example, TGBRI library provides this method to its user groups.

Use of Information and Communication Technology

Use of computers and networking technologies facilitates teaching and learning information skills to be more effective. The National Institute of Interdisciplinary Research in Science and Technology (NIIST) uses the bulletin board as a tool for IL programmes to their users and the National Institute of Oceanography (NIO) uses Intranet for this purpose.

Conclusion

In Kerala, there is still much to be done to promote integrated information literacy in libraries of R&D institutions. Teamwork between library professionals and researchers is well developed in some research institutions but many are only just beginning to realise what libraries can do for them. IL is very vital in influencing utilisation of e-resources. Information professionals are needed to pass on IL skills to library users, while library users should endeavour to find out what information is available online for their consumption.

References

American Library Association Presidential Committee on Information Literacy. 1989. Final Report. Washington, DC.

Darch, C., Karelse, C. and Underwood, P. (1997). *Alternative Routes on the Super Highway. Independent Online-Higher Education Review.* Independent Educational Media.

V

Open Access and Open Source Software

16

Open Access and Institutional Repositories: The New Scholarly Publishing Scenario

—V. Gopakumar and A. K. Baradol

The paper discusses the changes that open access and institutional repositories have brought in the scholarly publishing scenario at the international level, and their impact on libraries and librarianship. The need for open access, its mechanism involved, open access publishing and open access archiving are discussed.

Introduction

Open Access and Institutional Repositories are two buzzwords among the academia and the library and information science parlance. In the 80's the Universal Bibliographic Control was a dream of information scientists. Through the Universal Bibliographic Control, the universal availability of published literature or its bibliographic details was expected. This remained a dream because of the barriers of time, distance and language. But the advent of Internet, networked environments and huge server computers changed the scenario globally. Now time and distance are not at all barriers. Communication to the other end of the globe is a few mouse clicks away. The information revolution has made the world a global village.

In this changed situation the need for making available the research output from the academic and research institutions was felt seriously. This gave way to the concept of open access. Institutional repositories are the products of innovative ideas to make possible the concept of open access. This article discusses the changes that open access concept and institutional repositories have brought in the scholarly publishing Scenario globally and its impact on libraries and librarians hip as a whole.

Need for Open Access

The need for open access to scholarly literature is supported by several arguments. The different groups of stakeholders have their own arguments in respect of this concept. The academic and research institutions are consuming huge amount of funds for research with a view that the research would benefit the public. The public (taxpayer) feel that the research in academic as well as research institutions are funded by their money. Hence they are eligible to get access to the literature output of those research projects. This view is very much relevant in the case of medicine and applies to other subject fields too.

The view in support of open access held by researchers is exceedingly significant. An analysis of the traditional scholarly publishing scenario would reveal this. The scholarly publication is mainly centred on scholarly journals, where the journals have the monopoly in each areas of scholarship. The academic institutions and libraries of developing and under-developed countries have very little or even sometimes no access to such publications. So access to research was curtailed which in turn has adversely affected research globally.

"Most of the direct labor and much of the indirect cost required for the publication of a journal are derived from academic institutions that ultimately bear the cost of scholarly journals subscription fees. Faculty researchers produce the original research itself; academic editors and peer-reviewers select and validate the quality and priority of research; academic libraries process, house, and distribute the journals to end users, and library resources support archival preservation - all at little or no direct cost to the journals publishers themselves" (Crow, 2004).

Similarly, academic librarians all over the world were facing the so called 'Serials Crisis'. The cost of journal subscription was escalating, when academic institutions were not getting the

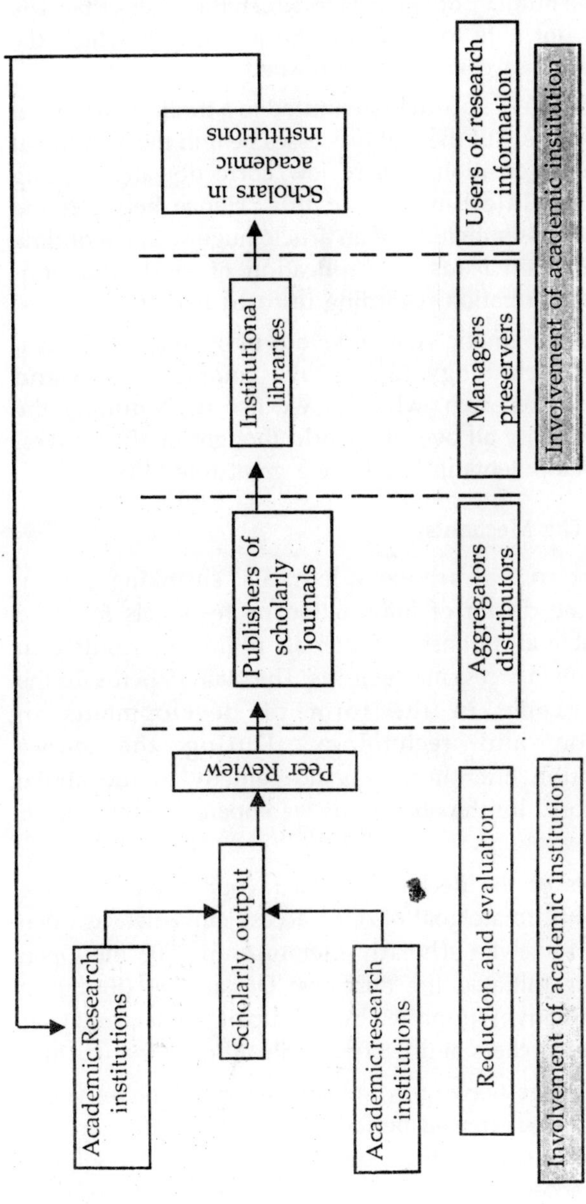

Figure 1: Traditional Scholarly Communication Process

required funding support. Librarians had no other choices than to cut down the number of journals to which they subscribe. The libraries were not able to purchase the journals in which the articles of their researchers were published.

The publication of an article submitted to a traditional journal took 36 to 52 weeks. But the real processes behind the traditional publishing like the creation, peer-review, correction and printing takes only very little time out of this. Hence between the production and dissemination of an article huge wastage of time occurs, which again leads to duplication of work and non-availability of information regarding research results.

Yet another pragmatic view in favour of open access is that, when there is technology to improve communication and dissemination of research, why not we use it? Naturally the academic community all over the world thought of alternatives, where the developments in ICT have a great role to play.

Open Access: The Mechanism

The exorbitant cost of scholarly journals, shrinking library budgets, and the dream of information professionals to make globally available all published materials ultimately resulted in the creation of open access mechanisms. The main impetus for the development came in the form of developments in communication and technology. During the paper based publication era, there was no remedy to the above disgusting factors. But the ubiquitous web opened pathways for open access.

An analysis of the declarations in favour of open access reveals that the ultimate goal of open access movement is open access to peer reviewed scholarly literature. In 2002 the Open Society Institute initiated the Budapest Declaration (Budapest Open Access Initiative) supported by a group of scholars and later seconded by researchers and professionals all over the world.

The BOAI suggests two mechanisms by which the universal availability of peer-reviewed periodical literature. They are the Open Access Publishing (OAP), otherwise called the "Golden" road to open access and the Open Access Archiving (OAA), otherwise called as the "Green" road to open access.

Open Access Publishing (OAP)

In this model of open access publishing the peer-reviewed journals are published as open access publications and they provide instant online open access to articles upon publication. A journal may be "full OA", meaning that it makes all of its articles available under open access principles, or "hybrid OA", meaning that some articles are made openly accessible whereas others are not. Open access journals generally publish under a copyright licence rather than an assignment of copyright, allowing authors to retain copyright ownership of their work. Some open access journals charge publication fees and some do not. By making content available online for free, OA journals guarantee that anyone with access to the Internet also has access to timely and useful research publications. A large number of journals have already come to exist providing free online full text access. A directory of the *open access journals* is available under the URL www.doaj.org. This site lists more than 3,000 journals. Major publishers also have come out with open access journals. Open access journals that do not charge publication fees are usually able to do so because they are supported by a hosting institution or university (for example, the *Harvard Human Rights Journal* is published and supported by Harvard Law School) or because they receive funding from external research or charitable sources. For example, *D-Lib Magazine* is produced by the Corporation for National Research Initiatives (CNRI) and *Ariadne* is funded by the Museums, Libraries and Archives Council (MLA), JISC and the European Union, and also receives support from the University of Bath.

There is a common misconception that OA journals do not provide peer-review at all or do not provide the same level of peer-review as toll access publishers provide. However, this is not true. Open access publishing is completely consistent with peer-review. OA journals provide a level of peer-review as rigorous and dependable as that provided by toll-access publishers. They use the same standards, the same procedures, and even the same reviewers as conventional journals

One perceived disadvantage of open access journals at present is their lack of recognised research impact. Research impact is defined as the extent to which a research articles is used for reading and further research.

Open Access Archiving (OAA)

This method of publishing is called the green road of open Access, where the authors are depositing their documents to a local repository which is available allowing open access. Wikipedia defines "institutional repository." "An Institutional Repository is an online locus for collecting, preserving, and disseminating - in digital form - the intellectual output of an institution, particularly a research institution."

For a university, this would include materials such as research journal articles, before (preprints) and after (post-prints) undergoing peer review, and digital versions of theses and dissertations, but it might also include other digital assets generated by normal academic life, such as administrative documents, course notes, or learning objects. The four main objectives for having an institutional repository are:

- to create global visibility for an institution's scholarly research;
- to collect content in a single location;
- to provide open access to institutional research output by self archiving it; and
- to store and preserve other institutional digital assets, including unpublished or otherwise easily lost ("grey") literature (e.g., theses or technical reports).

The Scholarly Publishing and Academic Resources Coalition (SPARC) defines "institutional repositories" as "digital collections capturing and preserving the intellectual output of a single university or a multiple institution community of colleges and universities."

What material will or will not be accepted for deposit in the institutional repository depends on an institution's open access policy. Usually, accepted material will include journal articles, research papers, book chapters and conference papers. Repositories have been designed to be interoperable through the use of common metadata standards developed by the Open Archives Initiative (OAI).

The institutional repositories are online locus for depositing the scholarly publications of an academic or research institution. The mechanism for submission of articles, its storage and backup, indexing of metadata, and the control of user interfaces are all controlled by software interfaces. There are many open source software packages available for this purpose. The leading names among them are DSpace, Eprints.

DSpace (*www.dspace.org*) software for developing institutional repository which is freely available as open source software and you can customise and extend. It captures, stores, indexes, preserves and redistributes an organisation's research material in digital formats. This digital asset management software is jointly developed by Hewlett Packard and MIT Libraries. DSpace facilitates the institutions and universities to operate an open access and interoperable institutional repository at the local level.

Eprints (*www.eprin.ts.org*) is another generic repository building software developed by the University of Southampton. It is intended to create a highly configurable web-based repository. There are about 300 Eprints based repositories according to the Eprints website. This also is highly customisable software.

Conclusion

The concept of open access has changed the scholarly publishing scenario globally. The extent to which we can attain bibliographic control is a matter of concern due to the limitations of policy matters of institutions involved in research and development.

References

Crow, R. (2004). The case for institutional repositories: A SPARC position paper.

Johnson, R. K. (2002). Institutional Repositories: Partnering with faculty to enhance scholarly communication. *D-Lib Magazine*, 8 (11).

Lynch, C. A. (2003). Institutional Repositories: Essential infrastructure for scholarship in the digital age. *Portal: Libraries and the Academy*, 3(2), 327--336.

Suber, Peter. (2007). Open Access Overview. Open Access News (blog), last revised 19 June 2007, Available at: http://www.earlham.edu/-peters/fos/overview.htm (Accessed on 4 March 2008).

Washington DC: The Scholarly publishing and academic resources coalition (SPARC).

17

Open Access Resources in S&T Field with Special Reference to Engineering and Medicine

—Susmita Chakraborty

The paper defines open access and its advantages. Open access publishers in the international level and in India are explained, and major open access publishers in the country are listed. An analysis of DOAJ is also attempted. A survey of open access institutional repositories is also given.

Introduction

Open access to scholarly literature is a movement led by eminent organisations like the Budapest Open Access Initiative (BOAI), Open Society Institute (OSI), Open Software Foundation, etc., which works against all barriers to worldwide information flow and tries to ensure anytime and anywhere information for all available literature. Some well-known names associated with open access movement are that of Richard Stallman, Steven Harnard, Peter Suber, Linus Torvald, etc. The call for open access is basically meant for researchers, librarians, administrators, students, publishers, foundation managers, learned society officers, government officials and citizens.

By *open access* BOAI means free availability of scholarly literature on the internet, permitting any users to read, download, copy, distribute, print, search or link to the full texts of these articles, crawl them for indexing, pass them as data to software, or use them for any other lawful purpose, without financial, legal or technical barriers other than those inseparable from gaining access to the internet itself.

The only constraint on reproduction and distribution, and the only role for copyright in this domain, should be to give authors control over the integrity of their work and the right to be properly acknowledged and cited.

Definitions

The most popular definition of open access journals is the definition by Budapest Open Access Initiative (BOAI): "Open access ensures the right of users to read, download, copy, distribute, print, search, or link to the full texts of ... articles as mandatory for a journal to be included in the directory prepared by BOAI." This definition may also be pertinent for other open access literature. Definition by DOAJ for open access journals: "Open access journals are journals that use a funding model that does not charge readers or their institutions for access" (Suber, 2009).

Advantages of Open Access

- Completely free and unrestricted online availability.
- Worldwide electronic distribution of the peer-reviewed journal literature
- Benefits scientists, scholars, teachers, students and other curious minds.
- Gives authors and their works vast and measurable new visibility, readership and impact.
- Helps global research and education community.

Candidates for Open Access

- Peer-reviewed journal articles
- Un-reviewed preprints for comment
- Important research findings to alert colleagues

Cost Considerations

Open access literature is not costless to produce though the overall costs are far lower than the costs of traditional forms of dissemination. For lowering the costs still further, strong involvement of the professional associations, universities, libraries, foundations and others are necessary. It will need new cost recovery models and financing mechanisms. Alternative sources of funding are:

- foundations and governments that fund research
- universities and laboratories research fund
- endowments set up by discipline or institution
- friends/activists of the cause of open access
- profits from the sale of add-ons to the basic texts
- funds freed up by the demise or cancellation of journals charging traditional subscription or access fees
- contributions from the researchers themselves
- other creative and innovative ways of funding

Ways of Open Access

Self-Archiving: these archives may be subject specific, institution specific or type specific.

Open Access Journals: OA journals can be born-OA journals or traditional journals shifted to OA mode, sometimes with a dual existence.

Key Players

Open access publishers have proved that open access is economically feasible. Some notable examples in the world scenario are:

a) PLoS: Public Library of Science (http://www.plos.org/)

The Public Library of Science (PLoS) is a non-profit organisation of scientists and physicians committed to making the world's scientific and medical literature a public resource. Its mission is to provide anytime, anywhere access to full-text of scholarly literature. PLoS received supports from the Gordon and Betty Moore Foundation, the Sandler Family Supporting Foundation, the Open Society Institute, the Irving A. Hansen Memorial Foundation, the Doris Duke Charitable Foundation, the Ellison Medical Foundation, the Burroughs Wellcome Fund, the John D., Catherine T. MacArthur Foundation and other foundations, universities, organisations and individuals.

PLoS journals charge a publication fee to the authors or research sponsors for each article they publish to recover a part of the cost of peer review, journal production and online hosting and archiving. PLoS journals are available at http://www.plos.org/journals/index.php

BioMed Central (http//www.biomedcentral.com)

BioMed Central is a for-profit open-access publisher, with a diverse group of peer-reviewed journals.

Budapest Open Access Initiative (BOAI) http://www.soros.org/openaccess

BOAI has published a number of open access journal business guides.

A meeting was convened by the Open Society Institute (OSI) in Budapest, Hungary on December 1-2, 2001 to explore strategies for economically self-sustaining open-access scholarly publishing. A statement of principle, strategy and commitment, commonly referred to as the Budapest Open Access Initiative was drawn and signed by:

- Leslie Chan: *Bioline International*
- Darius Cuplinskas: *Director, Information Program, Open Society Institute*
- Michael Eisen: *Public Library of Science*
- Fred Friend: *Director Scholarly Communication, University College London*
- Yana Genova: *Next Page Foundation*
- Jean-Claude Guédon: *University of Montreal*
- Melissa Hagemann: *Program Officer, Information Program, Open Society Institute*
- Stevan Harnad: *Professor of Cognitive Science, University of*
- *Southampton, Universite du Quebec a Montreal*
- Rick Johnson: *Director, Scholarly Publishing and Academic*
- *Resources Coalition (SPARC)*
- Rima Kupryte: *Open Society Institute*
- Manfredi La Manna: *Electronic Society for Social Scientists*
- István Rév: *Open Society Institute, Open Society Archives*

- Monika Segbert: *eIFL Project consultant*
- Sidnei de Souza: *Informatics Director at CRIA, Bioline International*
- Peter Suber: *Professor of Philosophy, Earlham College & The Free*
- *Online Scholarship Newsletter*
- Jan Velterop: *Publisher, BioMed Central*

Signatures were also invited (till today its open) and received from open access activists represented by researchers, universities, laboratories, libraries, foundations, journals, publishers, learned societies and similar open-access initiatives.

Budapest Open Access Initiative aims to

- Removing access barriers to this literature, especially the price barriers.
- Accelerate research.
- Enrich education.
- Share the learning of the rich with the poor and the poor with the rich.
- Lay the foundation for uniting humanity in a common intellectual conversation and quest for knowledge.
- Provides readers extraordinary power to find and make use of relevant literature.

Open Archives Initiative (OAI) www.openarchives.org

OAI creates standards for archiving materials in open access archives.

The Open Society Institute (www.soros.org)

The foundation network, founded by philanthropist George Soros, is committed to providing initial help and funding to realise this goal. It will use its resources and influence to extend and promote institutional self-archiving, to launch new open-access journals, and to help an open-access journal system become economically self-sustaining. While the Open Society Institute's commitment and resources are substantial, this initiative is very much in need of other organisations to lend their effort and resources.

Scholarly Publishing and Academic Resource Coalition (SPARC) http://www.arl.org/sparc/

Developed by the Association of Research Libraries in June 1998. It is an international alliance of academic and research libraries working to correct imbalances in the scholarly publishing system. SPARC is a partner of Public Library of Science.

A list of leading academic organisations that have endorsed SPARC is available at http://www.arl.org/sparc/about/endorsements/index.shtml.

Membership: It has nearly 800 institutions in North America, Europe, Japan, China and Australia and about 200 coalition members. It is also associated with major library organisations in Australia, Canada, Denmark, New Zealand, the UK and Ireland, and North America.

The Ligue des Bibliothèques Européennes de Recherche (LIBER) and other European organisations established SPARC Europe in 2001. Mission Statements are educating stakeholders, advocating policy changes and incubating real-world demonstrations of business and publishing models.

SPARC Open Access Newsletter (http://www.earlham.edu/~peters/fos/): is a newsletter written by Peter Suber of Earlham College. This site contains a tremendous amount of information about the open access movement, including a definitive guide, historical timeline and upcoming conferences. Peter Suber himself is a very popular name in open access arena. It includes Open Access Overview, Newsletter Archive, Open Access News blog, Discussion forum archive, SPARC home page for the newsletter and forum, Timeline of the Open-Access Movement, Conferences, Lists of OA-related sites and information, What we can do to promote open access and a Feedback form.

The Directory of Open Access Journals (DOAJ) www.doaj.org

It is a clearing house for free, full-text, quality-controlled scientific and scholarly journals since 2003. It aims to cover all subjects and languages. There are now 4,418 journals in the directory. Currently 1,686 journals are searchable at article level. As of 5 November 2009, 322257 articles are included in the DOAJ service.

Country Statistics: India is in 7th position with 132 Total number of journals in DOAJ. The first six positions go to United States with 961 journals, Brazil with 400 journals, United Kingdom with 375 journals, Spain with 257 journals, Germany with 168 journals and Canada 135. A detailed country statistics is to be found at http://www.doaj.org/doaj?func=byCountry.

Coverage: Four thousand journals from more than 2,000+ publishers in more than 50 different languages emerge. DOAJ is the authoritative source for open access journals with over eight million monthly hits, up to 4,000 journals published in almost 100 countries.

Sponsors: Lund University Libraries, the e-Depot of the National Library of the Netherlands (KB) (www.kb.nl/e-depot-en), the Swedish Library Association are the sponsors.

DOAJ tries to increase the visibility and ease of use of peer-reviewed and/or edited open access scientific and scholarly research journals with International Standard Serial Number (http://www.issn.org), thereby promoting their increased usage and impact. Owners of these journals are requested to supply the metadata when a journal has been added into the directory.

Access is free with free online user registration and open access without any embargo period.

Under Agriculture and Food Sciences, Agriculture (General) has 81 journals, Animal Sciences has 60 journals, Aquaculture and Fisheries has 10 journals, Forestry has 26 journals) Nutrition and Food Sciences (22 journals) and Plant Sciences (36 journals).

Subject Biology has 167 journals: Anatomy (6 journals), Botany (57 journals), Cytology (8 journals), Genetics (34 journals), Microbiology (36 journals) , Physiology (28 journals) and Zoology (70 journals).

Chemistry as a broad heading has four sub-areas. Analytical Chemistry (9 journals), Chemical Engineering (11 journals), Chemistry (General) (75 journals) and Organic Chemistry (8 journals).

Health Sciences has Dentistry (45 journals), Medicine (General) (318 journals), Nursing (28 journals) and Public Health (131 journals) under its wings. Medicine (General) is further subdivided into Allergy and Immunology (20 journals),

Cardiovascular (50 journals), Dermatology (14 journals), Gastroenterology (20 journals), Gynecology and Obstetrics (27 journals), Internal medicine (192 journals), Neurology (68 journals), Oncology (49 journals), Ophthalmology (18 journals), Pathology (23 journals), Pediatrics (43 journals), Pharmacy and materia medica (28 journals), Psychiatry (34 journals), Sports Medicine (12 journals), Surgery (62 journals), Therapeutics (49 journals) and Urology (17 journals).

In the Life Sciences category, Biochemistry has 34 journals and Biotechnology has 27 journals.

Mathematics has got 142 journals whereas Statistics has 32 journals.

Seventeen journals are there under Astronomy (General) and 61 journals under the subject heading Physics (General).

Under the broad heading of Science General, the subject Information theory has three journals and Science (General) has 57 journals.

Technology and Engineering consists of sub-headings like Chemical Technology (16 journals), Computer Science (162 journals), Construction (7 journals), Electrical and Nuclear Engineering (29 journals), Environmental Engineering (4 journals), Environmental Technology (5 journals), General and Civil Engineering (83 journals), Hydraulic Engineering (3 journals), Industrial Engineering (11 journals). Manufactures (6 journals), Materials (21 journals), Mechanical Engineering (20 journals), Military Science (1 journals), Mining and Metallurgy (7 journals), Technology (General) (56 journal) and Transportation (13 journals).

SHERPA www.sherpa.ac.uk/

It is a consortium of research-led universities and is based at the University of Nottingham. SHERPA is a portfolio of projects based on the philosophy of open access and repository run by a 33-member consortium of research-led universities. It has received SPARC Europe Award for Outstanding Achievements in Scholarly Communication 2007.

Services developed by SHERPA include ROMEO, JULIET and OpenDOAR.

ROMEO (http://www.sherpa.ac.uk/romeo/)

Funded by JISC and the Wellcome Trust, ROMEO uses a simple colour-code to classify publishers' copyright policies in relation to self-archiving and funding regulations. So far, ROMEO has reached 500 publisher policies on self archiving. It also provides searching of journal and publisher information by Journal Title, Publisher Name and ISSN. This journal information is provided by the British Library's Zetoc service hosted by MIMAS.

JULIET (http://www.sherpa.ac.uk/juliet/)

Research funders (i.e. funding agencies) open access policies are detailed in JULIET. These policies relate to (a) Self-Archiving, (b) publication of articles in open access journals or in hybrid journals and (c) depositing the raw research data in appropriate public archives or stores.

Directory of Academic Open Access Repositories (OpenDOAR) www.opendoar.org/:

OpenDOAR provides an authoritative, quality-filtered list of repositories and also provides searching for repositories and/or their contents. It also provides tools and support to both repository administrators and service providers.

The list of repositories is available at http://www.opendoar.org/countrylist.php. The repositories are listed under Continent, then Country and then by Institute. A list of Indian repositories may be found at http://www.opendoar.org/countrylist.php?cContinent=Asia#India

A search interface by many access points (subject, language, etc.) has been provided at http://www.opendoar.org/find.php

PubMed Central http://www.ncbi.nlm.nih.gov/pmc/

PubMed Central is a free digital archive of biomedical and life sciences journal literature at the US National Institutes of Health (NIH) developed and managed by NIH's National Center for Biotechnology Information (NCBI) in the National Library of Medicine (NLM). A complete list of its journals may be found at http://www.ncbi.nlm.nih.gov/pmc/journals/

SciDev.Net (www.scidev.net/scipub)

The Quick Guide on Science Publishing offers insight into the discussions on this topic and an overview of new initiatives to make science literature more accessible.

Digital Library/Archives Developed Using Free and Open Software

Many digital libraries have been developed worldwide using digital library software like Greenstone Digital Library Software, ePrint or Dspace. Archives developed in India using Greenstone Digital Library Software is available at http://greenstonesupport.iimk.ac.in/indiandls.htm

Eprints and related Archives: A quality list is available at http://tardis.eprints.org/discussion/eprintarchivessubjecttable9103.htm

Open Citation Project (The Open Citation Project- Reference Linking and Citation Analysis for Open Archives) gives many quality lists of ePrint archives at

http://opcit.eprints.org/explorearchives.shtml#general, http://opcit.eprints.org/explorearchives.shtml#OAI-services,

Open Access Institutional Repositories at http://opcit.eprints.org/explorearchives.shtml#institutional-lists.

Open Access Journal Archives at http://opcit.eprints.org/explorearchives.shtml#journal

Dspace Archives: There are over 700 DSpace repositories around the world. An evaluative list may be accessed at http://www.dspace.org/Repository-List.html.

Indian Open Access Scenario

To conclude this deliberation on open access resources, let us look a bit on the Indian scenario. We have repositories that are Institution-Specific, Subject-Specific, Document Type Specific, etc.

Institution-Specific

In many premier Indian institutes like the Indian Institute of Science; Indian Institute of Management, Kozhikode; Indian Statistical Institute, Bangalore; Indian Institute of Technology, Delhi; National Institute of Technology, Rourkela; National Aerospace Laboratories, Bangalore; National Chemical Laboratory, Pune; Information and Library Network (INFLIBNET), Ahmedabad; National Institute of Oceanography, Goa; Raman Research Institute, Bangalore, etc. are the repositories.

Table 1: Institutional Repositories in India

Name	*Host Institution*	*URL*	*No. of Items*	*Types of Documents*	*Software Used*
Librarian's (LDL)	Documentation Research & Training Digital Library Centre (DRTC)	https://drtc.isibang.ac.in/	236	Research Papers, Articles, Reports, etc.	DSpace
DSpace at GBPUAT University	G.B. Pant University of Agriculture & Technology	http://202.141.116.205/dspac e/	82	Research Papers, Articles, Reports, Thesis, etc.	DSpace
IIA Repository	Indian Institute of Astrophysics	http://prints.iiap.res.in/	725	Research Papers, Articles, Reports, Thesis, etc.	DSpace
EPrints@IIITA	Indian Institute of Information Technology, Allahabad	http://eprints.iiita.ac.in/	22	Research Papers, Articles, Reports, etc.	EPrints
DSpace@IIMK	Indian Institute of Management, Kozhikode (IIMK)	http://dspace.iimk.ac.in/	133	Research Papers, Articles, Reports, etc.	DSpace

(Contd...)

(Contd...)

EPrints@IIMK	Indian Institute of Management, Kozhikode (IIMK)	http://eprints.iimk.ac.in/	25	Research Papers, Articles, Reports, etc.	EPrints
EPrints@IISC	Indian Institute of Science (IISC)	http://eprints.iisc.ernet.in/	3645	Research Papers, Articles, Reports, etc.	EPrints
ETD@IISc	Indian Institute of Science (IISC)	http://etd.ncsi.iisc.ernet.in/	153	Theses & Dissertations	DSpace
EPrints@IITD	Indian Institute of Technology, Delhi (IITD)	http://eprint.iitd.ac.in/dspace/	1296	Research Papers, Articles, Reports, etc.	DSpace
DSpace at INSA	Indian National Science Academy (INSA) (Metadata only)	http://61.16.154.195/dspace/	818	Conference Papers, Articles, Reports, etc.	DSpace
ISI Library, Bangalore	Indian Statistical Institute, Bangalore	http://library.isibang.ac.in:80 80/dspace/	10	Research Papers, Articles, Reports, etc.	DSpace

(Contd...)

(Contd...)

DSpace at INFLIBNET	INFLIBNET	http://dspace.inflibnet.ac.in	428	Research Papers, Articles, Reports, etc.	DSpace
NAL Institutional Repository	National Aerospace Laboratories (NAL)	http://nal-ir.nal.res.in/	418	Research Papers, Articles, Reports, etc.	EPrints
DSpace at NCRA	National Centre for Radio Astrophysics	http://ncralib.ncra.tifr.res.in/dspace/	22	Research Papers, Articles, Reports, Theses, etc.	DSpace
EPrints at NCL	National Chemical Laboratory (NCL)	http://dspace.ncl.res.in/	290	Theses, Research Papers, Articles, Reports, etc.	DSpace
OpenMED@NIC	National Informatics Centre (NIC)	http://openmed.nic.in/	1035	Research Papers, Articles, Reports, etc.	EPrints
	National Institute of Oceanography	http://drs.nio.org/drs/	55	Journal articles, conference proceeding Digital Repository Service of NIO articles, Technical reports, theses, dissertations, etc	DSpace

(Contd...)

(Contd...)

Dspace@NITR	National Institute of Technology, Rourkela	http://dspace.nitrkl.ac.in/dsp ace/	223	Theses, Research Papers, Articles, Reports, etc.	DSpace
Digital Repository of RRI	Raman Research Institute	http://dspace.rri.res.in/	1064	Research Papers, Articles, Reports, Theses, etc.	DSpace
Vidyanidhi	University of Mysore	http://www.vidyanidhi.org.in /	1835	Theses & Dissertations	DSpace

(As on 01/03/2006, Ghosh and Das, 2006)

Subject-Specific

OpenMed@NIC, maintained by National Informatics Centre, New Delhi is subject specific. We also have MedInd or Indian Medlars site at NIC. They provide access to free and full text biomedical literature.

Librarian's Digital Library (LDL): It is by Documentation Research and Training Centre (DRTC), Bangalore in the field of library and information science.

Document Type-Specific

Vidyanidhi of University of Mysore collects these is from Indian universities. It stores any thesis or dissertation of any researcher or student that is accepted in any of the Indian universities or institutions, and provides access to theses and dissertations.

Open Access Publishers in India

Some of the examples of open access publishers in India are Indian Academy of Sciences (http://www.insa.ac.in/), Indian National Science Academy (www.ias.ac.in/pubs/journals/), Indian Medlars Centre of National Informatics Centre (http://medind.nic.in/), Medknow Publications (www.medknow.com/journals.asp), indianjournals.com (http://www.indianjournals. com) and Kamla-Raj Enterprises (www.krepublishers.com/KRE- New-J/).

Conclusion

To conclude, we may say that open access has come to stay. Despite some inhibition and initial reluctance on the part of researchers, publishers and other stakeholders, it already has gained a sound footing and many admirers. We can safely hope that India as well as the world outside will march forward towards the ever-increasing horizon of anytime, anywhere access of scholarly literature.

References

BioMed Central. Available at: http//www.biomedcentral.com. (Accessed on 24th September 2009).

Budapest Open Access Initiative. Available at: http://www.soros.org/openaccess. (Accessed on 23rd September 2009).

DOAJ: Directory of Open Access Journals. Available at: http://www.doaj.org/doaj?func=loadTempl&templ=about. (Accessed on 20th September 2009).

DSpace Archives. Available at: http://www.dspace.org/Repository-List.html. (Accessed on: 25th September 2009).

Eprints and related Archives. Available at: http://tardis.eprints.org/discussion/eprintarchivessubjecttable9103.htm. (Accessed on 25th September 2009).

Ghosh, S B and Das, A K. (2006). Open Access and Institutional Repositories - a Developing Country Perspective: A Case Study of India. Presented in World Library and Information Congress 2006 and IFLA Conference, Seoul, August 2006. Available at: http://eprints.rclis.org/6391/

Indian Archives using Greenstone Digital Library Software. Available at: http://greenstonesupport.iimk.ac.in/indiandls.htm. (Accessed on 25th September 2009).

JULIET. Available at: http://www.sherpa.ac.uk/juliet.

Open Archives Initiative. Available at: www.openarchives.org.

Open Citation Project Eprint archives. Available at: http://opcit.eprints.org/explorearchives.shtml#general. (Accessed on 25th September 2009).

Open Society Institute. Available at: www.soros.org/

Open Software Foundation. Available at: www.en.wikipedia.org/wiki/Open Software Foundation. (Accessed on 23rd September 2009).

OpenDOAR: Directory of Academic Open Access Repositories. Available at: www.opendoar.org.

PLoS: Public Library of Science. Available at: http://www.plos.org/

PubMed Central. Available at: http://www.ncbi.nlm.nih.gov/pmc.(Accessed on 25th September 2009).

ROMEO. Available at: http://www.sherpa.ac.uk/romeo.

Scholarly Publishing and Academic Resource Coalition or SPARC. Available at: http://www.arl.org/sparc.(Accessed on 25th September 2009).

SciDev.Net. Available at: www.scidev.net.

SHERPA: a consortium of research-led universities. Available at: www.sherpa.ac.uk.

Suber, Peter. Budapest Open Access Initiative:Frequently Asked Questions Available at: http://www.earlham.edu/~peters/fos/boaifaq.htm (accessed on 20th September 2009).

18

Open Licenses and Radical Shift in Digital Content Distribution

—V. Vimal Kumar and S. Chitra

This paper discuses Open Content Licences (OCL) in the digital content distribution. OCL give content creations the freedom to publish their works for free access without losing their ownership. The history and characteristics of OCLs are mentioned. Some of the popular OCL are discussed briefly. Open licence initiatives are on the way to develop more activities and tools to promote open content. The paper concludes that more business models should be introduced for open content distribution to attract more content development.

Introduction

World Wide Web is becoming the most preferred location for academic community, librarians and other professionals for communication, content generation and transfer. They are extensively making use of web services such as blogs, podcast, wiki's, digital libraries and institutional repositories for the transfer and access of information content in digital format. Text, images, audio and video in digitised format facilitate easy creation, transfer and duplication of information throughout networks. Reckless use and transfer of digital content through Internet invokes threats to copyright claims of commercial content creators. This situation force commercial pu' ,hers to make use of technology and law to ensure security and prevent unauthorised access of digital content.

Users have been enjoying the freedom to read published print works found in traditional libraries without seeking permission from the copyright owner. But the same freedom is restricted in a publicly accessible digital collection (Samuelon, 1998). Making and distribution of an unauthorised copy of digital content may invite provisions relating to the violation of copyright. Copyright can prevent libraries from providing open access to the digital information they collect and make barrier to the development of digital library collection (Kuny, 1996).

Existing intellectual property rights are designed to protect the interests of commercial publishers and curtail the user's freedom to share the content. This situation would not be good for innovation and consumer welfare in the long run (Samuelson 2001). Copyright laws make hindrances to authors and users to share and make use of copyrighted materials. Open licences are designed on the foundations of open source principles and protect the right of content creators and make sure public access of creative works. Open content licenses give content creators the freedom to publish their works for free access without losing their ownership.

Background Setting for Open Content Licences

A content licence is a document that states the freedoms and limitations that you apply to your work – an explanation of what someone can and cannot do with what you make (Roberts). Traditionally creative content is published and distributed through tangible objects like books, manuscripts, sheet music, video tape, microfilm and audio cassettes. Copyright laws provided protection for publishers from unauthorised use of content in physical materials, including literary, dramatic, musical, artistic and other intellectual works. It is considered as illegal if anyone violates the rights provided by the copyright law to the owner of copyright. Libraries and its users survived copyright restrictions by using the provisions of 'fair use' and 'library privilege' clauses. These exclusive provisions allow public to access and make copy of documents in libraries. Copyright laws give protection to creative works for a limited time, after which the work is added to public domain.

With the increasing popularity of Internet, the movie, music and publishing industries failed to implement copyright law in networked environment. As the result, commercial content creators hopefully turned towards technology to protect the content from unauthorised use and distribution. Digital content publishers implemented DRM (Digital Rights Management) to control the copyright threats. DRM is an umbrella of technologies that allow right owners to set and enforce terms by which people use their intellectual property. This system combines an encryption scheme to protect the content and authentication systems to open content for only authorised users. Online music sellers, bibliographic database vendors, and journal publishers are successfully make using DRM to control the use of content. They developed authorised softwares, water mark, IP based access, user name and password schemes to monitor and restrict the access of the content only in user's computer.

Brief History of Open Content Licence

Open content licences are built on the basics of open source software licences. Richard Stallman drafted 'GNU General Public Licence' in 1984 for the free distribution of software. David Wiley's GNU Free Documentation Licence in 1984 is considered as the first non-software open licence. Contributions of Tim O'Reilly and Andy Oram made open content licences more suitable for the online versions of printed books and journals. As a result, Open Publication Licence (OPL) was released in 1999. Larry Lessig constituted Creative Commons in 2001 for the distribution of literature, art, music and film in public domain. This initiative designed a variety of licensing options to public access of creative works. Later a range of open content licences appeared, and most of them contain the spirit of Creative Commons licenses.

Characteristics of Open Content Licences

Copyright laws are not user friendly for public access of digital content and is crafted with provisions advisable to accredit the monopoly of commercial publishers. Open content licenses are attributing the principles fostering free culture and have commitment to society. Lawrence Liag, an exponent of open content licenses noted its key characteristics:

– Open content licences give users right to copy, distribute, modify, perform, display and create derivative works.

– It ensures a work based on original work should get license under the terms and conditions of the open content licence.

– Open content licences include the provisions for both commercial and non commercial usage.

– Open content licences strictly instructs the appropriate credit to be given to the author of the work.

– This model of licences ensures community participation in content development and distribution.

Most of the open content licences terms are more or less same. Open content licences give dual advantages: it protect creator's right on the content and at the same time it give free access for users. The freedoms of usage allow for non-commercial purpose only. In certain context, permission of the creator is necessary for commercial usage of content and derivatives based on original work.

Nature of Community Content Development in Internet

Community participation is the main feature of content development in public domain; both developers and users actively engage in the effort. Main players associated with open content development are professionals, amateurs, libraries, archives academic institutions and public broadcasting companies. Amateurs and professionals participate in open content development to gain respect and accreditation from community. Public organisations engage in content development and distribution to satisfy the information needs of tax payers. Research institutes and researchers are very keen to publish their research output with the hope that "it brings increased visibility, usage and impact for their work." Online institutional repositories of academic institutions and libraries enable the free public access of scholarly content. Institutional repositories archive peer reviewed scholarly literature created by faculty members and research scholars. Academic institutions also distribute course content including lecture notes, multimedia, exams materials, presentations and reusable learning objects for seamless access by academic community and public.

Wiki-based content development process arrange global participation of experts in content creation and editing. A wiki is a Web application whose content is collaboratively added, updated, and organised by its users. A wiki's content is editable through a Web page interface (Scott). Wikipedia is the best example of collaborative effort to build an open content encyclopedia. This multilingual encyclopedia is a community endeavor of volunteers around the world. A large group of peer reviewers ensures high quality articles. 'Flu Wiki' (www.fluwikie.com) is another example of collaborative conformation to build a knowledge base for local communities to defend communicable diseases. A group of volunteer editors inspect the content quality and suggest modifications wherever needed.

'LibriVox' (http://librivox.org) is a public project instituted to publish free audio books on the Internet. In this project, books for reading are chosen on the basis of user's suggestions. Volunteers read and record the book content in digital format and coordinators upload the files on project website.

Open access journals and institutional archives or repositories are mainly used to manage digital scholarly content, especially research articles. Open journals conduct peer review. Archives do not perform peer review and can contain preprints, post prints, or both (Suber). Open Journal Systems, Eprints and Dspace are the popular software platforms for the management of online scholarly content. All these systems are facilitated online submission, peer reviewing, subscription, indexing and notifications.

Open content development model encourage both solo and collaborative content development. Various services are available online for content management and they can handle different types of digital content format. Such services have provisions to promote open licensed content and they are encouraging authors to publish content in public domain.

Popular Open Content Initiatives

Project Name	*Content Type*	*Licence*
Wikipedia	Encyclopaedia	GDFL
Librivox	Audio books	Creative Commons
Flickr	Image database	Creative Commons
Open Clip Art Library	Clip arts	Creative Commons
PLoS (Public Library of Science)	Medical literature	Creative Commons
OpenLearn and MIT Open Courseware	Educational resources	Creative Commons

Popular Open Content Licences

Open content licences are developed to distribute free content which does not contain any harmful licensing terms same contain in commercial digital contents. It also promote ethical, legal framework for the distribution and use of digital content.

Creative Commons

Creative commons is considered as most popular and flexible licence for free content distribution. The Creative Commons initiative designed this licence with the support of practitioners and theorists of law and technology. James Boyle, Michael Carroll, Lawrence Lessig, MIT computer science Professor Hal Abelson, cyber law expert Eric Saltzman, and public domain Web publisher Eric Eldred founded Creative Commons in 2001. Creative Commons is a set of legal licences from which creators can select the rights they wish to retain and those that they are willing to give to the public. A Creative commons licence is based on copyright. So they apply to all works that are protected by copyright law. The kinds of works that are protected by copyright law are books, websites, blogs, photographs, films, videos, songs and other audio & visual recordings. Popular projects make using Creating Commons are MIT Open Courseware, Public Library of Science, Flickr, Ourmedia and Wikinews.

GNU Free Documentation Licence (GFDL)

The GNU Free Documentation Licence is a copy left licence for free documentation, designed by the Free Software Foundation

(FSF) for the GNU project. GFDL mainly applied to the distribution of manual, text book and other documentations of free software. Projects which make use GFDL for content distributions are:

- Wikipedia
- PlanetMath - a free, collaborative, online mathematics encyclopaedia.
- Japanese History Documentation Project (http://www.openhistory.org/jhdp/)
- Free Online Dictionary of Computing (http://www.foldoc.org/)

Free Art Licence

Free Art License is developed from as a result of the inspiration gained from the meeting "Copyleft Attitude" in Paris in 2000. With this licence users are authorised to copy, distribute and freely transform the work of art while respecting the rights of the originator. The basic aim of Free Art Licence is to promote and protect artistic practice freed from the rules of the market economy (Hietanen, 2007).

Open Music Licence

Open Music Licence is a set of customised licences which allow public to use the music and giving credit to the musician. In addition, this license contains provisions to earn money for musician. Three versions of Open Music License are available;

- The Green Licence – Free for copy, distribution and modification.
- The Yellow Licence – Free for all use, but prevents commercial use.
- The Red Licence – Personal use and distribution only.

The open Music Licence was drafted after consultations with several song writers, musicians and bands (Liang, 2004).

Design Science Licence

Design Science Licence is a general purpose copy left licence. This is a solo project of Michael Stutz. The licence enforces "object form" (executable or performable form of the Work) and the "source data" (origin of the object form) in the content. According to this licence the original work is copyrighted by the author and must give credit to him in derivative works.

Common Documentation Licence

This licence is developed by Apple computer, Inc for the distribution of software manuals and instructions.

Creative Commons outwits other open content licences in the case of popularity and usage. Ability to habitat any content format and flexibility in privilege customisation make Creative Common licence favourite option for content distribution. Creative Commons offers six types of licences with various rights for fair use. There is an increasing acceptance of open content licences. As per licence adoption estimate at 2006, 140 million web pages contain Creative Commons Content. Creative Commons licence leads in the popularity and considered as the most successful Open Content license format and proved its endurance in court. Adam Curry, a popular podcaster and former MTV VJ won law suit against a magazine which published photos of his family under Creative Commons non-commercial license on Flickr without his permission.

Money Matters

Content creation and distribution is a money-tinkling business of commercial content distributors. Content companies act as intermediary between content creators and end users and a great portion of profit and reputation goes to content companies and not to original creators. Copyright of the content is loose from the author's side and it restricts him to further manipulation of his own creation. Traditional content distribution practice is not suitable for voluntary content creators who like to earn reputation than money. Online commercial content distributors possessed the technology and expertise in digital content publication. Now online content distribution scenario has entirely changed with the popularity of World Wide Web. There author can directly publish their content with the help of user-friendly online tools. And many alternative business models are introduced for content creators without hurting the user's freedom of free content access.

Following are the business models currently being used by digital open content (audio, video and image) distribution services (Hietanen, 2007):

- Distribution of content charging nominal subscription fee.
- Selling extra services for users is a popular strategy of open content business. Flickr is an online photo sharing service which provides free limited space for image uploading. If users pay an extra charge, they would offer unlimited storage space.
- Open licensed content are free to share and can be used to generate profit by organising and distributing content in packaged media. Here users need to pay only the cost of media (CD, DVD).
- Advertisement with free content is the most popular income generation practice. Video sharing services (e.g. YouTube, Revvr) displays a hyperlinked advertisement frame at the end of each video. If the viewers click on the promotional frame, the advertiser is charged and the fee is shared among content creator and video sharing service.

Open Access scholarly publishers follows different types of business models to meet the expenses of online publishing. Innovative income models currently being used to support the open-access distribution of peer-reviewed scholarly and scientific journals are (Swan):

- *Article processing fees*: A few number of open access journals charge fee from authors for article processing.
- *Hardcopy sales*: MedKnow, an Indian medical publisher earns money by sales of the print version. Their journals are freely accessible online.
- *Sponsorships*: Institutional or corporate offers to take over journals operating expenses in exchange for publicity.
- *Donations and fund raising*: Fund raising campaigns and donations from individuals and institutions ensures stable income.
- *Internal and external subsidies*: BioMed Central's membership program allows societies to offer the right to

publish without article processing fees as a member benefit.

- *Institutional membership schemes*: Institutions to pay a lump-sum annually in advance for articles that their authors will publish.

Education and research is a public funded activity in most of the countries. Open access journals and repositories of educational and research institutes are not drive by financial motivation. They believe that, open access publishing model increase access to its published research and this lead to better research communication. Free content use, worldwide access and reputation are the advantages of adopting open content distribution model.

Conclusion

Content creators are using a range of open content licences which suitable for free distribution of content socially and economically. Open Content licensing projects should work together for better inter operability and handle copyright management issues (Hietanen, 2007). Open licence initiatives are on the way to develop more activities and tools to promote open content. They concentrate on coordinating legal experts around the world, translation of project documents, development of licence metadata integration tools, search engines to find open licenced content, establishing open licenses within academic and scientific community. More business models should be introduced for open content distribution to attract more content creators into community based content development. In sum, open content licences could radicalise the content use and distribution to endorse community based content development.

References

Free Art License. Copy left Attitude. Available at: http://artlibre.org/licence/lal/en/

Frequently Asked Questions. Creative Commons. Available at: http://wiki.creativecommons.org/FAQ

Hietanen, Herkko. (2007). Community Created Content; *Law, Business and Policy*. Helsinki: Multiprint.

Income models for Open Access: An overview of current practice, SPARC. Available at: http://www.arl.org/sparc/publisher/incomemodels/

Kuny, Terry. (1996). The digital library: myths and challenges. 62nd IFLA General Conference. Beijing. August 25-31, 1996.

Liang, Lawrence. *A Guide To Open Content Licences*. Piet Zwart Institute. Available at: http://pzwart.wdka.hro.nl/mdr/research/lliang/open_content_guide. (Accessed on 11 June 2009).

Midyear license adoption estimates. Creative Commons. Available at: http://creativecommons.org/weblog/entry/5936

Q&A: What is DRM? BBC, Available at: http://news.bbc.co.uk/2/hi/technology/6337781.stm

Roberts, *Sharing Creative Works, Creative Commons* Available at:, http://wiki.creativecommons.org/Sharing_Creative_Works (Accessed on 12 July 2009)

Samuelson, Pamela, (2001). Intellectual property for an information age. *Communications of the ACM* 44, 66-68 .

Samuelson, Pamela. (1998). *Encoding the law into digital libraries. Communications of the ACM*, 41, 13-18.

Scott, Mitchell. Easy Wiki Hosting, Scott Hanselman's blog, and Snagging Screens. Available at: http://msdn.microsoft.com/en-us/magazine/cc700339.aspx

Suber, Peter Open Access Overview: Focusing on open access to peer-reviewed research articles and their preprints. Available at: www.earlham.edu/~peters/fos/overview.htm

Swan, Alma and Chan, Leslie. Open Access Journals: business models In *Open Access Scholarly Information Sourcebook*. Available at: www.openoasis.org

What's in it for me? SURFfoundation, Available at: http://www.openaccess.nl

VI

Electronic Resources and Services

19

Availability and Use of Electronic Information Resources in the Arts & Science College Libraries in Kerala: A Case Study

—V. Jalaja, and A. Vijayakumar

Electronic Information Recourses constitute major components in disseminating information and knowledge in the modern world. This study investigates the availability and use of electronic information resources in college libraries in Kerala. It is found that even though they have electronic information resources to some extent, the resources and services are not reaching the users to the expected extent.

Introduction

Information technology is the forerunner of the information society and the information age. IT provides easy access to a wide spectrum of information through computer, networking, CD-ROMs and Internet.

Information technology in its wider sense can be defined as any technology related to recording presentation and communication of information or knowledge emerged from time immemorial. On the other hand new information technology connotes the massive applications of electronic or digital technologies for the recording presentation and communication of information and knowledge.

In the changing environment of information technology the production and distribution of electronic information resources are growing day-to-day by its number and content. Any information resource that is accessible through a computer or network can be termed as electronic resources. For the past few year's electronic resources like e-journals, e-books and e-data bases have increased considerably. So the study about the availability and use of the electronic information resources in the college library is relevant.

Definition of Terms

The Library of Congress in its draft interim guidelines for cataloguing electronic resources defines electronic information sources as "manifestation of a work encoded for manipulation by computer. The manifestation resided in a carrier accessed either directly or remotely." It goes on to further define a directly accessed electronic resource as an "electronic resource whose carrier is 'touchable', e.g., a CD-ROM" and a "remotely accessed electronic resource as an electronic resource whose carrier does not embody a direct 'touchable' physically, (e.g., an electronic journal, or a database accessed through the Internet, or a website)."

AACR 2, defines an electronic resource as "material (data and/or program(s) encoded for manipulation by a computerised device. This material may require the use of a peripheral directly connected to a computerised device (e.g., CD-ROM drive) or a connection to a computer network (e.g., the Internet)."

Research Design

To attain the aim and specific objective of the investigation, a combination of quantitative and qualitative research methodologies along with a comprehensive literature review has been employed. Two main methods have been used in data collection: questionnaire surveys and semi-structured interviews with librarians.

Objectives of the Study

The major objectives assumed for the present study are as follows:

1) To assess the current use of electronic information resources in the college libraries in Kerala.
2) To find out the most favorable electronic information resources in the college libraries.

3) To suggest measures for improvement of existing electronic information resources and services.
4) To highlight the impact of electronic information resources on college libraries and its results.
5) To explain the concept, need and various type of electronic information resources available in college libraries.
6) To identify the impediments &challenges, in general, faced by the users of college library in regard to e-resources.

Analysis of Data

Use of Internet

The Internet has become an indispensable resource for the arts and science college libraries to enhance the collection, improve services and operations. The Internet has made easy and speedy purchase of information sources/documents like books, journals, electronic publication, etc. Itcan be successfully utilised for providing reference service because various primary and secondary sources of information are available online from many sites. Libraries can use the Internet to communicate with publishers, booksellers and vendors. Librarians can also use Newsgroups for getting information. It is possible to access the resources of other libraries through the Internet. It is also possible to browse the entire collection of a library through WebOPAC and can make a request for a document through e-mail. Librarians were asked to indicate the extent of the use of Internet in the library.

Use of OPAC

OPAC is an excellent source of bibliographic information in libraries. It provides access to the documents of libraries. It provides access to the documents of libraries through different modes of searching. The analysis of the data shows that majority of the arts and science college libraries in Kerala have no OPAC, even though most of them are computerised or at various stage of computerisation.

Use of Database for Information Retrieval and the Nature of Information Retrieved

Electronic databases form sound foundation for providing efficient information services in college libraries. In recent years the demand for database services is increasing, since most of the latest information is available in online database. Further, some of the information is available only on the CD-ROM format. Image database and multimedia databases are also becoming predominant. Similarly, personal reference databases and internal records enrich the knowledge of the users. Librarians were asked to indicate the types of databases and the nature of information retrieved, that is, bibliographic information or full text with choices ranging from commercial online databases to those containing internally generated records.

Extent of End-User Access to Databases

The data was collected to identify the prevalence of access to electronic databases by end users of the service. Librarians were asked to indicate which database types could be accessed from within the library, and also whether access was available either via terminals situated elsewhere within the organisation premised or from offsite using telecommunication links. The analysis shows that every few libraries are using commercial online databases and it is accessible both via terminals situated in the library and outside the library.

Use of Electronic/Online Journals

Some of the college libraries under the study are providing access to electronic journals. Most of them are under the management of private organisations.

Factors Influencing the Provision of Electronic Information Resources and Services

The budget allocations to majority of the arts and science college libraries in Kerala are not adequate. The IT skill and expertise of library staff of majority of the libraries are as just satisfactory. Most of the librarians have stated that training in the use of electronic information resources is only satisfactory or inadequate. Majority of the librarians have stated that electronic information resources are only satisfactory or inadequate.

Use Pattern of Electronic Information Resources

Influence of E-resources on Reading Habits

Electronic sources have increasingly become the focus of research and development institutions in the recent years. Academic libraries also could not remain behind, and many academic institutions have created digital virtual libraries for their users to access electronic journals; because accessing the web has become very convenient. Web-based full text electronic journals have naturally become the most popular tool for academic library users for locating desired resources. A question is asked to the respondents that whether they think the electronic resources influencing your reading habits more than before, and the results are given in Table 1.

Table 1: Influence of E-resources on Reading Habits (Course-wise)

Type of Course	*Influencing*	*Not Influencing*	*Total*
Undergraduate	270	84	354
	45 %	14 %	59 %
Postgraduate	210	36	246
	35 %	6 %	41 %
Total	480	120	600
	80 %	20 %	100 %

The students are of the opinion that the e sources available in the college library as well as the internet center and the university infonet centres are helping their reading habits more than ever before.

Gender wise Distribution of Influence of e-resources

Table 2: Gender wise distribution of influence of e resources

Gender	*Influencing*	*Not Influencing*	*Total*
Male	276	30	306
	46 %	5 %	51 %
Female	204	90	294
	34 %	15 %	49 %
Total	480	120	600
	80 %	20 %	100 %

Table 2 shows the wide spreading habits of using electronic resources in the colleges in Kerala.

Satisfaction of Respondents while Using E-sources

For measuring the use of electronic information resources in the college libraries in Kerala, the respondents are asked whether electronic information resources available in their college library are satisfying their information needs.

Table 3

Satisfaction of Respondents while Using E-sources

Course	*Yes*	*No*	*Total*
UG	222	132	354
	37 %	22 %	59 %
PG	174	72	246
	29 %	12 %	41 %
Total	396	204	600
	66 %	34 %	100 %

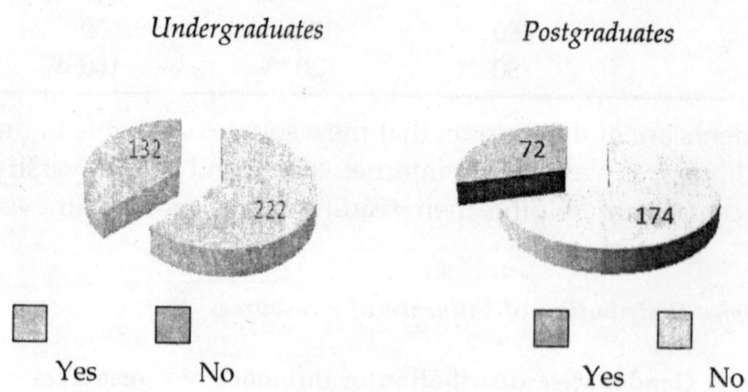

Figure 1

Satisfaction of Respondents while Using the E-sources

A grand total of 132+72=204(34 %) undergraduate and postgraduate students said that they are satisfied with the e-resources available in their college library.

Preferred sources of information (Course wise)

Here an attempt has been made to find out whether electronic resources or printed books are most preferable to the college students at the graduate and postgraduate levels. A grand total of 222+174, that is, 396(66%) undergraduate and postgraduate students said that they are satisfied with the e-sources available in their college library.

Table 4

Preferred Source of Information (Course-wise)

Course	*E-resources*	*Printed Books*	*Missing Responses*	*Total*
Undergraduates	183	123	48	354
	30.5 %	20.5 %	8 %	59 %
Postgraduate	162.00	36	48	246
	27.00 %	6.00 %	8 %	41 %
Total	345	159	96	600
	57.50 %	26.50 %	16 %	100 %

Table 4 shows that the use of electronic information resources in the college libraries in Kerala is increasing day by day.

Table 5

Preferred Source of Information (Gender-wise)

Course	*Missing Responses*	*E-resources*	*Printed Books*	*Total*
Undergraduates	183	123	48	354
Male	60	168	78	306
	10 %	28 %	13 %	51 %
Female	36	177	81	294
	6 %	29.5 %	13.5 %	49 %
Total	96	345	159	600
	16 %	57.50 %	26.50 %	100 %

Table 5 shows that only a negligible 96 (16 %) students did not answer this question because their colleges have no Internet connectivity. More female students compared to male students preferred e-sources.

Use of e-books in relation to conventional books

With the advent of modern technology in the publication field, the composition, printing and storage techniques changed to be not only more efficient and faster, but the final product becomes aesthetically pleasing. The revolution in the field of communication technology has ushered in an era of the electronic communication and electronic publishing along with e-commerce electronic books or 'e-books'. These are texts designed to be read solely on a computer screen using proprietary hardware devices or multi-purpose PCs.

Table 6

Usage of E-books in Comparison with Conventional Books

Course	*Missing Responses*	*Very High*	*High*	*Moderate*	*Low*	*Total*
Undergraduates	6	18	54	204	72	354
	1 %	3 %	9 %	34 %	12 %	59 %
Postgraduate	0	24	96	126	0	246
	0	4 %	16 %	21 %	0	41 %
Total	6	42	150	330	72	600
	1 %	7 %	25 %	55 %	12 %	100 %

A majority are of the opinion that the use of e-books has increased day by day when compared to the conventional books. The students said that the internet and IT have considerably helped their education system more than before.

Role of E-resources

The places of exploitation of Internet by the libraries and information centers are unlimited and endless. The Internet provides a wealth of information such as online e-books, e-Journal, e-newsletter, e-databases, etc. Theses vast resources can be accessed by the library and information centres and can be provided to the users. The respondents are asked to prove whether or not an electronic resource acts only as a supplement to the print medium.

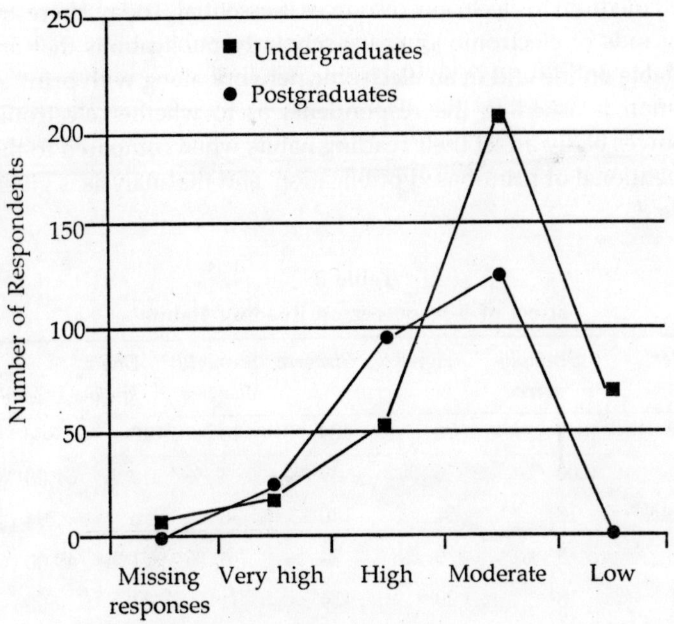

Figure 2

Usages of E-books in Camparison with Conventional Books

Table 7

Role of E-resources (Gender-wise)

Gender	*Strongly Agree*	*Agree*	*Disagree*	*Total*
Male	42	24	240	306
	7 %	4 %	40 %	51.00 %
Female	18	126	150	294
	3 %	21 %	25 %	49.00 %
Total	60	150	390	600
	10.00 %	25.00 %	65.00 %	100.00 %

Effect of E-Resources on Reading Habits (Gender-wise)

This is the information revolution era, and the shift from print-based medium to electronic resources is essential. Today, there are thousands of electronic journals, scholarly publications that are available online and in an electronic network along with print. A question is asked to the respondents as to whether electronic resources badly affect their reading habits when compared to the conventional or print-based publication, and the analysis is given Table 8.

Table 8

Effect of E-resources on Reading Habits

Gender	*Strongly agree*	*Agree*	*Disagree*	*Strongly disagree*	*Don't know*	*Total*
Male	0	36	234	18	18	306
	0.00 %	6 %	39 %	3 %	3 %	51.00 %
Female	18	54	180	36	6	294
	3 %	9 %	30 %	6 %	1 %	49.00 %
Total	18	90	414	54	24	600
	3.00 %	15.00 %	69.00 %	9.00 %	4.00 %	100.00 %

The Importance of E-resources in the Academic Activities

Electronic resources facilitated the researcher to have a quick and precise search for scientific information. Knowledge plays a vital role to the modern society and in this modern age. The information in the print format is now being added with electronic information resources. People want to get pinpointed information in speediest way. Electronic resources can organise, handle and disseminate, vast amount of information effectively. The undergraduates and postgraduates were asked to explain how they rate the value of electronic resources for conducting your study and research.The details are given in Table 9.

Most students said that electronic resources is very valuable for their study and research.

Table 9
Importance of E-resources in Academic Activities (Gender-wise)

Gender	*Very much important*	*Unimportant*	*Not responded*	*Total*
Male	252	54 0	306	
	42 %	9 %	0.00 %	51 %
Female	240	30	24	294
	40 %	5 %	4 %	49 %
Total	492	84	24	600
	82.00 %	14.00 %	4.00 %	100

Table 10
Importance of E-resources in Academic Activities (Course-wise)

Course	*Very Important*	*Unimportant*	*Not Responded*	*Total*
Undergraduates	312	36	6	354
	52 %	6 %	1 %	59.00 %
Postgraduates	180	48	18	246
	30 %	8 %	3 %	41.00 %
Total	492	84	24	600
	82.00 %	14.00 %	4.00 %	100

Table 10 shows that a majority found the electronic resources to be very important and a must for their study and research.

Improvement of Academic Activity Due to E-resources

Electronic information sources become an effective means of enriching and updating of information. The networks are the important systems for effective communication of information. Information Communication Technology (ICT) is a scientific, technological and engineering discipline with management techniques used in handling information, its application and association with social, economical and cultural matters. Another question asked of the respondents is whether with the influence of the electronic information sources their quality of learning/ research improved or not.

Figure 3 shows that a majority 510 (85 %) said that with the influence of electronic information sources, the quality of learning and research has improved very much.

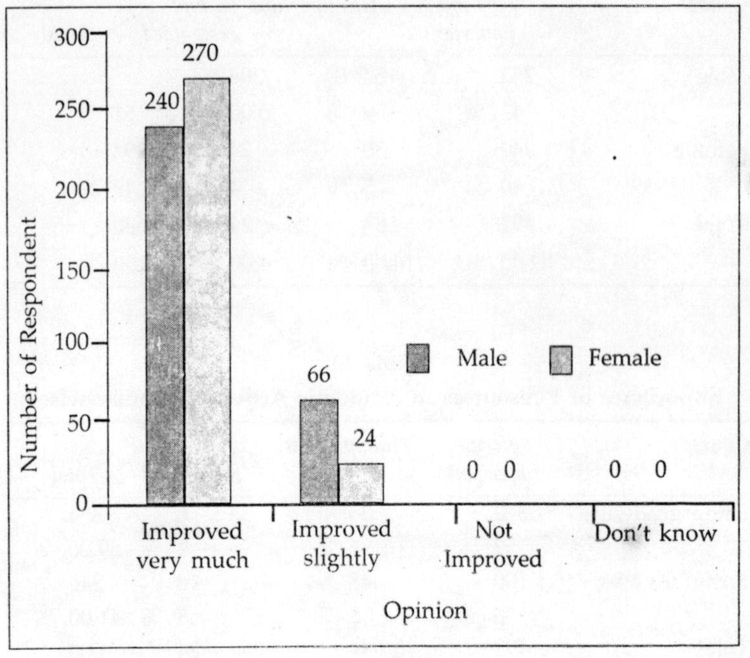

Figure 3

Improvement of Academic Activity Due to E-resources

Reason for Opting for E-resources

The respondents were asked why they opted for electronic information sources, whether it was (1) The information available in electronic form was easy to search (2) The search output was taken conveniently on floppy/CD/Printout 3) Information not available elsewhere was avilable (4) Latest techniques in research were available.

Table 11 shows that a majority of male and female students sought electronic information sources for the information available, and were easy to search and store.

Table 11
Reasons for Opting for E-resources (Gender-wise)

Gender	*1*	*2*	*3*	*4*	*Total*
Male	120	72	42	72	306
	20 %	12 %	7 %	12 %	51 %
Female	78	54	54	108	294
	13 %	9 %	9 %	18 %	49 %
Total	198	126	96	180	600
	33 %	21 %	16 %	30 %	100 %

Table 12

Reasons for Opting E-resources (Course-wise)

Course	*1*	*2*	*3*	*4*	*Total*
Undergraduate	138	60	18	138	354
	23 %	10 %	3 %	23 %	59 %
Postgraduate	60	66	78	42	246
	10 %	11 %	13 %	7 %	41 %
Total	198	126	96	180	600
	33 %	21 %	16 %	30 %	100 %

Table 12 shows that most students said they selected the electronic information sources because they got the latest knowledge for their research.

E-Resources-based Curriculum

Education systems or curricula around the world are changing rapidly in response to technological advancement. The sphere of education has been influenced by the twin phenomena of globalisation and liberalisation. The rapid technological change affects many aspects of human lives, including the way one learns. The challenges for students today is to acquire skills such as how to learn, how to make critical judgements, and how to communicate intelligently, to be flexible, adaptable and tolerant to other creeds and cultures, and to make contributions to the society and to the well-beings of others. Based upon the new curriculum and syllabus the students were asked, does their curriculum recommend using the e-resources. Table 13 and figure 4 show the results.

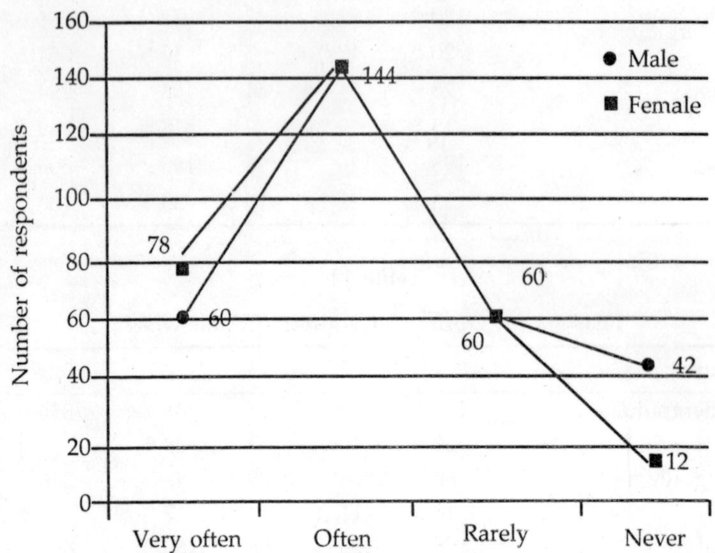

Figure 4
Opinion of Respondents

Table 13
E-resources-based Curriculum (Gender-wise)

Gender	*Very Often*	*Often*	*Rarely*	*Never*	*Total*
Male	60	144	60	42	306
	10 %	24 %	10 %	7 %	51 %
Female	78	144	60	12	294
	13 %	24 %	10 %	2 %	49 %
Total	138	288	120	54	600
	23 %	48 %	20 %	9 %	100 %

E-Resources-based Curriculum (Course-wise)

Table 14 and figure 5 describe the course-wise analysis of the e-resources-based curriculum and its results.

Table 14

E-Resource-based Curriculum (Course-wise)

Course	*Very Often*	*Often*	*Rarely*	*Never*	*Total*
Undergraduates	24	210	84	36	354
	4 %	35 %	14 %	6 %	59 %
Postgraduate	114	78	36	18	246
	19 %	13 %	6 %	3 %	41 %
Total	138	288	120	54	600
	23 %	48 %	20 %	9 %	100 %

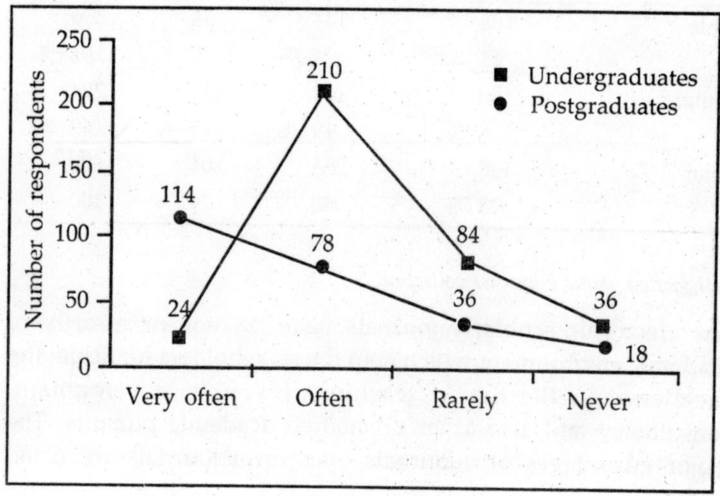

Figure 5

Opinion of Respondents

As per the figure 5 the 24(4 %) undergraduates and 114 (19 %) postgraduates said that their curriculum recommends of using e-resources where as 210 (35 %) UGs and 78 (13 %) PGs said it is often and 84 (14 %) UGs and 36 (6 %) PGs said rarely and 36 (6 %) UGs and 18 (3 %) PGs said that their curriculum never recommends the e-resources for their study. Most of the UGs and PGs 288(48 %) opine that their curriculum recommends of using e-resources.

Use of Electronic Journals

Places Sought for Accessing E-Journals

The respondents were asked from where they accessed 'e-journal': college library, university library or online. Table 15 shows the results

Table 15

Place Access of E-journals (Gender-wise)

Gender	*College Library*	*University Library*	*Any Other Place*	*Total*
Male	108	144	54	306
	18 %	24 %	9 %	51 %
Female	30	114	150	294
	5 %	19 %	25 %	49 %
Total	138	258	204	600
	23 %	43 %	34 %	100 %

Satisfaction of the e-journal collection

The electronic scholarly journals have become necessarily of academic environment which help the stakeholders for achieving excellence in the era of teaching, research, development, consultancy and also other diversified academic pursuits. The major advantages of e-journals over print journals are listed below.

- Speedier delivery
- Easy and effective search
- Multidimensional interaction
- Dynamic hyperlinks
- Multimedia effects
- Downloads
- Cost-effective options
- Flexibility
- Operating cost-free

So the students were asked whether they were satisfied with the total e-journal collection available in the college library or not. To this following. Table 16 shows the the results.

Table 16

Satisfaction Over the E-journal Collection (Course-wise)

Course	*Satisfied*	*Partly Satisfied*	*Not Satisfied*	*Total*
Undergraduate	138	174	42	354
	23 %	29 %	7 %	59 %
Postgraduate	90	156	0	246
	15 %	26 %	0	41 %
Total	228	330	42	600
	38 %	55 %	7 %	100 %

Conclusion

In the past the dial-up online information sources and services prevailed today it is the CD-ROM and the Internet. On the Internet, World Wide Web is playing the central role, pushing aside traditional resources like Telnet and FTP. The survey achieved its aim of providing an update summary of the current state-of-the art use of electronic information resources in arts and science college libraries in Kerala. Though the college libraries in Kerala have electronic information resources to some extent, resources and services are not reaching the users to the expected extent. This state of affairs has been largely due to inadequate finance, and inadequately trained library professionals. To overcome this unfortunate situation, college management needs to review their policies, and instead of heavily depending on traditional information resources, it should set aside adequate electronic information resources.

References

Anglo-American Cataloguing Rules (2002) 2nd rev. ed.

Haneefa, Mohammed. (2005). Electronic Information Resources in the special libraries of Kerala. *Kelpro Bulletin*, 9 (1&2), 53-57.

Jalaja, V and Dineshan, K. (2007). The Problem of digital divide among the Academic Community. *University News*, 42(03).

Library of Congress (2002). Draft Interim Guidelines for Cataloguing Electronic Resources. Available at: www.loc.gov.

Schuler, M. (1998). Will the paper trial lead to the e-books? *Computers in Libraries.*

Sharma, C.K. (2005). *Information Technology.* New Delhi: JDB.

Sicilia, F. (1996). *Electronic publishing and libraries.* London: MacMillan.

Suseela. V. J. (2003). Academic Use of Electronic Resources, *Kelpro Bulletin,* 7 (1&2), 26.

20

Electronic Journals: An Outlook

—Khushpreet Singh

This paper attempts to bring out the meaning of the term 'electronic journal' from the definition given by various authors. It traces the historical development of e-journals and their types. It mentions standardised codes used for presentation, and the medium of availability of journals. The paper concludes the advantages and disadvantages of e-journals in information search.

Introduction

Electronic publishing has brought significant changes in the global communication process. It has revolutionised the format of recorded knowledge in much the same way as the invention of the printing press did in 1440. The electronic transfer of knowledge by the electronic medium is becoming sophisticated each passing day. The widely accessible and networked interface is attracting users towards electronic information services. Likewise a similar scenario in the library environment has arisen ensuing the need and use of e-journals along with the print version. Electronic journals bring along new challenges before the information professionals to give full text access to scholarly publications both in print and electronic version to its end users

Electronic Journals

Different experts have a different impression or understanding of the term "electronic journals". Electronic journals are often referred to interchangeably as "electronic publishing", "electronic serials", "online journals" and "electronic periodicals."

The Encyclopedic Dictionary of Computer Science (1989) defines "The electronic journal, in its simplest form, is the all electronic counterpart of a conventional print on paper scholarly journal. The concept originated in experiments based on computer conferencing system the approach currently envisaged is based on a large main frame computer, which acts as a central store."

Lancaster (1995) defined it as "A journal created for the electronic medium and available only in this medium."

Darrel Ince. (2001) [A Dictionary of the Internet] defines: "Electronic journal is an academic journal which is only published on the World Wide Web. It carries out all its activities including peer review and publishing using net technologies such as conferencing, email, and the use of web sites. Such journals pride themselves on the rapid publication of articles and are often referred to as e-journals."

Reitz, J. M. (2007) [ODLIS] difines: "A digital version of a print journal, or a journal-like electronic publication with no print counterpart (*example*: First Monday, Webology), made available via the Web, e-mail, or other means of Internet access. Some Web-based electronic journals are graphically modeled on the print version. The rising cost of print journal subscriptions has led many academic libraries to explore electronic alternatives."

Initiation Phase of E-journal

The electronic journals historical evacuation has been traced to a 1960 UNESCO report that advocated use of computer technology to help solve the problems of traditional journal publishing. "Mental Workload", dealing with human–machine interactions in complex systems, has been identified as the first full-fledged electronic journal. It was issued in 1980 at the New Jersey Institute of Technology and funded by the National Science Foundation. The best-known e-journal within the discipline of library and information science is the *Newsletter* on *Serials Pricing Issues*. This news letter was first issued on February 27, 1989, in both paper and electronic format.

Types of E-journals

The electronic journals are categorised in many types according to the purpose. On the basis of distribution methods the following types of e-journals have be identified:

- *Internet applications e-journals*: These e-journals are available through Internet applications, which are also known as classic electronic journals. Originally they were distributed via the e-mail but now have been available on the web and only announcements regarding issues are distributed by e-mail.
- *Parallel e-journals*: These types of journals are published simultaneously in both forms: print and electronic. The online version may include the full text of journal, selected articles or only the table of contents. The website provides previews and excerpts of issues. The electronic version is always available much more quickly than its print counterpart.
- *Database model*: Another type of e-journal is called database model. It is also known as the software model. Here article reside in centralised database and the publishers and subscribers are given permission to access the database and use search software on the central computer to locate and download articles. The database model provides a piece of software that runs on an Internet connected computer which connects to the database of the journal's central computer
- *CD-ROM journals*: Commercial publishers have also made journal titles available through the CD-ROM. The full text of journals and other serial publications have been made available by the means of a CD-ROM.

On the basis of accessibility, e-journals are divided into two categories:

- *Commercial E-journals*: These e-journals are not available freely. Readers and libraries have to pay for the subscription of these e-journals. Many big publishers publish commercial e-journals.
- *Open Access E-journals*: Open access journals are those which use a funding model that does not charge readers or their institutions for access. Open access provides users the right to "read, download, copy, distribute, print, search, or link to the full texts of these articles" as mandatory for a journal to be included in the directory.

Formats of Information Stored or Presentation

The format of presentation made available should strike at the nerve centre of the human mind, bringing about a platform where the information source and seeker go on to perform at there optimism level. There are standardised codes for such presentations and a few which accepted the core essence have been mentioned below:

- *American Standard Code for Information Interchange (ASCII)* This is the commonly used encoding scheme. Typically what is stored is the text of each article, broken into paragraphs, along with bibliographic information in a simple tagged format. The major advantages are compact in size, economic, displayed on any computer terminal, full text available for searching, compatible with electronic mail and bulletin boards and the major drawbacks are no figure available, no special character display, no formation of text like italic, bold or size change.
- *Image Format:* Page images are most easily thought of as facsimile images of the page and as a matter of fact, these are typically stored in CCITT (Presently ITU) group 4 facsimile format because that is one of the most compact ways to store scanned images of text. The major advantages are ease and being inexpensive to capture, retains the format of the original; the disadvantages are the text is usually available only via Optical Character Recognition, display and printing is limited to the resolution of the original scan and not editable document.
- *Microsoft Word file:* Microsoft Word is currently the most common word processor on the market. Because it is so common, the .doc and .docx (available in 2007 and 2008 version) format has become the *de facto* format for text documents. Word files can also be used to create other file formats, such as PDF and HTML. There are several things that can be done to make content created in Word more accessible. The biggest advantage is easy to prepare files and edit the document.
- *Portable Document Format (PDF):* This is a file format developed by Adobe Systems. PDF captures formatting information from a variety of desktop publishing

applications, making it possible to send formatted documents and have them appear on the recipient's monitor or printer as they were intended. To view a file in PDF format, you need Adobe Reader, a free application distributed by Adobe Systems.

- *Standard Generalised Markup Language (SGML):* This is system for organising and tagging elements of a document. SGML is used widely to manage large documents that are subject to frequent revisions and need to be printed in different formats. Because it is a large and complex system, it is not yet widely used on personal computers. However, the growth of Internet, and especially the World Wide Web, is creating renewed interest in SGML because the World Wide Web uses HTML, which is one way of defining and interpreting tags according to SGML rules.
- *Hyper Text Markup Language (HTML):* This is the predominant markup language for Web pages. It provides a means to describe the structure of text-based information in a document by denoting certain text as links, headings, paragraphs, lists, and so on and to supplement that text with interactive forms, embedded images, and other object.

Medium of Availability of E-journals

The e-journal is a presentation for a variety of networked publication's are provided with e-journal by the means of the e-mail listserv, file transfer protocol, gophers, etc., offline resource like the floppy disk and the CD/DVD-ROM allow for there utilisation.

- *CD/DVD-ROM:* This is a small plastic optical disk used as a publishing medium and for storing information in digital format. The data encoded on a CD-ROM can be searched and displayed on a computer screen but not changed or erased. Example: LISA PLUS and Sensors & Transducers Journal.
- *Electronic Mail (e-mail):* The e-mail is a system of exchanging digital messages between the Internet users. It is a rapid and effective medium for communication and discussion. Electronic Social Psychology (ESP), a paid e-journal of psychology published in the mid-1980s, was distributed

via email. Nowadays, the content and publication notification is disseminated through email.

- *Listserv:* Mailing list management software designed to scan incoming e-mail messages for the words "subscribe," "unsubscribe," and other housekeeping commands and update the subscriber list automatically. E-journals are often distributed via listserv, e.g. Electronic Journal of Differential Equations (subs@ejde.math.swr.edu) and Michael Strangelove's directory of Electronic Serials. New Horizons in Adult education, a refereed e-journal first published in fall 1987 was distributed for free on a BITNET listserv.
- *File Transfer Protocol (FTP):* The TCP/IP protocol that allows data files to be copied directly from one computer to another over the Internet regardless of platform, without having to attach them as in e-mail.
- *Gopher:* Files and resources available on the Internet are accessed by means of a hierarchical menu system installed on a *Gopher server.*
- *World Wide Web (WWW):* A hypertext interface to the Internet and an alternative to menu based interfaces. Links can go any direction from one document on one server to another document on another server.
- *Blog or Weblog:* A shared on-line journal where people can post diary entries about their personal experiences and hobbies; postings on a blog are usually in chronological order. It is a new medium of communication. Example: Scholarly Electronic Publishing Weblog (http://digital-scholarship.org/sepw2/).

Advantages of E-journals

The most significant advantage of the e-journal is that the user does not need to search for them in the libraries or the other places as they are available at the desktop of the user. Thus the e-journal possesses an endless outreach capability and can be accessed anytime on the networked global village. Moreover e-journals can be read by an infinite mass of users at anytime. The entire text can be searched within a single click that saves time as well as storage space of users and professionals. E-journals can include multimedia and graphics, in colour, wherever necessary, at a marginal cost. These can be published a lot more quickly than the paper publications. Furthermore, they can make use of hyperlinks both internally and to other publications. An article or a research paper can be retrieved directly accessing abstracting and indexing databases. The content of the e-journals can be reproduced, forwarded and even modified. Thus providing with a more creative and quick way of having their information queries answered. As the publishers, research groups, authors can be easily contacted whenever required. Furthermore, e-journals are quite cost effective as compared to the printed version the user can quickly access to the back issues. Moreover, e-journals save paper and hence can be considered as an eco-friendly mode of disseminating the information.

Drawbacks of E-journals

This is a cold medium of communication as it blocks imaginations and creativity. It incurs great expense particularly at the beginning of its establishment. The bulky cost of required infrastructure is not affordable by all institutes. Even today, e-journals are not accepted or accessible in the rural and under developed areas, because of unreliable and low connectivity. Furthermore, the e-journals save the time spent only in the postal delays. They do not reduce the time required to review, correct and finalise the papers.

The Bottom Line

With the advancement and outflow of information and communication technology among the masses, the e-journal has created a benchmark in this field and its relevance is instilled in its ever groming users, providing them with an unintreputed desemination path, with users from the technocrat to the layman. The chaos of information on the www bemuses the user but e-journals bring peer reviewed have proved their relevance and critical worth. With the open access movement the results that were envisaged from the e-journal's, have not only been met but they have crossed some unseen barriers that were never to be imagined.

References

Brichford, M. and Maher, W. (1995). Archival Issues in Network Electronic Publications. *Library Trends* , *43* (4), 701-12.

Chandra, H. (2001). Management of Electronic Journals at the Central Library of IIT Madras. In H. K. Kaul and E. R. Reddy (Ed.), *NACLIN*, 71-81.

Encyclopaedia Dictionery of Computer Science, Vol. II. (1989). New Delhi: Anmol Publication, 15.

Harrison, T. M. and Stephen, T. D. (1995). The Electronic Journal as the Heart of an Online Scholarly Community. *Library Trends,* 43 (4), 592-608.

Ince. Darrel (2001) *A Dictionary of the Internet*. Encyclopedia.com: http://www.encyclopedia.com/doc/1O12-electronicjournal.html (Accessed on 10 March 2009).

Johnson, I.M. (2008). Electronic Publishing is Librarianship and Information Science in Latin America - a step Towards Development? *Information Research,*13 (1).

Khode, S. (2004). Print and Electronic Journals: Advantages and Disadvantages. In H. K. Kaul and S. K. Patil (Ed.), *NACLIN,* 204-212.

Lancaster, F. W. (1995). The Evolution of Electronic Publishing. *Library Trends,* 43 (4), 518-27.

Mounissamy, P., Kaliammal, A. and Rani, B. S. (2005). Users' Attitude Towards Electronic Journals. *IASLIC Bulletin, 50* (2), 91-95.

Nandi, S. G. (2007). E-publications as Helpful Resources for Researchers of Indian Libraries: an Overview. In D. S. Jaswal (Ed.), *Recent Trends in Library and Information Science*. Hamirpur: Arun Publication House. 22-27.

Natarajan, M. (2001). Users' Attitude Towards Electronic Journals: Comparison and Evaluation. In H. K. Kaul and E. R. Reddy (Ed.), *NACLIN,* 56-69.

Reitz, J. M. (2007). *ODLIS-Online Dictionary for Library and Information Science*. Libraries Unlimted. Available at: http://lu.com/odlis/odlis_e.cfm (Accesed on 10 March 2009).

Smecher, A. (2008). The Future of the Electronic Journal. *NeuroQuantology,* 6 (1), 1-6.

Sreekumar, M. G. and Sunitha, T. (2005). E-journal Collection Development Prospects: the IIM Consortium Experience. In H. K. Kaul and G. Sen (Ed.), *NACLIN,* 192-205.

Swan, A. and Needham, P. (2005). Developing a Model for E-Print and Open Access Journal Content in UK Further and Higher Education. *Learned Publishing*. 18: 25-40.

21

Impact of Digital Information Culture on the Academic Libraries

— Puttaraj A. Choukimath and Muttayya M. Koganuramath

The process of change in the digital age has been the focus in 'Digital Information Culture'. The present paper makes an effort to know how best the academic libraries and information professionals cope with the constantly shifting terrain of digital information culture, and how they manage the challenges posed by the emerging information communication technologies and social spheres of the digital age. An effort has been made to understand the impact of 'digital information culture' on the information sources and services of the academic libraries within their cultural sphere by the way they experience that change as well as the way in which they confront the digital world. It also describes with illustrations how best the libraries and librarians have been adapting to the changes in the complexities in relationships between the concepts of 'digital information culture' in the digital environment. An effort has been made to showcase that "digital information culture' has had and having a transformational impact on the academic libraries and their cultural values. It also deliberates how the 'Digital Information Culture' has transformed the information profession and their appropriateness in the digital age.

Introduction

The human society is undergoing a sea change due to phenomenal growth of information and application of IT in the form of high degree of computerisation and transmission of electronic information. In the information society which is not only producing the huge amount of information but also tremendous developments in the computer hardware and communication technology along with the necessary software tools have made possible the quick retrieval of the desired information merely on the pressing of a button. This paper explains the growth of digital culture and role of information professionals while performing information services in the libraries.

Digital Diversity

The advent of globally networked information is a historic change. Educational, commercial and industrial institutions depend on its effective exploitation for their success but cultural and human factors are the biggest obstacles. The evolution of information culture and how professionals and users do or don't adapt to networked services will help LIS professionals to achieve change with deeper understanding.

Changing Scenario

Digital technology will be the next bit-based information stream. The Internet has already occupied the major role while disseminating the digital information in the form of e-books, e-journals, newspapers, magazines and other online databases. The information we want, in whatever form, will be smart enough to find us, delivered like milk to our doorstep. We will not have to go out and look for the information that interest to us. With the new technology, not just our texts, but also our culture, will become more visual. While technology allows such changes, it doesn't offer any simple solutions.

The existence of a physical book even comes into question. "If we take the book in its broad sense to refer simply to bound, printed volumes, then most books will likely to disappear soon." A future no one can know, the introduction of digital technologies will certainly change, somehow, not only the form of our information, but also the way we store, present, and access it. As our information changes, so will our libraries and librarians would like to change? The change has already begun. Where it will end is the question. With such questions, the future of libraries is being decided. As professionals address the instability of their profession, they develop ideas of what libraries could be a blending of what a users would like to see, and what technology might allow or force. These ideas are possible blueprints for future libraries, as the professionals of LIS will shape our libraries in the years to come.

The future of libraries is for the future librarian, not just technology to decide—the future, and how the public, as well as librarians, must deal with the institution's shifting technology and shifting role in society. People will always want objects from their past preserved for sentimental value if nothing else. We can understand the sentimental value of libraries and the books for them. But we don't agree with the stereotype of a librarian as a holder of books. It should be as a holder of ideas in any form – print or electronic. A lot of information is coming in the print form, and we still have papers and letters and historical documents which need to be catalogued. But maybe part of our responsibility of making information accessible to everyone, part of our tradition of 'access,' is to 'be digital'. The future library might actually be a building filled with file servers and people sitting behind terminals thinking up the ways of effectively organising and presenting ideas, if they are in text, audio, or visual form. Maybe libraries will be the apt place where information is turned digital.

Acceptance Threshold Theory

Bill Gates, the founder of Microsoft, has a theory called the "Acceptance Threshold", when people come to accept a new innovation or technology. After reaching the threshold, the new technology is common — getting there is the difficulty. At a certain point, after that threshold has been crossed, the choice between the old and the new has been made for us. We won't be able to go back.

For example, think about a record store. Right now we have music in many forms—cassette, CD, records— but we don't have eight tracks. We can't go back. The Acceptance Threshold has been crossed, and certain things will fall out of being. We are at the same point in libraries, where we have the old and new right next to each other. There are card catalogues next to online catalogues, though the card catalogues are being phased out.

User Needs

Users are comfortable with what we know. They have probably done print searches for long years. Now they are faced with this new technology that they are not been trained on, and is not confident with. Hence, the role of LIS professionals is much more important than ever before. We are trained in this new technology, and it will be our role and our responsibility to teach to the users how use these new tools. It is not as comfortable to go up to a computer and learn your way through it, trial and error, as it is with a print index. We grew up with print.

Digital Citizenship

Libraries are providing easy access to vastly more information than ever before through the Internet. They enable all citizens to have access to information and service, and are central to the delivery of electronic government.

Democratised Information

The digital technologies in a positive way, each new development in the history of communication, has further democratised information. From oral traditions to print, to the printing press, now to electronic communication – we can reach more people. It is very positive that someone who may never have taken an interest in art can now access it. In a way it is a great bank of knowledge, and people might be more comfortable going to it from their computers at home.

Preservation

The issue is the new technologies do bring up preservation? Do you preserve old books that are acid damaged, brittle, in poor condition? The new technologies answer to that is 'no,' we don't preserve the objects; we digitise them so people will still have access to them. The information of the objects can still be accessed digitally. But if that is the case, where does that leave our libraries? Are our libraries going to become just warehouses for old objects, actually museums? Will the term 'library' primarily be used for a place where old communication artifacts are stored?

Professional Competency

Since the recent past, the library and information profession has witnessed a sea change. The impact of information and communication technologies has made us ask ourselves the following:

- Why would students like to enter a profession, which could change beyond recognition, and possibly cease to exist, in the near future?
- Why do students enter a profession that is totally changing under their noses?
- How can they make a library user-friendly if people don't like technology and have no choice now that it is here?
- What do they expect to find?
- Why do they come?
- What are the other functions of a library?

If that 'warehouse' scenario is a possibility, we have to ask what will be lost. Is a library a community? Is it a place for people to go? An interesting parallel to that is to look at the popularity of bookstores right now and the popularity of coffee houses that have access to the Internet. Why are these places so attractive? People like to go and look at books, they like to socialise, they like to go and have coffee, some like to try out new technologies. So if it is true, if it is the climate of our time right now, then why can't we make a library that place? Why can't we learn from the Internet cafes? Maybe we needed to change our definition of what a library is. Maybe we don't want it to be a warehouse for old stuff. Maybe we want it to be a place in the community where people can go and drink coffee, can go to an electronic database and find out about things, can email, can exchange ideas. May be we need a paradigm shift. It is up for grabs that librarians will be checking out books. What isn't up for grabs is that new technologies are evolving and that people will need to learn them. It's not a question of if the new technologies are good or bad, it is a question of how we can make our jobs successful with professional competency and use our profession to adapt to what users need.

In fact, there is no answer to how libraries or librarians will be changed by digital technologies—society itself is unsure what these technologies will be in a few years, or exactly how they will be used. But the technologies are here. The future library, unknown to us now, does exist somewhere in the minds of the people who will be building, changing and maintaining them in the years to come. Therefore digital libraries are cornerstones of every community, but they are also elements of a great national experiment in free and democratic access to information and resources in the different formats.

Influence of Digital Technology on Librarianship

E-Commerce Architecture in Library

E-commerce system is part of a larger, internal digital nervous system. It provides much more than just an electronic sale. A digital nervous system that integrates knowledge management, business operations and electronic commerce allows an organisation to communicate and accomplish. Its takes digitally while simultaneously enabling the sharing of information throughout the organisation. Collaboration via technology is by connecting all computers in an organisation and encompassing all computer-to-computer exchange of information.

The flow (Fig. 1) of information through a business via a digital nervous system is as unique as the specific organisation and its business partners. Yet, in order to capture and maintain a competitive advantage in its markets, the organisation and its partners need to create these information systems. 'A' system user accesses the transaction server through a PC or workstation. The PC in vendor 'A' is used to update data in a database server. When the data is correct, the user tells the system to transmit the data via web the server. To transmit the data, the web server uses the transactions of the data over the Internet to library via the router. The web server at the library reverses the process that occurred in the vendor. The web server at library stores the data in the database through the transaction and database server. A library user accesses the data through a PC via the transaction and database servers from vendor server.

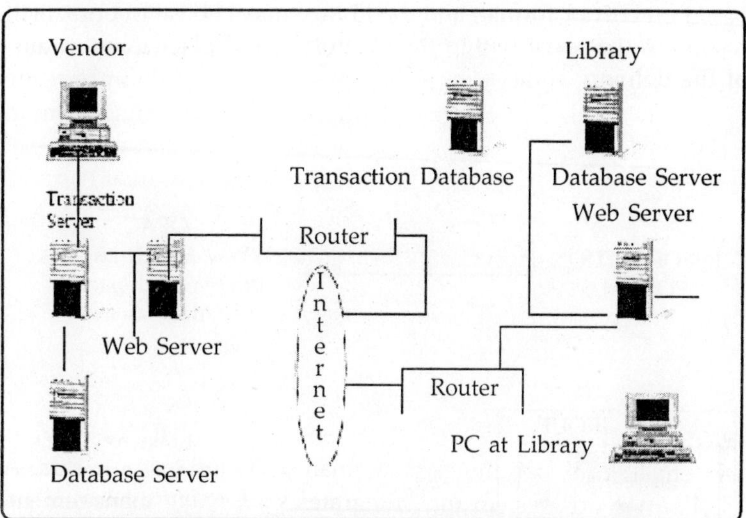

Figure 1: E-commerce Architecture in Library

Digital Services through Information Portals

Technology in the form of portals offers great opportunities for library and information professionals to give their services to existing users a real boost. At its simplest level, an information portal can offer users one place where they can search across a multitude of resources, and get electronic and book resources in one place. Both of these make it easier for users to interact with library services.

Services provided by LICs today must be about more than just discovery—more than just links. Information portals can provide integration of sources for searching and for the location and delivery of materials—in whatever format they exist. This content may be located anywhere—internal or external to the organisation—and may be in any format, physical or digital. It is important to remember that even with the explosion of digital content, we still operate in a mixed media environment. Information portals can add value in both arenas and can offer the most appropriate delivery choices for students, staff and researchers, and the library can control how resources are presented. For example, sources can be presented to the user based on cost or format, and the library may choose to prioritise resources that exist within the institution and place them at top of the delivery choices.

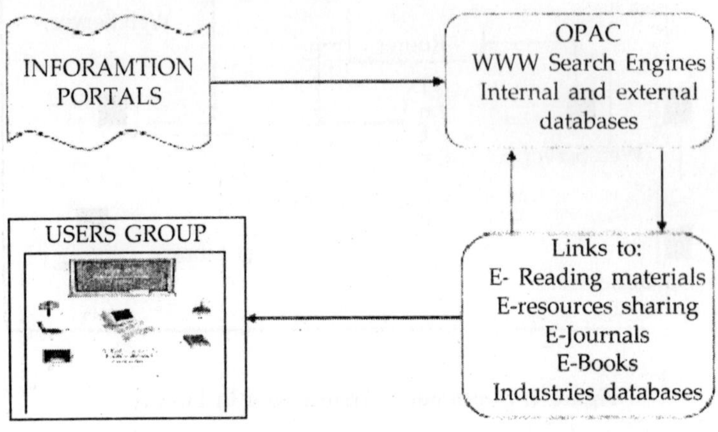

Figure 2

Digital Information Services through Portals

Implementing of portal is bringing the opportunity to develop digital services as a key learning support tool, and in so doing make it more appealing and rewarding to use library services. Portals can also bring new services to meet the growing expectations of today's users population (Fig.2).

If institutions do not provide information portal services, or if academics, students and researchers cannot or do not engage with the new theme, then they will continue to miss out on the highly useful information—and highly expensive—tools which have been bought in to make it easier for users to achieve their potential. So it is important that LIS professionals ensure that their users do not just use search engines, and in so doing, miss out on library provided resources that is in an increasing percentage of cases and can be delivered to them in real time.

Therefore the information portal is a browser-based application that allows information access to, collaborate with, make decisions and take action on a wide variety of information regardless of the location of the information or the format in which the information is stored. It has several features that are used to implement information management initiatives in an organisation:

- A constant view of your library and information centres.
- Information organisation and search capabilities.
- Direct link and access different resources.
- Direct link to relative data and experts.
- Individual identity and personalised.
- Better decision making capabilities.
- Improved semantics.
- Improved information organisation and search capabilities.
- Direct access to knowledge and resources.
- Direct links to reports, analysis and query or relative data points.
- Personalised access to content.

ATM Technology in Libraries

The design of a library network involves ATM technology. ATM (Asynchronous Transfer Mode) operates in a much different way than Ethernet. All data packets are broken into fixed size cells, and switching technology is used to set up virtual circuits between senders and receivers on the network. ATM switches either can be used in a pure computers as ATM adapters rather than Ethernet or TokenRing cards or they can be used as backbone network that operates with other routers, switches and hubs. ATM offers faster performance and data through-put than competing technologies such as FDDI, Ethernet Fast Ethernet, or Token Ring. Most ATM equipment operates at a speed of about 145 megabits per second.

In many ATM environment it is possible to establish multiple Emulated Local Area Networks (ELANs). While all computers can participate in the same switching matrix, computers can be assigned to various ELANs. Once assigned to an ELAN, the computers within that group can operate only with the other devices that share that ELAN, regardless of physical proximity.

Figure 3

ATM Technology for Self-Checking System

The 3M has been using the ATM technology for Self-Checking System (SCS) transactions (Fig.3) in the library. This technology has provided all-new way of functioning to meet the ever growing needs of library users and services. Today SCS enables library users to check out their resources without having to locate optical barcodes. It processes RFID (Radio Frequency Identification) tags and optical barcodes, allowing libraries to plan for an orderly migration to RFID technology – without compromising security – and is perfectly safe for all media types.

The library users can check out their own materials without the assistance of library staff, using one of digital Self-Check Systems in the library. The systems require no line of sight to "read" information from the digital identification tag, and will process both barcoded and digital identification items. The system actually checking the item in or out and re-sensitising or desensitising the security strip in each item. Check-in is an optional feature; it has to respond to the digital identification tag placed within each library item, allowing library staff and users to check items in and out without having to position books in a certain way or align materials with scan lines. It will allow patrons to manage one of the most labour-intensive functions in a library. LIS professionals have the time and resources to concentrate more specifically on the growing and changing needs of their patrons.

Collection management

The RFID (Radio Frequency Identification) technology and its products have successfully used in libraries. It offers a variety of products based on radio frequency identification, or the transmission of signals between information stored on a "smart tag" and a "reader". The use of digital identification technology requires neither direct contact with a reader, as does magnetic stripe technology, nor a direct line of sight with a reader, as does barcode technology. An additional benefit of this technology is that it saves time.

Digital ID collection management benefits both library staff and patrons by making the library a more efficient place to retrieve information, a concept developed by library technology experts. The library staff can spend less time on time-consuming, routine tasks and focus more of their time on the varied needs of patrons. As library budgets get tighter and patrons' needs increase, materials flow management offers better use of limited library resources. The ability to streamline nearly the entire materials flow cycle reduces expenses and raises library efficiency.

Libraries are constantly looking for ways to streamline the processes and provide a higher level of service to their patrons. Digital ID collection management brings many revolutionary applications to libraries, such as being able to restore shelf order in minutes. One digital identification tag can hold up to 256 bits of information. This allows for much more to be stored than just the item's identification, which is all the traditional barcode stores. Digital identification tags can store an item's identification code, the media type of the item, an identification for the library system that owns the item and an identification for the branch within the library system where the item currently resides.

In addition to the digital identification system the IT products has also having features of (Fig.4) detection systems to prevent the unauthorised removal of library materials. For the 3M detection systems have provided the highest level of security available to the library.

Figure 4: 3M Detection System

Managing the collection

To manage the collection quickly and efficiently, the library staff can use the Digital Library Assistants (DLAs) products. The DLA is a hand-held device that reduces the amount of time needed to manage time-consuming routine tasks, like finding lost items, weeding the collection, properly shelving items and performing shelf reading in a fraction of the time and at a fraction of the cost (Fig.5).

The DLA's ability to conduct "shelf reading", finding an item in the stacks not in its proper shelf order, and "weeding", removing items that are outdated or no longer circulating in the collection, were most impressive. They can be collected and moved to the proper location. The proper location is reported graphically and by title on the DLA screen, with the titles of the items to the left and to the right of the proper location also indicated on the DLA screen. Getting materials back on the shelves after check-in is a time-consuming and labour-intensive action that many libraries have a hard time keeping up with. The DLA cuts re-shelving time dramatically. It helps to identify cataloguing errors and identify items with inconsistencies between call numbers in the database and call numbers on the spine label.

Fig.5 Digital Library Assistant Hand Held Device

Figure 5: Digital Library Assistant Hand-Held Device

The Digital Data Manager facilitates the transfer of item information from the library's automated circulation system to the DLA. The shelf order and search list information is written to a memory card, similar to the compact flash card technology used in digital cameras. The digital data manager allows the DLA to perform shelf reading, re-shelving, and searching in the stacks in real time. It is among the most revolutionary technologies to affect the way libraries could manage the information.

Digital Information Culture and Research

'Digital information culture' has immensely influenced the ideas of retaining and restoring human culture, authentication, examination and reinterpretation, and heavily supported by digital technological innovations, applications and institutional policies. Library users continue to influence the information materials that are collected, preserved in all possible formats, and made accessible, in either formats: analogue and digital. Research interests in digitised information materials and increased institutional commitment to digitise conventional material reflects the rise in demands of 'digital information culture' from the libraries, and forms the force of continuing interest in doing so. But the nature of 'digital information culture' in which the difference of digital information materials and the increasing volumes of digital material are produced, the expectations of online access by 24x7 mode have an impact on notions of collecting. The use of cutting-edge technologies like knowledge management, semantic tools, graphics, interfaces empowers applications that improve the meaningful use and experiences users get from cultural resources, including the archival material. Research in the application areas of digital libraries and archives are exploring methods and tools for automatic indexing and semantic description of textual and non-textual objects such as music, speech, images, etc. Simultaneously, they have to enhance retrieval of information and knowledge through efficient search engines able to deliver results from complex multimedia and multilingual resources.

Research Data

Research in many areas now has been influenced by digital preservation and conservation. The collaborative research projects yield a wide range of research data from their experiments and analyses. Such research output is being used to bring together and network the institutions and organisations holding cultural and scientific content such as libraries, archives, museums, academic institutions, research centres, ICT corporate houses and companies, publishing agencies, Internet and multimedia service providers, and others.

Digital Preservation and Web Archiving

The rapid pace of change of electronic devices and formats represents a threat to the long-term accessibility of digital objects. Research seeks to mitigate this risk through novel concepts, techniques and tools, such as software agents, emulation or virtual environments. Some projects are developing test beds and systems facilitating long-term access to multi-sourced, multi-formatted and highly distributed resources. Other projects are supporting cultural institutions and other stakeholders in preserving their digital resources, for example, in the form of competence centres. The preservation and long-term accessibility of the Web history has high value e.g., for scholarly studies, market analyses, intellectual property disputes, etc. Web content, thus, is important because of its typical characteristics such as varied formats, highly dynamism, volatility, interactivity and context-dependent. Therefore, adequate web archiving has become a big challenge, which is being addressed by Information Communication Technologies.

Digitisation Technologies and Tools

Though high costs, other technical and organisational problems hinder their success, considerable efforts and resources are being put in for the digitisation projects across the world. Research explores how ICTs can facilitate large-scale digitisation and make digitisation more cost-effective. Projects are concerned both with new technology solutions and with best practice guidance, and are establishing centres of excellence for digitisation. Tools and methodologies being developed range from recognition and enhancement of printed text and audiovisual material to ICTs for capturing and rendering cultural artifacts.

Professional Challenges

Today's information society is passing through various challenges due to various reasons. Some of these can be deliberately mentioned as below:

Lack of Professional Knowledge

The lacuna of professional knowledge which may affect digital information culture can be as follow:

- Identification of users' information needs
- Analysis and anticipation of user and organisational information needs
- Presentation, editorial and publication skills
- Ability to organise and store information for effective retrieval

- Training, education and consultancy skills
- Knowledge delivery mechanisms
- Ability to add value to information
- Methods of disseminating information
- Awareness of technology skills and subject expertise
- Knowledge of disparate information resources and how to access / integrate them
- Familiarity with research methods
- Ability to evaluate information
- Knowledge management
- Knowledge of legal, economic and political aspects of information

Lack of Managerial Skills

Information is considered the most important resource and therefore, in the context of decision making, information, is also treated as the life of management. In the absence of awareness regarding various kinds of management, the information manager can't enjoy the right benefit of the right information in the undertaken stage of decision making. So, management skills are required by information professional at various stages of the information cycle. A few of these skills which are of utmost importance include:

- Understanding the organisational culture
- Project management
- Change management
- Strategic planning
- Financial management
- Human resource management
- Communication skills
- Marketing skills
- Vision and creativity
- Liaison and negotiating skills

Growth of Subject Knowledge

An information professional must keep one of his/her eyes on the present and another on the future. A professional should not be confined to his subject but in the light of technological innovation, availability of better software development tools, better techniques of communication, etc., must update himself. So, an information professional needs the following:

- Present trends and developments in hardware, software and communication technologies
- Information exploration and visualisation
- Means of preservation for information
- Internet and its efficient use for quick access of desired kind of information
- Technology for intellectual property protection.

Role of LIS Professionals in the Digital Culture

It is the responsibility of information professionals to become an agent between the users and the information. In the events of lack of poorly disseminating of information, it loses its value and the same may cause negative effects on the emotions of its users. In order to overcome such a situation, the LIS professionals have to:

- Analyse the user's needs from time to time.
- Regular and constant watch on the information flow within the enterprise.
- Analyse the information seeking behaviour.
- Help the user in learning the techniques for efficient retrieval of information.
- Make the appropriate use of information in a suitable situation.
- Be aware of the consequences of the misuse of the information and its impact.
- Strike a balance between the existing needs and changed needs of the system.
- Take necessary steps to implement the expected changes maintaining a balance between supporting and opposing forces.

- Evaluate systems and procedures from time to time.
- Review policies from time to time in the light of emerging trends.

There are very large chances of misusing information, which may further cause very erroneous and awkward decisions. Attempts should be made to minimise the misuse and abuse of information. A few specific suggestions to avoid misuse and abuse of information within an enterprise are;

- Emphasising on developing system standards
- Evolving an effective information policy
- Employing timely provision of service for avoiding delays
- Evolving effective bibliographic control devices
- Developing a good organisational environment
- Coordinating relations with the users
- Re-orienting users from time to time
- Training users in the latest tools used for information retrieval
- Building up ethics in the users
- Constantly reviewing the procedures
- Educating means of information maintenance.

Conclusion

The library systems are looking to the future of the library and how to communicate the benefits of new digital technology to professionals and users. The new technology products for libraries are changing how users are retrieve information at the library. Dedicated libraries and innovative products provide staff with greater capabilities for exceeding patrons' expectations both today and tomorrow. The future for libraries looks bright. The implications for the future of library workflow utilising digital identification products are promising. Information communication technologies allow the information professionals to perform duties more comfortably and effectively so that the library users should benefit in several ways. The new technological innovations have provided libraries around the world with new way of functioning and set up the new trends in information services, professionals work and performed library tasks. 'Digital information culture' is experienced through social, cultural, political and economic activities that are undertaken using digital technologies. The application of digital technologies and the centrality of its use distinguish the ultra-modern digital libraries from the traditional libraries in many respects.

References

Breeding, M. (1997). Designing Secure Library Networks. *Library Hi Tech,* 15 (1-2), 11- 20.

Clair, S.G. (1996). *Entrepreneurial Librarianship: The Key To Effective Information Services Management.* London: Bowker, .167-168.

Fabbi, J.L, Watson, S.D and Marks, K. E (2002). Implementing of the 3M Digital Identification System at UNLV Libraries. *Library Hi Tech,* 20 (1), 104-110.

Holt, Glen. (2008). Digital Preservation's Impact on Libraries and Librarians. Books and Sources Technology, January 21, 2008.Available at:http://lln.lyrasis.org/node/67 (Accessed on 15August 2009)

Jordan, Matthew (2004). Looking for a Future Library: How Will Digital Technology and Digital Culture Change or Libraries and Librarians? Available at: http://zine375.eserver.org/issue1/online3.html

Mason, Ingrid. (2007). Virtual Preservation: How Has Digital Culture Influenced Our Ideas about Permanence? Changing Practice in a National Legal Deposit Library. *Library Trends,* 56 (1), Summer ("Preserving Cultural Heritage," edited by Michèle V. Cloonan and Ross Harvey), 198–215.

Murray, R (2003). Information Portals: Casting a New Light on Learning for Universities. *Campus Wide Information Systems,* 20 (4), 146-151.

Reid, J. B and Foster, W. (2000). *Achieving Cultural Change in Networked Libraries,* Cambridge: Gower.

Sirurmath, S. S. (2000). Challenges and Opportunities to Libraries. In: *'Reengineering of Library and Information Services in an I.T. Environment"*, Proceeding of the MDP, XLRI, Jamshedpur, May 8-12, 16-33.

______________ and Pani, A. K. (2004). The Role of XML in Information Portals" In *Road Map to New Generation of Libraries Using Emerging Tecnnologies,* Eds.: T.A.V Murthy and others, Ahmedabad, INFLIBNET Centre, 496-502.

______________ and Pani, A. K (2004). E-Commerce Strategies for Library and Information Services" In: *Digital Information Exchange: Pathways to Build Global Information Society*, Eds.: Harish Chandra and others, Chennai, OS-SIS-IIT Madras, 536 -542.

Yorkovich, D. J. (2001). Lied Library: At the Forefront of Technology with 3M Digital ID Collection Management. *New Library World*, 102 (1165), 216-220.

22

Mastering the Web Search: Tools, Techniques and Tips for Users

—Fayaz Ahmad Lone

The paper describes the concept of World Wide Web and its origin. The various search techniques like Boolean, phrase, nested, proximity, truncation and field searching are explained, The web tools such as search engines, subject directories, meta search engines and invisible search tool are illustrated with examples. Finally the paper provides valuable tips for using the Internet effectively and efficiently.

Introduction

The World Wide Web, abbreviated as www and w3, is commonly known as the Web. It is a system of interlinked hypertext documents contained on the Internet. With a web browser one can view web pages that may contain text, images, videos and other multimedia and navigate between them using hyper links.

The World Wide Web is a global information medium which users can read and write via computers connected to the internet. In 1980, the Englishman, Tim Berners-Lee, an independent contractor at the European Organisation for Nuclear Research (CERN), Switzerland, conceived the idea of World Wide Web and built the same.

Stages of Web Searching

The web is the largest unorganised repository of information and searching relevant information is like finding a needle in the haystack. Without an expertise in the field of searching, web searching is like surfing aimlessly with the waves of water. Successful web searching involves four key stages.

- Developing a Search Strategy
- Understanding Search Techniques
- Mastering the Search Tools
- Remembering the Search Tips

Developing a Search Strategy

The search strategy is the planning process used to create an efficient search statement for your topic that will help you to find larger amount of relevant information. It is done by deriving the main concepts from the topic, selecting the keywords representing the concepts and identifying a suitable search technique for searching the relevant information using the search tools. Developing a search strategy is very easy and is completed in few steps as:

Step One: State your topic

- Trade relations between India and Central Asia

Step Two: Choose the most important words or main ideas from the topic

1. Trade 2. India 3. Central Asia

Step Three: Think about alternatives (Related, Broader and Narrow Terms)

	Trade	India	Central Asia
Related Terms	Business	Hindustan	Inner Asia/Middle Asia
Broader Terms	Cooperation	South Asia	Asia
Narrower Terms	Import	Delhi	Tajikistan
	Export	Kashmir	Kazakhstan

Step Four: Search the selected keywords using different search tools like search engines, directories, metasearch engines, databases using various search techniques such as Boolean operators to retrieve relevant information from the web.

Step Five: Find the required information from the deep web also using invisible web search tools.

Step Six: Reassess the search strategy based on the results retrieved. If hits are many, narrow the search and if hits are few, broaden the search. Use related terms to retrieve hidden results

Understanding Search Techniques

The web can be searched using different search techniques. The user, who is well aware of these search techniques, is expected to retrieve the better results. So, I feel it necessary to discuss some of the prominent search techniques in this section to make user aware and expert in web searching.

a) Boolean Searching

Boolean searching is an important skill to learn; you'll need these operators to effectively search the library catalogue, electronic databases and the Internet. Using Boolean operators (AND, OR, NOT) will help to focus and define your search by specifying the logical relationship among your keywords and terms. They can help broaden (increase) and narrow (decrease) search results.

They narrow a search as ALL TERMS must be present in each hit. If you enter the following search:

— Women and Tajikistan

each hit should contain both the words 'Women' and 'Tajikistan'. Adding 'Tajikistan' to 'Women' is a good strategy to use when you only need to limit your search to information about women in the Tajikistan. 'Women' is such a broad subject that a search with just 'women' as the search word is likely to result in millions of hits, most of which will be irrelevant if you are only looking for Tajikistan related information.

Or they widen a search because each hit will contain either 'Women' or it will contain 'Tajikistan'. These terms may or may not appear in the same record. If you enter the following search:

— Women or Tajikistan

all the records containing the word 'Women', as well as all the records containing the term 'Tajikistan' will be retrieved.

The best way to use 'or' is when you want to make sure that you cover synonyms. Have a look at the following example:

— Education or Teaching or Schooling

not narrows a search by excluding records containing specified words. If you enter the following search:

– Women Not Men

the word 'Women' must be present in the records retrieved, but the word 'Men' must not be present. Use the Not operator judiciously as you may exclude relevant records inadvertently.

b) Phrase Searching

Phrase searching is a type of search that allows users to search for documents containing an exact sentence or phrase, rather than single keywords. It is a method of keeping specific words together by grouping them with punctuation, usually double quotes to force a search tool to find terms in a phrase only. For example:

– "Political instability in Afghanistan"

c) Nested Searching

Nested searching is a combination of more than one search technique. Many search engines, databases and catalogues allow you to create complex queries using Boolean operators, phrases and parentheses. This is called nested searching. Usually, operations enclosed in the parentheses will be performed first followed by the operators outside the parentheses. We can use all the three signs (AND, OR, NOT) together in the nested search as:

– Women and (Central Asia or Inner Asia)

d) Proximity Searching

Proximity searching refers to the ability to specify how close within a record multiple terms should be to each other. The most commonly used proximity search option in Internet finding aids is a phrase search that requires terms to be in the exact order specified within the phrase markings. The default standard for identifying phrases is to use double quotes (" ") as:

– "Women empowerment in Turkmenistan"

Beyond phrase searching, other proximity operators can specify how close terms should be to each other. Each search engine can define them differently and use various operator names, such as NEAR, ADJ, W, or AFTER. These operators indicate the search engine to find records with specified words near to each other.

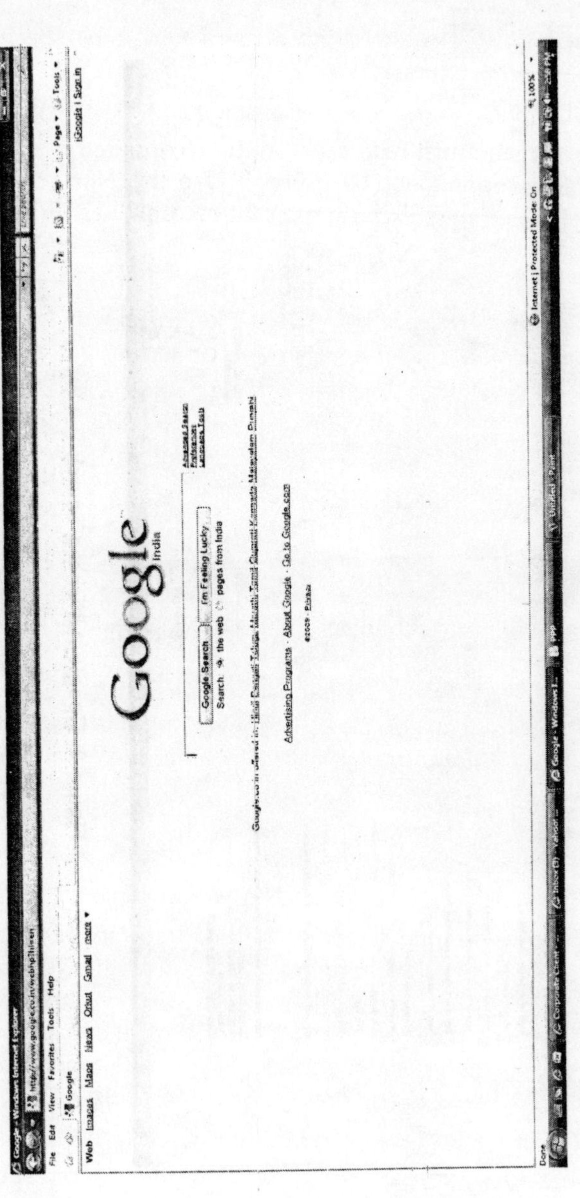

Figure 1: Google Simple Search

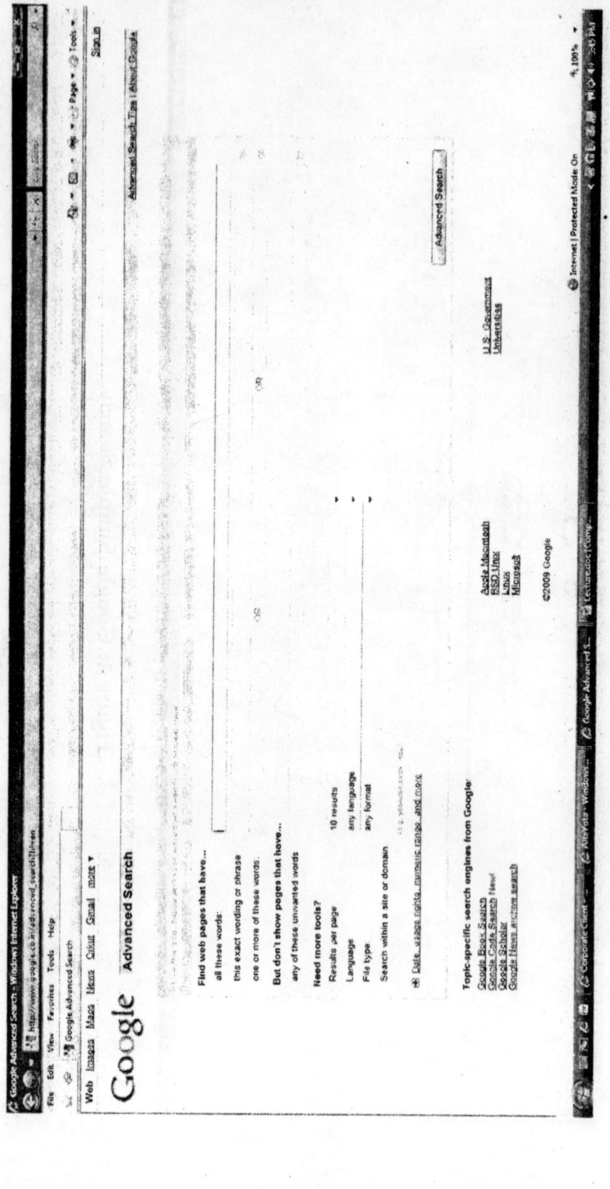

Figure 2: Google Advanced Search

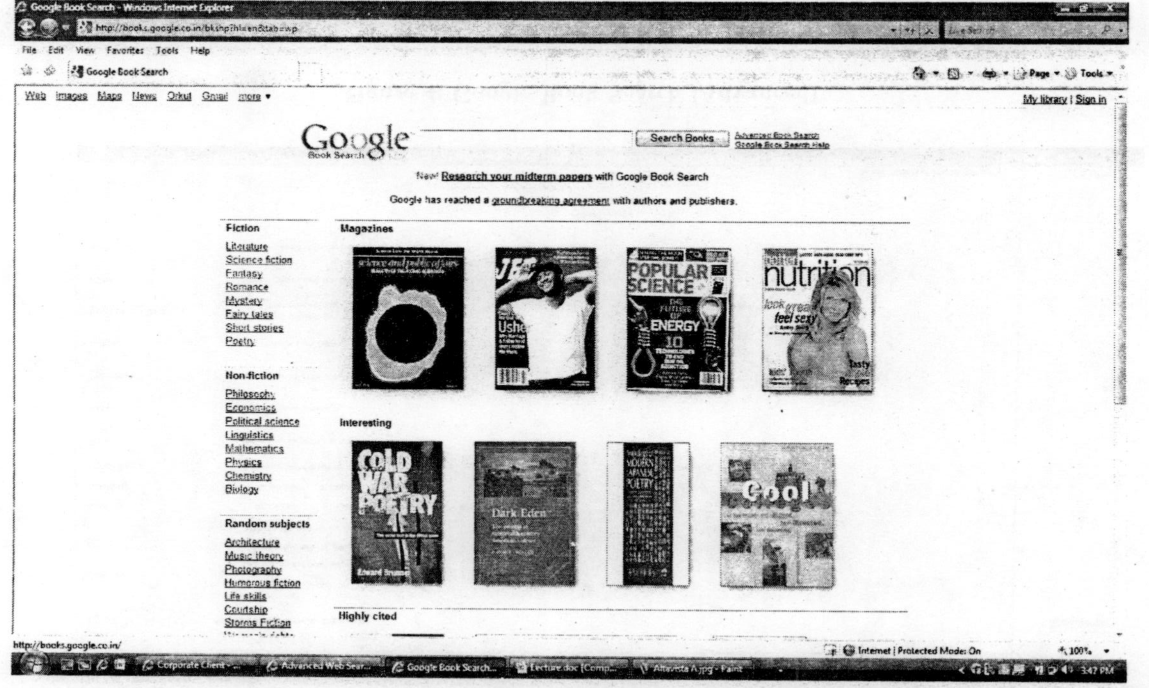

Figure 3: Google Book Search (Simple)

Advanced Book Search – Windows Internet Explorer

http://books.google.co.in/advanced_book_search

File Edit View Favorites Tools Help

Google Book Search Advanced Book Search

About Google

Find results	with all of the words with the exact phrase with at least one of the words without the words	10 results Google Search
Search:	All books Limited preview and full view Full view only	
Content:	All content Books Magazines	
Language	Return pages written in	any language
Title	Return books with the title	e.g. Books and Culture
Author	Return books written by	
Publisher	Return books published by	e.g. O'Reilly
Subject	Return books on subject	
Publication Date	Return content published anytime Return content published between	Jan 2009 and Dec 2009
ISBN	Return books with the ISBN	
ISSN	Return serials with the ISSN	

©2009 Google

Internet | Protected Mode: On 100%

Figure 4: Google Book Search (Advanced)

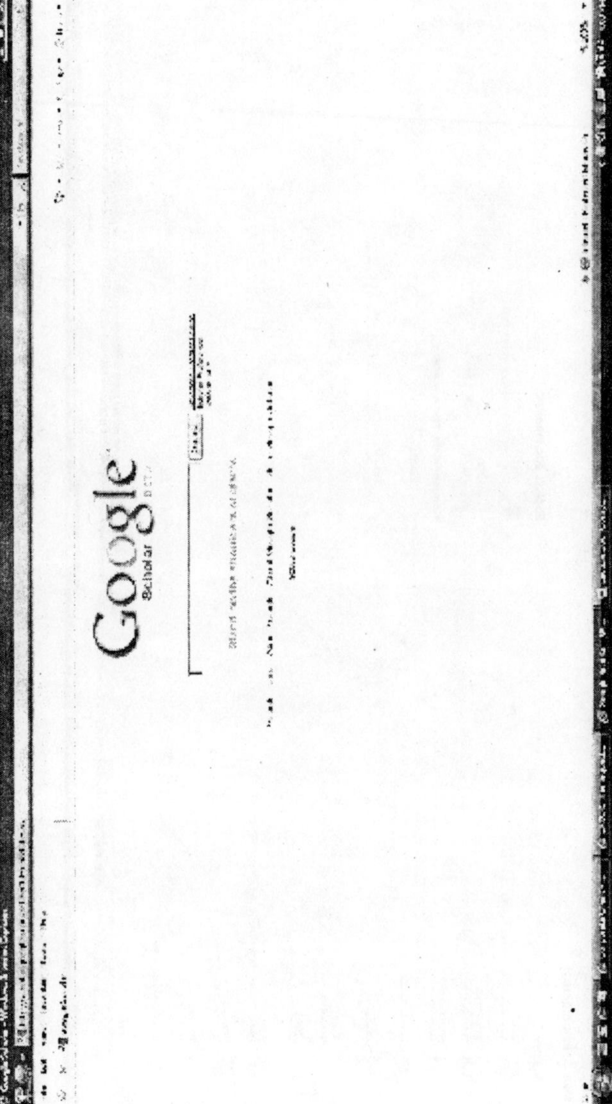

Figure 5: Google Scholar

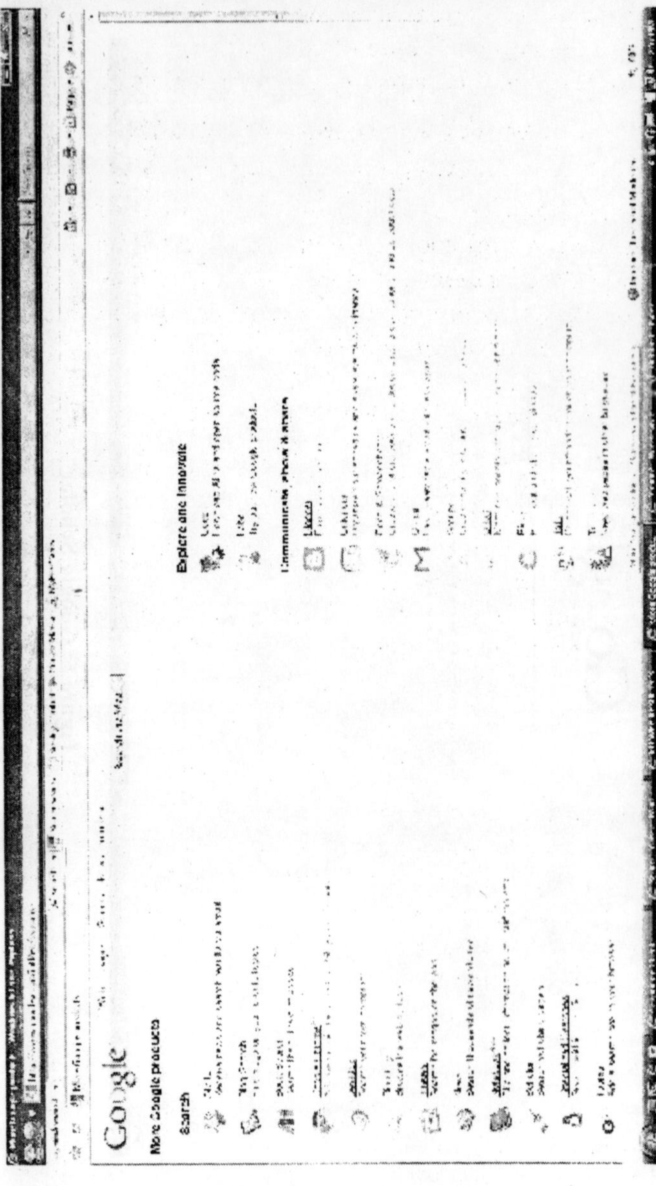

Figure 6: Google Services

e) Truncation searching

Truncation searching is used to retrieve variations in word endings or spellings. This search technique refers to the ability to search just a portion of a word. Typically, a symbol such as the asterisk (*) or dollar ($) or Plus (+) is used to represent the rest of the term. End truncation is where several letters at the beginning of a word are specified but the ending can vary. With internal truncation, a symbol can represent one or more characters within a word. For example, if you enter the word 'teach' your results might include records with the words 'teach', 'teacher', and 'teaching'. Different search engines and databases will use different characters to indicate truncation.

f) Field Searching

Field searching is the ability to limit a search by requiring that the search term is present in a specific 'field' (category of data) in the record. Field searching is often done with categories such as author and date that are common to most records. The ISBN, ISSN, DOI and URL can also be used in this technique.

Mastering the Search Tools

To facilitate efficient searching of information on the Internet, web search tools have come to the rescue of the users. The main Web search tools are:

- Search Engines
- Subject Directories
- Meta Search Engines
- Invisible Web Search Tools

a) Search Engines

Search engines are large, spider created databases of web pages that help searchers find specific information on any given subject. A web search engine is a tool designed to search for information on the World Wide Web (Wikipedia, 2008a). The search results are usually presented in a list and are commonly called *hits*. The information may consist of web pages, images, information and other types of files. Some of the search engines are:

- Google (http://www.google.com)
- Altavista (http://www.altavista.com)
- Alltheweb (http://www.alltheweb.com)
- Infoseek (http://www.infoseek.com)
- Yahoo (http://www.yahoo.com)
- MSN (http://www.msn.com)
- AOL (http://www.aol.com)

b) Subject Directories

Subject directories in general are smaller and selective than search engines. They use categories to focus your search, and their sites are arranged by categories, not just by keywords. Subject directories are handy for broad searches, as well as finding specific websites. Most subject directories' main purpose is to be informational, rather than commercial. The examples of the Subject directories are:

- About.com (www.about.com)
- BUBL (http://bubl.ac.uk/)
- Librarians Index to Internet (www.lii.org)
- Open Directory Project (http://www.dmoz.org/)
- The WWW Virtual Library (http://vlib.org/)

c) Metasearch Engines

Metasearch engines do not have their own database but get search results from several search engines. Users receive the best hits to their keywords from each search engine. Metasearch tools are a good place to start for very broad results, but do not (usually) give the same quality results as using each search engine and directory. The good examples of Metasearch engines are:

- Mamma (http://www.mamma.com)
- Dogpile (http://www.dogpile.com)
- Excite (http://www.excite.com)
- Metacrawler (http://www.metacrawler.com)
- Webcrawler (http://www.webcrawler.com)

d) Invisible Web Search Tools

The term "invisible web" mainly refers to the vast repository of information that search engines and directories don't have direct access to, like databases. Bright Planet estimates the invisible, or deep, web as being 500 times bigger than the searchable, or surface, web (Boswell, 2008). Unlike pages on the visible web (that is, the web that you can access from search engines and directories), information in databases is generally inaccessible to the software spiders and crawlers that create search engine indexes. The so-called invisible web is data that is locked up in databases and is hidden from search engines. The search tools of the Deep Web are:

- Infomine (http://infomine.ucr.edu/)
- CompletePlanet (http://aip.completeplanet.com/)
- Brightplanet (http://www.brightplanet.com/)
- Invisible-Web.net (http://www.invisible-web.net/)
- Geniusfind (http://www.geniusfind.com/)

The research is carried out throughout the world on search tools especially search engines to identify their strengths and weaknesses on the basis criteria like database size, relevance ranking, searching capability, update of database, display of results, automatic truncation, etc. On the basis of findings, the search engines are ranked. However, the ranks of search engines change frequently due to their dynamic nature but the search engines like Google, Altavista, Yahoo and MSN always succeed to maintain their place in top ten. Google, Yahoo! and MSN are widely recognised as the three biggest search engines today, with Google serving nearly 50 per cent of all web searches, and Yahoo! serving about 25 per cent. MSN has a share of less than 10 per cent, so we can see that there is a very big divergence, with Google emerging as the web searching superpower of our time (Aspland, 2008) Therefore, it is better to search the Web using this search engine.

Google (http://www.google.com)

Google was originally a Stanford University project by students Larry Page and Sergey Brin called BackRub. Finally, the project jumped off campus and became the private company Google and was launched in 1998 (Search Engine Watch, 2008). Google's lofty and altruistic mission is to organise the world's information and make it universally accessible. "We chose our system name, Google, because it is a common spelling of googol, or 10^{100} and fits well with our goal of building very large-scale search engines" (Brin & Page). It has quickly become the most successful search engines. It is voted four times as the "Most Outstanding Search Engine" by Search Engine Watch readers (Search Engine Watch, 2008).

Google started out with an index size of around 24 million web pages in 1996. By August of 2000, it had managed to increase their index size to approximately one billion web pages and on September of 2003 to 3.3 billion web pages. As its index continued to grow the number in their it page grew impressively large as well before it plateaus at eight billion web pages. This was around the time that Patterson filed the new patent. Then in September of 2005, as part of Google's 7th anniversary, Anna Patterson posted an entry on Google's official blog claiming that the index size was now 1,000 times larger than the original index. This pegged its index size to around 24 billion web pages, about a fourth of its goal of indexing a100 billion web pages. With the new system in place we can only wait and see how fast Google will reach the goal of a 100 billion web pages in its index (Wirken, 2009).

Google has a well-deserved reputation as the top choice for those searching the web not only due to its huge database size but also relevance ranking. The crawler-based service provides both comprehensive coverage of the web along with great relevancy. It's highly recommended as a first stop in your hunt for whatever you are looking for. A remarkable feature of Google is the capability of searching within the HTML, PPT, PDF, DOC, and other proprietary formats.

Google has "Simple" search mechanism (Fig. 1) as well as "Advanced" search mechanism (Fig. 2). In Simple search the user gets hits in thousands or even in lakhs mostly irrelevant (less Precision and more Recall), therefore, to limit the search results one has to go for Advanced search where user gets less hits but more relevant (more Precision less Recall). Google supports phrase searching (e.g., Russia in Central Asia), keyword searching (e.g., Central Asia, History), Boolean Operators (e.g., India AND itsCentral Asia OR Inner Asia NOT South Asia), proximity operator (NEAR) (e.g., Oil NEAR Caspian Sea), field searching like URL, ISBN (e.g., http://www.cagateway.org).

Google indexes different types of web documents like research papers, project reports, patents, seminar papers, conference proceedings, newspaper articles, books, reference sources, self publishing information like blogs, discussion forms and lots more. Thus, it provides opportunity to search separately for books, scholarly information, images, newspapers, self publishing information using Google Books search, Google Scholar, Google Image Search, Google News search, Google Blog search and so on.

Google Book Search also has Simple (Fig. 3) and Advanced (Fig. 4) search facilities. In Google simple search we can retrieve the books with no text available, limited text available and full text available as the Google indexes three types of books. No preview, Limited Preview and Full Text. The books with no preview and limited preview mostly serve the marketing purpose.

Google contains thousands of full text books that serve the purpose of users from general to specialist. The user should prefer to search for information in Advanced Book Search where he/ she can limit the search to full text only. In advanced search mode, he/ she can also search the books by title, author, publisher, subject, publication date and language.

Google Scholar (Fig. 5) provides a simple way to broadly search for scholarly literature. From one place a user can search across many disciplines and resources, peer-reviewed papers, theses, abstracts, articles from academic publishers, professional societies, preprint repositories, universities and other scholarly organisations.

In addition, Google has many services like "Google Directory", "Google Alerts", "Google Orkut", "Google Earth" "Google Groups" and many more. It has a spell-check mechanism and translation facility (translating web pages from one language to another with some limitations). In a nutshell, Google is the most comprehensive, largest growing and mostly used search engine available in modern networked environment.

Remembering the Web Search Tips

Several practical hints have been developed by experienced searchers for effective Web searching. The following are a few important ones:

- Using a "Simple" search will get so many more unwanted or garbage returns along with some relevant hits. By using "Advanced" search users get rid of those annoying results. So, it is better to go for advanced searching.
- For broad or general concept searches start with the directory-based services like (BUBL/Google/Yahoo Directory) so that you can see the range of what's available and take advantage of subject heading structure to move you towards more relevant documents.
- For highly specific or obscure topics, use the search tools. Often it can take a long time to figure out where in a subject hierarchy a particular term belongs.
- Look for a help page – search tools handle combining terms and searching for phrases in different ways; the help page will describe the correct way to state your search for that search tool.
- Have sufficient information on the search topic before starting the search. You should be aware of spelling variations, synonyms, broader and narrower terms that can be used in the search.
- Use the "refine" feature offered by many search tools. This will limit further searches to the retrieved set only.
- Many top-ranking documents will not be relevant. Before giving up scan through at least 5 pages of search results.
- Many search engines are sensitive to CAPITAL LETTERS. Therefore, as a rule, except for names, use lower case only while searching the web. However, if you can use them as abbreviations in searching as WHO for World Health Organisation.
- Use advanced technique to search documents in specific languages such as English and formats like pdf.
- Search the references of the relevant articles, as these may be also related to your topic of interest.

- Contact the author and request him for full text of article if the full text is not available or needs subscription.
- Use different web search tools like search engines to search information including invisible search tools, don't rely on Google only.

Above all, searching the information on the Internet is a systematic process. It is a series of activities as discussed above, each revealing new clues and avenues of search, and ultimately, leads to the relevant information.

Conclusion

Understanding how to perform sophisticated searches of online information will greatly increase your chance of finding relevant information you want. Using Google to search the internet will locate resources that are available to the public. While these resources are good for some purposes, serious research and academic work often requires access to good databases, quality articles and standard books and that even if they are available online, one can access only by subscription. Taking into consideration the amount of resources available easily on the Web, the methodologies that ease the search of information should be developed. Standard search engines are widely used for searching nowadays but they have limitations due to their pattern- search algorithm because they lack any kind of semantic content.

References

Aspland, M. (2008). *From Archie to Google*. Available at: http://www.articleclick.com/Article/From-Archie-to-Google/1020032(Accessed on 15 July 2008).

Berners-Lee, Tim and Fischetti, Mark . (2000). *Weaving the web: the original design and ultimate testing of the world wide web by its inventor*. San Francisco: Harper.

Boswell, W. (2008). *The Invisible Web: How to find and search the Invisible Web*. Available at: http://websearch.about.com/od/invisibleweb/a/invisible_web.htm (Accessed on 12 July 2008).

Brin, S and Page, L. (n.d). *The Anatomy of a Large-Scale Hypertextual Web Search Engine*. Available at: http://users.encs.concordia.ca/~kosseim/Teaching/COMP791-F06/Papers/google.pdf (Accessed on 15 June 2008).

Search Engine Watch (2008). *Major search engines and directories.* Available at: http://searchenginewatch.com/2156221(Accesed on 15 July 2008).

Wikipedia (2008). *Web search engine.* Available at: http://en.wikipedia.org/wiki/Search engine (Accessed on 12 July 2008).

Wirken, D. (2009). *The Google Goal of Indexing 100 Billion Web Pages.* Available at: http://www.streetdirectory.com/travel guide/187336/adsense tips the google goal of indexing 100 billion web pages.html (Accessed on 12 April 2009).

23

Proliferation of Electronic Resources: A Conjectural Approach

—Dillip K. Swain and K. C. Panda

Due to great information technology revelations during the last decade, there has been a significant demand for electronic resources everywhere. The information seekers have rightly shifted their focus from traditional printed documents to electronic resources. However, users are still unaware of some key aspects of e-resources that need to be unfolded. Therefore, this paper unveils some of the basic aspects of electronic resources pertaining to genesis of e-resources, sources and subject coverage of major e-resources, taxonomy of e-resources and future trends of e-resources that carry much significance and interest to the users of electronic information services.

Introduction

E-resources are simply the digital collections meant to provide solutions to regulate and control the fast rating information explosion in the recent years. Graham (2003) defines e- resources as information accessed by a computer, may be useful as bibliographic guides to potential sources but, as of yet, they frequently appear as cited references in their own right. In the words of Saye (2001) electronic resources are the information resources that are generated through some electronic medium and made available to a wide range of viewers both on-site and off-site via some electronic transferring machine or Internet. Moreover, electronic resources consist of materials that are computer-controlled, including materials that require the use of a peripheral attached to a computer: E-resources primarily include two types of resources (*IFLA*, 2000):

- *Data* (information in the form of numbers, letters, graphics, images, and sound, or a combination thereof); and
- *Programs* (instructions or routines for performing certain tasks including the processing of data).

In addition, they may be combined to include electronic data and programs (online services, interactive multimedia). Thus, electronic resources are treated in *two ways* depending on whether access is *local* or *remote*. *Local access*, on the other hand, is understood to mean that, a physical carrier can be described which is to be inserted into a computer or a peripheral attached to a computer (e.g., disc, cassette, tape and cartridge). *Remote access* is understood to mean that no physical carrier can be handled by the user-typically access can only be provided by use of an input-output device either connected to a computer system (e.g., a resource in a network or time-sharing environment) or by use of resources stored in a hard disk or other storage device.

Hence, electronic resources in its ambit include all kinds of digital collections in the form of databases, journals and books, image collections, examination papers, government and official publications, newspapers, patent resources, technical reports, standards, and theses/dissertations.

An ideal modern library must hold all the major types of electronic resources like e-books, e-indexes, e-journals, e-media, e-newspapers, etc. The statistical information of e-holdings of University of Toronto Library (Canada) given under Table 1 is a clear indicator of the scope of e-resources that cover different forms of materials available in electronic form.

Table 1 indicates that, out of the eight different categories/ forms of e-resources available, e-books collection is predominant with 347,870; followed by e-journals with 29,435; and e-newspapers with 3,068 titles, thus hold first, second and third rank in order respectively.

Genesis of E-resources

Some Internet veterans opine that real time communication started in 1970's with the advent of instant messaging in mainframe systems. In the late 1980's, the chart servicing was developed which gave rise to the emergence of documenting resources for communications.

Table 1
Sample Example of E-resources of University of Toronto Library (Canada)

Sl No	*Category/Form of E-Resources As of February 26, 2007*	*Licensed*	*Unlicensed*	*Total*
1	Journal Collections	20	0	20
2	e-Books	347,870	10,118	357,988
3	e-Indexes	734	100	834
4	e-Journals	29,435	4,375	33,810
5	e-Media	5	5	10
6	e-Newspapers	3,068	65	3,133
7	PDA/Handheld	3	8	11
8	e-References	940	125	1,065

(Source: http://main.library.utoronto.ca/eir/EIRwhatsnew.cfm)

Since then organisations developed their own e-resources and towards the end part of the 1980's, the concept of sharing their resources were worked out. Earlier, resource-sharing organisations were formed to handle physical resources, but the 1990s saw the broadening of access to e-resources through the development of institutions such as the Virtual Library of Virginia in 1994 and the Illinois Digital Academic Library in 1999. Aftermath, there has been a growing urge for the creation and utilisation of e-resources (Sloan, 2005) worldwide. The emergence of e-books as e-resources has grown since their inception in the early 1980s due to their usefulness in distributing large volumes of interactive multimedia information (Barker, 1998). However, the idea of e-books caught the popular imagination and showed a real promise of succeeding in the consumer marketplace after the mid-1990s. Several factors have converged to make this happen, namely, advances in computer hardware and software (fast, small and medium devices, lab tools, laptops and palm Pilots proliferation); the Internet has made it possible to exchange text and data electronically; and the World Wide Web has made it easy with enabling technologies such as Hyper Text Markup Language (HTML), Extensible Markup Language (XML) and Portable Document Format (PDF) as underlying standards (Rao, 2001) among other developments.

Table: 2 History and Origin of Major E-resources

Sl	*Type of e-resources*	*Product Name*	*Country of Origin*	*Chief Exponent/ Designer*	*Year of Origin*	*Key salient features*
1	e-book	Memex	USA	Vannever Bush	1945	Memex contained a microfilm with a reader and screens for reading from desk
2	e-journals	CHIMO	USA	New Jersey Institute of Technology	1976	The first journal accessed online
3	e-newspapers	Akbar e-Jahan	Pakistan	Mir Khalil-Ur-Rehman	1968	Urdu newspaper first made online
4	ETDs	Electronic Dissertations of Virginia Tech University	USA	Virginia Tech University	1996	Electronic dissertations of graduate programs
5	e-Patents & Standatds	USA electronic Patents	USA	Leon Riebman, American Electronic Laboratories	1975	Patents dissemination through electronic technologies

Source: www.e.u-tokyo ; www.jewishexponent.com ; http://books.google.co.in

Table:3 Major Sources of E-Resources

SN	*E-Resources/Databases*	*Publishers*	*Links*
1	ACM Digital Library (Computer Science)	Association for competing Machinery, USA	http://portal.acm.org/portal.cfm
2	Emerald Full-text	Emerald Group Publishing Ltd., UK	http://www.emeraldinsight.com/
3	IEL Online	Institute of Electrical and Electronic Engineers Inc, USA	http:// www...ieee.org/
4	IOP E-journal(Physics)	Institute of Physics, UK	http:// www.iop.org/
5	Royal Society of Chemistry E-Journals	Royal Society of Chemistry, UK	http:// www.rsc.org/
6	Science Direct (Full text Science Articles	Elsevier B.V. Netherlands	http:// www.sciencedirect.com/
7	Springer Journals	Springer Science+ Business Media Inc., USA	http:// www.springerlink.com/
8	Blackwell Synergy	Blackwell Publishing Ltd, USA	http:// www.blackwell-synergy.com/
9	Wiley On-line journals	Wiley Interscience, USA	http:// www3.interscience.wiley.com/

(Source: *Ghosh* and *Panda*, 2007, pp. 82-93)

Table: 4 Subject Coverage of Major E-Resources

Databases

Subjects	*ACM*	*Emerald*	*IEL*	*IOP*	*RSC*	*Science Direct*	*Springer Link*	*Blackwell Synergy*	*Wiley InterScience*	*Total*
Biology	Yes	-	-	-	-	Yes	Yes	Yes	Yes	05
Chemisty	-	-	-	-	Yes	Yes	-	-	Yes	03
Computer Science	Yes	-	Yes	-	-	Yes	Yes	-	-	04
Economics	-	-	-	-	-	Yes	-	-	-	01
Engineering	-	Yes	Yes	Yes	Yes	Yes	Yes	-	Yes	07
Geography	Yes	-	-	-	-	Yes	-	Yes	Yes	04
Law	-	-	-	-	-	-	-	Yes	-	01
Mathematics	-	-	Yes	-	-	Yes	Yes	Yes	Yes	05
Medicine & Health	-	Yes	-	-	-	Yes	-	Yes	Yes	04
Physics	-	-	-	Yes	-	Yes	-	-	Yes	03
Psychology	-	-	-	-	-	Yes	-	-	-	01
Social Science	-	Yes	-	-	-	Yes	-	-	-	02
Total	03	03	03	02	02	11	04	05	07	40

(Source: *Ghosh* and *Panda,* 2007, pp. 82-93)

At the advent of the twenty-first century, the publishers are more commonly revising the electronic files used in the production of print and some are re-engineering their respective editorial and production processes to produce files better suited to electronic products in the first place. Currently, several modes of electronic publishing are available. Journals are commonly delivered by subscription over the web; reference, legal and medical books are available on CD-ROM or DVDs and are becoming more web-oriented. In the context of e-books, they are more often referred to, a consumer product as a single volume, often a trade book that could be brought over the web and read in a laptop or desktop computer or Personal Digital Assistant (PDA) or a dedicated e-Book Device.

Thus, a great revolution of information technology during the last two decades has created a new era of electronic information with a great proliferation of e-books, e-journals, e-databases, etc., that fascinate the users with an advanced and promising fu ure of e-resources.

Sources of E-resources

E-resources are obtained from various sources, like online databases, individual e-journals, databases of ETDs , open access online journals, e-books, e-newspapers, e-standards/patents, Govt. portals, free websites developed by various organisations, universities, R&D institutions, different search engines, etc. However, online databases that hold detailed full text articles of a good number of journals form the major sources of e-resources. Some of the leaders of e-resources are hinted in Table 3 for an understanding.

The databases listed in Table 4 are the frontline sources of electronic resources that cover thousands of electronic journals covering major disciplines like Science, Engineering, and Social Sciences.

Table 4 depicts that Science Direct is the leading database that covers 11 subjects, followed by Wiley Inter Science 07 Subjects, and Blackwell Synergy 05 Subjects while, at the lower side, IOP and RSC cover two subjects each. On the other hand, Engineering is ccvered by a maximum of 07 databases, followed by Biology, and Mathematics (05 each) while, Economics, Law, and Psychology are each found in only 1 database.

Taxonomy of e-resources

Electronic resources are regarded as the mines of information that are explored through a variety of modern ICT devices, refined and redesigned, and more often stored in the cyber space in the most concrete and compact form, and can be accessed simultaneously from infinite points by a great number of audience (Swain and Panda,2009). The various types of electronic resources that are accessed via electronic media in day to day learning environment are broadly categorised as under:

- e-Books
- e-Journals
- e-databases
- e-Newspapers
- e- Dissertations/Theses
- CD/DVD- ROMs

Future Trends

The future of e-resources is in working with materials that are native to the electronic environment (Lynch, 2003). Many handbooks have years of history in their fields primarily trusted by their print resources, and that trust should be successfully passed on to the electronic formats (Webster, 2003). In an attempt to maintain a level of comfort for users and a level of credibility for sources, materials are not yet being envisioned and created in a completely electronic mode. Many of the print features like pages are still present. The shift is beginning, but it will likely be another generation or two before users are ready to fully abandon a print metaphor in online resources (Epps, 2005) and adapt to the fast growing information and communication technologies.

XML and other programming developments that will allow for meta searching may be the answer to cross-title searching without all titles having to be digitised by one company. Metasearch technologies allow simultaneous searching, from a single access point, across many different information resources (Fryer, 2004). To make meta searching work, all players in the field must agree to follow minimum standards and work with a system that will benefit everyone, not just themselves (Webster, 2003).

Meta searching is still in its infancy, and creating products that are capable of searching a variety of online sources from different publishers at one time has been a challenge. Similar to metasearching of electronic journal databases, the combined search would not provide power-searching capabilities. Those would continue to reside in the native interface for each resource. Standards development work has begun to look at authentication, standard search protocol, common descriptors and taxonomies, among other items (Fryer, 2004). While the future seems to reside with far-reaching meta searching capabilities, many product vendors, however, are not too enthusiastic about working toward this model (Webster,2003). However, the huge marketing of the electronic resources in the recent years would definitely push the vendors to march a few steps ahead of their thought in near future.

Conclusion

The Information Communication Technology (ICT) has created a sense of transformation and formed avenues for development of new products and delivery of electronic information services. Electronic resources which are likely to emerge in the near future may include notes and video of lectures from past courses as well as from other universities, as well as homework assignments in e-forms, e- term papers, e-project reports, context based e-references, e-indexes, e-subject bibliographies, and such other materials through the use of sophisticated searching techniques. Therefore, the users of electronic information keep track of the trends of electronic information for the successful utilisation of the aforesaid resources easily, comprehensively, confidently, and conveniently towards the achievement of the goals of their information seeking in electronic age.

References

Barker, P. (1998). The future of books in an electronic era, *The Electronic Library,* 16 (3), 191-198. Available at: www.emeraldinsight.com (Accessed 12 September 2009).

Epps, A. S. V. (2005). The evolution of electronic reference sources. *Library Hi Tech,* 23 (2), 287-298. Available at: www.emeraldinsight.com (Accessed 12th September 2009).

Fryer, D. (2004). Federated search engines. *Online,* 28 (2), 16-19. Available at: www.emeraldinsight.com (Accessed 12th September 2009).

Ghosh, T K., Panda, K C.(2007). Libraries in the midst of transitioning from print to electronic Collection : a challenge to the libraries of India in 21st century in respect to journal procurement. *Librarianship in 21st Century, National Seminar Proceedings*, Bhubaneswar, SBG, 82-93.

Graham, S R. (2003). Historians and Electronic Resources: A Citation Analysis. *JAHC*,3 (3), 18-24.

http://books.google.co.in (Accessed 27 October 2007).

http://main.library.utoronto.ca/eir/EIRwhatsnew.cfm (Accessed 27 October 2007).

IFLA (2000). Unimarc Guidelines No.60-Universal Bibliographic Control and International MARC Core Programme (UBCIM) Available at: www.pitt.edu/~agtaylor/courses/descbib.html (Accessed on November 3 2007).

Lynch, C. (2003). Digital library opportunities. *The Journal of Academic Librarianship*, 29 (5), 286-289.

Rao, S S. (2001). Familiarisation of Electronic Books. *The Electronic Library*, 19 (4), 247-256.

Saye, J. D. (2001). The Organisation of Electronic Resources in the Library and Information Science Curriculum. *OCLC Systems and Services*,17 (2); 71-78, Available at: www.emeraldinsight.com (Accessed on 12 September 2009).

Sloan, B. (2005). Evolution Takes a Leap. Available at: http://ww.libraryjournal.com/article/CA515807.html (Accessed on 3rd November 2007).

Swain, D. K. and Panda, K.C.(2009). Use of electronic resources in business school libraries of an Indian state: A study of librarians' opinion. *The Electronic Library*, 27 (1), 74-85. Available at: www.emeraldinsight.com/10.1108/02640470910934605

______________ (2009). Use of e-services by faculty members of business schools in a state of India: a study. *Collection Building*, 28 (3), 108-116(9). Available at: www.emeraldinsight.com/10.1108/01604950910971134.

Webster, P (2004). Meta searching in an Academic Environment. *Online*, 28 (2), 20-23. Available at: www.emeraldinsight.com (Accessed 12 September 2009).

______________ (2003). Implications of Expanded Library Electronic Reference Collection. *Online*, 27 (5), 24-27. Available at: www.emeraldinsight.com (Accessed 12 September 2009).

www.etd.uc.edu (Accessed 24 October, 2007).

www.e.u-tokyo (Accessed 27 October 2007).

www.jewishexponent.com (Accessed 27 October 2007).

24

Digital Reference Service: An Overview

— V. S. Midhula Soman and M. Varghese

The developments in ICT have been instrumental in bringing about drastic changes in all facets of Library and Information Science. The emergence of digital reference service, also called virtual reference service, during the early 1990s is one such development. This paper attempts to trace the origin of digital reference service, the different forms of it, its advantages over the traditional reference service, and mentions about the guidelines formulated by the IFLA and the ALA for the delivery of service.

Introduction

The exponential growth of digital information in a variety of formats coupled with the developments in Internet technology during the past few decades has brought in a sea change in all the facets of Library and Information Science (LIS). No activity in the field of LIS can be seen untouched by the influence of the Information Communication Technology.

Many of the libraries and information centres, the world over, today use the Internet as a means for delivery of information, and it has also been proved to be an efficient and cost effective alternative to traditional methods of communication.

In spite of the availability of search engines and other tools for the retrieval of information in response to specific queries, it has become necessary on the part of the LIS profession to extend personalised assistance to their patrons off the reference desk, or even beyond the walls of the library. This has resulted in the development of Internet-based reference services which today are referred to by terms such as digital reference service, electronic reference service, virtual reference service, e-mail reference service, chat reference service, 24/7 reference, etc. This paper attempts to trace the origin of digital reference service, the definitions proposed by different authors, the modes of delivery of service, and the system requirements to deliver the services. The advantages of digital reference service over traditional methods and the guidelines formulated by agencies like the American Library Association and the IFLA are also covered.

Origin of Digital Reference Service

Personalised assistance to library users in accessing the various resources and availing the services of the libraries was rather rare during the early days of libraries, as the main function then was preserving the documents which were rare entities. Once the libraries got transformed into service institutions, the librarians at least occasionally started to attend to what is called reference work. But it was since the third quarter of the nineteenth century that assisting readers began to be considered as part of the services in a library (Kaplan, 1947). Sam Rothstein (1955) traces the historical development of reference service in libraries in the United States. By 1896, reference work became a permanent part of the American library scene, and by 1906 it was made part of library school curriculum (Katz, 1969).

Some of the early definitions of reference work were: "that part of library administration which deals with the assistance given to readers in their use of the resources of the library" and "a direct or sympathetic and informed personal aid in interpreting library collection for study and research" (Wyer, 1930). Margaret Hutchins (1944) defined it so as to include "the direct, personal aid within a library to persons in search of information for whatever purpose and also various activities especially aimed at making information as easily available as possible.' Though one can point out differences in the scope of reference work as per these definitions, all of them agree in one point, namely, the importance of personal assistance to users. Katz (1969) has made a distinction between "direct" and "indirect" reference; the former covers person-to-person relationship between librarian and the patrons, especially in answering queries and in providing instructions. The latter consists of behind-the-scene activities in preparing for the direct reference. Preparation and maintenance of catalogues and bibliographies, development of reference collection, evaluation of reference books, inter-library loans, etc., are included here.

Ranganathan preferred 'reference service' to 'reference work' and he defined it as "the process of establishing contact between a reader and his document in a personal way." The term 'his document' is further clarified as to mean every one of the precise documents needed by him at the moment and also all the documents likely to be of use to him at the moment (Ranganathan, 1940).

For the first time in 1937 a post-designated as "reference librarian" was accepted at the Madras University Library. Subsequently terms like 'information service' and 'bibliographic instruction' were introduced to mean the various facets of readers assistance in libraries.

Bunge (1999) has categorised reference service into three broad groups. The first one is named 'information service' which involves either finding the required information on behalf of the users or assisting users in finding the information that they seek. The second group, broadly defined as 'information literacy skills', comprises training the users in making best use of the resources and services of the library. Guidance given to users in selecting the most appropriate information sources and services to meet a specific information need constitutes the third type of reference service.

Digital reference has emerged as a consequence of the application of the Internet in the field of Library and Information Science. From the very early stages of the development of the Internet, librarians have started using it to facilitate rendering services to their patrons. Initially it was in the form of bookmarking the sites, both free and subscription-based, which were found useful to their clientèle and making them available within the library. This may be considered as the first generation of the web-based reference service or digital reference. The second generation digital reference service is characterised by catering to the needs of the clientele who do not make their physical presence at the reference desk, but logg on to the site of the library either for consulting some ready reference source or for getting some information, say about the availability of a book or a journal. The first step towards this was providing the Online Public Access Catalogue, with the URL of the digital resources held by the library. However, access to the resources was restricted subject to the rules and regulations of the library, and may be free access from anywhere or restricted access through the Intranet within the library. The 'Electronic Access to Reference Service' (EARS), launched by the University of Maryland Health Services Library in Baltimore in 1984, is cited as one of the first reference service to go online (Padmini Kaza). The starting AskERIC in 1992 and the launching of Internet Public Library in 1995 have resulted in increased popularity and wide acceptance of Digital Reference Service at the global level.

Definitions

As already indicated the terms 'digital reference services', 'web-based reference services', 'electronic reference services', 'virtual reference service' and '24/7 reference service' are used interchangeably in the literature in LIS. Lankes (2005) prefers 'digital reference' and it is defined as "Internet-based questions and answer services that connect users with individuals who possess specialised subject or skill expertise." Janes, Carter and Memmott developed their own definition as a mechanism by which people can submit their questions and have them answered by a library staff member through some electronic means (e-mail, chat, web forms, etc., not in person or over the phone (Janes et al, 1999). According to Berlot et al (2000) digital reference services refer to a network of expertise, intermediation and resources put at the disposal of a user seeking answers in an online/ networked environment.

A digital reference occurs when a question is received electronically and responded to electronically. White (2001) prefers virtual reference service and he defines it as "an information access service in which people ask questions via electronic means (such as e-mail and Web forms). In turn knowledgeable individuals answer the questions, and responses are transmitted via electronic means." Sloan (2002) enumerates the different types of media used for the delivery of service. They include e-mail, web forms, chat, video, web customer call centre software, Voice over Internet Protocol (VoIP), etc. The Reference and User Services Association (2004) also favours 'virtual reference is reference service' in their guidelines, and while defining the term it is stated as being "initiated electronically, often in real-time, where patrons employ computers or other Internet technology to communicate with reference staffs, without being physically present. Communication channels used frequently in virtual reference include chat, videoconferencing, Voice over IP, co-browsing, e-mail and instant messaging." A technical note on virtual reference in the site of the Public Library Association, a division of the American Library Association, defines virtual reference as "online reference service that enables library patrons to ask reference questions through a library's website. The user may be at home, in an office, at school or in a library. Some virtual reference services also place answers to frequently asked questions (FAQs), selected reference tools, and access to selected databases on the website. The question answering service using the Internet technology is the essential component, without which the use of the name 'virtual reference, is misleading" (Boss, 2008).

Service Delivery

Service delivery models in digital reference are usually categorised into two, namely, asynchronous and synchronous based on whether a real time two-way communication is possible or not. The asynchronous model is characterised by a time delay in providing the service and communication only in one direction at a time. E-mail, web forms, Ask-a-service, etc., are typical examples. In the synchronous model transactions take place in 'real time' with an immediate response to the query.

E-mail

E-mail is the major form of information delivery in digital reference service. Users have the provision to click directly on the e-mail address given in the home page of the library so as to activate the email software, or they can send a message to the email address of the library using their own software. The easy availability of the service in the net has made it the most popular form of communication for the users. There is no need for any extra software. Though users can state the question with sufficient clarity by giving the necessary explanatory details, in the absence of reference interview, at least in some cases, it may not be possible to know the exact requirement. Moreover, the non-verbal elements that would give an indication of the specific requirement of the enquirer is also lacking. One of the advantages of e-mail is that it reduces the psychological barriers on the part of at least some of the users in asking the librarians for help face to face. While sending the answers it is possible to add images as well as other data files as supplements. The reference librarian can pool the answers delivered to various users so as to build a knowledge base for future use.

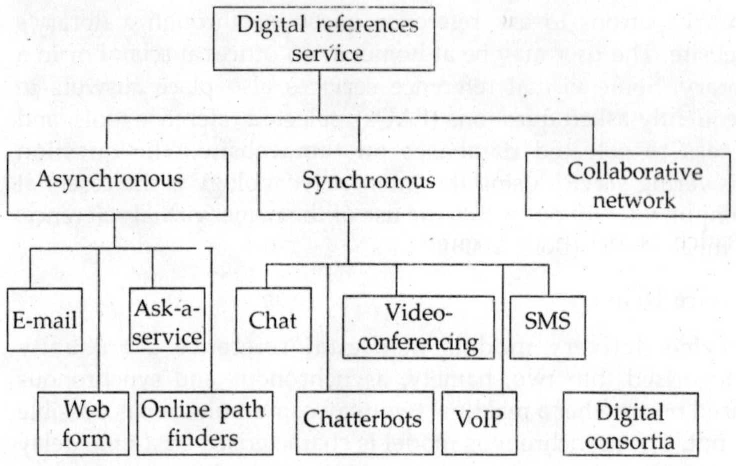

Figure 1

Web Forms

Some of the limitations of e-mail reference, especially the absence of sufficient details to clarify the query can be overcome by using a pre-designed web form for submitting the query. The web forms, made available on the site of the library, consist of several defined fields which have to be filled up by the users and submitted online. Some libraries use simple forms which contain essential data such as name and address, email id, telephone number and a statement of the query. Others include optional fields so as serve as a substitute for a reference interview. Patrons are therefore forced to give more detailed and structured information than in an e-mail. However, it is observed that in actual practice many users do not fill in these comprehensive forms which they consider superfluous. The answer will be sent to the user by e-mail. However the web forms have limitations in dealing with queries relating to complicated research problems.

Ask-a-Service

Ask-a-Services are usually corporate-sponsored websites that allow users to ask questions and receive answers free of charge from public information located mainly on the world wide web or from proprietary databases and networks of field experts. A typical example is the 'Ask-a-scientist' service offered by the 'Newton BBS', a free Electronic Bulletin Board System for science, mathematics, computer science and technology operated by the Argonne National Laboratory, one of the largest and oldest national labs under the Department of Energy, United States. The service is primarily aimed at K-12 students and teachers. Questions can be emailed and they will be attended by voluntary scientists who will send the answer by email. The number of questions handled by this service is in the range of 150 to 300 per day. It was started in 1991 and it maintains an archive of questions and answers handles since its inception. The US Geological survey offers a similar 'Ask-a-geologist' service. (http:/ walrus.wr.usgs.gov/ask-a-geologist). The 'Ask-a-librarian' service offered by the Library of Congress (http://www.loc.gov/rr/askalib/), the Cochin University of Science and Technology (http://library.cusat.ac.in/ask.php) the Central Library of the IIT Kharagpur (http://www.library.iitkgp.ernet.in/?q=node/20) are examples of similar services offered by libraries.

Chat Reference

Chat reference is also called Real Time Reference or Live Reference. Here librarians and users can 'speak' to each other in real time on the internet with the help of a special text-based software. The transaction involves a split web screen; in one screen users type questions and the response of the librarian can be instantly seen in the second screen. It can be used as a means for real time reference interview. The librarians can call the web pages or other electronic references where the required information can be found, and furnish it to the user, along with a copy of the whole dialogue. The libraries in the United States started to use chat software for reference purposes by the end of the nineties. The increasing popularity of chat among the youngsters favour the libraries to make use of it for reference service. However it is quite difficult to satisfactorily answer queries of long range type by chat. Moreover, it is also impossible to transmit documents like printed statistics, tables, illustrations etc. The language and jargon developed in chat circles also pose problems while using it for reference service. Therefore it may not be possible to fulfill all the requirements of an efficient and user-friendly information service through chat.

Chatterbots

In Chatterbots the questions submitted by the users are analysed by a computer software using the keywords contained in it, applying linguistic programmes and mechanisms. The knowledge base of the system may contain the answer to the question, and if so it is offered to the user. Here the user does not communicate with a librarian, and therefore some authors consider it as an asynchronous mode of delivery. The enquirers get the response from an interactive database that contains a range of answers prepared previously.

Chatterbots are technically similar to full-text search engines, but they portray the illusion of an online chat because the users enter their queries in the fields provided and receive immediate response. To increase the attractiveness, they make use of symbolic bodies in the form of animated images. They are often used as help assistants in computer software, as adverts on company websites and as additions to digital reference. They are available 24/7 and to several users concurrently. However, they only provide answers to standard questions and are in essence a simple FAQ which simulates a chat using artificial characters.

Voice over Internet Protocol

Voice over Internet Protocol, also termed as audio chat or Internet phoning, enables patrons to make a telephone call parallel to other Internet applications. Speakers and microphones installed to PC are needed at both ends. Software that allows communication via VoIP targeted to digital reference service are available in the market. Some web contact centres, e.g., LiveHelper (http://www.livehelper.com/), Click & Care (http://www.clickandcare.com) and LivePerson (http://www. liveperson.com/), already offer VoIP. This technique has the potential to take over from the comparably complicated synchronous chat communication on the Internet. VoIP offers the chance to improve and to speed up Internet communication. Since there is no need to use a key board to type the questions, many users favour this mode of digital reference service.

SMS reference service

SMS, also known as text messaging, is a form of digital reference in which users can send questions on their cell phones via SMS. It is an exciting new service designed specifically to allow libraries to expand their reference delivery methods to include the mobile/cell phone text messaging system so popular with the youth of today. The service is simple to use, highly effective, and can be implemented by any library anywhere in the world where SMS services are available.

Reference via Video

The software for videoconferencing has also been tested for digital reference service by several American libraries. There is an additional requirements of webcams and software packages at both the ends, and hence more expensive when compared to VoIP. Today videoconferencing is widely used for academic and administrative purposes, especially for disseminating lectures by eminent teachers to the students in different campuses.

Collaborative Reference

Access to the resources of a group of libraries would enable rendering reference service of a better quality and wider coverage than with that of an isolated library. It would also result in sharing of workload so that the service will be available for a longer duration per day. Some of the major projects in this area include the "Enquire" of the British public libraries (now seems to be stopped), the Danish project "Biblioteksvagten" (http://www.biblioteksvagten.dk/) which includes over 60 public and academic libraries and "QuestionPoint" (http:/

www.questionpoint.org/). an ambitious project jointly lead by OCLC and the Library of Congress. Though the QuestionPoint has a worldwide participation of libraries from Australia, Asia and Europe the focus is on American libraries. There is a library profile module used to coordinate the collaboration amongst the participating libraries. This profile module stores information about each library's central subject areas and main competencies, which enables the software to automatically forward specific queries to the most relevant library available at that point in time.

How Do Digital Reference Services Work?

Although there are variations among the different forms of services, all digital reference and Ask-a-service functions in a more or less similar manner. Human intermediaries evaluate incoming questions via e-mail or web interface and then decide on an appropriate course of action. New questions may be checked against an archive of previously answered questions for an appropriate answer, and if no suitable answers found, passed along to an expert for answering. The expert supplies the necessary information, which may consist of an actual answer or a pointer to additional resources, or some combination of the two. Responses are sent to the user's e-mail address or posted to a website for the user to access later. In some smaller Ask-a-services, the experts themselves may also monitor the incoming questions.

The task of creating and managing internet-based question and answer services is complicated by the ever-changing nature of the Internet. Services receive questions electronically, then route the questions to an appropriate expert according to a set of Internet rules. The questions progress to a pool of possible respondents, where they are qued according to some criteria, such as user need data received, etc. In services staffed by multiple experts some sort of triage may be initially performed to help expedite the answer process such as selecting the best expert to answer a particular question. The expert composes an answer in compliance with service policy, and replies are sent to the users.

A digital reference system involves the use of appropriate software also, a commonly used one is that of the LSSI, a commercial library solutions company. They have worked with a number of commercial software vendors to create various products and services for libraries interested in providing digital reference. They offer both software and a web reference centre for outsourced virtual reference. Subscribers to LSSI need not install any hardware or software locally. The servers supporting the system operate on an application service provider (ASP) model. The library operator uses a Web browser to control the remote sessions. LSSI has also developed a fully functional 24x7 web Reference Centre. The centre operates out of their headquarters in Germantown, Maryland, and is staffed remotely with professional librarians trained in online reference. Their reference staff provides everything from backup and overflow reference support, and second-level and after hours reference services, to a fully staffed 24x7 online reference service. The librarians come from a variety of backgrounds including special, academic, and public libraries, and are trained by LSSI to meet specific library requirements.

Guidelines and Standards

Agencies such as the International Federation of Library Associations and Institutions (IFLA) and the American Library Association have formulated guidelines and standards on digital reference service (DRS). The revision of the guidelines on digital reference by IFLA as on 6 March 2008 is available in http://archive.ifla.org/VII/s36/pubs/drg03.htm. It is in two sections administration of DRS and practice of digital reference. The former gives guidelines relating to policy issues such as the scope, target group and type questions, planning, staffing, training of staff, factors to be considered while designing the user interface, legislation issues, publicity and promotion, evaluation, and collaboration with other institutions. The second section dealing with the practice of digital reference, gives general guidelines on standard of service, the points to be considered while organising the answer to queries, and a rather detailed guidelines on chat service and chat sessions.

The MARS Digital Reference Guidelines Ad Hoc Committee, of the Reference and User Services Association (RUSA), which a division of the American Library Association, prepared a set of guidelines and got approved by the RUSA Board of Directors June 2004. It is available in http://www.ala.org/ala/mgrps/divs/rusa/

resources/guidelines/virtrefguidelines.cfm. The guidelines are grouped under five subheads, namely, definition of virtual reference, preparing for virtual reference service, provision of service, organisation of service, and privacy. The need for integrating VRS with other services of the library, the involvement of administration and computing staff and evaluation are covered under the preparation aspect. Guidelines on the scope of clientele, parameters of service, service behaviour particularly the behaviour and competency of the staff and detailed guidelines on collaborative virtual reference are given in the second section. The section on organisation deals with integration of Virtual Reference Service with the existing reference service, infrastructure requirements, finance, personnel, marketing of the service, and evaluation. Guidelines on the privacy aspect of the communication between the library stall and patrons are given in the final section.

Advantages of Digital Reference Service

Digital reference service has several advantages over the traditional reference service. Some of them are as follows.

- The service offered by consortia of libraries in a region offers the member libraries the opportunity to share reference questions with each other using the Internet and other communication technologies.
- Collaborative digital reference service allows individual institutions to share expertise as well as resources.
- The hours of service can be expanded, if necessary on a shared basis so that it will be available round the clock.
- Enables to provide access to a large collection of knowledge, serve the patrons in a better way by providing valuable information on a timely fashion.
- Ensures international visibility.
- Enhanced public relations benefits by having satisfied users and by providing information of a high quality.
- Geographically unrestricted access. Digital reference service may be accessible to users from any place.
- Multimedia and hyperlink facility.
- Online retrieval system is more flexible than other retrieval systems.

- Electronic catalogue provides enhanced access to the collection of a library.

Disadvantages

Digital reference service cannot be considered free from any demerits, particularly because of the lack of direct interaction between the patrons and reference librarian. The following are identified as the major limitations:

- Digital reference transaction is more complex and time consuming than traditional reference service.
- It is difficult to predict the cost of online retrieval system and therefore not easy to estimate the budget allocation.
- Although many databases are common among the several information service providers, some databases of preference may be available in only one system.
- Search interface of the same database may vary across systems and it will affect the effectiveness of search.
- Librarians often juggle real-time patron requests with those of walk-in or phone patrons.
- The cost of software does not make digital reference service cost effective. Coffman and Arret (2004) even argues that the costs associated with software, training and staffing may not justify continuing the service.
- Staff training is needed to use selected real time tools.
- Ongoing technical support must be available to maintain the system.

Conclusion

Digital reference service has now been got established as a powerful means for the free exchange of information and the promotion of interactive learning. Thousands of organisations have already implemented it for the delivery of information to their clientele as an efficient alternative to traditional methods. But very few of the Indian libraries have started offering digital reference service through their sites. By proper planning and implementation of digital reference practices, libraries in higher education institutions can ensure effective creation and maintenance of exemplary digital reference service for the patrons to the best of their satisfaction.

References

Bertot et al (2000). *Statistics and performance measures for public library networked services*. Chicago: American Library Association.

Boss, Richard W (2007). Virtual reference. *In Public Library Association, Technical,* Notes. Available at: http://www.ala.org/ala/mgrps/divs/pla/plapublications/platechnotes/virtualreference.cfm (Accessed on14 August 2007)

Bunge, C. A. (1999). Reference services. *Reference Librarian,* 66, 185-199.

Coffman, S. and Arret, L., (2004). To chat or not to chat: taking another look at virtual reference. *Searcher,* 12(7), 38-46.

Hutchins, Margaret (1944). *Introduction to reference work*. Chicago : American Library Association.

Janes, J. et al, (1999). The Internet public library handbook [review]. *Managing Information,* 6(8). 87.

Kaplan, Louis (1947). The early history of reference service in the United States. *Library Review,* 83, 286-90.

Katz, William A (1969). *Introduction to reference work,* Vol. 2, Reference services. New York : McGraw-Hill Book Company.

Lankes, David R. (2005). Digital reference research: fusing research and practice. *Reference and User Services Quarterly,* 44(4), 320-326.

Penka, Jeffrey T. (2003). The technological challenges of digital reference: an overview. *D-Lib Magazine,* 9(2).

Ranganathan, S.R. (1940). *Reference service*. Bangalore: Sarada Ranganathan Endowment for Library Science, 2006 reprint, 53.

Reference and User Services Association (2004b). Guidelines for implementing and maintaining virtual reference services. Available at: http://www.ala.org/ala/rusa/rusaprotools/referenceguide/virtrefguidelines.htm (Accessed on 20 September 2005).

Rothstein, Samuel (1955). *The development of references services through academic traditions, public library practice and special librarianship*. Chicago: American Library Association.

White, M. D. (2001). Digital reference services: Framework for analysis and evaluation. *Library & Information Science Research, 23,* 211-231.

Wyer, James I. (1930). *Reference Work*. Chicago: American Library Association, 4.

Zanin-Yost, Alessia (2004). Digital reference: what the past has taught us and what the future will hold. *Library Philosophy and Practice,* 7(1).

VII
Scientometrics/Webometrics

25

Authorship Pattern and Collaborative Research in the Field of Hepatitis

—B. Ramesh Babu and J. Ramakrishnan

This paper presents a scientometric analysis of the authorship pattern in the field of hepatitis covered in three bibliographic databases, namely MEDLINE, CINAHL and IPA for the period 1984-2003. MEDLINE covered the maximum of 75,750 records during the study period 1984 to 2003, followed by CINAHL and IPA databases. In this paper only authorship pattern in the field of hepatitis discussed. About 81 per cent of the total contributions represent collaborative research. The degree of collaboration has been arrived at 0.84. The value of Co-Authorship Index (CAI) for single author paper shows a declining trend from one block year period to another block. The pattern of Collaborative Coefficient results reveals that a majority of the countries have shown a higher degree of collaboration research. It is found that when the number of contributors increases, correspondingly the number of contributions decreases.

Introduction

The study of authorship pattern or productivity is one of the important aspects in the scientometric analysis. This study was aimed at to examine the authorship pattern and collaborative research in the field of 'Hepatitis' with the help of bibliographic databases namely MEDLINE, CINAHL and IPA. Generally it is necessary to concentrate on authorship pattern to assess the research contributions in a field and hepatitis research is not an exception.

We have already discussed the "Trends in the Growth of Literature on Hepatitis" and "National Patterns of Research output and Priorities in Hepatitis" in our previous papers. The first paper analysed the growth of literature output in the field of hepatitis covered in three bibliographic databases namely MEDLINE, CINAHL and IPA. It has been analysed by using bibliometric indicators such as Relative Growth Rate (RGR) and Doubling Time (Dt) (Ramesh Babu and Ramakrishnan, 2007). The second paper presents a scientometric analysis of National Patterns of Research output and Priorities in the sub-fields of Hepatitis covered in three bibliographic databases, namely MEDLINE, CINAHL and IPA. The literature covered in three databases for the period 1984-2003 was considered (Ramesh Babu and Ramakrishnan, 2008). This paper represents a revised part of the doctoral dissertation of the second author (Ramakrishnan, 2006).

Literature Review

Authorship pattern and collaborative research in Psychology has been analysed by Karisiddappa et al. (1990) based on the data collected from 'Psychological Abstracts'. Narendra Kumar and Ramesh Babu (1999) analysed the literature published in ILA bulletin during the year 1986-1996 discussing authorship pattern, citation pattern, subject covered, ranking of the contributors, nature of contributions, bibliographic forms, of cited documents, etc. Bhagavathi Sudha and Ramesh Babu (2000) analysed the Indian contributions on 'Information Technology' covered in the Indian Library and Information Science Literature during the period 1990-1993, with respect to degree of collaboration, bibliographic forms, sub-fields of information technology, etc. Farahat (2002) examined the pattern of authorship in 19 Egyptian journals of agricultural sciences. The scientific productivity of authors in theoretical population genetics was examined by Karisiddappa et al. (2002). Shirabe and Tomizawa (2002) studied on the likelihood of overseas access to international co-authorships, proposed a new index for international scientific co-authorship, which was based on a simple model of domestic and international co-authorships. Wilkes et al. (2002) have reported investigations on Nursing Research published by Australian authors from 1995-2000 in 11 Nursing journals, from Australia,

UK and the USA. Dutt, Garg, and Bali (2003) analysed 1317 papers published in the volumes of the international journal *Scientometrics* during 1978 to 2001. They noticed that the single authored papers dominated the scientometric output, but however, multi-authorial papers were gaining momentum. Koteswara Rao and Raghavan (2003) in their study on collaboration in superconductivity research in India indicates an increased interaction between countries, institutions, and disciplines, leading to "global research networks". The Indian output on Air Pollution research covered in E-CD was analysed quantitatively by Parameswaran, Ramesh Babu and Gopalakrishnan (2003). The various bibliometric indicators have been used in the analysis, with regard to the authorship pattern, Relative Growth Rate, Doubling time, Ranking of core journals, and core research institutions in India. Mapping global science using international co-authorship and a comparison of 1990 and 2000 using the Science Citation Index (CD-ROM version) for 1990 and 2000 were examined by Wagner and Leydesdorff (2003). Rajendran, Ramesh Babu and Gopalakrishnan (2005) analysed the global output of "fibre optics" research with regard to Growth of literature by year-wise, country-wise, authorship pattern, bibliographic forms, ranking of core journals and nature of research have been analysed.

Hepatitis

Hepatitis is a disease as old as the Greek and Roman hills. Hippocrates was the first to note the occurrence of jaundice epidemics – the telltale yellowing of the skin that heralds the fact that the liver can no longer properly cleanse the blood (Turklington, 1998).

According to Stedman's medical dictionary (2000) "Hepatitis is an inflammation of liver, due usually to viral infection but sometimes to toxic agents. Previously endemic throughout much of the developing world, viral hepatitis now ranks as a major public health problem in industrialised nations. The 3 most common type of viral hepatitis (A, B, and C) affects millions worldwide".

For the past 25 years, worldwide clinicians, epidemiologists, microbiologists, pathologists, molecular biologists and other basic scientists have contributed immensely to the knowledge on Hepatitis.

A large number of articles, papers, reports and so on are being published on research work in hepatitis. Since there is a continuous generation of information in this field, it is warranted to study quantitatively the output of literature by applying Bibliometric/Scientometric indicators. The study of this nature would benefit to identify the authorship pattern of literature in the field of hepatitis.

Objectives

1. To analyse the extent of authorship pattern. i.e. Single Vs. Multiple authors in the field of hepatitis.
2. To examine the author productivity and degree of collaboration in hepatitis literature output.
3. To analyse the Co-Authorship Index (CAI) and Collaborative Coefficient (CC) in the field of literature on hepatitis.
4. To identify the ranking of authors in the field of literature on hepatitis.

Methodology

The three databases, namely, MEDLINE (Medical Literature Analysis and Retrieval Systems Online) CD-ROM, CINAHL (Cumulative Index to Nursing and Allied Health Literature) CD-ROM and IPA (International Pharmaceutical Abstract) CD-ROM, were used for the purpose of data collection on hepatitis research. MEDLINE CD-ROM, the world leading international bibliographic database produced by the National Library of Medicine of United States, has been used. It deals with the biomedical literature, containing references to articles from more than 4,800 journals which cover from 1950 to the present. The CINAHL CD-ROM database is the only compact disc designed specifically to meet the information needs of nurses and allied health professionals. It covers records from 1982 to the current period. IPA CD-ROM began in 1964 as a print service and become computerised in 1970 which includes Clinical and Technical Drug Information, Pharmacy practice, Pharmaceutical education, Legal aspects of pharmacy, and Drugs, covering over 850 journals. In order to limit the chance of missing related articles, it is thought just and necessary to cover more than one database and therefore MEDLINE, CINAHL and IPA databases have been taken into consideration for searching in order to achieve a comprehensive coverage of hepatitis in literature for the analysis. The data thus collected from the source databases on the literary production of 'Hepatitis' for the period 1984-2003 has been analysed by using scientometric indicators such as Degree of Collaboration (DC), Co-Authorship Index (CAI), Collaborative Coefficient (CC) and Author Productivity (AP).

Analysis and Discussion

Quantum of literature published on Hepatitis during 1984–2003

A total of 82,617 records covered in three databases and the duplicate records are about 4 per cent (3,305) of total productivity. After the elimination of duplicate records, there are 79,312 records in the hepatitis literature has been presented in Table 1 according to year of publication. It is found that there is a gradual growth of literature in the subject of study by year after year. The year 2002 has marked a maximum of 7.59 per cent out of total productivity in the study period.

Authorship Pattern

To identify author productivity and authorship pattern the paper has attempted to analyse the following aspects:

1. Extent of authorship pattern. i.e. Single Vs. Multiple authors.
2. Degree of Collaboration (DC).
3. Pattern of Co-Authorship Index (CAI).
4. Collaborative Coefficient (CC).
5. Ranking of Authors.

Single Vs Multiple Authors

The year-wise distribution of contributions according to number of authors is shown in table 2. It is evident from the Table 2 that nearly one-third (31.98%) of the contributions were by more than five authors. About 85 per cent represent two and more authors, which mean collaborative research is evident in the hepatitis field and it is same in most of the scientific fields. (Figure 1).

Table 1

Quantum of Literature Published in Hepatitis by Year-wise

S.No.	*Year*	*Frequency*	*%*	*Cumulative %*
1	1984	2,538	3.20	
2	1985	2,516	3.17	6.37
3	1986	2,566	3.24	9.61
4	1987	2,715	3.42	13.03
5	1988	2,679	3.38	16.41
6	1989	2,993	3.77	20.18
7	1990	3,382	4.26	24.45
8	1991	3,543	4.47	28.91
9	1992	3,919	4.94	33.85
10	1993	3,976	5.01	38.87
11	1994	4,084	5.15	44.02
12	1995	4,584	5.78	49.80
13	1996	4,311	5.44	55.23
14	1997	4,458	5.62	60.85
15	1998	4,697	5.92	66.78
16	1999	5,083	6.41	73.18
17	2000	5,440	6.86	80.04
18	2001	5,560	7.01	87.05
19	2002	6,019	7.59	94.64
20	2003	4,249	5.36	100.00
Total		79,312	100.00	

Data in Table 3 reveals the state of authorship pattern. As already mentioned multiple authors' papers constitute the major percentage (81.46%). However, it was noticed that a meager percent (2.96%) represent anonymous authorship. The ratio of single and multi-authored papers is 1:5.3. The high incident by multiple authorship is the phenomena of scientific research. (Figures 2 and 3).

Table 2: Authorship Pattern in Hepatitis

Authors	*1984*	*1985*	*1986*	*1987*	*1988*	*1989*	*1990*	*1991*	*1992*	*1993*	*1994*	*1995*	*1996*	*1997*	*1998*	*1999*	*2000*	*2001*	*2002*	*2003*	*No. of records*	*%*
Single Author	518	463	440	439	485	535	585	582	631	628	572	700	597	621	673	761	838	810	907	574	12359	15.58
Two Authors	426	379	390	382	371	413	480	431	482	517	498	615	480	545	549	564	674	736	711	538	10181	12.84
Three Authors	382	381	386	429	392	456	484	468	510	529	582	611	560	488	555	623	625	608	701	447	10217	12.88
Four Authors	383	370	397	376	390	400	444	492	513	504	519	581	540	527	542	533	597	617	692	474	9891	12.47
Five Authors	315	336	348	375	338	342	384	399	443	428	459	489	508	499	494	546	574	598	645	430	8950	11.28
More than Five Authors	465	529	557	648	627	764	923	1062	1206	1270	1359	1492	1513	1615	1739	1826	1953	2020	2171	1626	25365	31.98
Anonymous	49	58	48	66	76	83	82	109	134	100	95	96	113	163	145	230	179	171	192	160	2349	2.96
Total	2538	2516	2566	2715	2679	2993	3382	3543	3919	3976	4084	4584	4311	4458	4697	5083	5440	5560	6019	4249	79312	100.00

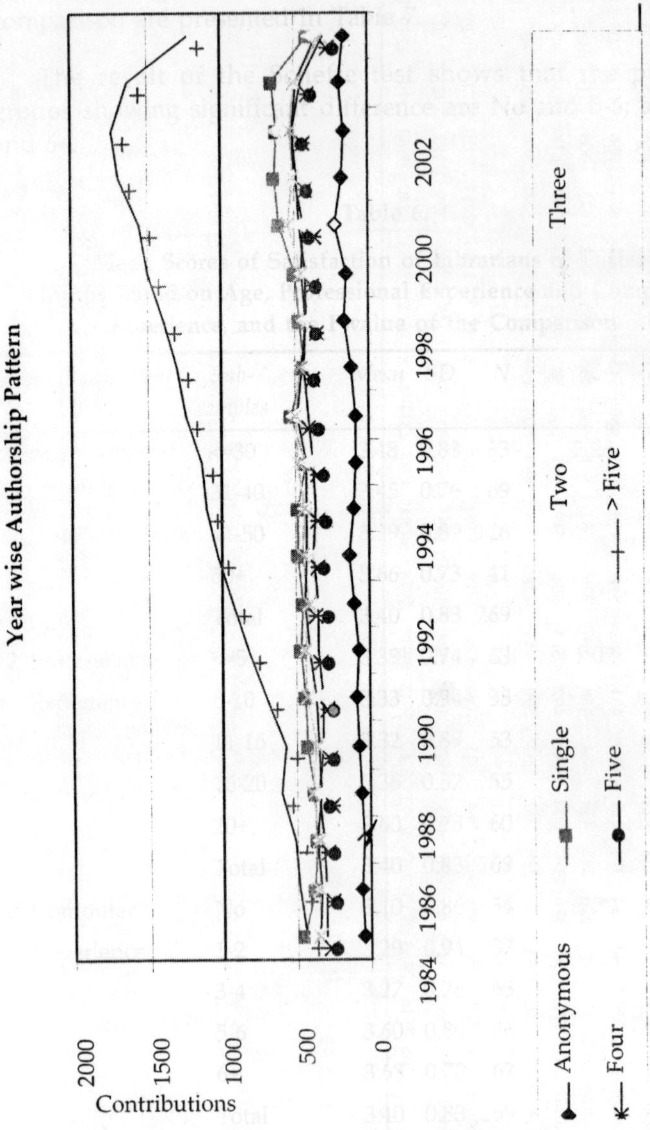

Figure 1: Year-wise Authorship Pattern

Similar studies in Phytomorphology (Maheswarappa and Nagappa, 1981), Applied Sciences (Mheswarappa and Mathias, 1984), Plant Breeding (Maheswarappa and Savadatti, 1990), Geology (Chakraborthy, 1981), Zoological Sciences (Begum and Rajendra, 1990), Agricultural Sciences (Munshi, Vashisht and Gautam, 1993), Medicinal and Aromatic Plants (Mishra and Mishra, 1991), and Environmental Genetic Toxicology (Reddy and Sharma, 1988) also showed that the number of single authorship papers are much less when compared to multi-authored papers.

Table 3: Single Vs Multi-Authored Papers in Hepatitis Research

Year	*Anonymous*		*Single Authored*		*Multi Authored*		*Total*	*%*
	Papers	*%*	*Papers*	*%*	*Papers*	*%*		
1984	49	1.93	518	20.41	1971	77.66	2538	3.20
1985	58	2.31	463	18.40	1995	79.29	2516	3.17
1986	48	1.87	440	17.15	2078	80.98	2566	3.24
1987	66	2.43	439	16.17	2210	81.40	2715	3.42
1988	76	2.84	485	18.10	2118	79.06	2679	3.38
1989	83	2.77	535	17.88	2375	79.35	2993	3.77
1990	82	2.42	585	17.30	2715	80.28	3382	4.26
1991	109	3.08	582	16.43	2852	80.50	3543	4.47
1992	134	3.42	631	16.10	3154	80.48	3919	4.94
1993	100	2.52	628	15.79	3248	81.69	3976	5.01
1994	95	2.33	572	14.01	3417	83.67	4084	5.15
1995	96	2.09	700	15.27	3788	82.64	4584	5.78
1996	113	2.62	597	13.85	3601	83.53	4311	5.44
1997	163	3.66	621	13.93	3674	32.41	4458	5.62
1998	145	3.09	673	14.33	3879	82.58	4697	5.92
1999	230	4.52	761	14.97	4092	80.50	5083	6.41
2000	179	3.29	838	15.40	4423	81.31	5440	6.86
2001	171	3.08	810	14.57	4579	82.36	5560	7.01
2002	192	3.19	907	15.07	4920	81.74	6019	7.59
2003	160	3.77	574	13.51	3515	82.73	4249	5.36
Total	2349	2.96	12359	15.58	64604	81.46	79312	100.00

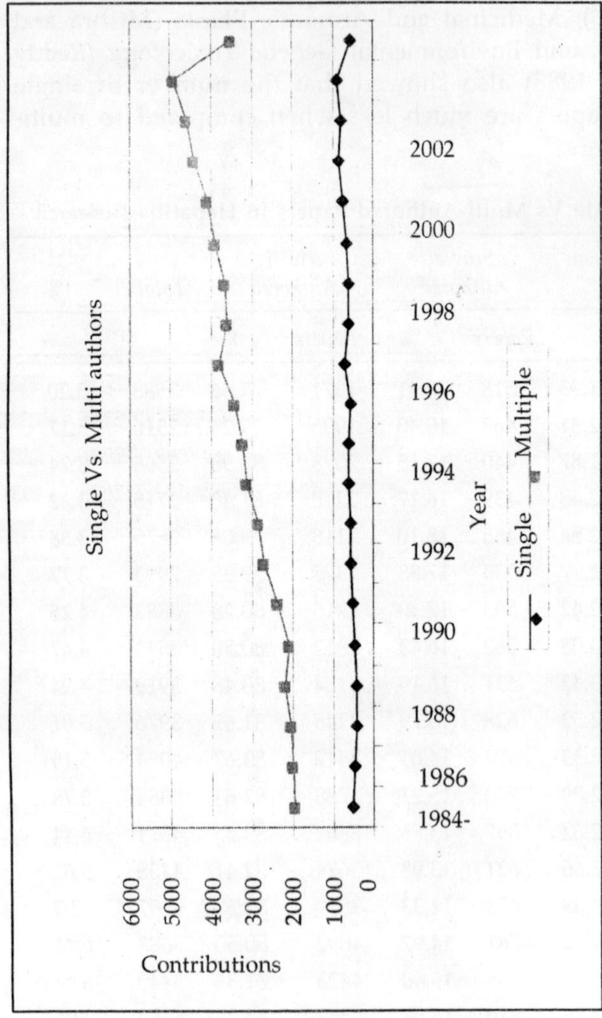

Figure 2 Single Vs. Multi-authored Papers in Hepatitis Research

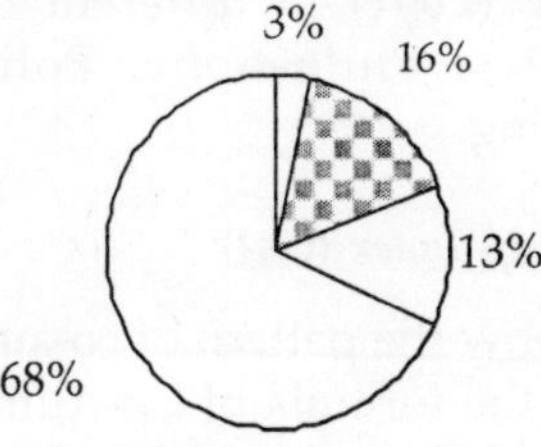

☐ Anonymous ☐ Single ☐ Two ☐ More than two

Figure 3 Authorship Pattern in Hepatitis

Degree of Collaboration

The Degree of Collaboration of authors year-wise is shown in Table 4. The extent of Degree of Collaboration in hepatitis research has been measured with the help of the formula devised by Subramaniam (1993).

The formula is

$$C = Nm / Nm + Ns$$

where

C = Degree of Collaboration in a discipline

Nm = Number of multiple authored papers

Ns = Number of single authored papers

Accordingly, the Degree of Collaboration has been calculated for the year 1984 is as follows:

$$C = \frac{1971}{1971 + 516} = \frac{1971}{2489} = 0.79$$

Likewise the Degree of Collaboration is calculated for every year and presented in Table 4.

The year-wise Degree of Collaboration falls between 0.79 and 0.86. The Degree of Collaboration for any subject ranges from 0.01 to 0.99 and it is always below 1 which has been proved by Karisiddappa, Maheswarappa and Shirol (1990) in Psychology and Bandyopadhyay (2001) in different disciplines such as Mathematics, Physics, Philosophy, Political Science and Mechanical Engineering.

Pattern of Co-Authorship Index (CAI)

In order to find out how the pattern of co-authors have changed during 1984 to 2003, the formula of Co-Authorship Index (CAI) suggested by Garg and Padhi (2001) has been used.

For calculating CAI the entire data set was divided into four blocks.

$$CAI = \{(Nij / Nio) / (Noj / Noo)\} * 100$$

Nij : number of papers having j authors in block I;

Nio : Total output of block I;

Noj : number of papers having j authors for all blocks;

Noo : total number of papers for all authors and all blocks;

$$j = 1, 2, 3\ ^{3}\ 4$$

CAI = 100 implies that co-authorship in a particular block for a particular types of authorship corresponds to the world average, CAI > 100 reflects higher than average co-authorship effort and CAI < 100 lower than average co-authorship effort in a particular block for a particular type of authorship.

For calculation of CAI the entire data were divided into four blocks as per the procedure laid down in the formula and the results of CAI given in Table 5. It is observed from the table 5 that the value of CAI for single author papers during 1984-1988 were highest (118.34) which started declining in other blocks. Similarly, for two authored papers, during 1984-1988, the CAI was 119.33, and started declining in other blocks. The CAI for multi-authored papers was lowest (96.54) in the first block and enhanced to 104.95 in the fourth block period from 1999 to 2003. This indicates that the team work in hepatitis research is in increasing trend.

Pattern of Co-Authorship among countries

To analyse the pattern of co-authorship, the entire data was divided into single, two and more than two authors for each country and the results shown in Table 6.

Table 4

Degree of Collaboration in Hepatitis Research

Year	*Anony-mous*	*Single author*	*Two authors*	*Three authors*	*Four authors*	*Five authors*	*More than five authors*	*Total*	*More than one author*	*Degree of collaboration*
1984	49	518	426	382	383	315	465	2538	1971	0.79
1985	58	463	379	381	370	336	529	2516	1995	0.81
1986	48	440	390	386	397	348	557	2566	2078	0.83
1987	66	439	382	429	376	375	648	2715	2210	0.83
1988	76	485	371	392	390	338	627	2679	2118	0.81
1989	83	535	413	456	400	342	764	2993	2375	0.82
1990	82	585	480	484	444	384	923	3382	2715	0.82
1991	109	582	431	468	492	399	1062	3543	2852	0.83
1992	134	631	482	510	513	443	1206	3919	3154	0.83
1993	100	628	517	529	504	428	1270	3976	3248	0.84
1994	95	572	498	582	519	459	1359	4084	3417	0.86
1995	96	700	615	611	581	489	1492	4584	3788	0.84
1996	113	597	480	560	540	508	1513	4311	3601	0.86
1997	163	621	545	488	527	499	1615	4458	3674	0.86
1998	145	673	549	555	542	494	1739	4697	3879	0.85
1999	230	761	564	623	533	546	1826	5083	4092	0.84
2000	179	838	674	625	597	574	1953	5440	4423	0.84
2001	171	810	736	608	617	598	2020	5560	4579	0.85
2002	192	907	711	701	692	645	2171	6019	4920	0.84
2003	160	574	538	447	474	430	1626	4249	3515	0.86
Total	2349	12359	10181	10217	9891	8950	25365	79312	64604	0.84

The pattern of co-authorship among different countries have been examined by making use of collaborative Co-efficient (CC) suggested by Ajiferuke (1988). The formula used for calculating CC is given below:

$$CC = 1 - \left[\sum_{j=1}^{k} (1/j)\ Fj/N \right]$$

F_j = the number of authored papers

N = total number of research published; and

k = the greatest number of authors per paper

CC= 1-[(4705/31667) + ½ (3954/31667) + 1/3 (21442/31667)]

= 0.56.

Table 5: Pattern of Co-Authorship Index (CAI) Year-Wise

Sl.No.	*Year*	*Single Author*	*Two authored*	*More than Two authors*	*Total*
1	1984-1988	2345 (118.34)	1948 (119.33)	8424 (96.54)	12717
2	1989-1993	2961 (109.81)	2323 (104.57)	12021 (101.23)	17305
3	1994-1998	3163 (94.31)	2687 (97.26)	15672 (106.12)	21522
4	1999-2003	3890 (98.21)	3223 (98.78)	18306 (104.95)	25419
	Anonymous				2349
	Total	12,359	10,181	54,423	79,312

According to Ajiferuke, the CC tends zero as single authored papers dominate, and on the other hand if the CC is in increasing trend that results in multi-authored papers. In other words, higher the value of CC, greater the probability of multi-authored papers on hepatitis. In this study it is found that the average CC has been arrived at 0.55 which indicates large share of papers were by multiple authors.

Table 6
Collaborative Coefficient (CC) Authorship Pattern

Sl.No.	*Country*	*Single authored paper*	*Two authored paper*	*More than authors*	*Two Total*	*Collaborative Coefficient*
1	USA	4,705	3,954	21,442	31667	0.56
2	UK	1,716	1,437	7,707	11117	0.55
3	Japan	716	499	2,993	4226	0.54
4	Germany567	571	2266	3,470	0.54	
5	France	574	345	1,927	2905	0.52
6	Netherlands	244	304	2,046	2611	0.59
7	Russia	343	369	1,675	2390	0.55
8	Switzerland	369	316	1,462	2198	0.54
9	Denmark182	174	1791	2,156	0.60	
10	China	495	182	1,217	1905	0.48
11	Italy	152	169	1,523	1858	0.60
12	Spain	176	216	1,285	1691	0.58
13	Australia	336	230	970	1578	0.51
14	India	164	185	585	947	0.52
15	Canada	205	113	386	815	0.52
16	Poland	151	137	456	746	0.50
17	Sweden	104	56	291	457	0.50
18	Greece	19	26	400	445	0.63
19	Austria	50	44	320	417	0.57
20	Ireland	36	45	302	397	0.60
21	Norway	60	44	275	379	0.54
22	Brazil	32	37	291	360	0.59
23	New Zealand	113	95	127	357	0.43
	Others	850	633	2,686	4,169	0.51
	Anonymous				2,349	
	Total	12359 (15.58%)	10181 (12.84%)	54423 (68.62%)	79,312 (100%)	0.55

The value of CC for Greece was highest (0.63) followed by Denmark (0.60) and Italy (0.60) and all the other countries except New Zealand (0.43) and China (0.48) where the CC is above 0.5. In other words the countries exhibiting CC as above 0.5 indicates that those countries have better collaboration in comparison to the countries with less than 0.5 as shown in Table 6.

6.2.5 Ranking of Authors in Hepatitis Research

The analysis of the research output on Hepatitis is also been made by ranking of highly productive authors. For this purpose, analysis has been made to rank the top ten authors and the details are shown in Table 7.

Table 7 Ranking of Authors in Hepatitis Research

S.No.	*Name of the Author*	*No. of Contributions*	*Address of the Author*
1	Czaja, A J	81	Division of Gastroenterology and Hepatology, Mayo Clinic and Mayo Foundation, Rochester, Minnesota 55905, USA
2	Laskus, T	67	Department of Immunopathology, Institute of Infectious and Parasitic Diseases, Warsaw, Poland.
3	Fabrizi, F	61	Nephrology Department, Hospital Lecco, Italy
4	Di-Bisceglie, A M	58	Liver Diseases Section, National Institute of Diabetes and Digestive and Kidney Diseases, National Institutes of Health, Bethesda, Maryland, USA.
5	Buti, M	52	Department of Internal Medicine, Hospital Valle Hebron, Universidad Autonoma, Barcelona, Spain.
6	Jilg, W	46	Max von Pettenkofer-Institute of Hygiene and Medical Microbiology, University of Munich, Federal Republic of Germany.
7	Kakumu, S	44	Third Department of Internal Medicine, Nagoya University School of Medicine, Japan.
8	Lok, A S	44	Department of Medicine, University of Hong Kong, Queen Mary Hospital.

9	Zuckerman, A J	44	Academic Unit of Travel Medicine and Vaccines, Royal Free and University College Medical School, University College, London, United Kingdom.
10	Kao, J H	42	Department of Internal Medicine, National Taiwan University College of Medicine and National Taiwan University Hospital, Taipei, Taiwan.

Author productivity

The study of author productivity is one of the parameters in analysing the research performance of a subject. The analysis of author productivity projects the prevailing trends of research. The analysis of number of contributors based on author productivity is presented in Table 9. It is observed that 76.30 per cent of authors have published single papers, followed by 12.72 per cent have contributed two papers. By and large authors who have contributed between one and 10 papers constitute 99.13 per cent of the total contributions. In other words, 99.13 per cent of the authors contributed papers ranging from one to ten.

From the above analysis, the following inferences could be derived:

1. The higher the number of contributions the smaller the number of contributors. In other words, the increase in the number of contributions decreases in the number of authors.
2. It is inferred that greater level of research performance is concentrated among few authors.
3. Of course, author productivity is normally influenced by the type of the institution where the researcher works, the area of specialisation and provision of necessary infrastructure facilities for the conduct of research, etc.

Conclusion

About 81 per cent of the total contributions represent the collaborative research. The degree of collaboration has been arrived at 0.84 during the study period. The value of Co-Authorship Index (CAI) for single author paper shows a declining trend from one block year period to another block. On the other hand for multi-authored papers the Co-Authorship Index reveals an increasing trend. The pattern of Collaborative Coefficient result reveals that a majority of the countries have shown a higher degree of collaboration research, since the collaborative coefficient is above 0.5. A total of 43 authors have been identified, who have published 50 and above contributions in the study period and out of which 10 belongs to USA. It is found that when the number of contributors increases, correspondingly the number of contributions decreases.

Table 8: Author Productivity in Hepatitis Research Output

No. of Papers	*No. of Authors*	*Percentage*	*Cumulative Percentage*
1	36,580	76.30	76.30
2	6,099	12.72	89.02
3	2,263	4.72	93.74
4	1,067	2.23	95.96
5	584	1.22	97.18
6	359	0.75	97.93
7	238	0.50	98.43
8	162	0.34	98.76
9	105	0.22	98.98
10	70	0.15	99.13
11	64	0.13	99.26
12	61	0.13	99.39
13	44	0.09	99.48
14	37	0.08	99.56
15	32	0.07	99.62
16	29	0.06	99.69
17	17	0.04	99.72
18	14	0.03	99.75
19	9	0.02	99.77
20	12	0.03	99.79

(Contd...)

(Contd...)

21	8	0.02	99.81
22	8	0.02	99.83
23	8	0.02	99.84
24	4	0.01	99.85
25	9	0.02	99.87
26	3	0.01	99.88
27	9	0.02	99.90
28	4	0.01	99.90
29	3	0.01	99.91
30	3	0.01	99.92
31	1	0.00	99.92
32	12	0.03	99.94
33	4	0.01	99.95
34	1	0.00	99.95
35	2	0.00	99.96
36	2	0.00	99.96
38	2	0.00	99.97
39	1	0.00	99.97
40	1	0.00	99.97
41	3	0.01	99.98
42	2	0.00	99.98
44	3	0.01	99.99
46	1	0.00	99.99
52	1	0.00	99.99
58	1	0.00	99.99
61	1	0.00	100.00
67	1	0.00	100.00
81	1	0.00	100.00
Total	47,945	100.00	

References

Ajiferuke, Q., Burrel, J and Tauge. (1988). Collaborative coefficient: A single measure of the Degree of Collaborations in research, *Scientometrics*, 14, 421-433.

Bandyopadhyay, A.K. (2001). Authorship pattern in different disciplines, *Annals of Library and Information Studies*, 48(4), 139-147.

Begum, K.J. and Rajendra, N. (1990). Research collaboration in Zoological Sciences, *IASLIC Bulletin*, 35(2), 79-82.

Bhagavathi, Sudha and Ramesh Babu, B. (2000). Indian Literature on Information Technology: A bibliographic study. In: *Trends in library and information science (Essays in honour of Prof.G.D.Bhargava)*. New Delhi: Gyan Publishing House. 273-286.

Chakraborthy, A.R. (1981). Trend towards team research in Geology, *IASLIC Bulletin*, 26, 141-146.

Dutt, Bharvi, Garg, K.C., and Bali, Anita. (2003). Scientometrics of the International Journal Scientometrics. *Scientometrics*, 56, 81-93.

Farahat, Hashem. (2002). Authorship patterns in agriculture sciences in Egypt. *Scientometrics*, 55(2), 157-170.

Garg, K C and Padhi, P. (2001). A study of collaboration in laser science and technology, *Scientometrics*, 51, 415-427.

http://library.dialog.com/bluesheets/html/bl0074.html.

http://www.cinahl.com/prodsvcs/cinahldbbody.htm

http://www.nlm.nih.gov/pubs/factsheets/medline.html

Karisiddappa, C.R., Gupta, B.M. and Kumar, S. (2002). Scientific productivity of authors in theoretical population genetics. *Scientometrics*, 53(1), 73-93.

______________ Maheswarappa, B. S. and Shirol, M.V. (1990). Authorship pattern and collaborative research in Psychology, *IASLIC Bulletin*, 35(2), 73-78.

Koteswara Rao, M. and Raghavan, K.S. (2003). Collaboration in knowledge production: a case study of superconductivity research in India. In: International Conference on Scientometrics and Informetrics Proceedings, Dalian, China. 230-40.

Maheswarappa, B.S. and Mathias, S.A. (1987). Research collaboration in different disciplines of applied sciences in India (1965-1983): a bibliometric study, *IASLIC Bulletin*, 32, 105-114.

______________ and Nagappa, B. (1981). Dynamics of scientific communications: an analysis of contributions in

Phytomorphology, *Journal of Library and Information Science*, 6, 16-22.

____________ and Savadatti S.G. (1990). Authorship pattern and collaborative research in Plant Breeding (1934-1989), *IASLIC Bulletin*, 35, 119-123.

Mishra, Sanjay and Mishra, Manoj. (1991). Collaborative research in Medicinal and Aromatic Plants, *Library Herald*, 30, 30-34.

Munshi, U.M., Vashishth, C.P. and Gautam. (1993). Research Collaboration in Agricultural Sciences, *ILA Bulletin*, 28, 57-60.

Narendra Kumar, A.M. and Ramesh Babu, B. (1999). ILA Bulletin (1986-1996): an analytical study. In: *Readings in Library and Information Science (S.P.Sood festschrift)*. Jaipur: Raj Publishing House. 237-256.

Parameswaran R, Ramesh Babu B and Gopalakrishnan S. (2003). Quantitative Analysis of Air Pollution Research output from India during 1993-1998 paper presented in 9th ISSI Conference held at Beijing, China during August 25-29.

Pulla Reddy, V and Sharma C.B.S.R. (1988). Bibliometric study of research publications in Indian Environmental Genetic Toxicology, *IASLIC Bulletin*, 33, 7-14.

Rajendran, P, Ramesh Babu, B and Gopalakrishnan, S. (2005). Bibliometric Analysis of "Fiber Optics" literature. *Annals of Library and Information Studies*, 52 (3), 82-85.

Ramakrishnan, J (2006). *Scientometric Analysis of Literature on Hepatitis: A Study Based on Bibliographic Databases*. Chennai: University of Madras (Supervisor: Prof. B. Ramesh Babu).

Ramesh Babu, B and Ramakrishnan, J (2007). Trends in the Growth of Literature on Hepatitis (1984-2003), *Journal of Korean Library and Information Science Society*, 38 (2), 31-50.

____________ and Ramakrishnan, J (2008). National Patterns of Research output and Priorities in Hepatitis, *Journal of Information Science and Technology*, 39 (4), 215-240.

Shirabe, M. and Tomizawa, H. (2002). Likelihood of overseas access to international co-authorships. *Scientometrics*, 53(1), 123-129.

Stedman's Medical Dictionary. (2000). 27th ed. Lippincott: Baltimore.

Subramanyam, K. (1993). Bibliometric Studies of Research Collaboration: A review. *Journal of Information Science*, 6, 33-38.

Turkington, Carlol. (1998). *Hepatitis C: the silent Killer*. Lincolnwood (Chicago): Contemporary Books.

Wagner, C S and Leydesdorff, L. (2003). Mapping global science using international co-authorships: a comparison of 1990 and 2000. In: Proceedings of the 9th International Conference on Scientometrics and Informetrics. 330-340.

Wilkes, L., et al. (2002). Measuring the Outputs of Nursing Research and Development in Australia: The Researchers. *Australian Journal of Advanced Nursing,* 19, 15-20.

26

A Bibliometric Analysis of Doctoral Dissertations in English Language and Literature

—R. Rajani and S. Humayoon Kabir

A bibliometric analysis of 11,466 citations collected from the doctoral dissertations in English Language and Literature accepted by the University of Kerala was done to determine the literature use pattern of the researchers in the subject area. This provides information about the bibliographic forms used, geographical and chronological distribution of citations, etc. The ranking of the cited books and journals show that British and American books still have their sway. Though less in percentage, some alien language and alien discipline citations are also present.

Introduction

Citations are signposts left behind after information has been utilised, and they provide information by which one may build pictures of user behaviour without even confronting the user himself (Smith, 1981). In a discipline like literature, in which the libraries play an important role, such studies help the information professionals, to provide, need-based user oriented services. Madeline made a use-based citation analysis by selecting three writers and three movements in literature (1983). Deo et al made a bibliographic study of dissertations in English Language and Literature (1995). All these studies confirm lesser use of sources other than books, lesser degrees of obsolescence etc.

Objectives

The objectives of the present study are to determine:

i) The number of citations in the theses.
ii) The authorship pattern of cited books.
iii) The bibliographic forms cited, their language, country of origin, etc.
iv) The rank list of cited books and journals.
v) The chronological distribution and the frequency distribution of the cited journals.
vi) The half life of the journal literature and the productivity of journals.

Methodology

The total population for this study is 11,466 citations that figured 70 theses accepted by the University of Kerala for the award of Ph.D. degree from 1965 to 1999. The year 1965 is the year of submission of the first Ph.D. thesis in this subject. The details of citing documents and the cited documents were entered in catalogue cards which were then tabulated and analysed.

Analysis of Data

Number of citations per thesis

Out of the 70 theses examined, one submitted during 1965 and another one submitted during 1972, contain 717 and 614 citations respectively. Majority of theses contained 50 to 200 citations. The number of citations are tabulated in Table 1.

Table 1 : Number of Citations in the Theses

Sl. No.	*Number of Citations*	*No. of Theses*	*Percentage*
1	NIl	4	5.71
2	1 – 100	14	20.00
3	101 – 200	35	50.00
4	201 – 300	10	14.29
5	301 – 400	3	4.29
6	401 – 500	2	2.86
7	More than 600	1	1.43
8	More than 700	1	1.43
	Total	70	100.00

Information Sources Cited

Books reign supreme in literature with a clear cut majority of 87.04 per cent. This phenomenon is unique in this subject area. Journals form the most sought after information source in science and social science disciplines. But the difference ends here. When the citations were examined, it was found that all the information sources used by scientists and social scientists were also used by the literary researchers. About 20 types of sources are cited. The major sources cited are given in Table 2.

Table 2: Information Sources Cited

Sl. No.	Source Cited	No. of Citations	%	Cumulative No. of Citations	Cumulative Percentage
1	Books	9,979	87.04	9,979	87.04
2	Journals	916	7.99	10,895	95.03
3	Interviews	173	1.51	11,068	96.54
4	Letters	142	1.24	11,210	97.78
5	Dictionaries	60	0.52	11,270	98.3
6	Newspapers	40	0.35	11,310	98.65
7	Encyclopaediae	40	0.35	11,350	99
8	Others	116	1	11,466	100
	Total	11,466	100	11,466	100

The Place of Publication of Cited Books

The geographical distribution of citations are given in Table 3.

Table 3

The Country of Origin of Cited Books

Sl. No.	Place of Publication	No. of citations	Percentage
1	Britain	5,020	50.31
2	America	2,036	20.40
3	India	1,512	15.15
4	Others	129	1.29
5	Not known	1,282	12.85
	Total	9,979	100.00

Books from about 15 countries are cited. British sources hold their sway with about 50 per cent of the total citations. This is followed by American and Indian sources perhaps the ready availability of materiaıs prompted their use.

View to the practice of giving incomplete citations 12.85 per cent of citations contained no publication details.

The language citations

The language in which a particular literature is written forms not only the medium of expression but also the cause and effect in the case of a particular literature. So language is not just the medium of expression, as far as literature is concerned. If it is so, other literatures need not be used by literary researchers. But the analysis of citation show this concept row. Though English books are cited more, about 10 other Western and Eastern languages are see cited in Table 4.

Table 4

Language of Citations

Sl. No.	*Language*	*No. of Citations*	*Percentage*	*Cumulative Citations*	*Cumulative Percentage*
1	English	11,137	97.13	11,137	97.13
2	Malayalam	130	1.13	11,267	98.26
3	French	62	0.54	11,329	98.80
4	Russian	40	0.35	11,369	99.15
5	Sanskrit	40	0.35	11,409	99.50
6	Latin	39	0.34	11,448	99.84
7	Bengali	10	0.09	11,458	99.93
8	Greek	6	0.05	11,464	99.98
9	Chinese	1	0.01	11,465	99.99
10	Spanish	1	0.01	11,466	100.00
	Total	11,466	100	11,466	100.00

Alien Discipline Citations

Though literary scholars are accused of their self-centred nature, the analysis of citations prove that about 11 per cent of the total citations were of alien disciplines. Not surprising since inter disciplinary studies held a small majority. So scholars cannot help, but rely on sources from other disciplines to solve the textual problems confronted in such studies. Table 5 gives a more detailed picture.

Table 5

Alien Discipline Citations

Sl. No.	*Discipline*	*No. of citations*	*Percentage*
1	Religion	264	20.59
2	Linguistics	254	19.77
3	Sociology	208	16.19
4	Psychology	202	15.72
5	Philosophy	152	11.83
6	Mysticism	55	4.29
7	Political Science	40	3.11
8	Fine Arts	39	3.04
9	History	39	3.04
10	Law	12	0.93
11	Economics	7	0.54
12	Science	5	0.39
13	Education	3	0.23
14	Anthropology	2	0.16
15	Demography	1	0.08
16	Useful Arts	1	0.08
17	Library Science	1	0.08
	Total	1285	100.00

The Chronological Distribution of Cited Books

The time span in this study is about 50 years. The theses submitted for Ph. D. from the 1960 to 1999 are included. A period of about 100 years is seen covered in the cited works. The chronological distribution of cited books is given in Table 6.

Table 6
Chronological Distribution of Cited Books

Sl. No.	*Age of Citations*	*No. of Book*	*Percentage*	*Cumulative Citations*	*Cumulative Percentage*
1	Less than 1 year	6	0.07	6	0.07
2	1 to 10 years	2,006	20.10	2,012	20.17
3	11 to 20 years	2,718	27.25	4,730	47.42
4	21 to 30 years	1,971	19.75	6,701	67.17
5	31 to 40 years	1,130	11,32	7,831	78.49
6	41 to 50 years	739	7.40	8,570	85.89
7	51 to 60 years	451	4.52	9,021	90.41
8	61 to 70 years	235	2.35	9,256	92.76
9	71 to 80 years	285	2.86	9,541	95.62
10	81 to 90 years	57	0.57	9,598	96.19
11	more than 100 years	381	3.81	9,979	100.00
	Total	9,979	100.00	9,979	100.00

Literary rsearchers' craze for antique materials is notorious. But this study shows otherwise. The literary researchers are reluctant to use very much recent materials. So both very recent and very old materials are seen less cited. The maximum number of books cited (78.41%) are between 1 and 40 years were as the books more than 50 years older only 11.11 per cent.

Authorship Pattern of Book Citations

Collaborative efforts are very less in this subject area. So naturally, very less number of works of shared responsibility are seeing cited as shows table 7.

Table 7: Authorship Pattern of Book Citations

Sl. No.	*Authorship pattern of Citations*	*No. of Citations*	*Percentage*
1	Single author citations	9,587	95.88
2	Two author citations	343	3.46
3	More than two authors	44	0.44
4	Corporate body as author	2	0.02
5	Self-citations	2	0.02
	Total	9,979	100

Rank List of Cited Authors

The rank list of cited authors are given in Table 8, which gives a surprising picture. Many literary wizards get far less number of citations, were as less popular writers get more citations. The following table contains the rank list of authors cited more than 50 times.

Table 8
Rank List of Cited Authors

Sl. No.	*Author*	*No. of Citations*	*Rank*
1	Walter de La Mare	390	1
2	John Galsworthy	344	2
3	John Steinbeck	285	3
4	G. M. Hopkins	270	4
5	Thom Gunn	126	5
6	Endora Welty	112	6
7	Flannary O'Connor	102	7
8	Samuel Beckett	98	8
9	N. N. Kakkad	90	9
10	H. V. Marrot	87	10
11	D. H. Lawrence	86	11
12	Sylvia Plath	82	12
13	Raymond Williams	74	13
14	Nayantara Sehgal	71	14
15	M. K. Naik	69	15
16	Arthur Miller	68	16
17	Srinivasa Iyengar	58	17
18	Mulk Raj Anand	53	18

Many major authors have received lesser number of citations. Jacques Derrida has received 24 citations – rank number 30. R.K. Narayan is on 33rd position with 20 citations. W. B. Yeats, the notable twentieth century poet and William Shakespeare, the all time wizard of English literature, are on 37th position with only 16 citations each. All these show that the age-old - classic author, concept is not current among literary researchers. Not surprising since the majority of studies are based on recent authors.

The Content of Citations

Literary scholars are notorious for their incomplete, unstructured citing behaviour. This study proved otherwise. The date elements of citations are given in Table 9.

Table 9
The Content of Citations

Sl. No.	*The Content of Citations*	*No. of Citations*	*Percentage*
1	Full citations	7,188	72.03
2	Author, title, pagination	1,081	10.09
3	Author, pagination	83	0.83
4	Title, pagination	489	4.89
5	ibid/op.cit	943	9.43
6	Notes	195	1.95
	Total	9,979	100

Table 10
Ranklist of Cited Journals

Sl. No.	*Title the Journal*	*Country of Origin*	*No. of citations %*	*Rank*
1	Modern Indian Studies	U.S.A	33	1
2	Journal of Indian Writing in English	India	27	2
3	Twentieth Century Literature	U.S.A	21	3
4	Osmania Journal of English Studies	India	18	4
5	The Literary Criterion	U.S.A	18	4
6	College English	U.S.A	17	5
7	Black American Literary Forum	U.S.A.	15	6
8	The Scrutury	U.S.A	13	7
9	Mark Twain Quarterly	U.S.A	13	7
10	Litt Crit	India	12	8
11	Journal of South Asian Literature	India	11	9
12	Modern Drama	Britain	10	10

Some of the notes run to pages describing the author's intention in making a particular statement.

The Format of Citations

The format of almost all the citations are author, title (place, publisher, year) pagination as given in the M. L. A. Style Manual 4th edition. No other style manual is seen followed.

Rank List of Periodicals

Journals cited more than 10 times is given in Table 10 with their countries of origin and ranks. The list contains the details of 12 journals covering 22.71 per cent of the total journal literature cited.

American journals cited more unlike in the case of books where British books had the supremacy. The journal literature shows wide distribution; 409 titles are cited. The total journal citations number of 916. The concentration of citations are on a very few journals. For example, Modern Fiction studies, the most cited journal, is cited only 33 time, i.e., it contains only 3.6 per cent of the total journal citations.

Application of Bradford's Law

Bradford's law states that if a group of journals are arranged in a order of decreasing productivity, that is, the journal that yields the most relevant articles comes first and the most unproductive last, then the journals will be grouped into a number of zones each producing a similar number of relevant articles. However, the number of journals in each zone will be increasing rapidly. The relationship between the zones and will be 1: a: a2. The application of Bradford's law is given in Table 11.

Table 11
Application of Bradford's Law

Sl.No.	*No. of Journals Articles*	*No. of*	*Ranking*	*Cumulative Citations*	
1	1	33	1	33	33
2	1	27	2	27	60
3	1	21	3	21	81
4	2	18	4	36	117

(Contd...)

(Contd...)

5	1	17	5	17	134
6	1	15	6	15	149
7	2	13	7	26	175
8	1	12	8	12	187
9	1	11	9	11	198
10	1	10	10	10	208
11	5	9	11	45	253
12	6	8	12	48	301
13	3	7	13	21	322
14	6	6	14	36	358
15	11	5	15	55	413
16	3	4	16	12	425
17	40	3	17	120	545
18	81	2	18	162	707
19	209	1	19	209	916

First zone covers 10 journals
Second zone covers 18 journals
Third zone covers 180 journals
The ratio is 1:18:180
This does not fit into Bradford's formula.

Table 12
Half Life of Journal Literature

Age of Citations	*No. of Citations*	*Cumulative Citations*	*Percentage of Citations*	*Cumulative Percentage*
Upto 1 year	10	10	1.09	1.09
1 to 10 years	360	370	39.3	40.39
11 to 20 years	272	642	29.69	70.08
21 to 30 years	114	756	12.45	82.53
31 to 40 years	58	814	6.33	88.86
41 to 50 years	43	857	4.67	93.55
51 to 60 years	23	880	2.51	96.06
61 to 70 years	17	897	1.85	97.91
71 to 80 years	2	899	10.86	100.00
Not known	17	916	10.86	100.00
Total	916	916	100.00	100.00

Obsolescence of Journal Literature

The use literature will decrease with time. After sometime, it may become out dated or obsolescent. This is calculated through the half life period. Half life period is a turn borrowed the from radio activity. There, it is the period which any radio active element will become half ifs mass by due to radiation. In Information Science, half life means the age or period of time up to which it receives half of its total citations it will ever receive. The half life of journal literature is given in Table 12.

The half life of journal literature is given in figure 1.

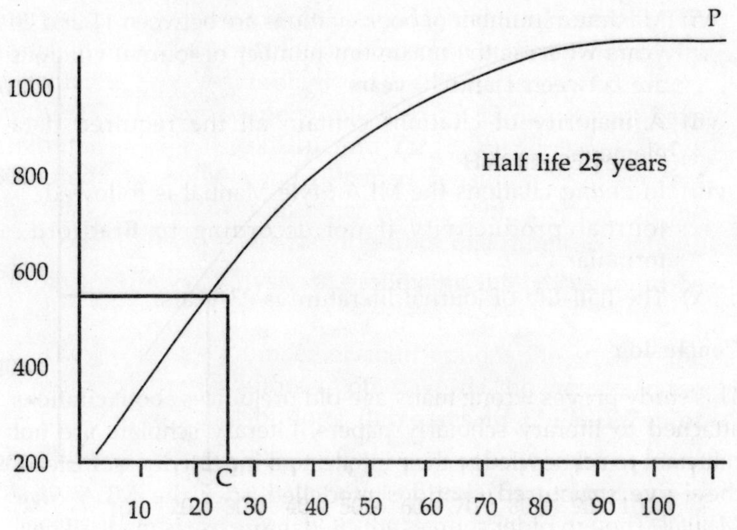

Figure 1: Obsolescence of English Literature

Half life of journal literature

The graph of plotted by taking period on X axis and cumulative number of citations in Y axis. The maximum number of citations cuts at point P. Half the number of total citations meet at point D on Y axis. A line drawn from point P parallel to X axis cuts the curved graph at point B. Again another line is drawn from B parallel to Y axis. This line meets X axis at point C. The distance from D to C is the half life of the total literature published during the period.

Findings

The major findings of this study are:

i) The average number of citations per thesis is 164.

ii) Books are the predominant bibliographic form cited contributing 87.04% of the total sources cited.

iii) Among the cited books, British books have the sway with 50.31 per cent of the total book citations.

iv) 2.87 per cent of citations are from alien languages.

v) 11.2 per cent of citations are from alien discipline.

vi) Maximum number of book citations are between 11 and 20 years whereas the maximum number of journal citations are between 1 and 10 years.

vii) A majority of citations contain all the required data elements.

viii) In giving citations the MLA Style Manual is followed.

ix) Journal productivity if not according to Bradford's formula.

x) The half-life of journal literature is 23 years.

Conclusion

This study proves wrong many age-old prejudices about citations attached to literary scholarly papers. Literary scholars are not reluctant to acknowledge their intellectual indebtedness. Instead, they give structured citations modelled after the MLA *Style Manual*. Though older sources are cited, more use is made of new sources. A wide variety of information sources are also cited. Classic authors are less preferred to recent once. No citation is given to digital materials.

References

Deo, V. N. et. al. (1995). Bibliometric study of Doctoral Dissertations in English Language and Literature. *Annals of Library Science and Documentation,* 42 (3), 81- 95.

Madeline, Stern. (1983) .Characteristics of literature of Literary Scholarship *College and Research Libraries,*. 43 (3), 190-209.

Smith, L C. (1981). Citation analysis. *Library Tends,* 30, 83-106.

27

Publication Productivity of Physics Researchers of Indian Institute of Science: A Scientometric Study

—K. G. Sudhier

This scientometric study analyses the publication of physics researchers at the Indian Institute of Science (IISc), Bangalore. There were 267 research papers published by the IISc physics researchers during 1999-2003. The highest number of publications was in the year 2001. The average number of publications per thesis was 3.7. The journals most preferred for publishing were Phys. Rev. B, J. Cryst. Growth and J. Phys. Cond. Matter. The average number of authors per article is 4 and the degree of collaboration of publications is 0.94. The collaboration trend was multi-authored publications.

Introduction

The term *Naukometriya* (the Russian for 'scientometrics') was coined by the Russian Statisticians Nalimov and Mulchenko (1969) for the quantitative methods for studying the development of science. Over the years scientometrics and bibliometric techniques have become tools to evaluate the productivity of research institutes, individual researcher and to map the growth of subject. Publication and citation counts are being extensively used for evaluation purpose of an institute.

Physics research in India is basically an institutional activity, pursued countrywide with funding coming from several sectors including academic, R & D, government and industry. The academic sector constitutes universities, institutions of higher learning and colleges. There are nearly 435 physics-based research institutions in the country employing more than 5,000 PhDs and several thousands Masters' engaged in research programmes in the major areas of physics. A large number of universities are engaged in post-graduate teaching and research and doctoral programmes. As a result, around 7,000 PhDs are awarded each year in physics (Dhawan and Gupta, 2007).

Even though physics institutions are spread throughout India, the research activity in physics is confined mainly to select few institutions only in the country. These institutions are regarded as R & D leaders in this area. The Indian Institute of Science (IISc), Bangalore, comes under this category of institution.

Research and development can not be envisaged without the communication of results of research and development. According to Boyer (1973), "the research process is incomplete if the research results are not used or not made readily accessible to the potentially interested researchers." The dissertations and the publications serve the purpose of communicating significant research results for the advancement of human knowledge.

IISc is one of India's oldest research institutes celebrating its centenary in 2009. The institution ranks as the foremost centre for research in Science and Engineering in the country. A quiet and conservative institution until the 1960's, IISc has grown dramatically in size and the breadth of its scientific activity over the past 30 years. Its character, which blends the ambience of a university with the advantage of a research institution, has helped IISc to maintain a steady level of academic performance.

In the present study an attempt ha been made to study the contributions of the physicists of IISc during the period of their doctoral research.

Previous Studies

A number of scientometric analyses have been carried out during the last two decades to evaluate the research productivity of Indian scientists.

Scientometric analysis of 67 theses and 610 articles (based on theses submitted by the scholars during 1960-2000 in the Dept. of Physics at the University of Burdwan) scattered in eight subdivisions of Physics were analysed by Nandi and Bandyopadhyay (2009).

Girap et al., (2009), in their scientometric study, analyse the publication productivity of the Technical Physics and Prototype Engineering Division at Bhabha Atomic Research Centre. There were 704 research papers published during 1986-2006 scattered in diverse domains.

Sevukan and Sharma (2008) presented a detailed analysis of research performance of Biotechnology faculties in central universities of India from 1997 to 2006. The data analysed for the study were retrieved from two database sources, namely, PubMed, NCBI and ISI *Web of Science* database.

Sudhier (2007) presented a citation study comprising 690 journals containing 11,412 references collected from seven doctoral theses awarded by the IISc, Bangalore during 1999-2003. It was observed that journals are the most frequently cited bibliographic form of citations.

Gopikuttan (2004) in his scientometric study deals with the research output in terms of journal articles, reports, books, etc., produced by the teachers of science departments, Faculty of Science, University of Kerala between 1980 and 1999 (20 years). The analysis of the data revealed that journal articles are the main vehicles of information transfer of faculty members, which accounts for 61.68 per cent followed by conference papers 31.52 per cent. Department-wise analysis of journal articles shows that Physics department produces 306 articles (19.94%) followed by Biochemistry 288 (18.68%).

Soman (2001), as part of his doctoral research programme, attempted to assess the scientific information productivity of physical scientists in the universities in Kerala, to find out the factors that affect the scientific information productivity, and to examine the role of information technology in augmenting the scientific productivity of the physical scientists. The study revealed that the average scientific productivity of physical scientists in terms of published research papers was greater in Electronics followed by Physics and Chemistry.

Garg and Rao (1998) made a scientometric analysis of the publication data of the scientists of an Indian Physics Laboratory (New Delhi). They found that the scientists preferred to publish their communications in foreign journals included in the SCI. They also found that the productivity of the laboratory in terms of the published papers per 100 scientists remained constant during 1965-1982.

Sangam and Nargund (1997) studied the trends in physics research publication and institutions-wise contribution to the physics research publications reported in *Indian Science Abstracts*.

Even though several studies have done to study the scientific productivity of scientists in the country, no specific effort has been made to evaluate the research contributions of physics researchers of IISc.

Objectives

The main objectives of this paper is to assess the publication behaviour of physicists of IISc, and

i) To study the research publication productivity of physics researchers.

ii) To ascertain the authorship and collaboration pattern of researchers.

iii) To examine the communication channels preferred for publication.

iv) To prepare a rank list of journals preferred for publication.

v) To find out country- wise distribution of journals.

Source Data

Scientometric analysis of 267 research publications by the physics research scholars published during their research period were collected for the period 1999-2003, which formed the basic data for this study. All the bibliographic details of publications which are included in the doctoral dissertations were collected and analysed as per the objective of the study.

Results and Discussions

Number of Publications

An analysis of number of publications included in the doctoral dissertations of IISc scholars are included in Table 1.

Table 1: Number of Publications

Sl. No.	*No. of publications*	*Count*	*%*
1	Nil	39	54.9
2	1-5	6	8.5
3	6-10	18	25.4
4	11-15	8	11.2
	Total	71	100.0

Gender-wise Productivity of Research Publications

Table3: Gender-wise Analysis of Research Publications

Sl. No.	*Year*	*Male*	*Female*	*Total*
1	1999	61	11	72
2	2000	33	2	35
3	2001	75	30	75
4	2002	18	7	25
5	2003	16	14	30
Total		203	64	267

It can be seen from Table 3 that out of the 267 publications, 203 publications are produced by male scholars and 64 are produced by female scholars. This is because of the dominance of male research scholars in IISc.

Gender-wise Average Number of Publication Productivity

Comparative analysis of average number of publications of male and female scholars is shown in Table 4.

Table 4: Gender-wise Analysis of Average Number of Publications

Sex	*Mean*	*SD*	*t*	*p*
Male	3.9	4.6	0.41	p>0.05
Female	3.4	4.9		

Authorship Pattern of Publications

The authorship pattern of publications of scholars are presented in Table 5.

Table 5: Authorship Pattern of Publications

Sl. No.	Authors	Count	%
1	1	16	5.99
2	2	55	20.60
3	3	42	15.73
4	4	59	22.10
5	5+	95	35.58
	Total	267	100.0

Degree of Collaboration of Publications

To determine the degree of collaboration of publications, the number of single authored and multi-authored publications is calculated, and the values are shown in Table 6.

Table 6: Degree of Collaboration of Publications

Single Authors	Multiple Authors	Degree of Collaboration
16	251	0.94

Preference of Channels of Publication by Physicists

Table 7 shows the preference of channels of communication by Physicists.

Table 7: Channels of Publications of Physicists

Sl. No.	Channels	Count	%
1	Journals	131	49.1
2	Communicated	53	19.9
3	International seminars	30	11.2
4	National seminars	27	10.1
5	Manuscripts	23	8.6
6	Technical reports	2	0.7
7	Books	1	0.4
8	Patents	0	0
	Total	267	100.0

Choice of Journals for Publication

The analysis of the preference of channels of communication of physicists shows that journals are the most preferred channel of publication of IISc physicists (49.1%).

The rank list of the most preferred journals by the physicists are presented in Table 8. The journals preferred more than four times are included in the table.

Table 8: Ranked Journals for Publication

Journals	*Country**	*Rank*	*Count*	*%*	*Cum %*	*IF***
Phys.Rev.B	USA	1	16	9.58	9.58	3.075
J.Crystal Growth	Netherlands	2	8	4.79	14.37	1.707
J.Phys-Condensed Matter	UK	2	8	4.79	19.16	2.049
Liq.Cryst.	UK	3	7	4.19	23.35	
Solid State Commun.	UK	3	7	4.19	27.54	1.523
Phys.Rev.Lett.	USA	4	6	3.59	31.14	7.218
App.Phys.Lett.	USA	5	5	2.99	34.13	4.308
Bull.of Astron Soc.	India	5	5	2.99	37.13	
Chem.Phys.Lett	Netherlands	5	5	2.99	40.12	2.438
Euro.Phys.Lett.	France	5	5	2.99	43.11	2.120
J.Appl.Phys.	USA	5	5	2.99	46.11	2.255
Acta Cryst.	Denmark	6	4	2.40	48.50	1.829
Astro. and Astorphys.	France	6	4	2.40	50.90	3.694
Astrophysical J.	USA	6	4	2.40	53.29	6.237
Mon.Not.Roy. Astr.Soc.	UK	6	4	2.40	55.69	5.238
Phys.Rev.A	USA	6	4	2.40	58.08	2.902

* Data from Ulrich ** Data from JCR-2006

The analysis shows that the IISc Physicists prefer to publish their research findings in world renowned journals with high Impact Factors (IF).

Ramasesan (1978) in one of his articles on the consideration of scientist in the choice of journals suggested that a scientist chooses (i) a journal which he feels would give him a fair criticism by competent referees (ii) a journal which deals with his own subject (iii) a journal where most papers are of high quality (iv) a journal that is well edited and well printed, and (v) a journal that gives free reprints.

Country-wise Distribution of Journals for Publication

A study of countries of journals preferred for publications are shown in Table 9.

Table 9: Country-wise Distribution of Journals of Publications

Country	*Rank*	*Count*	*%*	*Cum %*
USA	1	66	43.42	43.42
UK	2	38	25.00	68.42
Netherlands	3	19	12.50	80.92
India	4	10	6.58	87.50
Germany	5	6	3.95	91.45
France	6	5	3.29	94.74
Swiss	6	5	3.29	98.03
Denmark	7	2	1.31	99.34
Singapore	8	1	0.66	100.00
Total		152	100.00	

Language-wise Analysis of Journals of Publication

The language-wise analysis of journals preferred for publication by physicists are given in Table 10.

Table 10: Language-wise Distribution of Journals

Sl. No.	*Language*	*Count*	*%*
1	English	138	90.79
2	Dutch	13	8.55
3	French	1	0.66
	Total	152	100.00

English is the universal language and a majority of the physics journals are in English or in multi-language. This may be the reason for this result.

Publishers of Journals for Publication

In order to study the publishers of the journals preferred for the publication of research results, the following Table 11 is used.

Table 11: Publishers of Journals

Sl. No.	*Publisher*	*Rank*	*Count*	*%*	*Cum %*
1	APS	1	27	17.65	17.65
2	Elsevier Science	2	16	10.46	28.10
3	AIP	3	13	8.50	36.60
4	North Holland	3	13	8.50	45.10
5	IOP	4	11	7.19	52.29
6	AAS	5	7	4.58	56.86
7	Taylor & Francis	5	7	4.58	61.44
8	Academic Press	6	5	3.27	64.71
9	EDP Science	6	5	3.27	67.97
10	IAS	6	5	3.27	71.24
11	Kluwer	6	5	3.27	74.51
12	Wiley-VCH	6	5	3.27	77.78

The analysis of the publishers of journals shows that scholars prefer to publish in internationally published journals.

Analysis of Frequency of Journals for Publication

A study has been made to analyse the periodicity of publication of journals used by the scholars, and the results are shown in the Table 12.

Table 12: Frequency-wise Analysis of Journals

Sl. No.	*Periodicity*	*Count*	*%*
1	12	38	25.17
2	52	34	22.52
3	48	23	15.23
4	24	17	11.26
5	36	8	5.30
6	6	7	4.64
7	68	6	3.97
8	108	5	3.31
9	4	4	2.65
10	15	3	1.99

The results of the analysis of frequency of journals show that weekly and monthly journals are the most preferred journals for publications of research results.

Conclusion

The study revealed that majority theses of (54.90%) IISc do not include the list of publications of the research scholars. The average number of publications per theses is 3.7, because a majority of theses of IISc do not include the list of publications by the scholars. Publications produced by male scholars (3.9) are predominantly higher than that of female scholars (3.4).

The study also revealed that the authorship trend is towards multi-authored papers. The average number of authors per article of IISc researchers is four and the degree of collaboration of publication is calculated to be 0.94.

Journals are the most preferred channel of publication followed by *communicated* type of publications and International seminars. The study shows that the *Phys. Rev. B* tops the list of IISc Physicists choice of journals for publication of research findings with 16 publications (9.58%). Physicists prefer to publish their research result in world-renowned journals with high IF.

The country-wise analysis of the journals preferred for publications shows that USA, UK and Netherlands are in the first three positions in the ranking order, and researchers publish a majority of their articles in the English language journals (90.79%). The researchers publish 17.65 per cent of articles in journals of American Physical Society (APS), followed by *Elsevier Science* (10.46%). Monthly journals are the most preferred journals for publication by the researchers, and weeklies are in the second position.

The publication behaviour indicates that the physics scholars are highly selective in publishing their research results in specialised and high impact factor journals. It would be quite interesting to study other scientometric indicator based on citations and impact factors, participation in international seminars, academic achievements and awards received by the research scholars.

References

Boyer, C J. (1973). *The doctoral dissertation as an information source: a study of scientific information flow*. Metuchen: The Scarecrow Press, 1-46.

Dhawan, S. M. and Gupta, B. M. (2007). Physics research in India: A study of Institutional performance based on publications output. *DEIDOC Bulletin of Information Technology,* 27 (1), 55-67.

Garg, K. C. and Rao, M. K. D. (1998). Bibliometric analysis of scientific productivity: a case study of Indian Physics laboratory. *Scientometrics,* 13, 261-268.

Girap, Priya., et al. (2009). Publication productivity of the Technical physics and Prototype Engineering Division at Bhabha Atomic Research Centre. *DEIDOC Journal of Library &Information Technology,* 29 (2), 39-54.

Gopikuttan, A. (2004). Scholarly publication pattern in Science: A case study of University of Kerala. *Kelpro Bulletin,* 8(1&2), 21-24.

Nalimov, V. V. and Mulchenko, Z. M. (1969). Naukometriya: Izuchenie Razvitiya Nanki Kak Informatsionnogo Protsessa [Scientometrics: Study of the development of science as an information process]. Russia: Nauka. 169p. Cited by Hood and Wilson, *Scientometrics,* 52 (2), 2001, 291-314.

Nandi, Amitava and Bandyopadhyay, Amit Kumar (2009). Contribution in Physics research: An analytical study with special reference to the University of Burdwan, West Bengal. *IASLIC Bulletin,* 54(3), 131-146.

Ramasesan, S. (1978). Proceedings of the seminar on primary communication in S & T in India, 4-8 Dec., Bangalore. R.N. Sharma and Seetharama, Eds. New Delhi: Publication & Information Directorate, .73.

Sangam, S. L. and Nargund, I. N. (1997). *Trend in research publications by Indian Physicists: A bibliometric analysis*. In Bibliometric studies. Ed by G. Devarajan. New Delhi: Ess Ess Publications, 99-112.

Sevukan, R. and Sharma, Jaideep. (2008). Bibliometric analysis of research output of Biotechnology faculties in some Indian Central universities. *DEIDOC Journal of Library &Information Technology,* 28 (6), 11-20.

Soman, K.N. (2001). A study of the scientific productivity and information use pattern of scientists in the context of new information technology with special reference to universities in Kerala. PhD thesis. University of Calicut.

Sudhier, K.G. (2007). Journal citations in Physics doctoral dissertations of Indian Institute of Science. *Annals of Library & Information Studies,* 54(4), 177-184.

28

Visualising Academia: Contributions of Scientometric Ranking Algorithms to the Study of Universities in Karnataka

—K. Manjula and K. S. Chudamani

Examines the contributions and performance of six universities of Karnataka in seven subjects, viz., Physics, Chemistry, Botany, Zoology, Geology, Biology and Mathematics. For the ranking of the universities, h- index is used. The study concludes that Mysore University has the highest scientific productivity. Scientific productivity according to subject-wise distribution differs from one university to another university.

Introduction

Science & Technology have played a very important role in the overall development of mankind. Scientific knowledge has led to remarkable innovations that have been of great benefit to society. Rapid advancements in science & technology have brought the tremendous changes in the global scientific knowledge and information at a faster rate. The twenty-first century is going to be driven by science & technology. The national developments are going to be increasingly dictated by the knowledge strength than by access to national resources and capital. It is science & technology, which are going to provide access to new knowledge and to economic benefits arising out of this knowledge. Thanks to the sustained efforts during the last five decades, today India can boast of a strong base more than 230 universities, a large network of research institutions from academic, R&D units. All science & technology based activities presumed their success on the availability of trained manpower. It is in this context, that the study and contribution of academic science is important.

Science and scientific research have obviously been growing at a faster rate during recent years resulting considerable increase in the number of institutions and manpower engaged in scientific education and research. Research is an indispensable component for any discipline for the generation of new knowledge and is a means of continuously developing a discipline, endowing capability to utilise the knowledge generated in other disciplines. It admits to learn and admits of organisation. Diffusion of R&D performed in Universities, especially the state universities is less noticeable when discussing about university R&D. Therefore, this study intends to carry out a study of their contributions.

R&D in Universities

The government established the University Grants Commission (UGC) by an Act of Parliament in 1956. It discharges the Constitutional mandate of coordination, determination, and maintenance of standards of teaching examination and research in the field of university and higher education. UGC serves as a vital link between the union and state governments and the institutions of higher learning. It monitors developments in the field of collegiate and university education; disburses grants to the universities and colleges; advises central and state governments on the measures necessary for the improvement of university education; and frames regulations such as those on the minimum standards of instruction.

UGC has no funds of its own. It receives both plan and non-plan grants from the central government to carry out the responsibilities assigned to it by law. It allocates and disburses full maintenance and development grants by law. Besides, it provides financial assistance to universities and colleges under various schemes/programmes for promoting relevance, quality and excellence as also promoting the role of social change by the universities.

History of S&T Research in India

The tradition of science and technology (S&T) in India is over 5,000 years old. A renaissance was witnessed in the first half of the twentieth century. The S&T infrastructure has grown up from about Rs. 10 million at the time of independence in 1947 to Rs. 30 billion. Significant achievements have been made in the areas of nuclear and space science, electronics and defence. The government is committed to making S&T an integral part of the socio-economic development of the country. India has the third largest scientific and technical manpower in the world.

Science and technology, however, is used as an effective instrument for growth and change. It is being brought into the mainstream of economic planning in the sectors of agriculture, industry and services. The country's resources are used to derive the maximum output for the benefit of society and improvement in the quality of life. About 85 per cent of the funds for S&T come directly or indirectly from the government. The S&T infrastructure in the country accounts for more than one per cent of the GNP. S&T in India is entering a new frontier. If one analyses the history of science and technology in India, since independence, it won't be too difficult to decipher the reasons. Scientific inquiry in India was launched under the aegis of several discreet groups like the universities, semi-autonomous organisations of research including cooperative researh associations like CSIR, NPL, NCL, ICAR, the Atomic Energy Commission, research and development organisation of the Ministry of Defence among others. Each of these organisations have a history, an organisational pattern, conditions of work, a vision and a mission, which were to be guided by the policy decisions.

Need for the Study

Science and technology are complementary in knowledge domain, wherein science symbolises discovery and knowledge generation, and technology symbolises innovations using knowledge. Technology is a mechanism for delivering the benefits of science to the people and society. Recognising the importance of science and technology in the economic and industrial development, the government of India reemphasized the need to view them together in its "Science and Technology Policy 2003" – following the scientific Policy Resolution of 1958" and the "Technology policy Resolution of 1983." While stating that "the nation continues to be firm in its resolve to support S&T in all its facets," the policy recognises the central role of our S&T system "in raising the quality of life of the people, particularly the disadvantaged sections of the society, in creating wealth for all, in making India globally competitive, in utilising natural resources in a sustainable manner, in protecting the environment and ensuring national security.

Despite the glorious record achievements and the progress made in the recent past, the pace of growth of the scientific enterprise in India has been comparatively slow. Universities and colleges have not been able to retain their good image in science and technology education. The University Grants Commission has recently initiated steps for improving science education at all levels. There is an urgent need to establish a fair and transparent system for reviewing research output. The present study attempts to assess and monitor the status of Karnataka States universities scientific productivity. Therefore, there is a need for visualising the academia using some acceptable measures.

There are six state universities in Karnataka which will be part of this study. They are:

- Mysore University www.uni-mysore.ac.in
- Mangalore University www.mangalore university. ac.in
- Karnatak University www.kud.ernet.in
- Bangalore University www.bangaloreuniversity.net
- Kuvempu University www.kuvempu.ac..in
- Gulbarga University www.gulbargauniversity. kar.nic.in

Methodology

For visualising the academia, one can make use of scientometric ranking algorithm as one of the means. One such measure is h-index. This is described as the methodology for the study.

For the present study, data is taken from Scopus database during 2000-2007. The assessment of research performance is carried along with publications of each university. These included number of publications, citations and cited articles including authorship pattern.

The quality and quantum of scientific research in India have been declining over the years due to inadequate infrastructure facilities, insufficient funding of research activities and particularly lack of sufficient number of committed scientific workforce. Our universities and laboratories have thus failed to respond to the needs of time. The consequences are clearly visible in the system. The enrolment in basic sciences over the years has declined. Our research laboratories do not get adequate number of competent personnel at the lower as well as at the higher level. Besides, there is an acute shortage of qualified teachers in basic sciences, engineering technology and medicine.

Scientometrics is a branch science of science. It explains output in terms of organisational structure and resources inputs, develops benchmarks to evaluate the quality of information sources; packages information for decision making in science; defines appropriate data aggregation producers and methods for diachronic analysis; empirically describes the constantly changing relationships between science, technology and the market; and forecasts productivity of scientists, so that the dynamics of scientific research and technological development can be understood.

Scientometrics

The term 'scientometrics' originated as a Russian term for the application of quantitative methods to the history of science. This term was introduced and came into prominence with founding of the journal named *Scientometrics* by T. Braun in 1977, originally published in Hungary and currently from Amsterdam. Scientometrics used to mean communication process in science including socio cultural aspects and appears to be almost synonymous with science with more stress on quantitative aspects; it also used as a generic term for a system of knowledge, which endeavours to study the scientific (and technological) system using a variety of approaches within the area of science and technology studies. Thus scientometrics is a part of the sociology of science and has application to science policy making.

According to Pouris, "Scientometrics is for science what econometrics is for economics." Therefore it is application of quantitative techniques (systems analysis, mathematical and statistical techniques, etc., to scientific communication science output, science policy, science administration etc.) with the objectives of:

- Developing science indicators
- Measuring the impact of science on society
- Comparing the output as well as the impact of science at national and international levels.

According to Tague–Sutcliffe scientometrics is "the study of the quantitative aspects of science as a discipline or economic activity." Thus Scientometrics involves studies in:

- Sociology of science.
- History of science.
- Growth of science & scientific institutions.
- Behaviour of science & scientists.
- Science policy and decision-making.

One of the interesting features of the bibliometrics/scientometrics/informetrics discipline is the fact that there are three related terms used to describe part or all this discipline. Each of these terms has a particular historical origin which is generally well documented. In addition, each of these terms has a range of definitions that have been applied to them by the authors who are working in this field. Theses definitions indicate considerable overlap in meaning of the terms, but they are not necessarily synonymous.

Over time, the popularity (or usage) of the terms has changed, with the older term 'bibliometrics' fairly stable and the newer terms, 'informetrics' and 'scientomerics' gaining in usage. The growth rate of the literature of this combined field has also stabilised over the last five years with an annual publication output of about 300 records.

As the interests of researchers in this field turn to the measurement of web pages or websites, new terms have been coined to describe the application of measurement techniques to the interest, web and cyberspace pages or sites (i.e., netometrics, webometrics, and cybermetrics). As with the mostly print-based metric terms, we can expect to see researchers choosing terms which they feel most accurately describe their work. In all likelihood, these electronic-based metric terms will co-exist for a time.

h-Index

The *h*-index introduced by Hirsch (2005), is a scalar index, an original, simple new indicator to characterise the cumulative impact of the research work of individual scientists. It is the highest number of publications of a scientist that received *h* or more citations each, while the other papers have not more than *h* citations each. It is immediately recognised (Ball, 2005) as an easy computable indicator for a scientist's achievement, because it incorporates both publication quantity and citation quantity. Since its introduction, the *h*-index has received a lot of attention, as can be seen by the 72 citations that the original paper (Hirsch, 2005) has already accumulated within the first two years which is more than sufficient to enhance Hirsch's h-index. Bornmann and Daniel (2007) reviewed the research literature on the *h*-index after one year. They have recently compared nine different variants of the *h*-index (Bornmann, Mutz, and Daniel 2008).

Objectives of the Webometrics Ranking of World's Universities

The original aim of the ranking of world universities was to promote web publication, not to rank institutions. Supporting open access initiatives, electronic access to scientific publications and to other academic material are our primary targets. However web indicators are very useful for ranking purposes too as they are not based on the number of visits or page design but global performance and visibility of the universities. As other rankings focused only on a few relevant aspects, specially research results, web indicators based ranking reflects better the whole picture, as many other activities of professors and researchers are showed by their web presence.

The web covers not only formal (e-journals, repositories) but also informal scholarly communication. Web publication is cheaper and also maintains the high standards of quality of peer review processes. It could also reach much larger potential audiences, offering access to scientific knowledge to researchers and institutions located in developing countries, and also to third parties (economic, industrial, political or cultural stakeholders) in their own community. The webometrics ranking has a larger coverage than other similar rankings. The ranking is not only focused on research results but also in other indicators which may reflect better the global quality of the scholar and research institutions worldwide.

They intend to motivate both institutions and scholars to have a web presence that reflect accurately their activities. If the web performance of an institution is below the expected position according to their academic excellence, university authorities should reconsider their web policy, promoting substantial increases of the volume and quality of their electronic publications. Candidate students should use additional criteria if they are trying to choose university, webometrics. Ranking correlates well with the quality of education provided and academic prestige, but other non-academic variables need to be taken into account.

Comparison of the World Universities' Rankings

There are many variables considered for web ranking, such as size, links, etc. Other factors considered are:

- *Visibility (V).* The total number of unique external links received (inlinks) by a site can be only confidently obtained from Yahoo Search, Live Search and Exalead.
- *Rich Files (R).* After evaluation of their relevance to academic and publication activities and considering the volume of the different file formats, the following were selected: Adobe Acrobat (.pdf), Adobe PostScript (.ps), Microsoft Word (.doc) and Microsoft Powerpoint (.ppt). These data were extracted using Google, Yahoo Search, Live Search.

Scholar (Sc). Google Scholar provides the number of papers and citations for each academic domain. These results from the Scholar database represent papers, reports and other academic items.

The four ranks were combined according to a formula where each one has a different weight, but maintaining the ratio 1:1.

Webometrics Rank		
Visibility	Size	20%
(external inlinks)	(Web pages)	
50%	Rich files	
	Scholar	15%

The inclusion of the total number of pages is based on the recognition of a new global market for academic information, so the web is the adequate platform for the internationalisation of the institutions. A strong and detailed web presence providing exact descriptions of the structure and activities of the university can attract new students and scholars worldwide.

The number of external inlinks received by a domain is a measure that represents visibility and impact of the published material, and although there is a great diversity of motivations for linking, a significant fraction works in a similar way as bibliographic citation. The success of self-archiving and other repositories related initiatives can be roughly represented from rich file and Scholar data. The huge numbers involved with the *pdf* and *doc* formats means that besides others, administrative reports and bureaucratic forms are involved. PostScript and Power point files are clearly related to academic activities.

The flaw with this approach is that those universities that have a well-developed web presence get a high rank. In India, as universities are very large, more focus is on training, research, etc. Therefore, they may not get high visibility. Therefore, other measures need exploration. One such measure is h-index.

Data Analysis

The research involves the ranking of the selected university using h-index. The data collection involves the determination of the research output, citation counts, etc. For this purpose the Scopus database has been used.

Scopus is the largest abstract and citation database of research literature and quality web sources. It's designed to find the information scientists need. Quick, easy and comprehensive, Scopus provides superior support of the literature research process. Updated daily, Scopus is the easiest way to get to relevant content fast. Tools to sort, refine and quickly identify results help you focus on the outcome of your work. You can spend less time mastering databases and more time on research.

In the present study an attempt has been made to examine the contribution and performance of six state universities of Karnataka to the mainstream literature in seven broad subject fields (Physics, Chemistry, Botany, Zoology, Geology, Biology and Mathematics) of Science and Technology and its impact during the period 2000-2006, using publications and their citations impact as criteria of research performance.

Scientific Productivity

Table 1: Scientific Productivity

Sl. No	*University*	*Total Article*	*%*	*Article cited*	*%*	*Citation*	*%*
1	Mysore University	1,178	28.75	556	28.91	2147	24.86
2	Bangalore University	915	22.33	406	21.11	1676	19.40
3	Karnatak University	761	18.75	380	19.76	2418	27.99
4	Mangalore University	686	16.74	345	17.94	1439	16.66
5	Gulbarga University	347	8.46	157	8.16	615	7.12
6	Kuvempu University	220	5.36	79	4.10	341	3.94
	Total	4,097	99.97	1923	99.98	8636	99.97

A total of 4,097 papers were published during 2000-2006 by the six state universities (Mysore, Bangalore, Karnataka, Mangalore, Gulbarga and Kuvempu) of Karnataka. Table 1 is self-explanatory.

Subject wise break up of publications

Table 2 Subject-wise Break-up of Total Publications

Subjects	*K.U.D*	*G U*	*MY*	*B U*	*M U*	*K U*
Chemistry	481	112	678	281	328	131
Physics	52	67	52	85	75	4
Biology	11	82	76	79	18	15
Botony	52	3	24	63	20	7
Zoology	77	6	50	82	35	8
Geology	3	1	13	5	11	6
Mathematics	13	0	18	6	10	0

h-index of Universities

Table 3 shows the impact or h-index of the universities computed based on productivity and citation.

Table 3
h-Index-wise Analysis of Productivity of Universities

Sl.No	*University*	*Total No Publication*	*%*	*Total No of citation*	*%*	*h-Index*
1	Mysore University	3,099	32.40	12,268	31.57	3.96
2	Karnatak University	2,490	26.03	12,387	31.88	4.97
3	Bangalore University	1,779	18.64	6,763	17.40	3.80
4	Mangalore University	1,346	14.07	5,168	13.30	3.84
5	Gulbarga University	646	6.75	1,852	4.76	2.87
6	Kuvempu University	204	2.13	412	1.06	2.02
	Total	9,564	100.00	38,850	99.95	21.46

- In scientific productivity it was found that Mysore University has the highest number articles published
- Mysore University has more citations in comparison to other universities.
- In subject-wise distribution these are differences from one university to another university. In all subject areas, each university has its own contribution. A university is the highest in one subject and another university is the highest in another subject. Therefore, it is difficult to judge how the impact factor alone can indicate all these facts.
- H-index as such may vary by subject. This needs further computation and examination on a large scale.

The study reveals that Mysore University had the maximum output in terms of number of publications, while Kuvempu University, Shimoga produced the least number of research articles. The proportion of papers in high quality journals was maximum in Karnatak University, Dharwad, whose IF is followed by Mysore and Bangalore Universities. The total normalised impact per paper depicted Karnatak University on the top, followed by the Mysore, Bangalore and Mangalore. The publication h-index of Karnataka University ranked first and the least was Kuvempu University.

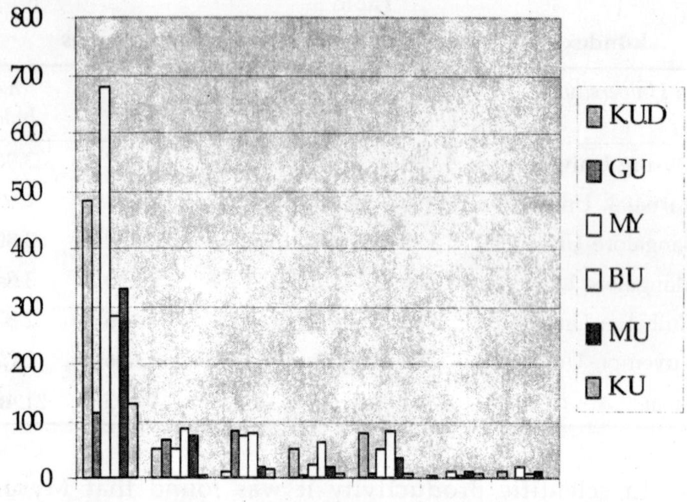

Figure 1: Subject-wise Productivity of Six Universities

Results of the study are only probable indicators for the state universities to evaluate the quality of their research publications in one dimension.

Recommendations

- New measures like h-index and impact factor need development for further testing of these ranks of universities.
- Broadening the scope is essential to examine the university contribution.
- Methods for improving productivity in cutting edge research needs development.Conclusion

Research performance is a multidimensional concept, which is computable using a single universal indicator. A number of indicators are available in the literature, which are useful to cope with the variety of the institutional locale of research, in the objectives of research, in the nature of output, and the purpose of measuring research performance. Measurement criteria vary with the type of institution. The scientists employed in R&D and academic organisations are more likely to be engaged in research leading to publication than those in government and industrial research institutions. Hence, publications in referred journals constituted the most important component of research output of academic institutions. Although many studies have been conducted with a view to assess the performance of various institutions in the field of science and technology, using scientometric indicators, only a few studies have been undertaken in India dealing with the assessment of universities.

Although there are several problems that has led to unsatisfactory scientific and technological advancement in the country, a rather pronounced one has been the insufficient diffusion of scientific knowledge in the country that could help promote a positive environment and attitude for better research and adoption of new technologies, generating feedbacks and posing new problems for scientific enquiry. A culture of scientific inquiry has not permeated in the masses and this has restrained the proper utilisation of scientific knowledge in the advancement of society.

References

Arunachalam, S. (2002). Is science in India on the decline? *Current Sciences*, 83 (2), 107-108.

Bornmann, L. and Daniel, H. D. (2007). What do we know about the h index? *Journal of American Society for Information Science and Technology*, 40.

Chidambaram, R. (2005). Measures of progress in science and Technology. *Current Science*, 88 (6), 856-60.

Hisch, J. E. (2005). An index to quantify an individual's scientific research output. *Proceedings of the National Academy of Sciences of the United States of America*, 102 (46), 16569-16572 Available at: http://www.pnas.org/egi/reprint/102/46/16569 (Accessed on 15 February, 2007).

McGraw Hill Dictionary of Scientific & Technical Terms: New York: MacGraw Hill, 1974.

Sangam.S.L. (1989). Obsolescence of literature in economics. *ILA Bulletin*, 25(2), 59.

Sengupta, I. N. (1989). *Bibliometrics and its application*. In *Information Science and Libraries*. Pushpa Dhyani, Ed.. New Delhi: Atlantic.

__________ (1985). Bibliometrics: A bird's eye view. *IASLIC Bulletin*, 30 (4), 167-174.

Tague-Sutcliffe, J. M. (1992). An introduction to Informetrics. *Information Processing and Management*, 28(1), 1-3.

VIII
Web 2.0

29

'Library One' – Forward from Library 2.0 and Further

— H. P. S. Kalra

The paper explores the term Library 2.0 and other similar terms, and suggests that the term 'library one' as an appropriate term be used for making and popularising 'library' as a brand. Rather than ride on the waves of terms created by the technology, librarianship should focus on its basics and roots in the information society environment. It argues that libraries have not progressed quantitatively, but have focused on quality and qualitative information. It lays emphasis on improving library systems and services in less developed countries like India. In the end, it hopes on the profession of librarianship coming out of Library 2.0 buzzword trap.

Introduction

Library 2.0 seems to be a neologism, which has been created to with a technological environment all around it. In spite of the benefits (Kelly et al, 2009) of all the technologies that help libraries and users reach an activated state called library 2.0, the concept is still ill-defined (Holmberg et al, 2009). But the term is increasingly used in library and information science journals, discussion forums, workshops, and conferences, though the concept has been coined in a blog in 2005 (Maness, 2006). For library 2.0 to have a clear and different context, we must be clear about the concept of 'Library 1.0', and about transition, if any, from Library 1.0 to Library 2.0.

Rather than ride on the waves of terminological jargon created by the technology, librarianship should focus on its basics and roots in the emerging information environment. New environments do necessitate coining of new words and terms to describe things and concepts, but rather than first create a term based on technology and then assign one or more contexts to it in librarianship would not be appropriate. Unfortunately, this seems to be the case with the term Library 2.0, although its creator Casey defines it very broadly arguing that it applies beyond technological innovation and service (Maness, 2006). Crawford (2006) compiled a list of 62 views and seven definitions of Library 2.0. If the present state of enthusiasm amongst library and information professionals remains at its present state and does not increase (which is highly unlikely), what would be the concept of Library 2.0, Library 3.0, ..., Library 5.0 and further; say a decade from now.

If we consider Library 2.0 (interpolated from Web 2.0) as a buzzword used to describe all sorts of activities that constitute a major transition by modern libraries in their outlook, services, resources, etc., to reach out to non-users and potential users, then a pertinent question in librarianship, particularly in the context of less and least developed countries, would be. 'What have been major transitions in the theory or practice of librarianship in the recent past?' Technologies might have changed the outlook of the libraries, but have Web 2.0 technologies in any way changed the way librarianship is commonly understood and practised in these countries.

From Web 2.0 to Web 1.0

There is no denying the fact that in the recent past change has been there, but it is riding on the wave of technology, and has less to do with changes in the theory and practice of librarianship. The activities that are sought to be undertaken under the broad umbrella heading Library 2.0 are similar to the activities that libraries and information centres have been carrying out in the pre-Web 2.0; but these activities are more complex in nature, perhaps larger in terms of scale and connectivity, and high-end technology driven, centred around library as a broad concept than its users. Adoption of library-centred approach by the proponents of Library 2.0 has been criticised (Plutchak, 2005). Therefore, it is time for libraries (whether of 1.0 or 2.0 or any other category) to reach out to their users adopting optimal technical environment with a philosophy: user is the king. So the library of the future is to be user driven, irrespective of the fact whether it is using Web 2.0 or Web 1.0 technologies, and systems that are designed for and marketed under Library 2.0 brand or otherwise.

Even the Web 2.0 world has not been free of criticism. Breeding (2006) argues that Web 1.0 technologies have not yet been fully achieved and a lot of potential still remains untapped in the application of Web 1.0 technologies, particularly in libraries. Thus, basic Web functionality needs to become ubiquitous towards building Web 2.0 concepts and technologies.

Qualitative Librarianship versus Quantitative Library#.0

Another feature of the terminology related to Web 2.0 and library 2.0 is the focus on quantitative change through whole numbers and parts. It clearly resembles the hangover from the numbering system for software versions. The essence of librarianship is not in quantification but in quality and qualitative information, though, most things with practice of librarianship are generally carried out with a quantitative perspective.

In the age of Web 2.0, Web 3.0 and further, librarians and information professionals should use 'One', not '1.0' as a suffix to the word library to symbolise the unity and strength of the library as a social institution. Library as the one and only primary social institution and as a concept represents preservation and access to knowledge and information.

It is high time that instead of using buzzwords like Library 2.0, we should concentrate on strengthening and making library, or in the terminology of Web 2.0 and Library 2.0, 'Library One' a popular and brand amongst at least all literate people, by coining appropriate terms in various languages. OCLC's report (2006) on a survey of 3,348 Internet users from Australia, Canada, India,

Singapore, the United Kingdom and the United States clearly indicate that library as a brand needs to be popularised, rather than focus on Library 1.0 or Library 2.0 or Library 3.0. Similar surveys should also be carried out for library users and non-users across India, preferably in their mother tongue, so as to understand the value of library for the users, and to find out the deficiencies in the library systems at local levels. The term 'Library One' should be discussed by library and information experts at national and international in the context of use of terms Web 2.0, Library 2.0 and the like, so that a library as a social agency should be promoted and developed rather than mired in needless discussion about 'library #.0'

The Perils of Library 2.0, 3.0 and Beyond

Extrapolating a little further into the world of books, documents, information, websites, blogs, social networking sites, and further would show even more advancements dominated by the technological tools and associated services and systems, but with core issues of quality of information and privacy of users dominated by technology remain unresolved (Rozenweig, 2006). Similarly, it has been stressed by Fister (2006) that "libraries need to find an ethical way to let our patrons do the kinds of record keeping and sharing they find useful and even natural while making sure such activities either are protected or that users are fully informed about the privacy they are giving up and its potential consequences." If we add an Orwellian-Ninteen-Eighty-Four perspective to the world of library 2.0., 3.0 and beyond, the library as a place and a concept would seem suddenly frightening.

Conclusion

"Don't move ahead without finishing the previous task or overlooking the past."

In Punjabi, a proverb can be roughly translated into what has been stated above in quotes. The brief discussion on librarianship and 'Library One' points to the meaning of the proverb. We should rather develop libraries and their collections rather than moving only along technology buzzwords. Plutchak (2006) has advised librarians to use the tools optimally in the following words:

"By all means, use all of the available tools, just don't get hung up on thinking that the tools provide the magic. Librarians do" (Plutchak, 2006).

Technology and its developments are important, and these would get incorporated into wherever these can be applied best. Shaping libraries, their collections and services solely on quantitative changes in technology would be disastrous for the libraries. The author is optimistic about the resilience of the profession of librarianship to come out of the Library 2.0 and other buzzword-traps in the near future.

References

Breeding, M. (2006). Web 2.0? let's get to web 1.0 first. *Computers in Libraries,* 26 (5), 30-33.

Crawford, Walt (2006). Library 2.0 and Library 2.0. *Cites and Insights,* 6 (2). Available at: http://citesandinsights.info/civ6i2.pdf

Danowski, Patrick (2007). [IFLA-L] Call for support: IFLA Library 2.0 discussion group. Available at: http://infoserv.inist.fr/wwsympa.fcgi/arc/ifla-l/2007-10/msg00046.html

Davis (2005). Talis, web 2.0 and all that. *Internet Alchemy blog.* Available at: http://internetalchemy.org/2005/07/lais-web-20-and-all-that

Fister, Barbara (2006). Do We Need Library 3.0? Available at: http://acrlblog.org/2006/06/08/do-we-need-library-30/

Holmberg, Kim et al. (2009). What is Library 2.0? *Journal of Documentation,* 65(4), 668-681.

Kelly, Brian et al. (2009). Library 2.0: balancing the risks and benefits to maximise the dividends. *Program: electronic library and information services,* 43(3), 311-327.

Maness, J. (2006). Library 2.0 Theory: Web 2.0 and its Implications for Libraries. *Webology,* 3(2) . Available at: www.webology.ir/2006/v3n2/q25.html

OCLC (2005) *Perceptions of libraries and information resources.* Available at:http://www.oclc.org/reports/2005perceptions.htm.

Plutchak, T. Scott (2005). *Librarian 5.0*. Available at: http://tscott.typepad.com/tsp/2005/12/librarian_50.html

Rozenweig, Mark (2006). The central problem of library 2.0: privacy. *Library Juice: on the intersection of libraries, politics, and culture.* Available at: http://libraryjuicepress.com/blog/?p=68

30

Online Social Networks and Their Impact on Information Communication

—Dineshan Koovakkai

Online social networks are means to connect with people in groups. The online social networking services such as MySpace, Facebook, Bebo, Skyrock, Hi5, Orkut, Friendster, CyWorld, etc., provide many facilities for information communication. They have great impact on personal group communication, business communication, professional communication, criminal investigation, teaching/learning, publishing, political campaigning and social activism.

Introduction

The ability to communicate distinguishes the living beings from the non-living. Communication is a process by which the feelings, emotions and ideas are exchanged with fellow living beings through gestures, symbols, signs, speeches or written words. Man, considered to be the most perfect creation of God, is communicating in a much better way by using written words and speeches apart from using other methods of communication.

Communication is a way of socialisation as well. It is a social process and means by which human beings keep in touch with one another. Communication may be verbal, written, audio-visual etc. (Arvind Kumar, 1999). Being a 'social animal' man maintains his relationship with his fellow beings by frequent communication. In the era of globalisation and social mobility where life is very fast and persons are dispersed, one cannot share his feelings with others in person always.

Speech was the first great step forward in the development of human communication. Inventions such as writing and printing were the important milestones in the history of human communication. The development of electronic way of communication has literally revolutionised the process of human communication.

The desire to communicate is generally natural to all living creatures. The fragrance of a flower, the grunt of a lion, cry of a baby, change in the facial expression—all are different methods adopted by the living beings to communicate different emotions and feelings. The use of electronic means of communication makes it possible to communicate with a greater speed to a wider audience. Online social networks provide a platform for sharing ideas and emotions in groups.

Online Social Networks

Online social networks are primarily web-based and provide various ways to interact through electronic media. They use software that enables people to connect and form virtual communities through Internet and provide communication facilities such as chat, messaging, e-mail, video, voice chat, file sharing, blogging, discussion groups and so on. Social networking has revolutionised the way people communicate and share information with one another. Various social networking websites are used by millions of people every day on a regular basis and it now seems that social networking is a part of everyday life (http://www.wikipedia.org)

The early efforts to support social network via computer-mediated communication include Usenet, ARPANET, LISTSERV, Bulletin Board Services (BBS) and Electronic Information Exchange Service. Early social networking websites include classmates.com, SixDegrees.com etc.

Social Network Services

Social network services build online social networks for communication of people who are willing to share interests and emotions. Most services are primarily web-based and provide various ways for users to interact. Many social networking services are means to connect with friends and professional groups. The social networking is now widely used in business, medicine and other areas of human activities. The most popular social network services include MySpace, Facebook, Bebo, Skyrock, Hi5, Orkut, Friendster, CyWorld, etc.

MySpace (www.MySpace.com)

MySpace is a social networking website which provides services such as bulletins, groups, instant messenger, mobile, news, karoke, classifieds, etc. It provides an interactive network of friends which includes personal profiles, blogs, photos, music and the like. MySpace allows users to customise their user profile pages by entering HTML into such areas as "About Me," "I'd Like to Meet," and "Interests." Users also have the option to add music to their profile pages via MySpace Music. Users can also change the general appearance of their page.

(*MySpace Home Page*)

Facebook (www.facebook.com)

Facebook is a free access social networking website launched by Facebook Inc. It allows users to join one or more networks of their interest or speciality to interact with others in the group. Users can post messages, upload albums, tag images, send virtual gifts and put classified advertisements through Facebook. Facebook allows users to upload an unlimited number of photos, compared with other image hosting services.

(*Home Page of Facebook*)

Bebo (http://www.bebo.com)

Bebo is an online social media network in which users can create account. When an account is created, it is private by default, which provides access to friends specially added. The users can also opt for public profile if he/she wishes to give access to his/her profile to any member. The other services of Bebo include Bebo music, Bebo authors, Bebo mobile etc.

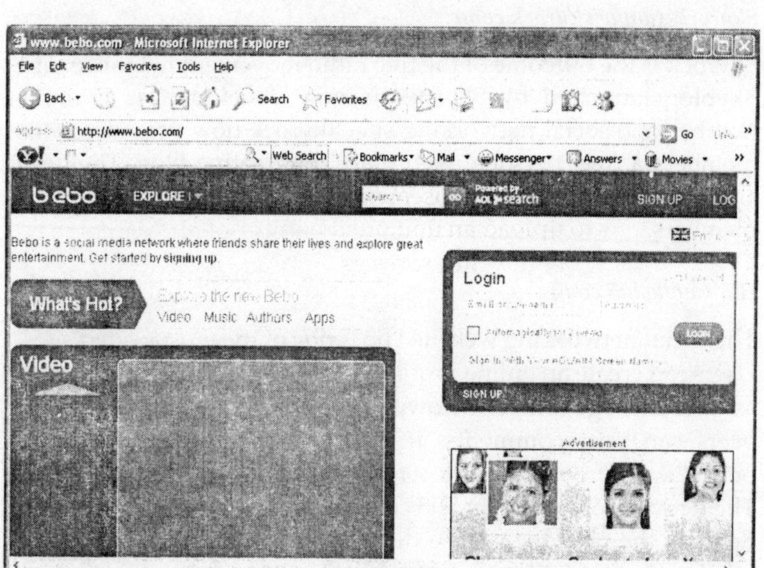

(Bebo Home Page)

(Home Page of Skyrock)

Skyrock (www.skyrock.com)

Skyrock is the outcome of the free radio movement in France. The Skyblog launched by Skyrock is now developed as France's number one social networking site. Skyrock now provides to its members a free, personal web space for creating blog. They can add profile and exchange messages with other registered members.

Hi5 (www.hi5.com)

The social networking website Hi5 is one of the most visited sites. Users can create an online profile in Hi5 to show information such as interests, age and hometown and upload user pictures where users can post comments. It also allows the users to create personal photo albums and set up a music player in the profile. The network of friends in Hi5 consists of users' direct friends (1st degree), the friends of those direct friends (2nd degree) and the friends of the friends of direct friends (3[rd]degree).

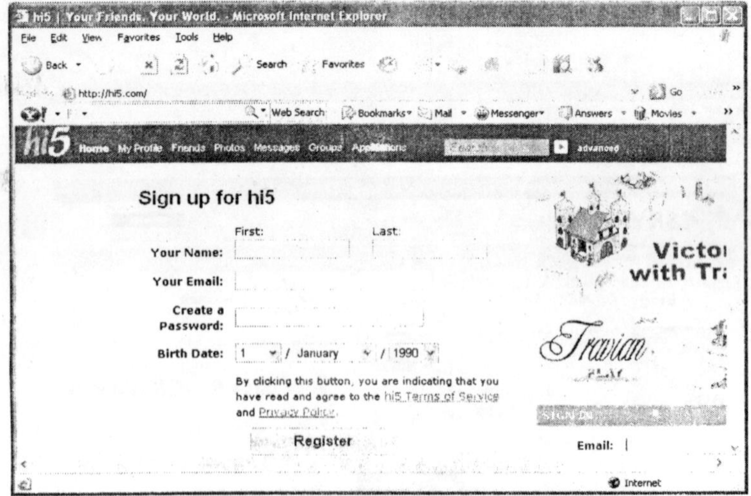

(*Home Page of Hi5*)

Orkut (www.orkut.com)

Orkut is one of the most visited social networking website in India which is run by Google. Users first create a profile in which the user provides his/her details. Users can also upload photos and videos into the Orkut profile. The communication is sent as scraps. Orkut users can also create communities and can post information to the group.

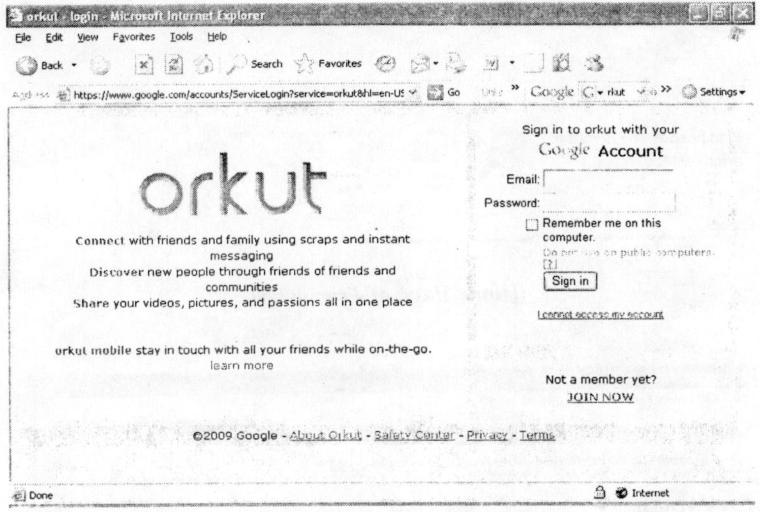

(*Orkut Home Page*)

Friendster (www.friendster.com)

Friendster is a privately owned Internet social network service. Friendster uses different techniques for networking individuals in virtual communities and demonstrates the small world phenomenon. A user of the system can determine the optimal relationship path (ie contact pathway) to reach desired individuals. A communication tool allows individuals in the system to be introduced (or introduce themselves) and initiate direct communication.

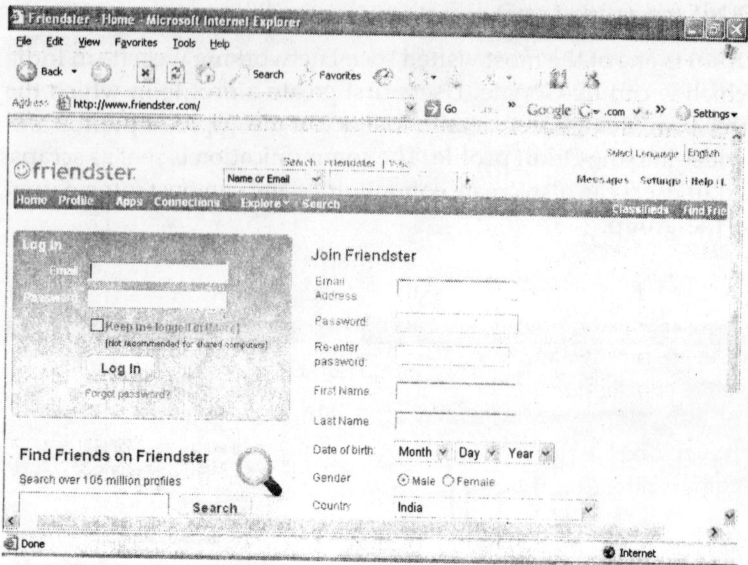

(Home Page of Friendster)

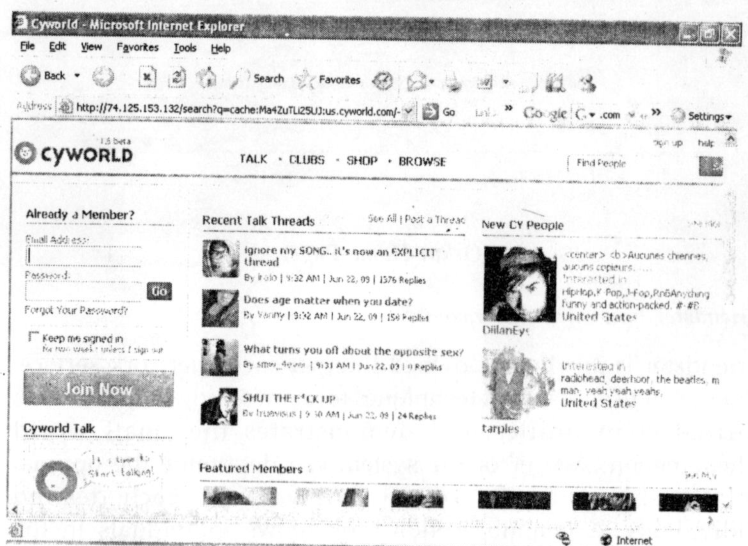

(CyWorld Home Page)

CyWorld (http://us.cyworld.com)

CyWorld is a web community site. Members cultivate online and offline relationships through a service called mini-homepage, which encompasses a photo gallery, message board, guestbook, friend list and personal bulletin board. CyWorld now provides more advanced services like Home2, club, paper etc.

Blog

A blog is a website, usually maintained by an individual or business establishment. Many blogs provide text, images and links to other blogs, web pages and other media. Readers can also leave comments in an interactive format. There are different types of blogs such as personal blogs, corporate blogs, political blogs, travel blogs, educational blogs etc. In the strict sense blogs do not come under the definition of social networking services.

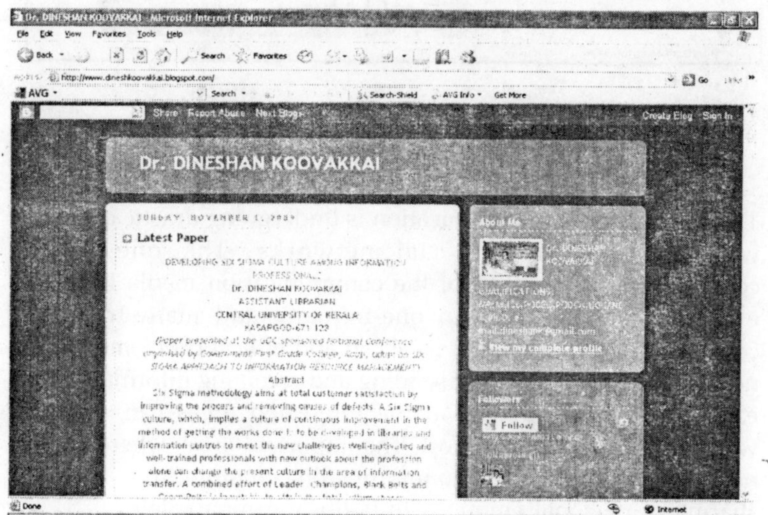

(Personal blog of the author)

Impact of Online Social Networks

Most of the on-line social network services provide more or less the same services. The main aim of these services is to connect people of similar interests and provide a platform for the exchange of their emotions and opinion.

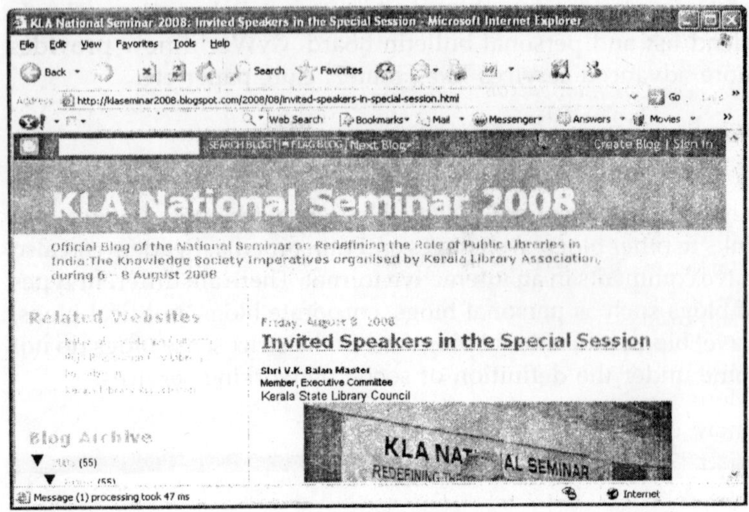

(Official blog of the National Seminar of Kerala Library Association)

The very mode of communication is undergoing drastic changes with the spread of social networks. The one-to-one communication in many of the communication media hitherto existing is giving way to one-to-many and many-to-many communication. In spite of its social and ethical problems, these networks provide a way of sending and receiving information so easily. The development in the interested areas can also be watched without much effort. The important areas where social networks have an impact on information communication include sharing of personal emotions to political campaigning.

Personal Group Communication

The online social networks help persons of similar interests like pet lovers, music lovers, etc., to exchange their feelings and discuss matters of interest. Persons of similar interest can send e-mail, post comments or take part in live chats through social networks. They enable friends to contact their school/college mates and share their ideas and emotions and lovers of sports, pets, flowers etc. can meet on the web and messages can be send in groups.

Business Communication

Entrepreneurs looking for expanding their contact base can use social networks at a lower cost. The social networks help them in better customer relationship management and better advertisement globally. Social networks can be used for marketing the products as well.

Professional Communication

Professional networking sites function as online meeting places. Members can post their own details in the form of blogs, share their experiences, interact with other professionals, discuss matters of interests, etc. Social networks also help the professional to know about the latest developments in their field of interest. LinkedIn.com is a good example of social networking being used by business professionals. In the medical field, Sermo.com is being widely used by American physicians to share their knowledge and discuss clinical subjects so as to update their knowledge and accurate patient care.

Criminal Investigation

The information posted on social network sites is used for many investigations. The content posted on these sites will give evidence about many criminal activities. The personal details and other information given by the students in sites such as MySpace, Facebook, etc., provides valuable information about adolescent crimes. School administrators and law enforcement agencies get valuable information through these sites.

Teaching and Learning

The social networking services can effectively be used in interactive teaching/learning. The students can post their reflections about their learning in class blogs. Social networks allow the students to receive feed back from teachers as well. The school blog can also be used to publish its newspaper, circulars and instructions to the students.

Publishing

Authors can create blogs to publish their works and express their experience in reading and writing. Bebo authors for example can upload chapters of their books and also get them reviewed. The readers can interact with the authors about their writings and other experiences.

Political Campaigning

Political organisations in many parts of the world are creating accounts on social networks like MySpace to keep in touch with their members. Many of the presidential candidates in America had set up MySpace profiles as part of the campaigning.

Social Activism

The social networking services are effectively being used in raising social issues and inviting live discussions. The environmental and social activists are also creating their accounts in social networks for expanding their membership base and campaigning.

Conclusion

The social networking services provided by various web service providers are revolutionising the pattern of information communication. They make the globe very small and connecting people and sharing of information among many is at the click ahead of every one who lives in the information society. They provide better environment for personal, business, professional and other communication.

Refereces

Arvind Kumar (Ed.). (1999). *The mass communication*. New Delhi: Anmol.
http://www.wikipedia.org (Accessed on 20th June, 2009).
http://www.myspace.com. (Accessed on 24th May, 2009).
http://www.facebook.com. (Accessed on 15th June, 2009).
http://www.bebo.com. (Accessed on 11th June, 2009).
http://www.skyrock.com. (Accessed on 12th June, 2009).
http://www.hi5.com. (Accessed on 24th June, 2009).
http://www.friendster.com. (Accessed on 24th June, 2009).
http://us.cyworld.com. (Accessed on 25th June, 2009).

31

Reaching Net Gen Students through Web 2.0: Challenges for University Libraries in India

—N. Nikesh and M. Ramina

This article brings out the skills of Net Generation students with Information Technology, and points out their preferences compared to the earlier generation. In this scenario, this paper analyses the Web 2.0 tools and services in which Net Generation students are more acquainted with and also describes how university libraries can incorporate such tools and services to deliver their information services. It also analyses some content management tools suitable for university libraries to develop their web portal.

Introduction

Much has been made about the new generation of technology-savvy students. Prensky (2001) called them *Digital Natives* and states that since they are born with all sorts of technology surrounding them, they have become 'native speakers' of the digital language. Many believe that these students possess unprecedented levels of skills with information technology and they think about and use technology very differently from their earlier generations. Many studies that have been conducted in different parts of the world in this regard endorse these believes (Diana, 2005 and Anoush). Indian Net Gen students are also not an exception to this fact. The survey conducted by Tata Consultancy Services (TCS) among school children said the new generation has shifted its social and academic life online. "The

TCS Generation Web 2.0 survey confirms that today's students are shifting their academic and social life online and embracing the digital world as true digital natives," said S. Ramadorai, Chief Executive and Managing Director of TCS. He also opinioned that "This societal trend has important implications for parents, educators, policy makers and future employers as well as companies and brands that want to sell to tomorrow's generation."

Another study conducted among Indian Net Gen Students across India by ISIM (not published) shows that majority of the Indian students are using one or more technological gadgets.

As a result of this ubiquitous environment and the sheer volume of their interaction with technology, today's students think and process information fundamentally different from their predecessors. Net Generation students value experiential learning, working in teams, collaborative learning and social networking. These all have a great implication on their information needs. As a result of this the present concept of university library is evolving. Today students mention Google more often than going to library. But ultimately they are not satisfied with the Internet search results for their information needs. Here is the space of a university library in providing what they want, but the present libraries need to realign their programs, services, and spaces with the Net Generation. Thus, a university library can become a part of campus life only if it is designed with genuine understanding of the needs of Net Generation (Net Gen) students. This does not just relate to the physical facilities of the library but, to all aspects of a library consisting of content, access, communication and services.

Indian University Libraries: Present Status

With the support of University Grants Commission and INFLIBNET university libraries in India are in their way of modernisation. Through its various programs it helps university libraries in India to improve their standards of services with latest technological aids. Notable two programmes are UGC INFONET and E-Journal Consortium. UGC-Infonet is an ambitious programme of UGC to interlink all the universities in the country with state-of-the-art technology. The network will overlay on ERNET backbone and provide Internet and Intranet Services. It is providing Internet Connectivity to more than 160 universities. INFLIBNET is responsible for executing and monitoring the entire project. E-Journal Consortium is a national initiative for providing access to scholarly electronic resources including full-text and bibliographic databases in all subject disciplines, to the academic community in India. It facilitates access to high quality e-resources to the academia in the country to improve teaching, learning and research. The Consortium provides current as well as archival access to more than 5,000 core and peer-reviewed journals and nine bibliographic databases in different disciplines from 23 publishers and aggregators. The access to all major e-resources was given to 50 universities in first phase in the year 2004. It has now been extended to 157 universities in three different phases.

So with the help of these now, university libraries in India are using technologies to access to scholarly databases, for circulation systems, and for online catalogues. With the explosion of Internet technologies, libraries incorporated a wide array of digital content resources into their offerings; updated the network with wired and wireless infrastructures of their buildings; and designed new virtual and in-person services. However, technology has resulted in more modernisation than transformation. There is an apparent disconnect between the culture of library organisations and that of Net Gen students. This paper will explore how libraries might better adapt to the needs of Net Gen students in a number of specific areas.

While examining the gap between present university library system and Net Generation students, we can observe that students are more depended on Google like search engines for discovery of information resources rather than coming to the library or library resources. Recent surveys exploring college students' use of Web-versus-the-library confirm this commonly held perception. Indian scenario is also not different from this. For the purpose of studying this, a survey was conducted among postgraduate and research scholars of Cochin University of

Science and Technology, Kerala, and the results were reinforcing this fact. Eighty per cent of the students prefer Information gathering through Internet search engines for their immediate information needs. Tata Consultancy Services also gives almost the same results in their survey. In that survey Google (41%) emerges as most preferred source of information.

The reason might be the fact that most of the library web pages are designed not in a user-centred mode. Net generation students are familiar and enjoying the Web 2.0 communication and collaboration features in the Internet. But library websites generally do not have the provision, software or support for student creation of new information products. So there are high chances that students get bored with the unilateral/monotonous presentations of library website without much user interaction facility.

In order to take remedial measures to bridge the disconnect between Net Generation students and university libraries, it is very much essential to get a thorough understanding regarding students habits of toying with web 2.0 technologies.

The survey result published by Tata Consultancy Services mentioned above very much speaks about this. The survey was conducted across 14,000 high school children in the age group of 12-18 in 12 cities across the country. It said about 80 per cent of the students surveyed have access to mobile phones and have embraced Web 2.0 tools like blogs and social networking sites.

According to the survey, Orkut and Facebook are the most popular destinations, and about 93 per cent of the students surveyed are aware about these sites. While 62 per cent have personal computers at home, one in four students owns laptop in metros.

The next question is how university libraries can befriend students by incorporating their technological toys with their library web portals.

Net Gen Libraries: Deliver Information Services with Web 2.0

The most important is the presentation of library web portals in an interactive mode. It is embarrassing to see that none of the university libraries in India have incorporated Web 2.0 features in their web portals. The following options might transform university libraries' information services by incorporating user participation and also by adopting interactive and collaborative tools according to user demands.

User Participation

In order to conceive the user's perceptions regarding their expectations and new services to be introduced, library patrons should ensure student participation in the design phase of the revamped system. Making use of the imagination, creativity, technical skills, and perspectives of Net Gen students is the best way to ensure that new services will be responsive to both their needs and their style.

Interaction Tools

Net Generation students will only be happier if they would get a chance of interaction with librarians and other experts as and when needed. Here two options can be made available for users. One is online interaction with library staff. This ensures support to users in working hours. Users can make use Library professional's expertise in seeking information from library resources and also from other resources. Here chances are more to get their relevant information rather than going directly to Internet search engines. This will slowly shift the preference choice of users from search engines to library portal. Another one is facilitating communication among users. Providing facilities in the library portal to create discussion groups for different interested groups will surely benefit academic community to discuss their topics of choice. This would provide option to throw their questions and get answers utilising the intellectual capacity of different users. This will help in socialising of information. Also the accumulated knowledge base would serve remarkably in future by providing search interface to this knowledge treasure. Many of the queries may get their solution from this base.

Visual aids

Visual aids Represent services and instructions visually and in multimedia modes. Users can make use of these facilities of library portals without attending library orientation programs. Instruction programmes should emphasise in giving the users a clear idea about the evaluation of various information resources in and out of the library. If needed a facility to link with the online support system could also be provided.

Personalisation

Some users may have their own knowledge about information resources in their subjects of interest. Personal space with customisation option should be given to each user to keep their information resources within the library portal. This can be made available to all the users in a collaborative way with search interfaces. This will produce fantastic results and thus become another knowledge base.

Online Reference Services

Many libraries have been offering e-mail reference services for a number of years. But Net Gen students are not satisfied with this. They are expecting simpler systems like Skype to facilitate voice interaction with librarians for their reference queries. VoIP technologies may be utilised for introducing these kinds of services. This would surely be an appeal to the multitasking Net Gen students so that they can continue their working and browsing as per the suggestions of the librarian over phone with or without webcam. This will feel like personalised attention of a librarian to the user though it is a virtual presence

Instant Messaging using twitter

Twitter (www.twitter.com) is a fast-growing, free messaging service for people, and it's one that libraries (and librarians) can make good use of—without spending much time or effort.

Twitter lets people send and receive short messages (called Tweets) via the web or via SMS using a mobile phone. Messages on Twitter are limited to a maximum of 140 characters, including spaces, and they're generally public. Because each message is just a sentence or two, a carefully crafted post can convey a good deal of information without taking a lot of time to read or write In addition, because Twitter has millions of users, it's a good place to find and connect with people interested, in your institution and/or your areas of expertise.

To automatically see what someone else is saying, you "follow" them. Those who regularly receive your posts are your "followers." You don't need to give each other permission to follow, and you can view Tweets without signing into Twitter, but you must sign in to follow someone.

Libraries can incorporate twitter APIs in their web portal. This will facilitate to share all kinds of news that users want. Short messages can tell people about events such as readings, lectures, and book release; newly available resources etc. Twitter posts can link to interesting news stories about literacy or about libraries. If needed, the posts can link to a library's own website and blog for more indepth information.

Social book-marking and tagging

Bookmarking and tagging are gaining popularity among Net users. Famous book marking site del.icio.us lets users bookmark web pages for themselves and others check out what others bookmark, and organise bookmarks at one place for portability. Besides its well-known basic tagging and bookmarking capabilities, del.icio.us offers a built-in tool set and application programming interface (API) that lets libraries do practically anything with their data. Its tag roll and link roll features, which update steadily, provide any account user with a snippet of JavaScript for any web page or blog, allowing easy access to a library's del.icio.us links. While library catalogs and databases rely on controlled vocabularies and traditional subject guides, and pathfinders often address only broad categories, tags allow library staff and users autonomy to assign worthy links multiple tags in natural language.

RSS

RSS, Really Simple Syndication or Rich Site Summary, allows a producer of information to broadcast the information across an Intranet or the Internet. It is created using XML language, an extensible markup language. XML allows the information producer to "tag" information creating metadata (data about data). The creation of metadata allows the specific information to be pulled from the document, converted into a script and displayed on a web page. XML RSS feeds can also be read through an RSS Reader. RSS can well be utilised in Library web portals in the following areas:

- To deliver selected targeted information to specific user groups.
- To offer website users the latest information from various sources.
- Efficient technique to use/update web pages.
- To deliver current awareness and news
- To deliver table of contents service
- Information can be pulled from catalogs or databases, converted into an RSS feed and displayed on web pages.

Once a user subscribes to a feed, the desired information is delivered to the user without them taking the time to search or browse for it. RSS feeds are read through an RSS Reader or placed as web content. Thus, work and personal email boxes are not overloaded with additional information for the user to read. This enables users to stay current on the latest information.

Explore services of mobile devices

A survey among Indian university students shows nearly all University students have access to mobile phone. So libraries need to utilise this powerful communication medium to deliver its services. Information services of all kinds or its snippets can be delivered through mobile phone. Library integration software can be linked with mobile phone for sending circulation details like reminders, reservation status, etc. Now it is possible to link other web 2.0 service like Twitter, Skype, other list servers, etc., to mobile phones to deliver instant information.

Development of wikis

The greatest example of information collaboration, the Wikipedia, is now evolving as the single largest source of knowledge in the world. Many institutions have started their own wikis for collaborative development of information systems. University libraries can take lead to develop and host wikis. Many open source wiki software are available now. Mediawiki *(www.mediawiki.org),* the software platform used for the development of Wikipedia, is having many robust features that can be utilised by library systems.

CMS for Library 2.0

In the dynamic web environment, collection, management, and publishing processes are too complex. Contents may be too much and rapidly changing. Contributors will be more in web 2.0 arena. In this context presenting useful contents in library portal is a complex task. Content is granular information. It could be text, graphics, pictures, sounds, videos, data, etc., Greater challenge of library and information science professionals is how to manage this granular information in the dynamic web environment. Here comes the importance of Content Management Systems. Content Management System manages contents in its overall lifecycle starting from creation to dissemination. Implementing content management system in library, library website environment needs the content management strategy. Next step is choosing content management software with robust features that suits library 2.0 implementation. There are many free and open source Content Management Software available. Three popular Software systems are Joomla, Wordpress and Drupal.

Joomla (www.joomla.org/)

Joomla enables you to build websites and powerful online applications. Many aspects, including its ease-of-use and extensibility, have made Joomla one of the most popular Web site software available. Many libraries have used Joomla to develop their portals. Joomla in libraries showcase the library sites developed using Joomla.

Wordpress (www.wordpress.org/)

WordPress is a blog publishing application and content management system. It was first released in May 2003. It is powered by PHP and a *SQL* data backend. As of September 2009,

Wordpress is used by 62.8 million websites in the US and 202 million websites worldwide. Many libraries have developed their web portals using Wordpress.

Drupal (*http://drupal.org*)

Drupal is a free software package that allows an individual or a community of users to easily publish, manage and organise a wide variety of content on a website. Tens of thousands of people and organisations are *using Drupal* to power scores of different web sites. Library Technology Reports of the American Library Asociation present an overview of Drupal for the library audience hoping to show why and how libraries can get started using Drupal.

Conclusion

The earlier concept of a library being a three dimensional model of user, staff and the physical component or documents have become outdated. Now it has taken a paradigm shift towards a multidimensional web environment where there are umpteen numbers of multifaceted aspects of information to be located from a cloud of information on the web each time.

As a majority of students and academic community treat web as the main source of information, libraries also need to change by adapting latest trends in the web information arena. Web has changed from its one dimensional Web 1.0 phase to two-dimensional or interactive /collaborative computing in the Web 2.0 phase, and is moving towards meaningful or semantic Web what we call as Web 3.0.

So it is high time to wake up and adapt to the dramatically changing environment. Library services and content has to be responsive pertaining to the NetGen students demands. A conscious efforts are called for from the part university libraries in India to address the deficiencies in the present system and transform to an environment that resonate with Net Gen students thus enriching their higher education and lifelong learning capabilities.

References

Anoush Margaryan and Allison Littlejohn. Are digital natives a myth or reality?: Students' use of technologies for learning, Caledonian Academy, Glasgow Caledonian University, UK . Available at: http://www.academy.gcal.ac.uk/anoush/documents/DigitalNativesMythOrReality-MargaryanAndLittlejohn-draft-111208.pdf (Accessed on 25 April 2009)

Diana G. Oblinger and James L. Oblinger, Eds. (2005). Educating the Net Generation. (Boulder: EDUCAUSE, 2005). Available at: http://www.educause.edu/educatingthenetgen.

http://drupal.org/cases

http://en.wikipedia.org/wiki/WordPress

http://wp4lib.bluwiki.com/#Library_Sites_That_Use_WordPress. http://www.techsource.ala.org/ltr/drupal-in-libraries.html)

http://www.joomlainlibrary.com/index.php?option=com_jashowcase&view=jashowcase&Itemid=70

http://www.tcs.com/SiteCollectionDocuments/TCS_News/TCS_PR_Generation_Web2.0_Survey_07_09.pdf5

http://www.techsource.ala.org/ltr/drupal-in-libraries.html

http://www.ugc.ac.in/new_initiatives/cons_subscription.html

http://www.educause.edu/Resources/EducatingtheNetGeneration/NetGenerationStudentsandLibrar/6067#3

Prensky, Mark. (2001). Digital Natives, Digital Immigrants: On the Horizon, MCB university Press, 9. Available at: http://www.marcprensky.com/writing/Prensky%20-%20Digital%20Natives,%20Digital%20Immigrants%20-%20Part1.pdf

www.inflibnet.ac.in

www.isim.ac.in

www.ugc.ac.in/

www.ugc.ac.in/new_initiatives/infonet.htm

IX
Meta Data

32

Metadata Standards for Cataloguing Indian Manuscripts: Some Refelections

—**N. S. Harinarayana** and **N. N. Prasad**

Cataloguing of manuscripts is one of the areas which has received a scant attention by the Indian cataloguers. Information technology has enabled not only to provide better opportunity to preserve the content of the manuscripts for posterity but also helped to provide efficient access from remote areas to these manuscripts. Creating metadata records for their resources is an important function in digital library initiatives. Although attempts have been made in this direction, no single standard has been universally accepted and adopted for cataloguing of manuscripts. This leads to a situation where inconsistency and non-uniformity in cataloguing practices of manuscripts exists. Hence, this paper aims to identify appropriate standards for the description of manuscripts, comprehensively and efficiently with a special reference to Indian situation. The standard such as AACR2R, MARC21, EAMMS, Digital Scriptorium and Text Encoding Initiative are discussed. The standards available for description of manuscripts such as 'Digital Scriptorium' and 'Text Encoding Initiative' (TEI-MSS) are examined and mutual mapping of the elements are done.

Introduction

Cataloguing has been a specialised activity in libraries. It requires a fair amount of training and practice. History has witnessed efforts to achieve uniformity and consistency in cataloguing activity. Right from Cutter to RDA, different rules and codes have been developed for holding the bibliographical details for storage and retrieval. In spite of strict rules and policies, variations can be observed in cataloguing practice. It is probably difficult for any one document to provide the rules required for all kinds of resources including manuscripts. Indeed, the heterogeneity of the nature of manuscripts demands to consider it as a separate class for cataloguing and poses a challenge for the cataloguers engaged in descriptive cataloguing.

Cushioned in the hoary antiquity of several millennia, the cultural heritage of India descends down to us through manuscripts. These manuscripts constitute sources of very valuable information for the social, cultural and literary history of India. Thus manuscripts are the written ambassadors of our history; they are the cultural heritage reserves of our country. They contribute in threading up the cultural, literary, educational, economical and historical continuity of life, lived in different stages of cultural evolution.

India, an important country of the orient, possesses millions of manuscripts like the Arab countries. Manuscripts were produced in all parts of the country: they are in many languages and scripts and on a wide range of religious, philosophical, historical, literary and scientific subjects. Preservation and organisation of these valuable sources of information are big challenges to the information professionals. Issues and problems in handling these manuscripts, particularly cataloguing them, are being discussed in this paper.

Cataloguing of Manuscripts

Librarians have been engaged in resource description for as long as there have been libraries. The origin of modern Anglo-American cataloguing however is generally traced to Sir Anthony Panizzi's compilation of cataloguing rules for British Museum in the mid-nineteenth century. Contributions from Charles Jewett and Charles Cutter have been considered monumental in the history of cataloguing. Ranganathan has also come out with Classified Catalogue Code which did not become that popular when compared to his classification scheme – 'Colon Classification'. The development of Anglo-American Cataloguing Rules (AACR) has brought a significant uniformity among cataloguers of the world. The *Machine Readable Catalogue* (MARC), published and maintained by Library of Congress, provided a mechanism for encoding the catalogue data in computers. MARC is a very detailed ambitious standard which tries to accommodate all sorts of resources. However, it has been found that even MARC is not sufficient to suit the requirements of a very specialised resource like manuscripts. Manuscripts are special in their own right and provide unique set of issues for catalogues. The following paragraphs in this section highlights some of the issues in cataloguing of manuscripts with special reference to Indian manuscripts.

A manuscript is a unique book; there are no duplicates. Even if the text is same, as in the case of a model and it's copy, the two books are different in script, physical appearance and even text, because a handwritten copy always contains some changes in comparison with its source. According to M L Saini, "If a collection of printed catalogues of Indian manuscripts were brought together at the present time it would extend over more than 50 feet (or about 15 metre) of shelving and would constitute in itself a specialist library. We have reason to suppose that more than one million of Indian manuscripts are deposited in libraries public or private, and that more than 6,00,000 different manuscripts have been listed in some manner in printed catalogues since the origins of Indian studies a century and a half ago." And so many other features of the Indian manuscripts pose challenges to the organisers and cataloguers. However, to highlight a few, the problems in cataloguing of Indian manuscripts are summarised as follows:

- Uncertain authorship. Authors are almost bee-hived in obscurity and the variants in Indian name only add confusion to obscurity.
- Proliferation of the different manuscripts of the same text both in India and abroad and also the mass of related peripheral literature render the task of identification and authentication difficult.
- Overwhelming enormity of anonymous works.
- Lingual and scriptural variations also contribute to confusion. Synonymy in sounds and signs leads to interchangeability. Errors of scribes have lead to the complete divergence between the meanings of the text of the original and its manuscripts.

- Loose-leaf practice of manuscript maintenance has resulted into mutual shuffling of pages.
- Indian manuscript catalogues swarmed up inordinately both in quality and quantity, quite unrelated and independent of one another even in the same very language.
- Hence, cataloguing a manuscript is a difficult task, which requires a skill and competence. However, with the advent of IT, using Metadata standards, a comprehensive cataloguing and access to manuscripts can be made easier and simpler.

Metadata Standards

Metadata is structured data, which describes the characteristics of a resource. The term *Meta* derives from the Greek word denoting a nature of higher order or more fundamental kind. It shares many similar characteristics to the cataloging that takes place in libraries, museum, archives, and manuscripts, etc. This enables people searching for electronic information to find the information they are seeking more efficiently. Metadata is invaluable for both discovering and using resources because it succinctly describes, manages catalogues, and retrieves the resources, efficiently and effectively.

Some of the most popular metadata schemes that could be used for cataloguing for manuscripts include:

- AACR-2 (Anglo-American Cataloguing Rules 2nd Edition)
- APPM (Archives, Personal Papers, and Manuscripts: A Cataloging Manual for Archival Repositories, Historical Societies, and Manuscript Libraries)
- MARC21 (United States Machine Readable Cataloguing)
- DC (Dublin core)
- EAMMS (Electronic Access to Medieval Manuscripts)
- Text Encoding Initiative (TEI)
- Digital Scriptorium

Each metadata scheme will usually have the following characteristics:

- A limited number of elements.
- The name of each element.
- The meaning of each element.
- Guidelines as to how the data values have to be rendered/ stored in these elements.

Syntax, though, is not strictly part of the metadata scheme, the data will be unusable, unless the encoding scheme understands the semantics of metadata scheme. The encoding allows the metadata to be processed by a computer programme. A few of these are:

- HTML (Hyper Text Make-up Language)
- SGML (Standard Generalised Make-up Language)
- XML (Extensible Make-up Language)
- RDF (Resources Description Framework)
- MIME (Multipurpose Internet Mail Extension)

Typically, the semantics is descriptions of the contents, location, physical attributes, type (e.g., text, image, map or model.) and form (e.g., print copy, electronic file, and manuscript). The metadata elements supporting access to published documents include the originator of work. When and where it was published and the subset areas it covers, where the information is issued in analogue form, such as print material, additional metadata, is provided to assist in the location of the information e.g.: call numbers, accession numbers, used in libraries. The resource community may also define some logical grouping of the elements or leave it to the encoding scheme.

Metadata Standards for Manuscript Cataloguing

A few metadata standards are available for cataloguing of manuscripts, out of which AACR2R, MARC21, EAMMS, Digital Scriptorium and Text Encoding Initiative are briefly discussed here:

AACR2R

The Anglo-American Cataloguing Rules is the most widely used cataloging rules for printed materials. The first edition of AACR appeared in 1967, a cooperative effort of cataloguers in the US,

UK, and Canada. The second edition, published in 1978 and revised in 1988, was developed by the Joint Steering Committee for Revision of AACR, Michael Gorman and Paul Winkler, editors. The revised edition was published in the year 1998. Amendments were brought out in 2001.

Rules for descriptive cataloguing of all types of materials are likely to be found in general Library collections. Individual chapters cover books, pamphlets, and printed sheets; cartographic materials; manuscripts; music; sound recordings; motion pictures and video recordings; graphic materials; computer files; three-dimensional artifacts; microforms; and serials. Rules guide cataloguers in (1) constructing descriptions to identify and represent bibliographic works in catalogues; and (2) constructing uniform headings (for persons, corporate bodies, geographic places, and titles) to be used as access points in catalogues. They do not cover subject cataloguing. AACR 2, Chapter 4, "Manuscripts," focuses on description of individual manuscript items, particularly literary manuscripts and letters. The rules of AACR2R form the broad basis for the data entry in other standards such as APPM, MARC21, Digital Scriptorium etc.

Archives, Personal Papers, and Manuscripts: A Cataloguing Manual for Archival Repositories, Historical Societie and Manuscript Libraries (APPM)

APPM proves rules for descriptive cataloguing of archival materials in any physical format, focusing on collections or groups and the historical context of creation rather than on individual items, although they will accommodate item-level description. In the US it replaces AACR 2 Chapter 4 for repositories that wish to emphasize aspects of archival control in their cataloguing. By following the general structure and approach of AACR 2, APPM provides for the integration of information about archival materials with information about other research resources in bibliographic systems. Rules guide cataloguers in (1) constructing descriptions to identify and represent archival material in catalogues, and (2) selecting and constructing uniform headings (for persons, corporate bodies, geographic places, and titles) to be used as access points in catalogues. The chapters on headings borrow heavily from AACR 2 and incorporate some Library of

Congress Rule Interpretations and they do not cover subject catalogueing.

MARC21

MARC is not a cataloguing code, but as widely used as an encoding standard for cataloguing data. It can be thought of like a framework for holding the bibliographic data. MARC is an acronym for MAchine-Readable Cataloging. The five MARC 21 communication formats—Bibliographic Data, Authority Data, Holdings Data, Classification Data and Community Information—are widely used standards for the representation and exchange of bibliographic, authority, holdings, classification, and community information data in computer readable form. Each MARC format provides detailed field descriptions and guidelines for applying the defined content designation and identifies conventions to be used to insure input consistency. The tags normally used for manuscripts include 001, 003, 005, 006,007, 008, 035, 040, 080, 082, 100, 110, 240, 245, 246, 250, 260, 300, 440, 500, 505, 506, 520, 530, 533, 535, 546, 561, 581, 600, 650, 700, 710, 752, etc. However, many feel that MARC21 does not meet all the requirements of manuscript cataloguing.

EAMMS

Electronic Access to Medieval Manuscripts is a recent project to develop guidelines for encoding and storing catalogue descriptions of medieval and Renaissance manuscripts in electronic form. The project receives funding from the Andrew W. Mellon Foundation, and is affiliated with another Mellon-funded project, the Digital Scriptorium. The goal of EAMMS is:

- to identify the type of information contained in a summary catalogue record and determine how such information might be encoded for storage in a relational database;
- to identify and classify additional categories of information contained by a full, scholarly catalogue record, and determine how this information might also be encoded;
- to test and refine the guidelines for encoding by creating a database of electronic catalogue records encoded according to the guidelines, and to allow online access to this database.

Digital Scriptorium

Digital Scriptorium is a project started in 1996 with a grant of the Andrew W. Millon Foundation to the Bancroft Library of the University of California at Berkeley, and the Rare Book and Manuscript Library of Columbia University in New York. Consuelo W. Dutschke, Curator of Medieval and Renaissance Manuscripts at Columbia, says, "Digital Scriptorium is a web-based visual union catalogue of medieval and renaissance manuscripts: web based, in that it was intended form the start as on expendable and correctable tool, in the way that the static media of print or even CD-ROM cannot be; Union, because it meshes into one database the holdings of a number of institutions; and visual, because it includes at least one image of every manuscript described, thus allowing the user to test and eventually correct the catalogued information by means of his own specialised knowledge."

At present Digital Scriptorium contains about 2,200 entries and 2000 images. It has been created with an access database compatible with the TEI-DTD. The Digital Scriptorium database dictionary accompanies the Microsoft. "Access 97" database structure, designed in 1997 at the University of California, Barkeley by John Hassan and Merrillee Profitt in consultation with C.W Dutschke (Curatov of Medieval and manuscripts at Coloumbia) and Martha Rust (then at Berkely), has been incorporated over a period of time. The database in intended to collect in an efficient and organised manner basic information about manuscripts held by the Digital Scriptorium partners, and to provide searching prints for images form these holdings.

The database is divide into two sections (1) Document and (2) Image, The document containing ownership, i.e. (historical) information about the manuscript, then the descriptive (i.e., physical) and bibliographic (i.e., textual) information about the manuscript, as well as the caption information for individual images. Thus document section has four parts:

a) Manuscript

b) Part

c) Test

d) Image

In practice to first level "manuscript" identifies the single codex; the second level "part" contains most of the physical information about the codex; the third level, "text" holds bibliographic information; the fourth level, "image" refers to what the end-user sees on the web. Each successive level is dependent upon the proceeding level (s), in a potentially, but not necessarily many-to-one relationship, to its predecessor. The second section called 'Image' which is not defined here, contains the processing data about the image (i.e., image capture metadata, for example, type of capture, film type, shatter speed, frame etc.). In this database totally 67 fields are provided to describe the given manuscript among which 14 fields are required fields.

Text Encoding Initiative For Manuscripts Cataloguing (TEI-Ms)

Text Encoding Initiative (TEI) is an interaction and interdisciplinary project, established in 1987, to develop guidelines for the encoding of textual material in the electronic form for research purposes. TEI became a consortium in 2000. The University of Oxford, the Brown University, the University of Bergen and the University of Virginia host the TEI-Consortium; a sub-group is devoted to manuscript cataloguing. TEI is an international standard that helps libraries, museum, publishers and individual scholars to represent all kinds of literary and linguistic texts for online research and teaching, using an encoding scheme that is maximally expressive and minimally obsolescent. TEI is an interchangeable format; it continues to develop and maintain encoding standards. It has a specific mark-up syntax as well as well defined tag set, but few tags are mandatory.

TEI Header is a set of descriptions prefixed to the TEI encoded document that specifies four components:

a) File description (a full bibliographic description)

b) Encoding description (level of detail of the analysis—the aim or purpose for which an electronic file was encoded; editorial principles and practices use during the encoding of the text.

c) Text profile (classificatory and contextual information such as text's subject matter; the languages and sub-languages

Table 1

	TEI – MS Data Elements		Digital Scriptorium data elements	
Sl No.	*Name of the element*	*Definition of the element*	*Name of the element*	*Definition*
1.	<idno>	Supplies the string of abbreviations and numbers, usually referred to as the 'call number', 'shelfmark', 'accession number', etc., that is used to identify the item.	Shelf mark	Collection name, item number, size designate that the particular institution uses to identify on specific manuscript.
2.	<altname>	Contains any form of alternative identifier used for a manuscript. E.g., Nick name, former catalogue no., ocellus nominum, etc.	Nick name	Names commonly used to refer to certain more famous manuscripts
3.	<country>	Contains the name of a geopolitical unit	Country	Country of origin of the manuscript
4.	<region>	Contains the name of a smaller geopolitical unit, intermediate between country and settlement.	Region	Modern political subdivision of a country (Region, country, department land, Province, etc.,)

(Contd...)

(Contd...)

5.	<settlement>	Contains the name of the smallest component of a place name.	City	Name of the city where the manuscript is held.
6.	<institution>	Contains the name of the organisation, within which a manuscript repository is held.	Institution	Name of the institution where the manuscript is held.
7.	<repository>	Contains the name of the repository(usually a distinct a physical building) with in which manuscripts are stored, forming part of an institution.	Library	Name of the library where the manuscripts is held
8.	<author>	Identifies the primary author of the work or works contained in a manuscript.	Author	Name (s) of author (s)
9.	<title>	Supplier a title for the work or works contained in a manuscript, or a brief description of a manuscript.	Title	Title of the work.
10.	<respStmt.>	Supplies a name and	Other	Names of other associated with a description for someone associated given text.

(Contd...)

(Contd...)

		other than an author credited with intellectual responsibility for some aspect of the work/s within a manuscript.		names of authors.
11.	<origDate>	Contains any form of date, used to identify the date of origin for a manuscript or manuscript part.	Date, Begin date, end date Year = month = day	Date of origin of the manuscript, Date of the manuscript when it is dated by the scribe.
12.	<textLang>	Describes the languages	Language (s)	Names of the language used in the and writing systems used manuscript text. by a manuscript.
13.	<note>	Contains any additional descriptive information about a manuscript / item.	Note	A non defined slot to be adopted to the needs of a specific manuscript.
14.	<bibl>	Contains a conventional bibliographic description, for example, of a modern edition of item.	Bibliography	Bibliographic
15.	<decoNote>	Contains a note describing either a decorative component	Other Decoration	Any other significant decoration

(Contd...)

(Contd...)

	of a manuscript or fairly homogeneous class of such components.		
16. <explicit>	Contains the text of any explicit attached to a particular manuscript item, that is, the closing words of a text or a section of a text sometimes used as a kind of title, possibly followed by one or more rubrics or colophons.	Explicit	Ending words of a text often used to identify it.
17. <incipit>	Contains the text of any incipit attached to a particular manuscript item, that is the opening words of a text.	Incipit	Beginning words of a text, often used to identify it.
18. <rubric>	Contains the text of any rubric or heading attached to a particular manuscript item, that is a string of words where by a manuscript	Rubric	Author-and /or title-like information in the manuscript, often set off from the main body of the text by red ink, underlining, display script or spacing.

(Contd...)

(Contd...)

	signals a text division (begin, end) which is in some way set off from the text itself, usually in red ink, or by use of different size or type of script, lining, or other such visual device.		
19. <support>	Contains a description of the written materials making up the manuscript item.	Support	They physical material that support the script.
20. <extent>	Describes the approximate size of the manuscript specified in any convenient units.	Total Folios.	In reference to the individual part, the number of leaves in Arabic numbers.
21 <collation>	Contains a description of how theleaves or bifolia are physically arranged.	Span ofFolios	Number of leaves in Arabic numerals.
22. <watermarks>	Contains a detailed description of the watermarks identified in the paper of which a manuscript is composed.	Watermark	The identifying mark used by the paper maker.

(Contd...)

(Contd...)

23. <dimensions>	Element is available for use any where in a description, the cataloguer may choose to discuss (for example) dimensions of miniatures at the same time as describing the miniatures, rather than specify that information within the <extent > element.	Outer Dimensions	Dimensions of the book block.
24. <layout>	Contains a description of ruling technique and layout.	Layout	Indication of ruling technique and layout.
25. <music	Contains description of type Notation>	Music of musical notation.	Type of musical notation, when present.
26. <bindingDesc>	Describes the present and former bindings of a manuscript, either as a series of paragraphs or as a series of distinct binding elements, one for each binding of the manuscripts.	Binding	Book binding

(Contd...)

(Contd...)

27. <binding>	Contains a description of one binding, i.e. type of covering, boards, etc., applied to a manuscript.	Binding	Book Binding
28. <foliation>	Describes the numbering system or systems used to count the leaves or pages in a codex	Total Folios	In reference to the extent of leaves of the entire codex.
29. <provenance>	Contains any descriptive or other information concerning a single identifiable episode during the history of a manuscript or manuscript part, after its creation but before its acquisition.	Provenance	Successive owners, private and institutional.
30. <msPart>	Contains information about an originally distinct manuscript fragment now forming part of a composite manuscript.	Composite	Manuscript Statement as the whether or not the codex is composed of more than one part.

used; the situation in which it was produced, the participation and their setting)

d) Revision history (history of changes during the electronic files development) contains bibliographic information supporting use of the resources.

Mapping of TEI-MS and Digital Scriptorium Elements

An attempt has been made to identify the data elements prescribed by *Digital Scriptorium* and *Text Encoding Initiative* (TEI-MS) for preparing metadata manuscripts. It may be noted from the table given below that both the system provides a very detailed list of elements required for cataloguing of manuscripts. The tables given below provide the features of both the standards. Table 1 provides a corresponding data elements with definition of both the elements. As many as 30 data elements are common to both, however there 'name' and 'definitions' vary slightly and table 2 provides those elements not found in TEI but available in *Digital Scriptorium* and vice versa in table 3.

The Data Elements which are not Found in Text Encoding Initiative Set but Found in Digital Scriptium

Table 2

Data Elements	*Definition*
Physical issue (S)	Presence of seals if the item is an archival document; roll or other non-codex format; or printed book.
Reproduction	Container for notes on existence of microfilm, negatives, etc.
Acknowledgements	Public recognition of contribution to knowledge about the manuscript.
Source	Source of the information input into the database.
Inputter	Name of person responsible for selecting, organising and inputting the information about the manuscript into the database, with reference to all four levels

(Contd...)

(Contd...)

	(Manuscript; Part; Text; Image) even though the field "Inputter" is only present at the "Manuscript" level; date of initial/main inputting.
Reviser	Name of person revising a given record and date of the revision.
Revisit	Flag referring to any one or several fields in this level as a reminder that the level contains something that is incomplete/uncertain/possibly wrong.
Part number	A roman numeral designating the parts of a given codex that have independent origin from one another (frequently but not necessarily with differing place or date).
Span of folios	With reference to the individual part, the number of leaves in arabic numerals.
Cardinal point	Point of the compass or the word "central" for country of origin; second of four place-defining elements.
Document	Identifies reports of legal activity.
Alphabet	Indication of primary writing system of the manuscript.
Script	Type of script used, in practice usually a subset of the Latin alphabet.
Number of scribes	Number of readily distinguishable hands with span of leaves copied by each person.
Scribe	Name of the scribe.
Artist	Name of artist/decorator.
Sequence	Arabic numeral to ensure proper sequencing on the web.
Supplied title	Term that indicates a category of books, rather than a specific text.
Docket	Abridged outline of proceedings in a legal document, giving names, dates, action, etc.

(Contd...)

(Contd...)

Status of text	Statement as to type of problem when a text is not complete or disordered.
Folio number(s)	The location within the manuscript of the photograph.
Caption	Text accompanying image on the web, serving both to point out an interesting feature (justification for the choice of shot), and to allow for free-word searching.
Iconclass	A hierarchical code comprised of numbers and letters to identify iconography; see Iconclass manual/CD-Rom for the codes themselves; for overview, see website: http://iconclass.let.ruu.nl/home.html
Notes to photographer	Notes to photographer.

Table : 3 The Elements which are Not Found in Digital Scriptorium Set but Used in Tei

Data Elemetns	*Defintion*
<origPlace>	Contains any form of place name, used to identify the place of origin for a manuscript or manuscript part.
<mscontents>	Describes the intellectual content of a manuscript or manuscript part either as a series of paragraphs or as a series of structured manuscript items.
<msItem>	Describes an individual work or item within the intellectual content of a manuscript or manuscript part.
<colophon>	Contains the text of any colophon attached to a particular manuscript item: that is, an inscription, usually found at a break point such as the end of a text or codex, usually containing information about the production of the manuscript, such as the name of the scribe, the date and place of the copying, the person who commissioned the copying, etc.

(Contd...)

(Contd...)

<listBibl>	Contains a list of related bibliographic descriptions (standard TEI element).
<summary>	Contains a brief summary of the contents of an item provided by the cataloguer.
<form>	Contains a description of the physical format of the manuscript.
<msWriting>	Contains a description of all the different kinds of writing used in a manuscript.
<handDesc>	Describes a particular style or hand distinguished within a manuscript.
<condition>	Contains a description of the physical condition of the manuscript.
<additions>	Contains a description of any significant additions found within a manuscript, such as marginalia or other annotations.
<history>	Groups elements describing the full history of a manuscript or manuscript part.
<origin>	Contains any descriptive or other information concerning the origin of a manuscript or manuscript part.
<acquisition>	Contains any descriptive or other information concerning the process by which a ms or ms part entered the holding institution.
<additional>	Groups additional information relating to the modern bibliography for a manuscript, its current curatorial status, and and other associated materials.
<adminInfo>	Contains information about the present custody and availability of the manuscript, and also about the record description itself.
<surrogates>	Contains information about any digital or photographic representations of the manuscript being described which may exist in the holding institution or elsewhere.

(Contd...)

(Contd...)

<accMat>	Contains details of any significant additional material which may be closely associated with the manuscript being described, such as non-contemporaneous documents or fragments bound in with the manuscript at some earlier historical period.

Conclusion

A catalogue is a tool or pointer for archiving and providing access to old treasures of knowledge. Systematic arrangement, uniform and mutual consistent cataloguing of manuscripts is needed. In the present information technological era the information present in the manuscripts should be digitised, preserved and provide access to these old treasures of knowledge, by developing common suitable metadata standard and make them useful by providing efficient assessing points to them and opens the communication channels is needed.

After carefully considering the requirements of the cataloguing of Indian manuscripts, it is suggested that either *Text Encoding Initiative or Digital Scriptorium* schema may be used for recording the cataloguing details. Both being international and well-tested schema, the Indian libraries can really adopt them. In a recently concluded project, one of the authors of this paper has adopted the framework suggested by Digital Scriptorium for cataloguing of manuscripts available at the Kuvempu Institute of Kannada Study.

References

Caplan, P. (2003). *Metadata fundamentals for all librarians.* Chicago, ALA Editions.

Chakravarti, C. (1950). Value and importance of manuscripts in olden times. *Journal of Royal Asiatic Society Bengal* (letters), 16, 253-61.

Coveney , D. K.(1950). Cataloguing of literary manuscripts. *Journal of Documentation,* 6 (3), 125-139.

Digital Scriptorium. Available at:http://www.scriptorium.columbia.edu/

Electronic Access to Medieval Manuscripts. Available at: http://www.hmml.org/eamms/

Saini, M.L. (1969). Manuscripts literature in Indian language. *ILA Bulletin*, 5 (1), 6-21.

TEI: Text Encoding Initiative. http://www.tei-c.org/index.xml

William Y. A., Naomi D., David, F., and Carl L. (2003). A case study in metadata harvesting: the NSDL. *Library Hi Tech*, 21 (2), 228–237.

33

Mapping of Metadata Standards: Issues in Metadata Crosswalks

—V. Chandrakumar

The paper describes what is metadata, various types, its applications, functions, etc. The author further explores metadata standards and the issues involved in metadata cross walks. The key issues in mapping metadata standards are terminology, degree of interoperability, properties, organisation, process, semantic mapping, etc. Possible solutions to overcome problems concerned with metadata mapping are explained.

Introduction

Information Retrieval in Internet and WWW is greatly dependent on how to the contents are described in the form of search aids. Search engines fail to find the relevant information from the web pages and associates with some problems. To overcome these problems of search engines, metadata is used. Metadata is a structured, encoded description of an information package. It provides an intermediate level at which viewing or searching choices can be made in the light of data characteristics like content, quality, condition and usage.

There are three main types of metadata operating in digital environments: Descriptive metadata, Structural metadata and Administrative metadata (Monal and Jana). Descriptive metadata is used to describe or to identify information resources. In other words, it can be said that the main purpose of descriptive metadata is resources discovery and identification. It can include elements such as title, author, abstract, keywords etc. Structural metadata describes the relationship within or among related information resources. It includes how compound objects are put together, for example, how pages are ordered to form chapter and how chapters make up the book. It helps users to navigate through individual objects that are part of a complex entity— like administrative metadata used in managing and administering information resources, such as when and how it was created, file format and other technical information, and who can access it.

The key function of metadata is to facilitate and improve the retrieval of relevant information that is resource discovery in digital library environment. In addition to resource discovery, metadata can help organise digital or electronic resources, facilitate interoperability and legacy resource integration, provide digital identification and also support archiving and preservation (Monal and Jana).

- *Resource discovery*: Metadata serves the same function in resource discovery as in catalogues by: Allowing digital resources to be found by relevant criteria; Identifying digital resources; Bringing similar resources together; Giving right location information
- *Organising digital resources*: With the growth in the number of web-based resources, portals and gateways are becoming increasingly useful in organising links to resources. Lists of relevant resources can be incorporated into static web pages, which have their names and locations, encoded in the HTML. But for increased efficiency it has become customary to build such pages dynamically from metadata stored in database, from which various software tools can easily extract and reformat information for web applications as per demand.
- *Interoperability*: Metadata allows for interoperability, or, the possibility of the exchange of information with minimal loss of content and functionality between multiple systems constituted of different hardware and software platforms, data structures and interfaces. They are two approaches to interoperability, one is cross-system search and other is metadata harvesting. The z39.50 protocol is an example of cross-system search. With the help of this protocol, partners do not share metadata but map their own

capabilities to a common set of search attributes. On the other hand the Open Archives Initiative developed a protocol (OAI-PMH) which requires partners to translate their native metadata to a common core set of elements and expose this for harvesting.

- *Digital identification*: Most of the metadata schemes include some elements, which acts as a standard number to uniquely identify the object. It may also be given using a file name, URL (Uniform Resource Locator) or some more persistent identifier such as PURL (Persistent Uniform Resource Locator) or DOI (Digital Object Identifier).
- *Archiving and preservation*: The digital resources will survive and continue to be accessible into the future. Archiving and preservation are the important for the digital resources. It is necessary to require special elements to track the lineage of digital object (i.e., where it came form and how it has changed over time), to detail its physical characteristics and its behavior in order to emulate it on future technologies.

Besides these the functions of metadata also include verification of authenticity, intellectual property management, content-rating, authentication and authorisation of digital information resources.

Metadata Standards/ Schema

There are large numbers of metadata initiatives, formats / schemes are available in the digital environments. Metadata standards can be defined as a set of metadata elements, with associated semantics and syntax for describing a particular type of digital resources. Generally it comprises a conceptual model, a set of named components (terms, elements, etc.) and a specification of how represent a metadata instance in a digital format. There are different types of metadata standards are in operation for different purposes. Each one has some advantages and disadvantages.

Metadata schema provides a formal structure designed to identify the knowledge structure of a given discipline, and to link that structure to the information of the discipline through the creation of an information system that will assist the identification, discovery and use of information within that discipline.

Metadata schema transformations are more complex than purely structural transforms because they require a set of equivalences identified by human experts—Dublin Core title can be mapped to MARC 245, Dublin Core author can be mapped to MARC 100 and so on—but this important knowledge is recorded in a multitude of ways that are not standardised and not always machine-processible, including web pages, databases, spreadsheets, PDF documents, and the source code of many computer languages (Godby, Smith and Childress, 2004).

The term 'mapping' can be defined as "Intellectual activity that identifies semantically equivalent elements in different metadata schemes." Crosswalks may be defined as "Documentation resulting from mapping showing the equivalencies and conversion specifications" (Pierre and LaPlant). A crosswalk is a semantic and/or technical mapping (sometimes both) of one metadata framework to another metadata framework. Metadata crosswalks that associate three pieces of information: the crosswalk, the source metadata standard and the target metadata standard, each of which may have a machine-readable encoding and human-readable description (Godby, Young and Childress, 2004) . The following information about a metadata framework is required for metadata crosswalks:

- *Semantics:* The meaning of elements
- *Structure:* Human understandable and machine readable format (e.g., XML)
- *Syntax:* Grammar used to convey meaning and structure

A fully specified crosswalk provides the ability to create and maintain one set of metadata, and to map that metadata to any number of related content metadata standards.

The main objective of this paper is to explore the metadata standards and to examine the issues concerned with metadata crosswalk where a system follows one metadata schema want to change into other schema.

Methods of Mapping

A system to be designed to facilitate the use of crosswalks among metadata standards that must resolve differences between the metadata schemas. The system with the hypothesis that usable crosswalks must have the following characteristics (Godby, Young and Childress, 2004).

— A set of mappings between metadata standards that is endorsed by a stakeholder community.

— A machine-processable encoding.

— A well-defined relationship to source and target metadata standards, which must make reference to particular versions and syntactic encodings.

— Metadata conversions must be addressed in a fully specified crosswalk. The following are the methods of the mapping:

  — *Element to Element Mapping:* All metadata standards specify a number of properties associated with metadata elements. For crosswalk, these properties must be taken into consideration of each element between standards.

  — *One to Many:* An occurrence of the source element maps to more than one occurrence in the target elements. For example, a crosswalk for GILS to DIF would need to map the GILS 'contact name' element to the 'first name' and 'last name'.

  — *Many to One:* More than one occurrence in the source element maps to one element in the target element.

  — *Extra Elements in Source:* Another important case that requires resolution is the handling of a source element that does not map to any appropriate element in the target standard.

  — *Unresolved Mandatory Elements in Target:* There is mandatory elements in source standard and in the target that have no corresponding mapping in the target standard.

  — *Hierarchy:* The hierarchy of the elements may be fixed in some standards and the other cases the depth of the hierarchy is unlimited.

  — *Single versus Multiple Objects:* There are standards such as SDSM and IRDS are multiple object metadata which object includes system, programme, data, survey, documentation, datasets and frame. Unlike the single object metadata is always associated with only one item per use.

- *Logical Views:* A logic view enables users to see a specific set of metadata elements of the metadata standard organised in specific way. The standards that provide multiple logical views enable different users communities access to the same metadata elements using different organisations or hierarchy of those metadata elements.

Moen (2004) enumerates the mapping methodology between any two elements:

- One-to-one
- One-to-many (repeatable elements; unique more narrowly defined elements)
- Many-to-one (complete mapping; incomplete mapping)
- One-to-zero (no semantically equivalent element)

Hunter has listed a number of possible approaches to handling the semantic mapping problem. The chosen approach is a balance between simplicity on the one hand and flexibility or scalability on the other. Below is a list of mapping approaches in increasing order of both scope and difficulty:

- such as WordNet;
- Determine the semantic mappings from a dynamically generated ontology created by using differencing to merge multiple domain-specific ontologies.

Issues

There are issues in mapping the metadata standards. Some of the issues are:

- *Terminology:* Lack of common terminology currently exists among the different metadata standards. For example, MARC21 metadata is identified using the data elements as 'tag', a unit of the data elements 'subfield' whereas Dublin Core identifies the metadata as 'label'.

- *Degree of Interoperability:* Interoperability is the ability of two or more systems are components to work together to produce a common result or a common goal which is retrieval of information. The degree of interoperability is a measure allowing characterising the ability of interoperation between two schema.
- *Properties*: The metadata properties are varying one standard to another. The similarities need to be extracted and the concepts generalised and used in a common way across all metadata standards. The common metadata properties include:
  - A unique identifier for each element, e.g., tag, label, field name.
  - A semantic definition of each element.
  - Usage of metadata elements such as mandatory, optional, or applicable mandatory.
  - Repeatability of the metadata occurrence in the object.
  - Organisation of metadata elements in terms of both hierarchical and vertical relationship.
  - Limitation in value of data element (e.g., free text, controlled vocabulary, numeric value, or date).
  - Optional support for local / additional metadata elements.
- *Organisation:* The structure and organisation of elements in one schema may vary with another schema. The level of elements described in one schema may be listed in another level in another schema.
- *Process:* During the development of a metadata standard, there may be occasions where the choice of mechanism or process selected for use in the metadata standard is arbitrary, and there is an analogous process in another related standard. The analogous processes are chosen may be varying one to another.
- *Semantic Mappings:* The elements (or fields) in one metadata set are correlated with the elements of another metadata set that have the same or similar meanings. This is also sometimes called 'semantic mapping.'

Conclusion

Structural mapping and syntax mapping is possible between two metadata standards whereas 'Semantic mapping' is one that crosswalks between the standards. One of the solutions to overcome the issues/problems concerned with mapping metadata scheme is 'an interoperable core' (Pierre and LaPlant). Mapping is one way of translations between metadata standards via mapping to and from the core.

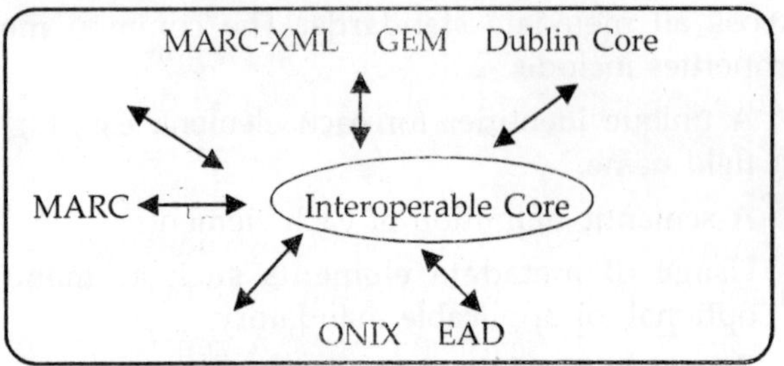

Figure 1: Mappings to the Interoperable core

Source: http://www.siderean.com/dc2003/103_paper-22.pdf

A schematic representation of the relationship between the metadata standards and the interoperable core is shown in the figure above. Godby et al (2003) describe the two-path interoperable metadata using translation technique. Translations between metadata standards are achieved via mappings to and from the core. These mappings may be more or less complete, as when translations for closely related standards, such as the various dialects of MARC, are submitted through the registry process for the purpose of record conversion. The interoperable metadata core can be made available by translation path method. The design of the long translation path has two desirable consequences. First, only two translation steps are ever required: from the source standard to the interoperable core, and from the core to the target standard. Second, the collection grows in power as more translations are submitted. In the previous model, the proliferation of mappings is a problem that leads to confusion and reduces the usability of a metadata translation service.

Another solution would be a 'Crosswalk Depository', a prototype for a repository of metadata crosswalks, called SchemaTrans. The repository improves the usability of the bibliographies by collecting all information required to document and execute a collection of crosswalks. Crosswalks in the SchemaTrans repository are initially modeled using METS, a standard for encoding metadata about objects in digital libraries. The resulting records are deposited into an OAI repository that can be searched by human or machine using the SRW/U protocol. SchemaTrans translates XML documents from the specified source to the target by matching the dependencies in the documents against the records in the METS database.

Semantic Mapping via a Mapping Matrix (Hunter) is another solution to interoperability. The mapping matrix explicitly defines the semantic mappings between a fixed set of metadata vocabularies from a number of different domains.

Metadata Term Thesaurus (Hunter): A generic approach is to extract the mapping dynamically from a thesaurus of metadata terms, generated by formally defining relationships between metadata terms from a number of different domains' standardised vocabularies rather then limiting the semantic mapping to a fixed number of domains/vocabularies (i.e., the number of columns in the mapping matrix). The metadata term thesaurus which was developed, MetaNet, contains only preferred terms (the ABC core vocabulary), equivalent/overlapping terms (ET), narrower terms (NT) and broader terms (BT) and attempts to encompass terms from the most significant and widely-used metadata vocabularies (Dublin Core, IFLA, IEEE LOM, INDECS). The scope of this thesaurus is limited to the most significant metadata models/vocabularies used for describing attributes and events associated with resources and their lifecycles. This encompasses metadata vocabularies from the bibliographic, museum, archival, record keeping and rights management communities.

References

Canadian Heritage Information Network. Available at http://www.chin.gc.ca/English

CC:DA (ALCTS/CCS/Committee on Cataloging: Description and Access). (2000). Task Force on Metadata: Final report, June 16,

2000. Available at: http://www.libraries.psu.edu/tas/jca/ccda/tf-meta6.html (Accessed on 12 July 2009)

Concept of metadata interoperability. Available at: http://www.dlese.org/Metadata/documents/interop.htm (Accessed on 17Augut 2009)

Crosswalks. Available at: http://www.dlese.org/Metadata/crosswalks/index.htm (Accessed on 12 June 2009)

Godby, Carol Jean, Smith, Devon, and Childress, Eric.(2003). Two Paths to Interoperable Metadata. Available at: www.oclc.org/research/publications/archive/.../godby-dc2003.pdf (Accessed on 12 July 2009)

Godby, Carol Jean, Young, Jeffrey A., and Childress, Eric.(2004). A Repository of Metadata Crosswalks. *D-Lib Magazine* 10 (12) December 2004. Available at: http://www.dlib.org/dlib/december04/godby/12godby.html (Accessed on 13 June 2009)

Hunter, Jane. MetaNet - A Metadata Term Thesaurus to Enable Semantic Interoperability Between Metadata Domains. Available at: http://dret.net/biblio/reference/hun01 (Accessed on 12 June 2009)

Learn more about the metadata crosswalk repository. Available at: http://www.oclc.org/research/researchworks/schematrans/default.htm (Accessed on 14 July 2009)

Monal, Mrinal Kanti and Jana, Sibsankar. The Core Concept of Metadata for Digital Information Resources with Special Reference to Dublin Core. Available at:http://drtc.isibang.ac.in:8080/xmlui/bitstream/handle/1849/374/p27 sibsankar jana mondal.pdf?sequence=1 (Accessed on 15 June 2009)

Moen, William E. (2004). NISO Workshop on Metadata Practices on the Cutting Edge, May 20, 2004, Washington, DC. Available at: http://74.125.153.132/search?q=cache:ECm6lLqQqTEJ:www.unt.edu/wmoen/presentations/NISO MD Workshop May2004.ppt+Moen,+W illiam+E.+NISO+Workshop+on+Metadata+ Practices+on+the+ Cutting+Edge,+May+20,+2004,+Washington, +DC&cd= 1&hl=en&ct=clnk&gl=in

Pierre, Margaret St. and LaPlant, Willian P.Jr. Issues in Crosswalking Content Metadata Standards. Available at: http://www.Niso.org/press/whitepapers/crosswalk.htm (Accessed on 12 June 2009).

34

Bibliographic Standards

—M. Parameswaran

This paper defines bibliographic standard. It distinguishes between the standard for bibliographic entry and standards for exchange of bibliographic data. It explains ISBD and its structure, and points to the revision ofAACR on the framework of ISBD. It discusses MARC, CCF and ISO 2709. It explains the Standard Book Numbering and briefly discusses the developments in India related to MARC and ISBN.

Introduction

Bibliography is a list of documents. It can appear either as a separate publication or at the end of chapters of books or at the end of scholarly treatises or research papers. When a bibliography appears as a separate publication its purpose is to give details of documents so as to identify it and procure it from publishers, printers, etc. When it appears at the end of scholarly articles its purpose is to give an authenticity to the statement of an author. In both cases bibliography consists of entries or descriptions on documents. A document description in a bibliography (which is briefly referred to as an entry) consists of the name of the author, title of the document, imprint, collation, etc. When a document is described in a bibliography it is desirable to have some standardisation. Standard is something that is established by authority or general consent as a model or example to be followed. If there is such an established pattern of description it is easy to distinguish the names of authors, editors, publishers, etc., without confusion.

A library catalogue is a list of documents available in the collection of a library. In this sense the library catalogue is also a bibliography. Therefore the library catalogues also should follow some bibliographic standards. Conformity to the rules of catalogue codes automatically achieves standardisation in catalogue entries. A bibliographic standard may be defined as a general framework or structure prescribing an order for the elements of description in a bibliographic entry along with standard punctuation marks to indicate each of them.

The following are the important types of standards available for bibliographic description.

1) International Standard Bibliographic Description (ISBD)
2) MARC formats
3) International Format of Bibliographic Information Exchange (ISO: 2709)
4) Common Communication Format (CCF)

The first one is meant for description of documents in bibliographies and catalogues while the other three standards are meant for exchange or bibliographic or cataloguing data in computer readable form, such as magnetic tapes or CD-ROM.

There are also standards institution at national and international levels which prescribe standards for bibliographic entries that appear as citations at the end of scholarly treatises, research articles, etc., American National Standards Institute (ANSI) New York, the British National Institute (BSI), the London and Bureau of Indian Standards (BIS), Delhi, have produced the national standards for bibliographic eiration In addition, there are various style manuals prescribing standards for bibliographic citation. *The Chicago Style Manual* and *MLA Style Manual* are two such style manuals. Prescriptions of these style manuals are used for citation of references in theses/dissertations.

International Standard Bibliographic Description (ISBD)

An international Working Party was set up by the International Meeting of Cataloguing Experts in Copenhagen in 1969 to study the possibilities of an International Standard for Bibliographic Description (ISBD). ISBD was prepared and officially adopted by the IFLA Committee on Cataloguing at a meeting held in 1971.

The First Standard edition of ISBD (M) was brought out in I974. This standard has been adopted by more than 20 national bibliographies and translated into over 14 languages.

The International Standard Bibliographic Description for Monographic publications ISBD(M) specifies the description of printed monographs. ISBD(M) has identified special areas (parts) in the bibliographic description of a monograph, and each area has been demarkated into several elements. ISBD (M) prescribes the following areas:

1. Title and statement of authorship area.
2. Edition area
3. Imprint area
4. Collation area
5. Series area
6. Notes area
7. International Standard Book Number binding and price area

The following is the order of elements in the descriptive part of an entry;

1. Title and statement of authorship area
   - 1.1 Title proper
   - 1.2 Parallel title and other title information
   - 1.3 Statement of authorship
2. Edition area
   - 2.1 Edition statement
   - 2.2 Statement of authorship relating to edition
3. Imprint area
   - 3.1 Place of publication
   - 3.2 Name of publisher
   - 3.3 Date of publication
   - *3.4 Place of printing
   - *3.5 Name of printer
4. Collation area
   - 4.1 Pagination and number of volumes

4.2 Illustration statement

4.3 Size

4.4 Accompanying material

5. Series area

5.1 Series statement

5.2 Subseries statement

5.3 Numbering within series

5.4 International Standard Serial Number

6. Notes area

7. International Standard/Book Number, binding and price area

7.1 ISBN

*7.2 Binding

-7.3 Price

Note: Items with * marks are optional.

Punctuations

ISBD(M) uses a number of punctuation marks such as equal sign (=). colon (:), semicolon (;) and diagonal slash (/).

Example of an entry

Education and the social order / Bertrand Russel . - Revised ed. - London: George Allen & Unwin, 1975. - viii, 301p.; 22 cm.

Previous ed. published as

— 'Educatin and the Modem World'. - London: Van Nostrand, 1932.

— ISBN 0 486 22876 9 Paperback.

The International Standard Bibliographic Description (General) has been brought out as a general standard for the description of all kinds of library material. A special feature of this standard is the provision for an area of details which are special to particular material or type of publication.

The areas of ISBD(G) are:

1. Title and statement of responsibility area

2. Edition area
3. Material (type of publication) specific details area
4. Publication distribution etc. area
5. Physical description area
6. Series area
7. Notes area
8. Standard number and terms of availability area

ISBD(G) is supposed to serve as a model for specific ISBDs of other materials. IFLA has brought out ISBDs for serials, old books, manuscripts, cartographic materials, printed music, computer files, etc.

ISBD and Revision of AACR

AACR2 and its 1988 revision have based on various ISBDs for the preparation of rules for descriptive cataloguing in its Part I. IFLA and the Joint Committee for Revision of AACR agreed that the revision of AACR will follow the framework of ISBD and their punctuations, but it need not be necessary for the code to follow the terminology used by ISBD exactly.

AACR2 further varies in certain optional provisions for example it is not compulsory to record the statement of responsibility.

Standardisation of Bibliographic Data Formats for Exchange Purpose

Due to computerisation of cataloguing data by national bibliographic agencies there was a need for standardisation in thisa rea. MARC is the acronym for Machine Readable Catalogue. The original MARC format was developed in the United States by the Library of Congress, and since then a number of formts have emerged such as USMARC, UKMARC and other national MARC formats. These have some differences in content designation. The difference in data contents in these formats mean that editing is required before records can be exchanged. As a solution an international (universal) MARC format was developed by IFLA in 1971. This is known as UNIMARC (Univesal MARC format). It is possible to convert records written in any one MARC format into UNIMARC and then be converted into any other format. This would require each national agency to write only two programmes - one to convert to UNIMARC and another to convert from UNIMARC instead of having to write a separate programme for each MARC format. The second edition of UNIMARC was brought out in 1980. *UNIMARC Handbook* was published in 1983. The main feature of UNIMARC is that it should have one set of tags or subfield identifiers covering all materials. There would be no specific order of subfields so that they could be placed in the order required by the catalogue codes. UNIMARC was developed as an exchange format and data would be converted to that format from other formats. In 1987 the Manual of *UNIMARC* was produced.

INDIMARC

The Bureau of Indian Standards published *Indian MARC* which was based closely on UKMARC in 1985. As a need for revision was felt soon after the formulation of Indian MARC, the National Information System for Science and Technology (NISSAT) developed INDIMARC on a framework prescribed by the CCF.

Common Communication Format (CCF)

Common Communication Format (CCF) is a bibliographic exchange format developed by PGI programme of UNESCO. It is intended for use by agencies having records of monographs, serials, journals, articles, etc., which wish to exchange bibliographic records with one another. It follows ISO 2709 in full for its structure but it does not follow any particular catalogue code. One of the specific features of CCF is that it has special techniques to indicate the vertical relationship (i.e., a monograph with its chapters) and the horizontal relationship (a work with its various versions in different languages).

The CCF record structure consists of four major sections or parts;

i) Record label
ii) Directory
iii) Data fields
iv) Records separator

Format for Bibliographic Information Interchange

ISO 2709 is an international standard that specifies the requirements for a generalised machine readable format that will hold any type of bibliographic record. It may be noted that this standard does not define the content of individual records or the meanings assigned to tag indicators or identifiers. Rather it only prescribes a generalised structure and can be used to transmit records describing all forms of material capable of bibliographic description between data processing systems. According to ISO 2709 the general structure of a bibliographic record can be shown schematically as shown below:

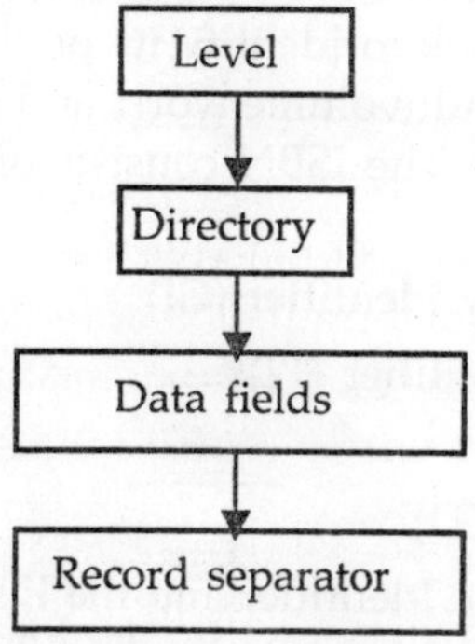

As per ISO 2709 a bibliographic record should include the following fixed and variable length fields:

i) a record label
ii) a directory
iii) a record identifier
iv) reserved field
v) bibliographic data fields
vi) field separator
vii) record separator

Standard Book Number

The genesis of the ISBN dates back to 1966 with the founding of an ISBN agency at Berlin. UK was the first country to introduce this system in 1967. The technical Committee of Documentation of the International Standards Organisation (ISO/TC46) set up a working group to investigate the possibility of adopting the system for international use. There were several standard book number systems followed by various countries. This Committee evolved an international standard on the ISBN system known as ISBN/ISO 2108-1972, which unified different national practices.

The purpose of ISO 2108 was to coordinate and standardise internationally the use of book numbers so that an ISBN identifies one title or edition of a title from one specific publisher and is unique to that title or edition.

The International Standard Book Number or ISBN is a unique number given to a book to identify its publisher, the individual title or a volume of multivolume work, and is unique to that title or edition or volume. The ISBN consists of 10 digits with four subparts:

a) Group/Country Identifier (GI)
b) Publisher's Identifier (PI)
c) Title Identifier
d) Check Digit (CD)

The Country or Group Identifier and the Publisher Identifier are given by the ISBN agency at Berlin. The Title Identifier will be allocated by the publisher and the fourth part which is the 10th digit will be a Check Digit. This number is computed as a result of an elaborate calculation on other digits.

Advantages of ISBN

1) It identifies every book uniquely.
2) It facilitates machine handling of bibliographic data.
3) It faciitates international exchange of bibliographic data.
4) It can be used by publishers and distributors for various purposes such as order, supply and manufacturing statistics.

Agency for ISBN in India

The National Educational Resource Centre (NERC) of the Raja Ram Mohan Roy Foundation was earlier responsible for developing an ISBN system for India. At present the Ministry of Human Resource Development has dismantled NERC and named it as National Agency for ISBN. The Agency is working under Book Promotion Division of the Ministry of HRD. THe National Agency for ISB, despite several constraints, is managing the registration of Indian Publishers under ISBN, of course with a very slow pace.

International Standard Serial Number (ISSN)

International Standard Serial Number (ISSN) is a unique identification number for serials. Its aim is to unambiguously identify and individualise each serial title. Here the word serial is taken to include periodicals, newspapers, annuals, journals, memoirs, proceedings, etc. and monographic series. ISSN is an eight-digit number in two blocks. The ISSN of *IASLIC Bulletin* for example is 0018-8447.

The responsibility for controlling the assignment of ISSN rests on the International Serial Data System (ISDS). This is an intergovernmental organisation established within the framework of UNISIST/PGI programme. ISDS has its International Centre at Paris. In addition it has a network of various national and regional centres. The Union Catalogue Section of INSDOC (NISCAIR) serves as Indian National Centre (INC) for ISDS. It started functioning in 1986.

Conclusion

Given above is a brief account of various international standards for bibliographic (or catalogue) entry format, bibliographic data exchange format and numbering systems for bibliographic identification. The MARC programme and shared cataloguing programme of Library of Congress initiated the conversion of bibliographic data of new publications into computer readable form and the exchange of bibliographic data files between national libraries and bibliographic centres. Standardisation of bibliographic formats at the international level was a prerequisite for the success of such programmes for exchange of computer readable bibliographic data files. The development of international standards in this field is due to the pressure of these processes. India, being a significant producer of books in English and in various regional languages, cannot ignore these developments.

Though late, India has also started to develop its own national standards in this field, and to cooperate with the international efforts for bibliographic standardisation.

References

Govind, Vijay. (2000). Implementation of International Standard Book Number System in India: Perspectives and Prospects. *ILA Bulletin,* 35(3&4), 67-73.

Gredley, Ellen and Hopkinson, Alan. (1990). *Exchanging bibliographic data: MARC and Other International Formats.* London: Library Association.

Guha, B. (1983). *Documentation and Information: Services, techniques and systems,* 2nd ed. Calcutta: World Press, 16.

X
Other Topics

35

Classification: A Universal Concept

—M. P. Satija and K.P. Singh

This paper begins with a conceptual analysis of the term 'classification' and its various manifestation. It describes the process of classification, Genus- species relations and classification as a tool for organising knowledge. It mentions the modern library classification system and the specific uses in organising library collection, and highlights the use of classification system in electronic environment.

Introduction

Classification is a process of making classes. A class is a set or group of entities (both abstract and concrete) having at least one common similarity. This similarity is called characteristics and is the basis of grouping or sub-grouping of entities. For example, all the students of a class, whether male or female, of any religion and caste, coming from different states or regions, speaking different languages, having different political ideologies, have one characteristic in common, that is, all of them are candidates for the same degree.

A class can be of any size. All human beings make one class called *homo sapiens*. All Indians make one class. Similarly, all Christians make one class, Roman Catholics make another class; Indian Roman Catholics make yet another class, or Keralitie Roman Catholics may further make another class. There seems no end to making classes and subclasses of people or of any other entity. A class may even be of a single member.

Meanings of Classification

Classification is a process of grouping of similar or like entities. It may be noted that there can be no grouping without division, as there can be no shadow without light, or no parting without meeting. Therefore, grouping implies division. Grouping and division are two sides of the same coin. We add a member to a group by separating it from others, in the process of grouping and regrouping. Therefore, grouping and division are the basic processes of classification. But classification is more than endless grouping and sub-grouping. After grouping starts the process of ranking, that is, arranging the member of a group in a sequence. Even a small family can be divided further by status or age of its members. This is ranking. For example, say all the 20 student of a class may be further arranged in a row by age, height, educational merit or even alphabetically by name. Let us take the case of candidates appearing in IAS examination. The final result by UPSC divides them into two groups: successful and unsuccessful. Successful candidates are further ranked according to the marks obtained. That ranking is very vital. All this is classification.

Classification is a systematic and predictable order. A group of chemical elements is a class by itself. Their grouping into Group 0, 1,2,3...8 is further classification. Their further arrangement according to their atomic number is classification and ranking. In the third sense, assigning each ranked entity a code or symbol to preserve their ranking is classification. For example, a class of 25 students may be first arranged according to educational merit, then each student may be ranked 1, 2, ... 25 or A to Z in order of merit for convenience of handling. This allocation of codes will mechanise and fix their ranking and consequent sequence.

Various Manifestations of Classification

Grouping and division seem primitive or elemental processes of classification. Looking at the bottom, classification is a corelation or discovering relations between entities. All members of a group are related to one another by some commonality. When we admit an entity into a group, a relation between that entity and group is discovered or created. For example, Physics is not only a member of the big class, science, but also bears a relation to

Mathematics on its left and Astronomy on its right. Mathematics, Physics and Astronomy are intrinsically related to one another. In a family, which is always a class by itself, all members are related by blood. Hence classification is relation.

Classification and Organisation

Since grouping and inter-group ranking are acts of organisation, thus classification is organisation. In fact, classification and organisation are inseparable. Now classification is considered as a tool for organising in every sense of the word. Since organisations have structure, so classification is structuring and mapping. Difference between a heap of bricks and a mansion is classification. In a mansion every brick is positioned in an organised way.

In an organisation all members are related and coordinated, so classification is coordination and control. The difference between a disciplined army and a chaotic mob is classification. Army men are coordinated and controlled while a mob is uncontrolled, though both the groups comprise of men.

Classification is matching and pairing this is implied in grouping of entities brought together;

When we are ranking and arranging we are sorting and tabulating. So, tabulating and sorting are acts of classification.

Uses of Classification in Daily Life Routines

Classification is a mental act and logical process of association and relation. It goes on every moment of life knowingly or unknowingly deliberately or unconsciously. Any system be it biological (man), social (government, libraries, institutions) or mechanical (computers, machines) has to classify for successful functioning. All human beings, what ever they do, have to classify in every sense of the word. The more sophisticated and intelligent a person, better his/her sense of classification.

A postman classifies postal items for efficient and timely delivery. For quick, efficient and easy delivery a postal items is sorted (classified) many times at different stages between posting and delivery. A fruit seller sorts his fruits into categories, say, oranges, apples, grapes, and so on. Further each group say of apples is further sorted into species say Kashmiri apples, Simla apples, Golden apples, Green apples, etc. An astute vendor may further sort each species by quality and price. At every step of grouping sorter is adding value to the items. Thus classification is value addition.

Record files in an office are arranged in some order, and within each file letters and memos are arranged in some known order. Without such an arrangement the previous record cannot be located and used. Books and other reading material in libraries are arranged, no doubt.

Scope of Classification

There is no act of life where classification is not used. It is applied everywhere. It is a basic process to learn. The opposite of classification is disorder and chaos. Classification can be done of all objects entities, actions, thoughts and concepts. We can classify people, countries, natural phenomena, plants, flowers, animals, libraries, philosophies, literature, artifacts, automobiles – what not. It is a universal constant. It is the only method to simplify, understand and comprehend a complex universe to discover its structure and impose some order over the otherwise chaotic world.

Classification is Knowledge Creation

English philosopher J.S. Mill (1806-1873) says that classification facilitates the operation of the mind in clearly conceiving and retaining in the memory the nature of the entity or phenomena. Someone has aptly and axiomatically defined empirical science as "a systematic classification of experiences". Therefore classification is training of the mind. It is often said that to learn to classify is itself an education. "Sharpness in thinking, clarity in expression, exactness in communication depend ultimately on classification," says Ranganathan (*Prolegomena*, X B2). The eminent educator John Dewey (1859-1952) was of the opinion that all knowledge is classification. Brian Buchanan quotes another English philosopher W. S. Jevons (1835-1882) as saying that all knowledge, "all reasoning, so far as it deals with general names or general notions may be said to consist in classification." Scientists seek patterns, that is, generalisations in nature.

Knowledge advances when a pattern is discovered. A new idea becomes knowledge only when it is related with some past knowledge. (All researchers cite references to previous works for acceptance of their research.) Information becomes knowledge when given some context and structure. Thus concepts, information, knowledge and classification are inherently related.

Process of Classification

Classification is a process of corelation. It is a way of thinking—thinking systematically and purposefully. It is an aid to memory and reasoning power. Nothing can be identified without it. It means to define an entity is to classify it first. For example, a gun is a firearm; a chair is a piece of furniture, a car belongs to the class of vehicles, and so on. All thought and reasoning contain some process of classification

A group is divided or a member is included into a group on the basis of some characteristic. A characteristic is an attribute, quality or property of an entity which relates it with or separates it from a group. For example, a group of people may be divided into males and females. Here "gender" is the characteristic of division. All the students of a university may be divided into undergraduate, postgraduate and research degree students. Here level of education is the characteristic. Books in a library may be arranged on the basis of their subject content. Thus a characteristic is the basis of division. Successive application of right and relevant characteristics produces deeper and finer classification.

Classification is a process, a logical visual method of simplification and understanding. No phenomena or object can be understood without classifying it. It organises all sorts of entities and depicts their due place in the universe. Classification can be both of abstract and concrete entities, of ideas and things. It is essentially a life process of learning, doing and living successfully. Human civilisation progressed as primitive humans learnt to classify the visible phenomena around. Let us say man learnt of edible and non-edible things; divided animals into useful and harmful groups. It was another (more sophisticated) act of classification when man related clouds with rain, and rain with growth of vegetation and life; and related certain herbs with certain diseases. All that became knowledge by and by. It has rightly been said that all knowledge is classification. Knowledge is defined as sum total of facts, beliefs, experience, memories, expressed feelings, arts, sciences, fiction and myths conserved by the society. Thinkers in all ages have tried to categories knowledge to understand its nature, categorise, boundaries and growth. That became knowledge classification. Knowledge classification is outlining and mapping to depict its structure and boundaries. It leads to better understanding of its history, nature, kinds, properties, growth and also gaps in it. It becomes a guide for the educationists, scientists and librarians. Knowledge classification is both speculative and empirical, and is a province of philosophers and scholars. One example of knowledge classification is Vedic categories (1500 BC) of knowledge in *Dharma, Artha, Kama and Moksha.*

Library classification is book or document classification. Documents are nothing but carriers of knowledge and information. In modern libraries documents are classified on the basis of their knowledge contents. Therefore, knowledge classifications have become basis of library classifications. But knowledge is abstract and fluid, and takes the shape of its container and carrier. Books, on the other hand, are physical and solid entities to be arranged on shelves. Documented knowledge has some non-subject aspects such as language, viewpoint of the author, format, media, etc. All these have to be accounted for in a library classification. Library classifications are in fact more detailed, have notations/symbols to be assigned to documents, separate common tables for physical aspects, and have also a detailed index of subjects. Therefore library classifications are more formal and complex than the knowledge classification on which these are based.

Genus-Species Relation

A class or group is logically called a genus, and the characteristic is the difference we add to produce species:

Genus + Difference = Species

Example Tables + Material = Glass tables, Wooden tables, Plastic tables, Metal tables, etc. Here material is the characteristic to divide the universe of tables.

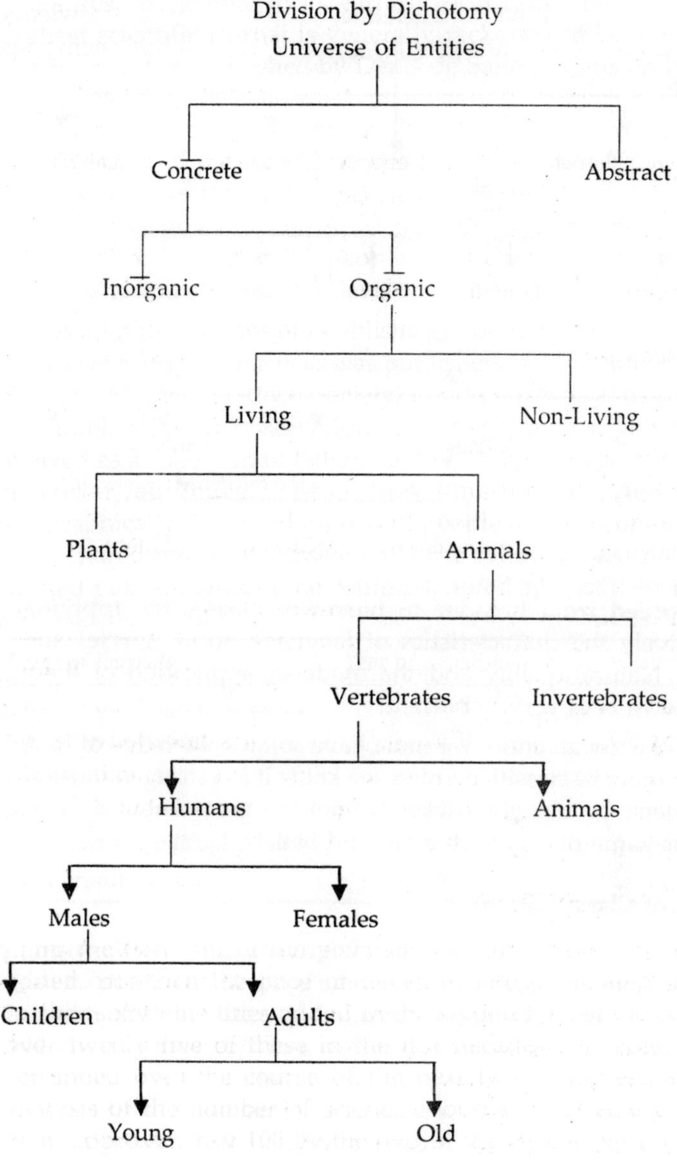

Let us apply the genus-species to literature by applying characteristics

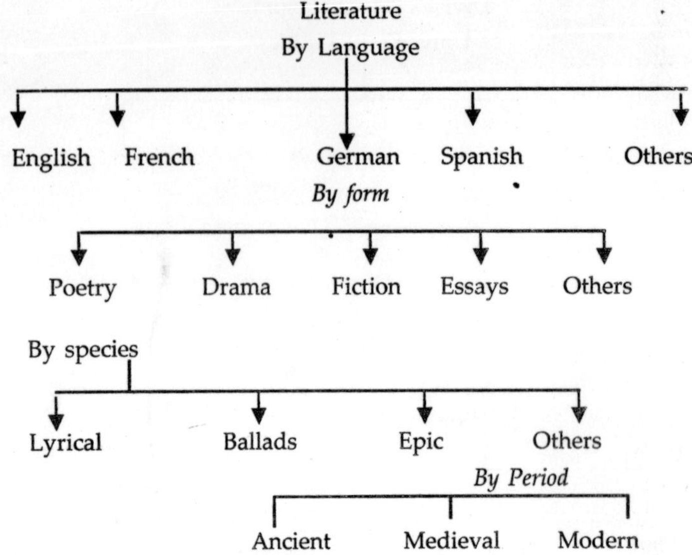

We proceed from broader to narrower classes by applying respectively the characteristics of language, form, species and period. Nature, quality and the mode of application of these characteristics is very important.

To classify an entity we must have some knowledge of it. A guitar cannot be classified unless we know it is a stringed musical instrument. To classify cricket (game) we must know it is an outdoor game played with a bat and ball.

Nature of Classification

Logically speaking classificatory groups are not absolute; classifications are relative as something is classified with reference to others. An entity cannot be classified or ranked in itself. It takes two to create a classification. It means a unique entity cannot be classified. It is a class of its own. No classification is absolute, it also means that classifications are not permanent. Classifications are not real even. No classification exists in Nature. All classifications are man-made, and made for a purpose. No classification is good or bad; these are unhelpful or helpful to a varying degree. It all depends upon the purpose of classification. A classification which serves its purpose well is best, whether logical or not. The logic of classification depends upon the characteristic chosen and the order in which these are applied. A large group of persons could be divided by age, gender, religion, race, nationality, mother tongue or colour of skin, hair or eyes, and many more characteristics. Each time it will result in different grouping. Choice of characteristics and the order in which these are applied one after the other will depend upon the purpose of classification. For example, a farmer would place birds, rats, insects and monkeys in one group as enemies of his crop. A scientist may laugh at such a classification. Both are correct, as their purpose in different. A farmer produces food while a scientist produces knowledge. A child or layman thinks that birds, butterflies and bats belong to the same class as all these can fly, while for a scientist all the three belong to different classes, each of its own. Different classifications produce different maps or depict different structure of knowledge depending upon the society and time of its origin. Classifications are not neutral. These are mirrors that reflect their time, place and society. Vedic classification in different from the one produce by Aristotle. Classification of knowledge by English philosopher Francis Bacon (1561-1626) is quite different of the two. No two classifications are similar.

Classification as a Tool

According to Aristotle (384-322 BC) classification is theoretical, practical and productive science. As the saying goes theory is the most applied knowledge, we can arguably say that classifications are always practical and designed for some purpose. As already said, classification is a tool for simplification, understanding and organisation. Without organisation nothing works. All the uses of classification may be summed up as : (1) Management (2) Aesthetics (3) Knowledge creation.

Organisation is for better management. Classification organises anything and everything : life to a shoe store; knowledge to libraries. A library, archive, postman, grocery shop all use classification to save time. It ultimately leads to economy of time, money and manpower.

Aesthetics is the science of beauty. An arranged store appeals visually to the visitors. Classification was also described as pairing and matching. So a housewife matching the colour of her room curtains with other items in the room is essentially doing an act of classification. A gentleman matching the colour of his tie with the suit he is wearing is an act of classification, too. Here the purpose is purely aesthetic to feel good and look good.

Philosophers, scientist, researchers classify to study and understand the growth and structure of knowledge. It is to outline and map the vast sea of knowledge. Without this map it will not be possible to navigate and further explore this boundless sea. A formal researcher has to select data, tabulate data and corelate data to create new information. All the three stages are acts of classification. Hence classification underlies research – the latter is knowledge production.

Classification is pattern making and pattern recognition. A computer retrieves information by patterns recognition and comparison, hence it works by classifying; so does our brain which always works by association, grouping (integration) and pattern recognition.

Selecting a life partner for marriage involves a series of classification acts. Marriage is selection and pairing – both are manifestation of classification. The characteristics selected for marriage are: age, religion, caste, physique, looks, job, financial status, values and attitudes, educational qualification, and many more. In which order you apply these characteristics depends upon your need and values. Marriage is selection, and every selection is classification.

Knowledge Classification

As said earlier, classification can be of any object, phenomena, concept or acts. Classification and categorisation of knowledge *per se* is called knowledge classification. From time to time philosophers, scientists, educationists and the likes have formally categorised entire known knowledge to outline its boundaries and show the structure of knowledge. For example, Hindu Vedas (1500 BC) divided knowledge into four categories in the order : *Dharama, Artha, Kama, and Moksha.* Aristotle (3rd century BC) divided knowledge into three parts: Theoretical, Practical and Productive, and further divided entire knowledge into ten categories. A propedia is classification of knowledge and vice-versa. Knowledge is defined as sum total of ideas, theories, experiences, history, feelings, values, sciences, symbols, arts, facts, fiction, myths conserved by a society.

Classification of knowledge is essential for its simplification, understanding and progress. Without its organisation no further growth and progress can be made. For example, a new idea or a discovered fact will not become knowledge until it is related and integrated with the existing knowledge. Therefore, it has aptly been said that all knowledge is classification.

Library Classification

Libraries are established to house and preserve books and other recorded intellectual and artistic heritage of mankind. Books and other information sources are knowledge objects and can also be classified like other physical objects. Since antiquity librarians have classified books to produce convenient groupings and to facilitate their location at the time of need. An unarranged collection is a heap of books, not a library by definition. To find a book from such a library will be like locating a needle from a huge heap of hay. In earlier times books were grouped and arranged on the basis of their language, size, colour of binding, authorship or broad subject categories. Those methods were perfectly useful in those times as the main aim of libraries was to store and preserve documents rather them to serve them to the scholars. Access to knowledge was the preserve of the privileged few.

Modern Library Classification

In the then emerging industrial society of the late nineteenth century there was an attitudinal shift in the values of education and libraries. The importance of literacy was recognised for aware and responsible citizens. In a democracy access to education was democratised and opened to all. "Education for all" became the objectives of the welfare state. To meet the needs of the society not only many new libraries were established by law, the doors of libraries were open to all and sundry — scholars, students, neo-literatures, poor, children, housewives, old and handicaps, and other marginalised sections of the society without any discrimination. Further to maximise their use books were placed in free stacks and users were allowed open and direct access to the books. That open access policy required new and better arrangement of books for the browsers. Then Melvil Dewey (1851-1931) designed his decimal classification which divided knowledge by academic disciplines of study and used decimal notation to denote subjects. The latter provided almost infinite capacity for expansion and insertion of new subjects at proper places. Since then the books are being classified predominantly on the basis of their subject content, that is knowledge. Thus library classification is knowledge classification as applied in libraries. In other words library classification is applied knowledge classification.

But library classification is lot more than knowledge classification as it has also to take into account the physical aspects of the documents, the way knowledge has been formatted and presented in them, as well as the viewpoint of the author. It includes aspects such on language, media, form, format, viewpoint and many more such things.

Formally and traditionally, library classification has been defined as the arrangement of books and other reading material in a way that is helpful to the users. Today's libraries are arranged by subject though different types of collections are arranged in different ways. For example, government documents, patents or standards are arranged by their own official codes. Current periodicals are arranged alphabetically by title. Maps, CDs, pamphlets, photographs indeed require different and separate arrangements. Making of library classification systems in also classification. The designer of a classification scheme is known as a classificationist. Operating a classification system to assign class numbers to documents in a library is also classification; such a person is called a classifier.

Uses of Classification in a Library

Classification is vital to library services. In fact classification is implied in definition of a service library. In supports all library services. Classification is to a library as skeleton is to human body on which all the body organs rest. Classification of a library collection is like map of a city. In a library, classification serves all the function given above, namely, it is a tool of management, aesthetics and knowledge creation. All the Five Laws of Library Science (1931, 1957) formulated by Ranganathan, support library classification and have specific implications to design quality classification systems. Without classification a library is an unorganised dump of books. Therefore, without it the full value of a library collection cannot be obtained. However, its specific uses can be broadly listed as:

- It brings together books on the same subject. Thus a patron gets all the books at one place which is much more convenient to the users.
- It facilitates the browsing function of a library. Browsing is to look at library collections without any specific purpose – a sort of window shopping. Browsing is a habit with the scholars. It is only possible fruitfully in a library organised by subjects. Browsing always leads to incidental discovery of long needed and valuable information. This accidental discovery is known as serendipity. Not only this, the general to specific order of arrangement with some notational manoeuvring has been turned into pedagogical order in schemes like the CC. Ranganathan calls it APUPA pattern on the shelves. It is quite helpful for the self-learners. Thus systematic arrangement of books in open access libraries is helpful in self-learning.
- It is a location tool; without it the library catalogue will not be able to function properly. It is also used for preparing shelf lists.
- Classification is the basis of all information retrieval systems and methods both in manual and electronic systems.
- It helps to replace the books at their correct places when the books are returned to the stacks after the home or inside use.
- It has been claimed that a library classification has three functions, namely, cognitive, information retrieval and shelf arrangement. Cognitive function is to represent the structure of knowledge and intra-relation of subjects. That is to produce a map of knowledge. Many library

classifications, e.g., Ranganathans CC, Bliss BC and BSO, have emphasized this function.

- Many bibliographies, catalogues, etc., are classified for better use. UDC was created to arrange entries in a universal bibliography.
- It has been found useful in reference service for facet-analysis of user's questions in reference interviews. It is useful for arrangement of circulation record.
- It helps in building a balanced collection of documents in a library.

Uses in Electronic Environment

Classification can be easily used to arrange and retrieve records in electronic databases. Online Public Access Catalogues (OPACs) function far better when class numbers are provided as another access point. In fact, in the electronic information era it has found so many new uses that it is rightly said that we are witnessing the second golden age of classification. Conventional classification systems, such as the DDC, UDC, LCC, have been used to organise and search information on the world wide web (WWW) search engines. Search engines like Yahoo, Google, AltaVista use broad classification methods for organising their information. Eccellio (http://science.eccellio.com) is a search engine which uses faceted classification which returns precise information. It uses Google database but adds an extra level of classification to refine search. They have defined it as Google^{++}. In the web environment at least seven functions have been identified by Professor Lois Mai Chan. These are location, browsing, hierarchical searching, retrieval, identification, sub-grouping (partitioning) and profiling. It has aptly been called mathematics of librarianship.

There are many day-to-day routine uses of classification in a library so much so that it will be impossible for a library to function properly and achieve its objectives without a sound classification. It has aptly been said that a book is the foundation of a library but classification is foundation of librarianship. Indeed there is no escape from or any substitute to it in libraries, or life.

Limitations of Classification

Classification was described as mathematics of librarianship, yet like the value of ð(pi) it is never exact. Classifications are social, not natural. These do not satisfy the needs of all the library users. Only a majority are served while some users with specialised needs require different arrangement. Classification, especially the library classification has many limitations and problems. It is a costly process and subjective, too. Two classifiers may differ widely on the correct classification of a given book. Not only this a classifier may class a given book differently at different times. No classification can comprehensively represent the total subjects dealt in a book. Even a monograph may deal with more than one subject at a time. In classification only the dominant subject is represented. A textbook on algebra and geometry is either placed at algebra, or geometry, not both. Further, let us say a textbook in cataloguing may have a very valuable chapter on history of cataloguing or on the life of C A Cutter. These side topics will not be represented by the class number, and may remain hidden from needy users. Classification by discipline also scatters subjects. For example, a book on "Family life" may be placed in different main classes such as Ethics, Sociology, Anthropology, Social Welfare, and Medicine. Hence the scattering. It is not incorrect to say that classification suppresses and scatters more than it reveals and collocates. A classification may not satisfy all the users as they have invidual needs. Classifications are not based on the survey of the needs of library users. A nineteenth century English philosopher, W. S. Jevons (1835-1882), had criticised classification as a logical absurdity. This is no less true of library classification of which there is no substitute. We have to work with imperfect tools.

References

Buchanan, Brian (1978). *Theory of Library Classification.* London: Clive Bingley, 37.

Chan, Lois Mai (2007). *Cataloguing and Classification : An Introduction.* 3rd ed. Lanham, M. D: The Scarecrow Press, 309-314.

Philip, H.W (1961). *A Primer of Book Classification,* 5th ed. London: AAL, 9-20.

Ranganathan, S. R. 1967). *Prolegomena to Library Classification,* 3rd ed. Bombay, Asia, 77-79.

Satija M.P. (1998). Classification: Some Fundamentals Some Myths *Knowledge Organisation,* 25 (1-2), 32-35.

_____________ (2000). Classification: An essay in Terminology *Knowledge Organisation,* 27(4), 221-229.

_____________ (2004). *A Dictionary of Knowledge Organisation.* Amritsar : Guru Nanak Dev University, 35-36.

36

Copyright in the Digital Environment: A State- of-the-Art Report

—K. N. Prasad

Digitising information has come as a boon to many., including library and information professionals. It reduces storage space, increases efficiency of retrieval of information. But along with it, it has brought copyright problems. This paper discusses the problems of copyright in the digital environment and the attempts made in solving them.

Introduction

Intellectual property comprises all entities arising from human intellect activity—ideas, inventions, words (facts or fiction), theatre or art. It includes documents of all kinds, archives, databases (whether online, CD-ROM or delivered by other mechanisms), material on the Internet, individual items in a database, computer software, and inventive pieces of hardware that are subject to patent coverage.

Intellectual Property Right connotes the rights to literary, artistic and scientific work; performances of performing artists; phonograms and broadcasts; inventions in all fields of human endeavour; scientific discoveries, industrial designs; trademarks, service mark and commercial names and designations; and all other products resulting from intellectual activity in the industrial, scientific, literary and artistic fields. It is a generic term covering patent, registered design, trademark, copyright, layout of integrated circuits, trade secrets, geographical indicators and anti-competitive practices in contractual licenses.

"Copyright" is understood as the right to copy or refuse copying. The original writer of a piece of literature is the author. Similarly, the original artist of a painting, drawing, etc., is the author of his artistic work; again the composer is the author of musical work. Any person who reproduces the work of the original author without his prior permission violates his right called "copyright." The same principle applies to making copies of software.

We seem to be moving toward a world in which most creative works - books—music albums, movies, television programs, software, and so on—exist as computer files. Because it is easy to make perfect copies of files, and because using such files may involve making copies as an incidental effect, copyright holders are understandably worried about whether existing technological, legal and cultural restraints on copying are adequate to protect their intellectual property in the future. But some citizens' groups are concerned that the changes proposed to address these worries go too far.

A variety of bills, such titles as the Collections of Information Antipiracy Act, the Digital Millennium Copyright Act, the Digital Era Copyright Enhancement Act, and the Sonny Bono Copyright Term Extension Act, are now making their way through the US Congress. It is hard to tell exactly what effects legislation will have until it has been enacted and interpreted by the courts, but these new laws could greatly change the balance between copyright holders' control of creative works and the public's interest in being able to use them.

Content companies fear new technologies will result in lost revenue, and technology companies fear IPR reforms proposals will cripple the Net.

Patent and copyright laws have evolved within narrow socio-economic and political contexts. Designed to protect individuals whose inventions/creations require safeguarding in view of their potential commercial value, they remain incompatible with traditional knowledge, which is collectively owned, whose "invention" extends across generations, and whose *raison d'etre* is not profit, but ecological understanding and social meaning. Due to these contradictions, legal rights may have impacts quite other than those intended. By protecting select elements in isolation from the larger cultural context, they encourage fragmentation of the cultural system. By designating knowledge "owners", they may trigger social dissensions between recognised proprietors and others who are excluded. Finally, as IPR's protect knowledge by setting rules for their commercial exploitation, they may facilitate the appropriation of traditional knowledge by the global marketplace. In short, extant legal arrangements are ill adapted for protecting traditional knowledge. Today efforts are turning towards the challenging task of defining new or *sui generis* systems.

There is clearly a need for novel approaches to traditional knowledge systems which can meet the challenges arising from their increasing prominence. One important step forward is to consider traditional knowledge, not as static sets of information, but as integral components of living and dynamic societies and cultures; a process, not a product.

Librarians and information professionals recognise, and are committed to support the needs of their users to gain access to copyright works and the information and ideas they contain. They also respect the needs of authors and copyright owners to obtain a fair economic return on their intellectual property. Effective access is essential in achieving copyright's objectives.

Librarians and Copyright

Librarians and information professionals recognise and are committed to support the needs of their patrons to gain access to copyright works, and the information and ideas they contain. They also respect the needs of authors and copyright owners to obtain a fair economic return to their intellectual property. Effective access is essential in achieving copyright's objectives.

Copyright law impacts on most of what libraries do. It affects the services that libraries can provide to their users, and the conditions on which they can provide access to copyright materials. It affects the way in which libraries can act as navigational agents and undertake effective archiving and preservation activities.

Libraries have a crucial role to play in controlling as well as facilitating access to the increasing number of local and remote electronic information resources. Librarians and information professionals promote respect for copyright and actively defend copyright works against piracy, unfair use and unauthorised exploitation, in the digital environment. Libraries have long acknowledged that they have a role in informing and educating users about the importance of copyright law and in encouraging compliance.

Is copying of articles from the newspapers considered an offence under copyright law? A copyright law suit decided in a UK court of appeals gives an overview of the situation under which copying from newspaper does not constitute infringement. According to British law, in a typical publication, copyright subsists both in content of a work and also in typographical arrangement and design element of work. Typographical arrangement covers style, compositions layout and general appearance of a page of a published work. The copyright in a typographical arrangement of a published edition rests with the publisher.

Copying material from the newspaper for "reporting current events" is considered fair use and not an infringement. The judgement effectively permits limited copying of articles from newspapers without infringing on typographical copyright. However, the court has not established a law that copying of articles from newspapers is not an infringement. In India, the law is well established that copying of any material from newspapers or books is an infringement of copyright and is punishable according to Copyrights Act 2000.

According to Marylyn Gell Mason, "The meaning of copyright in an electronic environment is still cloudy and hazy. The electronic environment makes it easy to alter content, either inadvertently or deliberately." Judy Holoviack feels that the users will require the means to ascertain that the version they are using is unadulterated. Sandra Whisler is concerned with the protection of intellectual property during the transition period from print to electronic format. On an optimistic note, she encourages electronic publishing. Copyright concerns won't go away, but the problem of protecting intellectual property rights will not be so overwhelming as to freeze development of online publishing.

In the US, strategies specific to print and broadcast sector began to find their way into copyright policies that are expected to operate in networked information system. New copyright policies that protect and regulate intellectual property in cyberspace constitute the major theme of many international meetings, as the information market transcends national borders and tends towards globalisation.

According to Peter Lyman, "While each nation strives to define a national information policy, the true future of intellectual property will be defined by the Global Information Infrastructure which will be crafted by treaties among nations."

Today, it is widely believed that personal computers, cable television, the Internet and the telephone system are converging into a giant hose that will spray huge amounts of data - intellectual property. As this occurs, according to the conventional scenario, the economic winners will be those who own the zeroes and ones, not those who make equipment that copies, transmits and displays them. Because copyright is the mechanism for establishing ownership, it is increasingly seen as the key to wealth in the information Age.

At the same time the transformation of intellectual property into electronic form creates new problems. If the cost of manufacturing and distributing a product falls, economic forces will drive down its price too. The net embodies this principle to an extreme degree. Manufacturing and distribution costs collapse almost to nothing online: zeroes and ones can be shot around the world with a few clicks of a mouse. Hence producers of digital texts, music and films will have trouble charging anything at all for copies of their works—competitors can always offer substitutes for pushing the price towards the vanishing point.

In addition creators deal with piracy, which is vastly easier and more effective in the digital environment. People have long been able to photocopy texts, tape record music and videotape television shows. If the document (film) is digitised into a computer file, it can be e-mailed to millions of people in minutes; because strings of zeroes and ones can be reproduced with absolute fidelity, the copies are perfect. And online pirates have no development costs. In other words, even as a digital technology drives the potential value of copyright to even greater heights, the same technology threatens to make it next to worthless.

The paradox has created two situations. One is to advocate eliminating copyright altogether. Anti-copyrightists believe that the increased ease of copying effectively obviates the (c) symbol and all it entails. In this view, copyright restricts what people can do with the intellectual property coming through the wires. It tries to fence the electronic frontier. It unjustly creates monopolies in the basic commodity of the Information Age. The other opposing reaction is to strengthen the hands of copyright owners.

The Library Association Copyright Alliance (LACA) of UK supports the effective enforcement of copyright and recognises that libraries, information services and archives have a crucial role to play in controlling as well as facilitating access to the increasing number of local and remote electronic information resources. Library, information and archive professionals promote respect for copyright and actively defend copyright works against piracy, unfair use and unauthorised exploitation, in both the print and the digital environment. Library, information and archive professionals have long acknowledged that they have a role in informing and educating their users about the importance of copyright law and in encouraging compliance.

LACA maintains that over protection of copyright could threaten democratic traditions and impact on social justice principles by unreasonably restricting access to information and knowledge. If copyright protection is too strong, competition and innovation is restricted and creativity is stifled.

Information is increasingly being produced in digital format. New communications technologies bring unprecedented opportunities for improving access to information, and technology has the potential to improve communication and access for those disadvantaged by distance or economic circumstances. However, technology also has the potential to further stratify society into the information-haves and the information-have-nots. If reasonable access to copyright works is not maintained in the digital environment, a further barrier will be erected which will deny access to those who cannot afford to pay.

If in future all access and use of information in digital format becomes subject to payment, a library's ability to provide access to its users will be severely restricted in order to maintain a balance between the interests of rights holders and users.

LACA Statement of principles

1. For works in digital format, without incurring a charge or seeking permission all users of a library should be able to:
   - browse publicly available copyright material;
   - read, listen to, or view publicly marketed copyright material privately, on site or remotely; and
   - copy or have copied for them by library and information staff, a reasonable portion of digital work in copyright for personal, or educational use.
2. Providing access to digital format of a protected work to user for a legitimate purpose, such as research or study should be permitted under copyright law.
3. The lending of published physical format digital materials (for example CD- ROMs) by libraries should not be restricted by legislation.
4. Contractual provisions, for example, within licensing agreements, should not override reasonable lending of electronic resources by library staff.
5. Legislation should give libraries and archives permission to convert copyright protected materials into digital format for preservation and conservation related purposes.
6. Legislation should also cover the legal deposit of electronic media.
7. National copyright legislation should render invalid any terms of a license that restrict or override exceptions or limitations embodied in copyright law where the license is established unilaterally by the rightsholders without the opportunity for negotiation of the terms of the license by the user.
8. National copyright laws should aim for a balance between the rights of copyright owners to protect their interests through technical means and the rights of users to circumvent such measures for legitimate, non- infringing purposes.
9. Copyright law should enunciate clear limitations on liability of third parties in circumstances where compliance cannot practically or reasonably be enforced.

In the world of Internet, a common practice is to forward e-mail messages, or portion thereof; to quote portions of Usenet and mailing list postings; and to make private non-commercial copies of texts downloaded from ftp, gopher, or websites. Under current definitions of fair use, these practices would be considered fair uses; and they are also acceptable norms of practice for Internet users. The Gray areas of fair use and potential copyright infringement activities would include:

- Scanning of photographs in GIF formats (these are usually copyrightable images; for instance a common Usenet practice is to scan in Playboy photographs, but these images are protected by copyright);
- Typing in newspaper or magazine articles (acceptable to type in portions with the correct citation and attribution);
- Posting articles or private e-mail written by someone else without their express permission.

Network culture must create a culture where fair use is understood alongside a level of compliance and responsibility, or else fair use will be stifled and negotiating fees and licences will become the norm.

In the United States, the National Information Infrastructure (NII) Preliminary Report, the Green Paper on "Intellectual Property and the National Information Infrastructure" was released by the Working Group on Intellectual Property Rights in July 1994. The Paper recommended that the Copyright Act of 1976 be amended slightly to accommodate the advent of digital information. The paper recommended that:

- Digital transmission of a copy of a copyrighted work be considered an act of copyright infringement;
- 'first sale' rules for works transmitted digitally be abolished; and
- copyright infringement could be constructed if technological devices are used to circumvent copy-protection schemes that copyright owners have created.

Four areas of copyright law and their applicably to digital transmission have been identified by the Green Paper. They include: right to browse; right of digital transmission; abolishment of first sale rule; and abolishment of fair use.

Copyright issues in the digital environment are global, not local issues. How can differing national laws and dictums be harmonised in the global context? Many commentators have suggested that a copyright clearing house to issue licences and cleat rights will become a necessary adjunct to creating multimedia content on the information highway.

'The primary objective of copyright is not to reward the labor of authors, but 'to promote the progress of science and useful arts'. To this end, copyright assures authors the rights to their original expression, but encourages others to build freely upon the ideas and information conveyed by a work. This result is neither unfair nor unfortunate. It is the means by which copyright advances the progress of science and art.

Copyright: Intern

Copyright has been the focus of protecting intellectual property on the Internet. As such, there have been both technological and legislative efforts to continue incentives for authors to create useful works.

Contributory infringement (and the consequent liability) is one of the most contentious areas of the copyright debate. For instance, is an ISP liable for contributory infringement when it allows its users to link to hacker sites? If an ISP closed a user's account when informed by an IP owner, would the ISP be liable for the violation of civil nights or breach of contract?

Bandwidth on the network is limited, and continues to be so. The traditional technical solution, caching, is to allow copies to be saved at distributed points throughout the network. However, caching raises two issues. First cached copies can be out of date yet still contains information which is time sensitive (such as prices or stock quotes). Second, some web sites derive revenue based on the amount and kind of access to then-servers, and they currently have no verifiable way of counting the number of access to their servers, their document cached elsewhere on the network.

Today the Internet in itself has become a medium for varied violations of copyright of data. The control over net-based activities has become a major cause for concern.

Copyright: Databases

Databases as a concept have undergone a change after the Internet has narrowed the distances for transacting business. Databases were initially seen primarily as stored information say, in the form of share prices, details of employees, products and such other information. Today the term databases constitute data stored in the world wide web, CDs, multimedia products, network and so on.

Networking and eventually the Internet in itself has widened the horizon of accessibility of all the databases. The result is that the column of data processed every day and the number of people get access have increased. A wide range of material is being accessed or is accessible to a much higher number of people through a wider medium of propagation.

Both the quality and quantity of the data have gained a lot of significance with the development of knowledge sharing which evolved with computer era.

The voluminous information being created everyday has highlighted the need for protection of databases. On account of this, adequate protection of databases has become very important.

The object of such a protection is to ensure:

a) that the owner gets his right to protect the data adequately;

b) accessibility of the data to all those who legitimately wish to use the same;

c) Prohibition of unauthorised use of data.

Owners of fonts want to distribute them for different purposes at different prices. They fear that freely distributing fonts for reading documents might allow people to author documents without paying for additional rights such as redistribution. Neither a purely legal nor purely technical solution is likely to be successful.

One of the best ways of protection of databases is by adhering to Intellectual Property Rights (IPR). In databases, copyright vests as soon as a database or any data for that matter, is created.

In India, copyright is available, for the form and the substance of the matter. However, any infringer can intelligently change the arrangement of pre-existing database and reuse the same material thereby avoiding the copyright law.

As per our laws today, compilation of data or documents, including material from the public domain, can receive protection by copyright if the compiler can show originality in the selection and arrangement of the data. However, the author has to still prove originality in terms of selection of the materials.

The protection under copyright law is not necessarily the best form of protection. Today, E-commerce being the major business generator, varied data are stored in the world wide web. The wide accessibility to information is the advantage. The flip side is the misuse of such information for purpose other than those for which it is intended.

The fact that "bits" of a new database can consist of pieces from other copyrighted material is causing a lot of concern among the academic community and there have been calls for pressure to be put on governments to loosen such restrictions.

Software patentability is controversial and goes two-ways for the seller and the buyer (user). It should be noted that there is a need to pay the fees of any software used, to pay royalties to the right holders of client software.

Copyright-Digital Format

One can produce perfect copies from works in digital format. When anybody downloads a digital work and prints or makes disc copies, each of these copies is a perfect copy. While accessibility can be increased because of the availability of digital formats, it also makes private copying of these works easier and more difficult to detect.

Copyright owners certainly want to preserve and expand their markets. However, not all authors share these same values; for example, academic authors often want wide dissemination of their works and are not so much concerned about market protection,

Because copyright works become part of the social record of a civilisation public access is especially important to librarians. The licensing digital resources as opposed to purchase of the work threatens public access, a core value for the public at large.

Information needs to be communicated and shared to be valuable. Certainly, copyright holders deserve fair compensation for their works, but licensing may or may not be fair.

One of the significant differences between analogue and digital works is that one can use a non-electronic work without making a copy of that work. If the work is in digital format, this is not true.

It is suggested that copyright law's focus on making a copy may simply no longer be relevant since access by computer by their nature make copies, but these ephemeral copies are not significant and should not be considered infringing copies. It is also suggested that copyright protection could be reexamined to consider how copyright could function without the notion of copying.

Copyrighted works are protected regardless of the medium in which they are created or reproduced; thus, copyright extends to digital works and works transformed into a digital format. Copyrighted works are not limited to those that bear a copyright notice. As a result of changes in copyright law, works published since March 1, 1989 need not bear a copyright notice to be protected under the statute.

The digital and networked environment has posed several problems to the copyright law. This is because :

a) *In the digital medium, works are more equivalent*: In digital form, all copyrighted works – pictures, sounds, texts, music or movies – consist of strings of bits. All therefore, fit the definition of "literary work."

b) *The plasticity of works in digital form:* Works in digital form are easily transformed form one form to another. They are also easy to alter, even without a change in the character of the work. With the right tools, it is easy to digitally edit photographs, texts, or anything else – and to do so in a manner which cannot easily be detected.

c) *Automatic generation of works in digital form:* The digital medium also permits new works to be created for which no human author can readily be designated.

d) *Technological and contractual means for overcoming digital replicability:* An well-recognised problem digital technologies pose for copyright arises from the ease and low cost with which multiple copies can be made and distributed in digital form, especially in a networked environment.

Legal Implications

Cases of newspapers suing others that link to them, or news services that link to others while keeping their own banner-laden frames on the screen are pressing our understanding of the technology and the related policy beyond the scope of what their originators conceived.

Copyright in the Digital Environment

Information is increasingly being produced in digital format. New communications technologies bring unprecedented opportunities for improving access to information, and technology has the potential to improve communication and access for those disadvantaged by distance or economic circumstances. However, we now know that technology also has the potential to further stratify society into the information- haves and the information-have-nots. If reasonable access to copyright works is not maintained in the digital environment, a further barrier will be erected which will deny access to those who cannot afford to pay.

WIPO

In 1996, the members of the World Intellectual Property Organisation adopted two treaties to update copyright law for the digital environment. In confirming that existing exceptions and limitations can be carried forward and extended in the digital environment, WIPO countries rejected the claim that "digital is different". Contracting parties are allowed to carry forward and extend such limitations in the digital environment, and create new exceptions where appropriate.

IFLA

IFLA is an international non-governmental organisation (NGO) which exists to undertake, support and coordinate research and studies, and disseminate information about all aspects of library and information work world wide, and to organise meetings and training in this field.

Traditionally, libraries have been able to provide reasonable access to the purchased copies of copyright works held in their collections. However, if in future all access and use of information in digital format becomes subject to payment, a library's ability to provide access to its users will be severely restricted. In order to maintain a balance between the interests of rights holders and users, IFLA has developed the following statement of principles.

Electronic Copyright Management Systems (ECMS)

There is no appropriate copyright management system designed to the environment of the web. It has, however, been felt that there is a need for consensus for standards for such a system We are all used to the notion that copyrighted works are of an intangible nature, and we are trained to make the distinction between the work as such, and a copy that work, the former being an intangible concept, while the latter is physical object. The characteristic for the digital environment is the disappearance of physical copies. A machine readable from is a copy, and one may trade with such copies as is seen in CD-ROMs, where the conventional systems for rights management may be successfully applied. But for business in the digital environment, copies are not traded.

The trade in physical objects is replaced by a trade in signs liberated from the media on which the signs more or less incidentally are stored, more or less temporarily. But here, there is a copy of the work. He may use it for personal benefit but also for re-distribution through an intranet.

Several attempts have been made at developing Electronic Copyright Management Systems (ECMS).One important effort is CITED (Copyright in Transmitted Electronic Documents) a project producing a generic model of how to achieve a solution for digital environment under which two demonstrators were implanted ADONIS for a collection of journals in machine readable form, and NRCISSE for fine art from several museums with accompanying explanatory texts.

IMPRIMATUR is another current project attracting lot of attention.

Development of ECMS

The elements necessary for the development of a viable electronic copyright management system may be:

- *Identification:* Identifiers are well known in the conventional environment, e.g., International Standard Book Number (ISBN). A better example is the International

Standard Recording Code (ISRC) which was developed by the International Standards Organisation (ISO), as an identifier for phonograms and audiovisual recordings known as ISO 3901. There are currently efforts in developing such codes for many categories of works. They are often referred to as "Copyright management information". The code will typically be a reference to a database that contains the details of the work, for instance the owner, or succession of owners, the licensing divided on geographical areas, media, etc.

A related method is that of fingerprinting which is a scheme for retaining information on the use of the work. There is emerging scheme of identifying each work by a code embedded in the work itself, a code which may be retrieved by a copyright management system, and used as a key for accessing databases containing detailed information on the rights associated with this work, for instance for distributing revenues.

- *Cryptography:* To protect the work, it should be subjected to encryption. This would make it possible only for somebody with access to the key to benefit from the works. The technology allows many legal issues to be solved, obviously identification and authentication of the parties are secured.
- *Payment:* It is important to find a scheme that allows on the spot purchases of items of rather low value.
- *User identification:* There must be some way of ensuring the identity of the user.

The transaction is indicated by the user who identifies a work he or she wants to purchase. The material is not necessarily residing on a database under the control of the right holder, as it is in encrypted form and therefore protected in this way. The system would rather identify and authenticate the end user, checking that the necessary credit is available at the account of the end user. It would retrieve the copyright management information from the work, perhaps accessing a database to determine how the payment should be distributed. The work would then be transferred to the user and decrypted by his device, at the same time the payment would be deducted from his or her account and credited to appropriate account of the right holders.

Copyright, Digital Environment, India

The Information Technology Bill 1999 which has been introduced in the parliament during November 1999 is a giant step to take India ahead in the new Internet era.

The protection of content on Internet, which in all its form covers the classic definition of IPR and Copyright Act, however, does not find a proper mention in the new IT Act given assent by the President.

The content on the Internet is the parameter for the success of any dot com. It is the backbone of the Internet business and IPR is related to it. Ironically care has not been taken about IPR issue in the IT Bill, which could prove fatal in the long term. Experts observe that the responsibility on the contents should be with the producer and not with ISP providers who act just as middlemen. Some, however, feel that being a web host ISP has responsibility to provide content after proper scrutiny.

It is unusual for authors of articles in scholarly journals to receive any recompense for their work. Many, if not most, authors assign rights to their work to the publisher without taking into account of such material might subsequently appear in other media.

Given the development of electronic journals however, perhaps it is time to look again at such issues as fair use, the relationship between information and intellectual property, copyright and the economic ramifications of the new technology, some moves in the direction have already been made.

Indian Scenario

Copyright is available for the form and substance of the matter. Any infringer can intelligently change the arrangement of a preexisting database and reuse the same material thereby avoiding the copyright law. Sec 2(v) of the Indian Copyright Act, 1957, as amended in 1994, defines 'adaptation' in relation to any work as 'any use of such work involving its rearrangement or alteration'.

The IT Act ensures a Cyber-Regulation Advisory Committee, a controller, and adjudicating officer to regulate cyber laws. There will also be a Cyber Regulation Appellate Tribunal.

The Law defines what constitutes cyber crime and also has provisions to punish cyber criminals. It sets up framework for transaction involving computer generated documents and communications. It also deems electronic documents as legally binding and acceptable in place of paper. Checks and bills, power of attorney, trusts, will and contracts of sale of immovable property, will not be accepted in a digital format.

Computer crimes recognised under this law would affect hackers and those who are not authorised to enter a system to download data, introduce viruses, damage data or the system, block access to authorised users.

The law would apply to anyone in or outside of India who tampers with a computer located in India.

Conclusion

The answers to the questions—Does the nature of the technology require us to change the legal understanding or status of copyright as it stands now? What rights should be associated with to Web content? and How should the rights be expressed, and should the expression of the rights be used for notification, enforcement, or payment negotiation? do not necessarily lie solely in technology nor policy, but the rational combination of both.

IPR is something that affects us every day. We should be conscious of its effects on our economy. It is not enough to have strong laws but strong mechanisms to enforce, like the judiciary, police and the customs.

It remains to be seen whether strict adherence to copyright laws is possible. If it is going to be meaningful protection, it has to be done on a global basis through international treaties that all nations are prepared to recognise and follow.

References

Anuradha, K.T. (2000). Copyright fair use and database in digital networked environment. In National Seminar on Information Policies and Cyber laws, 4-6 December 2000, Bangalore, Sarada Ranganathan Endowment for Library Science, Paper E.

Association of Research Libraries (ARL). Available at: gopher://arl.cni.org/ll/info/nii/conf/

Bing, Jon. Managing Copyright in a Digital Environment. Available at: http://tiepac.portlandpress.co.uk/books/tiepac/session2/ch3.htm

European Projects. Available at:http://www2.echo.lu/legal/en/hoer.html

Franklin, Jack. IPR and Copyright-Some Food for Thought. Available at: http://telescan.nk.nl/action/news/issue2noframes/actnf2c.html

http ://www2. echo. lu/libraries/en/projects/bibdel.html

http://amide.lp.lu

http://fairuse.stanford.edu

http://portico.bl.uk.ifla/copearms/html

http://potico.bl.uk/cro/

http://www.findlaw.com

http://www.ilt.columbia.edu/gen/reHLTcopy.html

http://www.imprimatur.alcs.co.uk/html/home.htm

http://www.infosafe.com

http://www.lse/ac/uk/decomate

http://www.mari.co.uk/copicat

http://www.w3.org/pub/www/pics/960314/steam.html

http://www.zurich.lbm.com:80/Technology/Security/extem/semper/Index.html

http://www2.echo.lu/le/en/ipr.html

http://www2.echo.lu/libraries/en/projects/copinet.html

http://www2.echo.lu/libraries/en/projects/ecupp.html

IFLA. http://www.ifla.org

Institute for Learning Technologies, Columbia University.

Ivey, Keith C. New Copyright legislation (http://www.eeicommunications.com).

Prasad, K.N. (1998) Intellectual Property Rights. *Information Studies*. 4 (2); 67-104

Intellectual Property Rights in India: An overview. In National Seminar on Information Policies and Cyber laws, 4-6 December 2000, Bangalore, Sarada Ranganathan Endowment for Library Science, PAPER A.

Library Association UK, Library Association Copyright Alliance (LACA) Position on Copyright in the Digital Environment. Available at: http:// www.la.hq.org.uk/groups/laca/laca4.html

Rights Issues. Available at: http://www.psg.com/nii.ipr/overview.html

Shade, Leslie Regan. Copyright in the Digital Networked Environment. Available at: http://www.ifla.org/ifla/documents/infopoVcopyright/shade01.htm

USACM (Association Computing Machinery) National Intellectual Property.

White paper on IPR Available at:URL:http://www.netrights.com/EnhancedAttribution.html

WIPO Treaty. Available at: http://www.wipo.org/eng/dipiconf/distrip/treaty01.ht. Critique of WIPO on IPR. Available at: http://www.ahccoalition.org/ wn/brochure.htm

37

Origin and Development of Library and Information Science Periodicals

—A. Gopikuttan and P. R. Hima

This paper traces the origin and development of Library & Information Science periodicals in the world as well as in India. The world's first library periodical is Bibliotek for Loeger *produced by Denmark in 1809. A comprehensive decade-wise analysis of world LIS periodicals in the twentieth century is made. India ranks fourth in the publication of LIS journals in the world.* Library Miscellany *is the first library periodical in India, started in 1912 by the Dept. of Libraries, Baroda. The chronology of LIS periodicals in India are listed in detail.*

Introduction

The whole world today is witnessing an unprecedented growth of scholarly publications in various disciplines through journals, magazines, conference papers, trade publications and monographs. Not only developed nations but the developing nations too, from time to time and in a variety of forms, have realised the need and importance of scholarly literature as they bring varied ideas from masterminds in their respective fields. Scholarly literature in the field of library and information science has been growing gradually as new facets are added to the subject progressively due to the interdisciplinary approach and information explosion. The field of library and information science is no longer confined to four walls of classification and cataloguing but has been broadened to embrace new concepts like automation, information retrieval, digitisation, wikis, metadata, blogging, podcasts, open access, and other web-related technologies. The present study aims to trace the origin and development of library literature so that the trend followed by scholarly literature in library science can be visualised.

Rise of Scholarly Journals

Prior to the development of printing, there was little formal communication because of the difficulties in creating and distributing copies of scholarly works to others. At that time scholars wrote extensively to one another but this communication was both slow and limited to narrow personal circles. The rise of scholarly societies and their associated journals changed all this. In fact, a number of strands came together in the late seventeenth century to cause the appearance of the scientific periodicals.

First, printing made easy production of multiple copies available and improved communication technologies especially postal and courier services made distribution of these copies possible. These technologies had existed for some time before they were taken up for scholarly communication and did not change significantly over the course of the seventeenth and eighteenth centuries.

Secondly, periodical publication in other areas had existed for up to a century prior to the first scientific journal: book catalogues, calendars, almanacs and newspapers. The technologies of the newspapers and almanacs suggested a possible format and distribution channel for scientific results.

Thirdly, the existing scholarly correspondence patterns lent themselves to transformation into print. The tone of the communications was already somewhat impersonal and contained items of news and recent discoveries. These scholarly letters also passed through the hands of a small number of learned men who acted as gatekeepers and redistributors.

Fourthly, there was a movement across Europe towards the establishment of scholarly societies as a way to communicate and cooperate better. The Royal Society was founded in London in 1600, followed by the Académie des Sciences in Paris in 1666 and the Kungliga Svenska Vetenskaps Akademie (Royal Swedish Academy of Science) in 1739.

In response to these technological potentials and to other pressures, the journal in its earliest form came into being. The earliest scientific journal is generally reckoned to be the *Journal des Scavans*, first published by Denis de Sallo in Paris on January 5, 1665 as a weekly. Sallo was a member of the French Parliament and belonged to a group of intellectuals which were to be the predecessors of the Académie des Sciences. *Journal des Scavans* dealt with news and discoveries in the arts and sciences, but was not formally linked to the Académie des Sciences, being rather intended for interested lay-people. This publication provided a model and impetus for the development of other journals.

Within two months of establishment of the *Journal des scavans*, the *Philosophical Transactions was* published as a monthly serial in March, 1665, by the Royal Society, London. It was a medium for the publication of observations and experiments, and can be viewed as a collection of letters now reaching (and addressed to) a wider audience. These 'new media' allowed small geographically dispersed groups of people to form communities with shared interests. Subsequently the following journals have started publishing from the countries noted against their names.

Name of Journals	*Year of establishment*	*Country*
Gionale dei litterati di Roma	1668	Italy
Miscellanea curiosa	1670	Germany
Acta medica et philosophica hafniensia	1673	Denmark
Collectanea medicophysica	1680	Holland
Acta eruditorum	1682	Germany

Later the first half of the eighteenth century saw another five added, but then the pace of development accelerated, with a further sixty nine titles added in the second half of the century, over twenty five of these in the last decade. This acceleration continued over the course of the next two centuries, with an analysis of the number of scientific journals available growing from approximately 100 by the end of the seventeenth century to perhaps 2,000 by the end of the eighteenth, 16,000 by the end of the nineteenth and perhaps 90,000 by the end of the twentieth century and so on.

Origin and Growth of Periodicals in India

The first true periodical published in India was *Asiatick Researches: or, Transactions of the Society instituted in Bengal, for Inquiry into the History and Antiquities, the Arts, Science and Literature of Asia.* The first volume of the periodical with the lengthy title appeared in 1788 and continued up to 1822 and later continued as *Asiatic Researches* up to 1939. Later it was replaced by the *Journal of the Asiatic Society.*

Other Early Periodicals

Tables containing Results of Meteorological Observations is considered to be the first serial on meteorology from India, which was published in 1796 by East India Company's Observatory in Madras. Another important periodical named *Indian Magazine and European Miscellany,* started publication from Madras in January 1807. But its publication ceased in 1808. *Dig Durshan* or the *Indian Youth's magazine,* a bilingual periodical in English and Bengali, started publication from Calcutta in April 1818 with monthly frequency.

In 1810, the first serial on astronomy, named *Meridional Observations* was published from India by East India Company's Observatory. The *Friend of India,* another periodical, started publication from Serampore in May 1818. In 1821 the quarterly series of *Friend of India* was started in order to publish long articles from 1835, a weekly series was also started.

Specialised Periodicals

Literary and scientific societies played a major role in the establishment of scientific periodicals. The first medical periodical to be published in India was the *Transactions of the Medical and Physical Society of Calcutta.* It started publication in 1825 from Calcutta and was the official organ of medical and physical society of Calcutta. From 1837 the title was changed to *Quarterly Journal of the Calcutta Medical and Physical Society.* It ceased its publication in 1845. *Gleanings in Science,* a monthly journal, started publishing in 1829 from Calcutta and was the first specialised periodical in general science. *Transactions of the Agricultural and Horticultural Society of India,* published in 1829 from Calcutta, is considered to be the first journal on agriculture from India.

Report of the Hon'ble Company's Botanic Gardens, published from Calcutta in 1836, is the first serial on botany from India. *Transactions of the Bombay Geographical Society,* published from Bombay in 1836, is the first journal on geography from India. *Ayurved Darpanah,* published in 1840 from Calcutta in Bengali, might be the first journal on ayurveda amongst Indian languages. *Journal, Archaeological Society of Delhi* published from Delhi in 1849, is the first journal on archaeology from India.

The earlier periodicals started making their appearance in India in the late eighteenth century, and most of them were published from the three presidency towns, namely, Calcutta, Madras and Bombay. In Engineering the oldest periodicals are the *Indian and Eastern Engineer*, and *Indian Engineering,* started in 1887 and published from Calcutta simultaneously. The growth of periodicals has kept pace with the growth of knowledge. Periodicals become numerous during the nineteenth century, and were available in almost all fields during the twentieth century. The explosion of scientific literature was so enormous that it became difficult for the readers to cope up with this huge literature. To meet this problem, secondary periodicals were published.

Origin and Development of Periodicals in LIS

Early History

According to the *Ulrich's International Periodicals Directory,* 21st edition, 1982, the world's first library periodical was produced by Denmark in 1809, namely, *Bibliotek for Læger* (literally: "Library for Doctors") as a quarterly by the Danish Medical Association in Danish. Until the end of the 1830s, *Bibliotek for Læger* was the primary choice for Danish physicians, but then a younger generation of doctors rebelled against the old medical institutions, including *Bibliotek for Læger*. They were organised in the so-called Philiatrien Society, and in 1839 they founded *Ugeskrift for Læger* (literally: "Weekly Journal for Doctors"), which quickly weakened the position of *Bibliotek for Læger*).

The second in line was the *American Antiquarian Society Proceedings* produced by US in 1812. It contains the hitherto unpublished records of the Society, together with a reissue of all the matter printed previous to October, 1849.

In 1840, Germany produced *Serapeum* (1840-1870) edited by Robert Naumann, and it contained news, notes and articles about libraries and literature. Another journal published in that period was *Anzeiger Fuer Literatur der Bibliothekswissenschaft* with varying titles from 1840 to 1886.

In 1876, the American Library Association started publishing the *American Library Journal,* the official journal of the American Library Association, later shortened to *Library Journal.* It was begun as a result of the interest and discussions between Frederick Leypoldt and Melvil Dewey, both of whom felt that it was time for the budding profession to have a journal of its own. The first issue contains articles on public documents, the profession, international library concerns, on the establishing of libraries, etc. News of some libraries in England, France, Germany, Italy and Sweden were included in a section called "General Notes". Today, *Library Journal* is a multi-purpose, independent, inclusive, broadly directed, usually lively periodical and one of the most widely read.

Some of the important periodicals published between 1884 and 1899 are *Zentralblatt Fuer Bibliothekswesen* published from East Germany in 1884; *Bulletin of the Board of Library Commissioners* of New Hampshire (1895); *New York Public Library Bulletin* started in 1897; *Assistant Librarian* started from UK in 1898 by the Association of Assistant Librarians; *New Library World,* formerly known as *Library World,* published from UK in 1898; and *Library Association Record* started in 1899 by the Library Association, London. *Library Association Record* is a monthly and it is the official publication of the British Library Association.

Early Twentieth Century Periodicals

Before the end of the nineteenth century, a number of state library associations had been formed in USA, but none began publishing a journal. It was by the early twentieth century that several associations had begun journals, among them some of which are significant publications.

American Libraries (1907) is one of the three major journals published from USA. The other two are *Library Journal* (1876) and *Wilson Library Bulletin* (1914). For about four decades, it was devoted almost exclusively to news and reports concerning the work of the association. Since World War 11, *American Libraries* has become a general interest periodical, publishing news and articles quite indistinguishable from those that appear in *Wilson Library Bulletin* (1914) and *Library Journal*, in addition to material relating to the organisation, conferences and work of the association.

Wilson Library Bulletin is the third important journal published from USA. It was started as the *Wilson Bulletin* in 1914, an irregularly issued house organ and promotional medium of the H.W. Wilson Company, and for years was supplied gratis to anyone who requested it. It is similar in context to *Library Journal* but it deals more with the practical work.

In 1916 *Ontario Library Review*, a quarterly journal started publication from Canada. In the same year *Biblioteksbladett Library Journal* (1916), from Sweden was published. In 1919 Illinois *Libraries* was started as a monthly publication by the Illinois State Library. *Library Review*, a quarterly publication from UK, started publication in 1927. *Catholic Library World* was published in 1929 as a monthly and it is the official journal of the Catholic Library Association (US). *Library Quarterly* began publishing in 1931as a journal of investigation and discussion in the field of Library Science by the Graduate Library School of the University of Chicago, with an international list of distinguished advisory editors. *Library Quarterly* provided for the first time a medium devoted exclusively to scholarly publication, and through the years it has maintained a high scholarly standard. The same year saw the birth of *OLA Bulletin*, published as a quarterly by the Ohio Library Association. In 1932, *Kansae Library Bulletin* was published as a quarterly. In 1934 Poland published *Bibliotekarz* as a bi-monthly and *Bok og Bibliotek* from Norway in the same year. In 1936 *KLA Bulletin* from US was published as a quarterly. In 1937 Huntington *Library Quarterly* was published by Henry E. Huntington Library and Art Gallery. The same year saw the birth of three other journals, namely, *Granthagar*, a Bengali publication from India by IASLIC; *Rutgers University Libraries Journal* (US); and *School Libraries* as a quarterly by the School Library Association (UK). In 1938 *Ohio Library Trustee* from US and *Municipal Library Bulletin* from South Africa were published. In 1939 *California Library Association* started publication as a quarterly. *Princeton University Library Chronicle* was also started in the same year by the Princeton University Library. In the same year *College and Research Libraries* was published as a bi-monthly from Chicago (US). It is the official journal of the Association of College and Research Libraries.

As one of the oldest and probably the best of the oldest is the ALA Divisional Publication's *College and Research Libraries*, which has achieved a solid position not only in USA but also internationally. From its first issue in December 1939, it did not limit itself to new and reports of Divisional Work and Meetings, although all of these have been and still are present. Even the earliest issues contain scholarly writings and increasingly the result of real inquiry and research.

Periodicals in the 1940s

In 1945, the *Journal of Documentation* devoted to the recording, organisation and dissemination of specialised knowledge was started by ASLIB (UK). In the same year *Idaha Libraries* from US and *Indian Librarian* from India were published. In 1946 *Top of the News* was published from US as a quarterly. This is the official publication of the Children's Services Division and the Young Adult Services Division of the ALA. In 1947, *Library World*, a bi-monthly from Japan, started publication. In the same year *Harward Library Bulletin* from US and *Unesco Journal of Information Science, Librarianship and Archives Administration* (originally known as *Unesco Bulletin for Libraries*), a publication from United Nations, was published. In 1949, *Florida Libraries* by Florida Library Association was published as a quarterly journal. In the same year *Aslib Proceedings* from UK which contains news and papers, given by members at meetings and conferences, was published.

Publications in the 1950s

In 1951, *Libri: International Review* was published from Denmark as a quarterly. In 1952 *Library Trends* was published as a quarterly by the University of Illinois Graduate School Of Library Science. *Library Trends* is distinctive among American journals in that each issue is entirely devoted to a single narrow topic.

Each issue contains contributions by ten or more contributors on various aspects of the topic, and some issues have become documents of considerable resource importance.

In the same year, *School Libraries* was published by ALA as a quarterly. *School Libraries* is the official organ of the American Association of School Librarians. *School Libraries* was also known as *School Media Quarterly*. At present it is known as *School Library Media Quarterly*.

American Theological Library Association News Letter, a quarterly publication was brought by US in 1953. In the same year *Library Scene*, a quarterly publication, formerly known as *Library Binder* of *US*, *NYLA Bulletin* by the New York Library Association, *Virginia Libraries*, a bi-monthly by Virginia Library Association, Washington State University Pullman; *Library Staff Association LSA Open Stacks* by Washington State University Library Staff Association as a half yearly, were published.

In the year 1954, a number of periodicals were published. Prominent among them are : *ASLP Bulletin* of the Association of Special Libraries of the Philippines; *Annals of Library Science and Documentation*, a quarterly publication by Indian National Scientific Documentation Centre, New Delhi; *Beta Phi Mu Newsletter* from US; *Bibliotekar* from Bulgaria; *City Business Courier* , newsletter of the City Business Library, UK; *Cleverland Medical Library Bulletin* (US); Japan Society of Library Science (originally published as Annals of Japan Society of Library Science) from Japan; *Medical Libraries* by the Medical Library Association, Japan etc.

In 1955, Italy published *Associasione Italiana Biblioteche Bollettino D Informasioni* , a quarterly publication. In the same year UK published *Society of Archivist Journal*. In 1957 *Library Resources and Technical Services* was published from US by merging *Serial Slants* and *Journal of Cataloguing and Classification* by ALA Resources and Technical Services Division. This is published as a quarterly. Between 1950 and 1959 over 110 new periodicals were published in LIS field.

Periodicals in the 1960s

In 1960, *Journal of Education for Librarianship*, the official publication of the Association of American Library Schools started publication as a quarterly. In the same year *RQ* (*Reference Quarterly*), a publication of ALA's Reference and Adult Service Division, was started as a modest newsletter that contained neither articles nor book reviews. But today it has both.

Some of the periodicals published between 1961 and 1970 are *V Mire Knig* (1961) published from USSR, *Bibliotheksdienst* published from West Germany (1961); *Bloomfield Public Library Highlights* (1962) published as a bi-monthly from US; *Buecherschau*, a quarterly publication from Austria (1962); *Bibliotecas* (1963) a bi-monthly from Cuba; *Information Processing and Management* (1963), a bi-monthly formerly known as *Information Storage and Retrieval* from US; *Brio* (1964) by UK branch of International Association of Music Libraries; *Library Technology Reports* (1965) an evaluative information on library systems, equipment and supplies published from US; *Research in Librarianship* (1965) published from Australia; and *Drexel Library Quarterly* (1965) published as a quarterly from US Drexel University, School of Library and Information Science.

Drexel Library Quarterly is another distinctive periodical published from UD in that each issue like *Library Trends* is devoted to a single narrow topic. There are no news items, book reviews , editorials or reports. Each issue with ten or more contributors write articles on various aspects of the topic has become important documents.

In 1966, the *Journal of Library History, Philosophy and Comparative Librarianship*, formely *Journal of Library History* was published from US. Also *Program*, a quarterly publication from UK was published in the same year. *College and Research Libraries News* is another publication which was published from US in the same year. It is a supplement to *College and Research Libraries* and contains more of ephemeral, less important matters so that *College and Research Libraries* itself contains only articles and other substantive material as well as book review, abstracts and notes. In 1967, *Library History* was published by the Library Association (UK). In the same year, *Informatika* from Yougoslavia was published. In 1968 it brought out Information for *Forskningsbibliotaker* (Denmark); and *Information Sciences: an International Journal* (US), *International Library Review* (New York and London); *Journal of Librarianship* (UK); and *Library and Information Science Abstract* (UK) were published in 1969. In 1970 *Sipapu* from US and *Law Librarian: Bulletin of the British and Irish Association of Law Librarians* were published. In 1971, *Unabashed Librarian* and *ASLA President's Newsletter* from US were published.

Periodicals in the 1970s

Some of the periodicals published from UK between 1971 and 1975 are *Interlending Reviews: Journal of the British Library Lending Division* (1971) and *International Cataloguing* (1972). These two journals have an international coverage. Some of the national periodicals from UK during the same period are *Librarians for Social Change* (1972); *LEG News* (1972); *Service Point* (1972); *Unisist Newsletter* (1973); and *International Classification* (1974) with international coverage. Some periodicals which are published during this period were expansion of previously published materials or changes of titles. For example, *Library World* which was started in 1897 was changed to *New Library World* in 1971; and *Aslib Information* (1973) expanded from *Aslib Proceedings*. In the same way *Radials Bulletin* (1974) expanded from a list in the *Library Association Yearbook; IFLA Journal* (1974) expanded from *IFLA News* which had ceases publication later; and *British Library Journal* (1975) replaced the *Library Association Sound Recordings Group Newsletter*, now jointly published with *Aslib's Audio Visual Group*. International Coordination in library and information science periodicals was stimulated by a 1972 symposium held in Paris sponsored by UNESCO.

In 1976, *Art Libraries Journal* from UK was published by the Art Libraries Society as a quarterly. Formerly this was known as *ARLIS News Letter*. In the same year France published a quarterly publication named Bibliothegue *Nationale Revue*. Some of the periodicals published between 1977 and 1982 are *Cabiers De I Analyses Des Donnees* (1977) from France; *Library Acquisition :Practice and Theory* (1977) from US; *Open Access* (1978) from UK; *Public Documents Highlights for Texas* (1978) from US as a quarterly; *Outlook on Research Libraries* (1979) from UK; and *Journal of Information Science* (1979) a bi-monthly from UK.

Periodicals in the 1980s

The prominent LIS periodicals in 1980s are *Science and Technology Libraries* (1980) from US as a quarterly; *Socialist Librarian's Journal* (1980) from UK; *Cataloguing and Classification Quarterly* (1980) from US; *Community Analysis Studies* (US) in 1980; *Special Collection* (US) in 1981; *Resource Sharing and Library Networks* (US) in 1981; *SAILIS Newsletter* (1981) from South Africa; *Medical*

Reference Service Quarterly (US) in 1982 and *Art Documentation* (US) in 1982.

Periodicals in the 1990s

A number of periodicals have ceased publication due to financial and other reasons, for example, Arizona *Libraries and D C Libraries*. Some others started publication as journals, which now become newsletters. Examples are *Missouri Library Association Quarterly; Florida Libraries; New Mexico Library Bulletin; Bulletin of the Maine Library Association; Montana Library Quarterly* and the *New Jersey Librarian*.

Some of the prominent periodicals which began publishing in 1990s are: *IFLA Series on Bibliographic Control* (1991) in English, published by International Federation of Library Associations and Institutions. Another one named *ISBN Newsletter* (1990) in English; which covers agency activities , current news of ISBN and efforts to encourage ISBN use around the world was published by International ISBN Agency, Germany. *Information Outlook*, published by Special Library Association, USA was formed by the merger of *Special Libraries* (1910-1997) and *Specialist* (1980-1997). It was in English language and started publication from 1997 onwards.

Periodicals in the Early Twenty-first Century

Some of the prominent periodicals which began publication after 2000 are *Archival Science*: international journal on recorded information (2000), published in English as a quarterly by Springer, Netherlands. *Indian Journal of Library and Information Science* (2007), published by World Information Syndicate, New Delhi in English came as a quarterly. *Journal of Information and Knowledge Management* (2003), which publishes original research and case studies by academic, business and government contributors on all aspects of information procession, information management, knowledge management, tools, techniques and technologies; published by Information and Knowledge Management Society, Singapore. *Journal of Information Science and Technology* (2004), id published by The Information Institute, USA in English. In January 2007, Elsevier published *Journal of Informetrics: an International Journal* with Leo Egghe as the Editor in Chief.

LIS Periodicals in India

Periodicals are responsible for creation of literature in a subject. India ranks fourth in world in the publication of LIS journals; USA, UK and Canada being the other three countries publishing 703 (41.43%), 155 (9.13%) and 75 (4.42%) periodicals, respectively, up to 2003.The first library periodical in India was *Library Miscellany,* a quarterly in English, Marathi and Gujarati; it was started in 1912 by the Department of Libraries, Baroda. W. A. Borden who was the Director of the State Library Department contributed a lot in starting the first periodical in Library science. However, its publication ceased in 1920. Later *Granthalaya Sarvaswamu,* a monthly journal in Telugu language, was started in 1915 from Vijayawada by Andhra Pradesh Library Association. Another journal, *Granthagar Karmi* in Bengali, was started in 1937 from Calcutta by the Indian Association of Special Libraries and information Centre (IASLIC). The journal *Modern Librarian* in English of pre-partition days of India was continued as the *Indian Librarian* from 1945-81 by Sant Ram Bhatia from Jallander which was ceased later.

Chronology of LIS Periodicals in India

The chronological listing of library science periodicals in India shows that the journal *Pustaklaya* started in 1924 is perhaps the oldest continuing periodical published by Gujarat Pustakalaya, Sahkari Mandal; followed by *Grandhalokam* published in 1948 from South India by Kerala State Library Council, Thiruvananthapuram. The *Annals of Library and Information Studies,* formerly *Annals of Library Science,* was started in 1954 by INSDOC, New Delhi, under the editorship of Dr S. R. Ranganathan, the Father of Library Science in India. Another periodical the *IASLIC Bulletin,* a quarterly organ of Indian Association of Special Libraries and Information Centres, Calcutta (now Kolkata) was started in 1956. West Bengal State has been a pioneer of another journal, the *Granthagar* (1958) in Bengali, published by the Bengal Library Association. The Delhi Library Association started its quarterly journal the *Library Herald* in 1958 under the editorship of Prof. P. N. Kaula. The Uttar Pradesh Library Association in 1962 brought out the journal *Lucknow Librarian.*

Other periodicals started in the same year were *Herald of Library Science* by Prof. P. N. Kaula and *Libra* by the Department of Library Science and Documentation, Rajasthan University, Jaipur. The Library Science Student Association of Karnataka University started its annual periodical *The Timeless Fellowship* in 1964. Another significant journal, the *Library Science with a Slant to Documentation,* commenced its publication in 1964; this was jointly sponsored by Documentation Research and Training Centre and Sarda Ranganathan Endowment for Library Science, Bangalore. Its name changed to *SRELS Journal of Information Management*. The Indian Library association started the *ILA Bulletin* in 1965 followed by the periodical *Indian Library Science Abstract* by *IASLIC Calcutta* in 1967.

A number of new periodicals were started in the 1970's, viz., *ALIS Bulletin* in 1976 from Trivandrum (ceased later), *Indian Journal of Library Science* in 1975 from Calcutta; *ISIS Bulletin* in 1976 from Bangalore; *Journal of Library and Information Science* in 1976 by Delhi University, Department of Library and Information Science; *Library History Review* from Calcutta, etc.

Similarly, during the 1980's a few more journals were brought out. Some of the important ones includes *Indian Journal of Library Science* in 1980 published by Institute of Librarians, Sanskrit College; *DESIDOC Bulletin of Information Technology* in 1981 from DESIDOC; *Information Technology and Tomorrow* in 1982 from NISSAT, and in the same year another important periodical, *International Information Communication and Education* commenced its publication from P. N. Kaula Endowment for Library and Information Science. *CLIS Observer* was started in 1984 from Centre for Library and Documentation Centre, New Delhi; and *MFCLA Bulletin*, a quarterly of Maharashtra Federation of College Library Association, in 1988.

Besides these the 1990's saw the emergence of few more periodicals like *Granthana: Indian Journal of Library Studies* in 1991 from Raja Rammohun Roy Library Foundation; *DELNET Newsletter* in 1994 by Delhi Library Association; *Information Studies* in 1995 by Ranganathan Centre for Information Studies, Bangalore; *INFLIBNET Newsletter* in 1995 by Information and Library Network Center, Ahmedabad; *JISSI: International Journal of Scientometrics and Informetrics* (1995) in English as a quarterly by Brzark Information Systems, New Delhi, *Kelpro Bulletin* (1998) by Kerala Library Professionals Organisation, Thiruvananthapuram etc.

The beginning of the twenty-first century also witnessed a number of periodicals published from India. Some of them are: *Trends in information Management* (2005) published by DLIS, University of Kashmir, *Information age* (2007) published by Dr.P.S.G. Kumar library foundation, Nagpur, *PEARL*: Journal of LIS (2007) published by University Library Teachers Association, AP, *Indian Journal of Library and Information Science* (2007) published by Red-flower Publications Pvt Ltd, Delhi and *World Digital Library* (2008) published by TERI. The Department of Library and information Science, University of Kerala, has started publishing *Journal of Information Science and Technology* (JIST) as a half-yearly publication from 2008 onwards. Society for the Advancement of Library & Information Science, Chennai started a new journal, *SALIS Journal of LIS* from 2009.

Conclusion

Periodicals constitute the most important segment of the science & technology literature and in other fields. It is an indispensable tool in the communication and acquisition of new ideas and knowledge. It provides a medium for the exchange of expert experiences. The regular and frequent appearance of the periodical ensures that it can remain close to the frontiers of knowledge by continuous addition, correction or even retraction. Because of these peculiarities, the periodicals are considered as the vehicle of nascent thought and carrier of current information in all fields of knowledge and library and information science is not an exemption. As in the case of all other disciplines, periodicals in LIS are also growing in number and this growth indicates that the subject of LIS is developing due to the promotion of the research activities in the field.

References

Collection Development Training – Selection: Periodicals & Newspapers Available at: http://www.lib.az.us/cdt/slrper.aspx (Accessed on 6 September 2009)

Danton, Periam J. (1976). The Library Press. *Library Trends,* 25(1), 162.

Fjallbrant , Nancy . Scholarly Communication – Historical Development and new possibilities . Available at: www.iatul.org/doclibrary/public/conf _Proceedings /.../Fjallbrant.doc (Accessed on 10 August 2009).

Goyal, S P. (1987). Seventy five years if Indian periodicals in Library and Information Science (1912-1986): Asurvey. *Herald of Library Science,* 26(1-2), 65-75.

Hypermedia Online Publishing: the Transformation of the Scholarly Journal. August 7, 2009. Available at: http://andrew.treloar.net/research/theses/phd/thesis-59.shtml#pgfId-139398 (Accessed on 7August 2009).

Khanna, J K and Khurana, S. (2007). *Handbook of Research Methodology.* New Delhi: Y.K. Publishers, 297-99.

Kronick, David A. (1976). *A History of scientific and technical periodicals.* 2nd ed. Metuchen: Scare Crow Press.

Mittal, R.L. (2007). *Library Administration: Theory and Practice.* New Delhi: Ess Ess Publications, 394-396.

Neena Singh and Panda K. C. (2003). Growth of LIS periodicals in India (1920-2000): an evaluation. *IFLA Newsletter,*1(23),17-28

Osborn (1973). *Serial Publications: their place and treatment in libraries.* 2nd rev ed. Chicago: American Library Association.

Periodical types. Available at: http://www.tarleton.edu/~library/library module/unit6/6types lm.html (Accessed on 2 August 2009).

Scholarly Journals. Available at:: http://www.csupomona.edu/~library/tutorials/scholarly journals.html (Accessed on 12 August 2009).

Sen, B K. (2002). Growth of scientific periodicals in India (1788-1900). *Indian Journal of History of Science,* 37(3).

The four functions of scholarly journals. Available at:: http://www.ariadne.ac.uk/issue7/fytton/ (Accessed on 6 August 2009)

Wani, Zahid Ashraf, Bakshi, Ishrat Majeed and Sumeer Gul (2008). Growth and Development of Library and Information Science Literature. *Chinese Librarianship: an International Electronic Journal* 26.

IX

Prof. C. V. Rajan Pillai: Reminiscences and Impressions

38

Prof. (Dr.) C.V. Rajan Pillai: A Towering Personality in Library and Information Science Profession

(Summary of an Interview Session by the Editors)

—S. Humayoon Kabir and **K. G. Sudhier**

Dr. C.V. Rajan Pillai hails from an agrarian family in central Travancore, namely, Changayil, Karichal, Haripad, Alleppey District, Kerala. His father Mr. M.N. Padmanabha Pillai, Mozhiyottu, Vazharmangalam, Kallissery, Chengannur, Kerala was a farmer who identified himself a communist with a concern for poor people and their problems. He passed away at the age of 90 in the year 2003. His mother Smt. L. Bhavani Amma is a housewife, aged 90, and she belongs to Changayil family.

Dr. Pillai was born on 31 November 1941. He had his primary education at St. Mary's School, Karichal, Haripad. He joined the 8th standard in Government Boys High School, Haripad, from where he was matriculated in the year 1958. He did graduation with physics main and mathematics as subsidiary subjects in St. Berchman's College, Changanacherry, affiliated to Kerala University at that time. Among the teachers he still remembers with due regards and respect two of them, Prof. S.L. Thomas, Head, Department, of Physics and Prof. C.A. Shepperd, Head, Department of English. According to him the desire to become a teacher originated in his mind through their classes.

After graduation in the year 1963 Dr. Pillai entered the service of the Kerala University as an Assistant in Oriental Research Institute and Manuscripts Library where

Dr. K. Raghavan Pillai was the director of the Institute. In the year 1968 he joined for B. Lib. Sc. in the Department of Library Science, University of Kerala under the guidance of Prof. K.A. Isaac. While he was working as Assistant Librarian in the Kerala University Library went on leave for higher studies and joined Banaras Hindu University, for M. Lib. Sc. course in the year 1972. Under the supervision and guidance of Prof. P.N. Kaula, he passed out with a rank. Prof. Kaula's classes inspired him for doing research in Library and Information Science. He was awarded Ph.D. from Kerala University in the year 1987, under the guidance of Prof. (Dr.) Puthussery Ramachandran.

In the year 1974 Dr. Pillai married Smt. R. Sreekumari Amma, Lecturer in Physics, College for Woman, Thiruvananthapuram. She is a native of Kanyakumari (Dist) in Tamil Nadu. Recently Prof. R. Sreekumari Amma retired as Principal, Maharajas College, Ernakulam. Her intelligent and wholehearted support in all matters contributed to the success of Pillai's life. They have two sons, R. Rajesh and R. Sreejesh. Both are well educated and well placed.

Dr. Pillai joined the Department of Library Science, University of Kerala, as a faculty member in 1978 where he got an opportunity for teaching both B.Lib.Sc and M.Lib.Sc. classes. Classification, theory and practice, Universe of Knowledge, Research Methodology were the subjects taught by him. During this period he could establish himself as one of the best teachers in library science and contacts with universities outside Kerala.

In the month of December 1984 Dr. Pillai joined the Cochin University of Science and Technology (CUSAT) as University Librarian. Within a small span of time, Cochin University Library was well organised and several information services were introduced for the benefit of the academic community of the university. 'Modernisation of Cochin University Library', was a project sanctioned by U.G.C, and Dr. Pillai was appointed as the principal investigator of the project. The project was a complete success in introducing computerised information services, and Cochin University Library became the first University Library in Kerala which introduced the computerised information services. No doubt the credit goes to Dr.Pillai. The U.G.C. Committee during their visit in CUSAT recognised Cochin University Library as the best university library in South India with respect to organisation and information services.

In the year 1997 Dr. Pillai joined the Mahatma Gandhi University as Professor and Head of the Department of Library and Information Science. B.L.I.Sc and M.L.I.Sc courses were organised. Because of his efforts, M.G. University sanctioned to begin B.L.I.Sc and M.L.I.Sc courses in some of the affiliated colleges. Dr. Pillai served as Professor and Head, Department of LIS, Mahatma Gandhi University, more than eight years, and at the age of 65 on his on request he relinquished for his service. During the period of his service in M.G. University he conducted several refresher courses, and organised a lecture series, namely, Library and Information Science Lecture Series. M.G. University constituted an expert committee for modernisation of Mahatma Gandhi University Library with Dr. C.V. Rajan Pillai as its chairman, and many of the recommendations of the committee were implemented.

Dr. Pillai worked in various capacities in several universities. At present he is a recognised research guide for Ph.D work in Library and Information Science of University of Kerala, Cochin University of Science and Technology and Manonmaniam Sundarnar University, Tirunelveli. Five Scholars were awarded Ph.D under his guidance. He was a visiting fellow of U.G.C and delivered guest lectures, keynote addresses, presented papers in seminars, published books and articles. He served as a member of Academic Council, Faculty of Arts, Doctoral Committee, Board of Studies of University of Kerala. He was also a member of the Doctoral Committee in L.I.S of Mangalore University, and M.S. University. He also served as a member of B.O.S. of Mangalore University, Calicut University, M.G. University and M.S. University. In fact he got many opportunities to participate the academic activities of Library & Information Science Departments in all the universities in Kerala and outside Kerala.

Dr. Pillai served as a member in selection committees of universities inside and outside Kerala. K.P.S.C and U.P.S.C are still utilising his services as an expert member in selection committees. As an adjudicator of Ph.D. theses and chairman of open defense, he served in several universities.

Dr. Pillai is closely associated with the activities of IASLIC, ILA, IATLIS, KLA and KELPRO. During the period of his service in Kerala University he organised the library staff of the university under the organisation, Library Staff Association. He was the founder secretary of the Association, and many of the grievances of library staff were studied in depth and solved under his able leadership.

Dr. Pillai has a wide circle of friendship inside and outside Kerala, from all walks of life. During the interview he mentioned names of several important personalities with whom he has close contacts for the last several years. Among them many have passed away even after their sad demise Dr. Pillai remembers with respectful regards two great scholars who helped him to develop his personality. They are Dr. K. Raghavan Pillai, former Director, ORI & ML and Mr. A.K. Panicker, Deputy Librarian, Kerala University Library.

From the discussion we understand that Dr. Pillai is a good conversationist. He is a teacher par excellence. Honesty, hard work, and punctuality are the basic qualities of his life. Prof. (Dr.). C.V. Rajan Pillai stands head and shoulders above others - a towering personality of the library profession.

We feel proud of him and pray to Almighty for his long life with multifarious activities to enrich the library and information science profession.

39

Rajan Pillai: My Student at BHU

—Prof. P.N. Kaula

Established : 1962

Phone : 351172

HERALD OF LIBRARY SCIENCE

Editor:
PROF. P.N. KAULA

Office:
C-239, Indira Nagar
Lucknow-226016

Ref: HL/760

Date: 17-01-2009

Dear Editors,

It was a pleasure to receive your letter informing me about the Festschrift being sponsored and presented to Dr. C.V Rajan Pillai.

Dr. Rajan Pillai had been our student at BHU and has grown as a specialist in the field, I will be pleased to write on his early years with us at BHU. I know Dr. Pillai very closely and have admired the work he has done in the profession. I was witness to his education and early formative years at Banaras and will be glad to write of it.

The deadline, however, given is short for writing about him.

With best wishes.

Yours sincerely,

(P. N. KAULA)

40

My Respects to Prof. C. V. Rajan Pillai: A Teacher Par Excellence

—Prof. A.K. Baradol

Our Student Days

Prof. C.V. Rajan Pillai and I were together during the academic year 1972-73 for our Master's degree course in Library Science (M.Lib.Sc.) at Banaras Hindu University, Varanasi. Our group was a very small one with only six students. All six of us were in the university hostel named 'Birla Hostel'. The stay was all the more comfortable because of the company of Prof. Rajan Pillai. My room was adjacent to his room. Both being south Indians in the group of six students, we were naturally closer.

On many evenings we used to visit the lone south Indian hotel known as 'Madras Hotel' in an area known as 'Lanka' outside the Banaras Hindu University campus. While going to the hotel we discussed some academic and personal problems. He always used to contribute to the discussion. We discussed about the themes for the dissertations which was part fulfilment of the Master's degree course.

His contribution to the Universe of Knowledge is significant. He had written a book on this theme. We used to discuss the Universe of Knowledge after Prof. Kaula P.N. delivered his lectures for the Master of Library Science classes. Prof. Rajan Pillai is an advocate of Colon Classification and Ranganathan's philosophy. He was an eager and studious student in the class and was above average in studies. His approach to the universe of knowledge was fresh which leads him into breaking new ground.

Prof. Rajan Pillai became one of the most respected senior students because he used to solve some problems in classification practical course/paper; and also because of his mild behaviour. He developed a method of deep thinking on technical subjects when he was studying the Master's course. He had already put in some experience in the library of University of Kerala, Trivandrum, which was advantageous for him to think about the problems academic libraries were facing in those days.

Association with Mangalore University, Mangalagangothri (Karnataka)

Prof. Rajan Pillai was closely associated with the Department of Library and Information Science of Mangalore University. He served as UGC visiting fellow at the Department of Library and Information Science, Mangalore University during 1991-92 and 2000-2001. The areas covered by him during his visit as visiting fellow were 'Universe of Knowledge and its Structure', 'Design of Depth Classification Schemes,' and 'Universal Decimal Classification.' During his tenure of visiting fellowship he used to conduct the classes regularly and systematically. He stayed at our university guest house. A few students of the department used to bother him in the evenings with their difficulties in some courses. He used to solve their difficulties in Organisation of Knowledge: Classification. I got this feedback from the students of our department. They had a very good opinion about his domain of knowledge and said that he is a teacher par excellence.

He attended the National Seminar on 'Women and Library Services' conducted at the Department of Library and Information Science, Mangalore University during January 29-30, 1990. He participated very actively in all the sessions of the seminar. This showed his interest in academics.

Prof. Rajan Pillai served as an external examiner for two doctoral (Ph.D.) students of Library and Information Science at Mangalore University. He was requested by the University to witness the open defence of the theses and conduct the Ph.D. vivavoce of examination. He did this work with perfection. He posed a lot of questions to the doctoral students pertaining to the themes of the research. He also suggested the points to be incorporated before the theses were published.

He served as a member Board of Studies during 1977-1980, i.e., for a term of three years. During the meetings of the Board of Studies he actively participated and gave enough inputs for the designing of syllabi and other issues.

He served as a member of the Board of Examiners for Bachelor's course in Library and Information Science at Mangalore University. He was also the examiner for practical examinations for B. Lib. Science and M. Lib. Science in Mangalore University. A day was always assigned for the preparation for practical examinations. He used to always attend the preparation work for the practical examinations and did the work meticulously.

My Visit to the Places where He Worked

I had an opportunity to be associated with the Cochin University of Science and Technology (CUSAT), Kochi, for doctoral programme in Library and Information Science. Whenever I visited Kochi for the work of Cochin University of Science and Technology (CUSAT), Kochi, Dr. Pillai was very kind to me. He used to receive me at the railway station so that we can have more time for discussions on academic issues. After the completion of the academic assignment we used to discuss some professional issues. The issues discussed included the curriculum/syllabus of Library and Information courses at different levels, etc.

It was a pleasure for me to have his company on various assignments, like the meetings, the lectures and seminars. He was invited by Mangalore University for serving as a resource person for the three refresher courses in Library and Information Science conducted by the Department. He was rated as one of the best resource persons by the participants of refresher courses at Mangalore University.

After the superannuation from the position of a librarian of CUSAT in a strange twist of career Dr. Rajan Pillai was invited for a the post of a Professor and Head of Library and Information Science at Mahatma Gandhi University, Kottayam, which duties he carried out very successfully.

More than anything else Prof. Rajan Pillai's attitude of listening to any problems first and then giving his opinion/verdict impressed me much. His opinion provided on any matter was firm; come whatever he never changed his decision taken once. As a scholar and as a straightforward administrator he made mark in the Library and Information Science profession.

He used to enquire about the career of M. Lib. Sc. class fellows which showed his concern about his friends. Being a simple and soft-spoken person he proved to be one of my best friends who always considered self-respect as important. He considered human dignity to be non-negotiable and that it was everyone's right. He did whatever he told, and at the same time he told whatever he did. Our friendship flourished for over 37 (thirty-seven) years and became stronger.

I pray to God for peace to Prof. C.V. Rajan Pillai. He is now leading a peaceful retired life which is the way one should live. With this I end my greatest respect to Prof. C.V. Rajan Pillai.

41

Dr. C. V. Rajan Pillai: A Rare and Good Friend

—Prof. P. Leelakrishnan

Although this note comes a little late, let me express my immense pleasure in contributing to the festschrift of Dr. C.V. Rajan Pillai.

In this complex society, people run after designed glories. Lore and open mind are strange commodities. A rare and good friend, Dr. Rajan Pillai lives in my thought as an exception and as a green meadow that never dries up. A man of vision and wisdom he has made richer the institutions he served. He has been the source of strength to the Cochin University Library which he built up into one of the best treasure houses of knowledge sought after by many. It is rather a privilege to get an occasion to write about a friend whose association with me is for more than two decades.

42

Guruvandanam

—Dr. K. P. Somanathan Nair

There are two kinds of people: Those who do the work and those who take the credit for others' work. Prof. (Dr.) C.V.Rajan Pillai (i.e., Dr. CVR) falls in the first group. Others enjoy the credit of his work in the library profession. He is a man with professional honesty and dedication to the cause of librarianship. It is befitting that Dr.CVR is honoured with a festschrift. He deserves it and even much more. I feel honoured to be associated with this task of honouring him.

Dr. CVR's life and work is a rare example of professional competence, hard work, dedication and leadership. He has attained a highly respectable and unique position among the professional librarians and library educators in India. He is a man of strong conviction. He possesses a peculiarity in his personality with his uncompromising nature and strong determination. He never bows down to any authority in the matter of principles.

Dr. CVR is a librarian turned to a teacher, a teacher turned to a librarian and again a librarian turned to a teacher. I feel very proud of being a student of him. When I first saw him, he was a library trade unionist. He was the leader of Kerala University Library Staff Association. He was elected to the Library Advisory Committee of Kerala University as the representative of Library Staff in the year 1973-74. Later he joined the teaching profession as Lecturer in the Department of Library and Information Science of Kerala University. Very quickly he proved himself as a very good teacher. I was then a student of MLISc and Dr.CVR taught me in the MLISc classification class. Even now I keep precious memories of his lectures in library classification.

Nearly half a dozen persons took their doctorates in Library and Information Science under the guidance and supervision of Dr.CVR. I happened to be the first among them. Moreover, I also got a chance to work under him as a faculty member in the Department of Library and Information Science of Mahatma Gandhi University, Kottayam. He served that University as Professor and Head for over 10 years. Even after retirement, he is magnanimous to associate with many programmes of this Department. Thus I have a very long and close association with the beloved teacher. I always got very valuable advice from him in many matters.

Let me humbly take this opportunity to garland him with my rejoicing reminiscences on this occasion of honouring him....*Dhanyavaad!*

43

Dr. Rajan Pillai as the CUSAT Librarian

—Prof. S.Balaraman

It gives me immense pleasure to know that Dr. C. V. Rajan Pillai, a well known Library and Information Scientist, is being honoured by the library professionals and his friends with the publication of a festschrift volume. Dr. Pillai served the library profession effectively for more than five decades, in different capacities. I was closely associated with him when I was in the Cochin University of Science and Technology (CUSAT) as Pro-Vice-Chancellor and Vice Chancellor.

In 1984 he joined the Cochin University of Science and Technology as a University Librarian. Under his leadership the library was well organised in modern lines, and he started several information services for the benefit of the academic community of the university. The credit of starting computerised information services in the Cochin University goes to Dr. Pillai.

As the Vice-Chancellor of CUSAT, I had enough opportunity to testify his dignified personality and ability. The Library and Information Science Lecture series of Cochin University Library was started by him, and the first lecture in this series was delivered by Prof. K. A. Isaac. Among other qualities of his character, honesty, hard work and sincerity are worth mentioning. He is also well versed in university politics, and during crises his friendship and advice helped me a lot. He is a very good friend of his colleagues and he would never let his colleagues and subordinates down at critical times; that is the secret of his success in administration.

In conclusion, I may add that Dr. C. V. Rajan Pillai is a very inspiring speaker and good organiser.

44

Dr. Rajan Pillai as a Researcher

—Prof. Puthusseri Ramachandran

My acquaintance with Rajan Pillai begins from the year 1969, when I joined the Department of Malayalam, University of Kerala. I had several opportunities to witness his academic and administrative abilities wherever he worked.

Dr. Pillai selected a topic, namely, 'Malayalam periodical literature till 1925' for Ph.D. work under my guidance. A large number of periodicals were published in Malayalam till 1925, and the articles published in them reflected the cultural, social, political, religious and educational ideas and aspirations of the people of that time.

The nature of the topic required continuous hard work for successful completion. The University of Kerala awarded him Ph.D for the work in the year 1987. As a research fellow I found him an intelligent and alert scholar.

It is usual to meet people with vision and fortitude. But it is very rare to see someone like Dr. Pillai with the will to win in difficulties and at the same time to keep the fellow workers with him. His power of creating lasting impression upon people he meets is admirable. No doubt, he is a good teacher with proved research abilities.

List of Contributors

Dr. Achutsankar S. Nair. Hon. Director, Centre for Bioinformatics Kariavattom Campus, University of Kerala, Thiruvananthapuram. 695 581 sankar.achut@gmail.com

Dr. Anas, K. Assistant Professor, Dept. of Library & Information Science, Pondicherry University, Pondicherry 14. anaskalib@hotmail.com.

Dr. Aswath, Lalitha. Professor & Chairperson, Dept. of Library & Information Science, Bangalore University, Bangalore-560056. lalithaaswath@yahoo.co.in

Dr. Balaraman, S. Former Vice Chancellor, Cochin University of Science & Technology; Former Member & Acting Chairman, Kerala State Human Rights Commission, *Swaram*, Mundackal Kollam- 691 001.

Dr. Baradol, A. K. Professor & Chairman, Dept. of Library & Information Science, Mangalore University, Mangalagangothri, Mangalore. akbaradol@gmail.com

Dr. Chakraborty, Susmita. Librarian, Bengal Engineering & Science University, Kolkata, West Bengal. susmita.chakraborty@ becs.ac.in

Dr. Chandra Kumar. V. Lecturer, Dept. of Library of Information Science, University of Madras, Chennai. vcakilan@gmail.com

Chitra, S. Officer. Library & Information Centre, Tata Consulatancy Services, Technopark, Thiruvananthapuram. 695 581. chitra3.s@tcs.com

Choukimath, Puttaraj A. Assistant Librarian, Tata Institute of Social Sciences, Mumbai- 400 088. choukimath@tiss.edu

Dr. Chudamani, K. S. Deputy Librarian, JRD Tata Memorial Library, Indian Institute of Science, Bangalore. 560012

Dr. Geetha, V. Associate Professor, Dept. of Library & Information Science, Sc. Bishop Heber College, Trichy. manogeeth@ yahoo.com

Dr. Gopakumar, V. University Librarian, Goa University Library Goa. gopakumar.v@rediffmail.com

Dr. Gopikuttan, A. Head, Dept. of Library & Information Science University of Kerala, Thiruvananthapuram. 695034 agopikuttan@yahoo.co.in

Dr. Harinarayana, N. S. Reader, Dept. of Library & Information Science, University of Mysore, Manasagangothri, Mysore-570006, ns.harinarayana@gmail.com

Hima, P. R. Research Scholar, Dept. of Library & Information Science, University of Kerala, Thiruvananthapuram. 695034

Dr. Jalaja, V. Head, Dept. of Library & Information Science University of Calicut, Kozhikode. Jalajadlis@yahoo.co.in

Jalajakumari, C. Reference Assistant, Kerala University Library Thiruvananthapuram-695 034.

Johnson, Sophia. Librarian, Al Ghurair University, Dubai International Academic City, Dubai, UAE. sofiyajohnson@hotmail.com

Dr. Kabir, S Humayoon. Associate Professor, Dept. of St. Library of Inforamtion Science, University of Kerala, Thiruvananthapuram-24. humayoonkabir@yahoo.co.in

Dr. Kalra, H.P.S. Associate Professor, Dept. of Library & Information Scince, Punjabi University, Patiala. 147002 hpskalra@gmail.com

Prof.Kaula, P. N. C- 239, Indira Nagar Lucknow. 226016.

Dr. Khan, Khaisar Muneebulla. Reader, Dept. of Library & Information Science, Mangalore University. Mangalagangothri, Mangalore, khaisarmk@yahoo.com

Khushpreet Singh. Research Scholar, Dept. of Library & Information Science, Punjabi University, Patiala. 147002, Punjab, khushpreet.singh@gmail.com

Dr. Koganuramath, Muttayya M. University Librarian Tata Institute of Social Sciences, Mumabi 400 088. koganuramath@r ediffmail.com

Dr. Koneru, Indira. Faculty Member, Dept. of Library Science ICFAI Academic Wing, Hyderabad. 500082 ind68@hotmail.com

Dr. Koovakkai, Dineshan. Assistant Librarian, Central University of Kerala, Kasaragod, Kerala. 671123 dineshank@gmail.com

Dr. Kumbar, Mallinath. Reader, Dept. of Library & Information Science, University of Mysore, Mysore. mallinathk@ yahoo.com

Dr. Leelakrishnan, P. Advocate, High Court of Kerala, *Shyam*, BMC Post, Kochi. 6820231, Ernakulam

Lone, Fayaz Ahmad. Documentation Officer, Centre of Central Asian Studies, University of Kashmir, Jammu & Kashmir. fayazlib@yahoo.co.in

Manjula, K. JRD Tata Memorial Library, Indian Institute of Science, Bangalore. 560012

Dr. Mohanakumar, T. Assistant Librarian, Kerala University Library, Thiruvananthapuram- 695034. Mohanakumar_t@ yahoo.co.in

Musthafa, K. Mohammed. Research Scholar, Dept. of Library & Information Science, Aligarh Muslim University, Aligarh. musthafa.lis@gmail.com

Nagarathna, H.C. JRD Tata Memorial Linrary, IISc, Bangalore-12.

Dr. Natarajan, M. Scientist 'F', NISCAIR, Satsang Vihar Marg, New Delhi-110 067, m_natarajan@hotmail.com

Nikesh, N. M Tech Student, ISiM, University of Mysore Mysore. nikeshn@gmail.com

Dr. Noushad Ali, P. M. Chairman, Dept. of Library & Information Science Aligarh Muslim University, Aligarh-202002. naushadali.amu@gmail.com

Dr. Panda, K. C. Head, Dept. of Library & Information Science Sambalpur University, Orissa, krushna52@yahoo.co.in

Prof. Parameswaran, M. Former Head, Dept. of Library & Information Science, University of Calicut, (15, *Sri Silam*, Green Park, Baypore, Kozhikode. 673 015).

Dr. Prasad, K. N. Executive Officer, Sarada Ranganathan Endowment for Library Science (SRELS), Rajaji Nagar, Bangalore-560 010, srels@dataone.in.

Prasad, N. N. MLISc Student, Dept. of Library & Information Science, University of Mysore, Mysore. 570006 prasad.happy@gmail.com

Dr. Radhakrishnan, N. Senior Librarian, BITS Pilani-Dubai Campus, UAE. radhakrishnan@bitsdubai.com

Dr. Rajani, R. Catalogue Assistant, Kerala Legislative Assembly Library, Thiruvananthapuram. 695033 rajaiunnikrishnan nair@gmail.com

Prof. Ramachandran, Puthusseri. Former Professor & Dean University of Kerala, (Puthusseri, Sreerangom Lane Thiruvananthapuram- 695010).

Dr. Ramakrishnan, J. Deputy Librarian, Regional Medical Library, TN Dr. MGR Medical Library Guindy, Chennai. 600032, dhanaram@yahoo.com

Dr. Ramesh Babu, B. Professor, Dept. of Library & Information Science, University of Madras, Chennai. beeraka52@ yahoo.com

Dr. Ramesha. Reader, Dept. of Library & Information Science, Bangalore University, Bangalore. 560056 bramesha@ rediffmail.com

Ramina, M. Professional Assistant, Cochin University of Science & Technology, Cochin. raminanikesh@gmail.com

Dr. Reena, K. K. Library & Information Officer, DOEACC Center Calicut NIT Campus, P.O. Kozhikode, Kerala- 673601.

Dr. Satija, M. P. Professor, Dept of Library & Information Science Guru Nanak Dev University, Amritsar.143005, Punjab. satija_mp@gmail.com

Dr. Singh, K.P. Senior Lecturer, Department of Library & Information Science, University of Delhi, Delhi. 110007. singhkp_1972@yahoo.co.in

Soman, V.S. Midhula. Librarian, Kerala Institute of Medical Sciences (KIMS), Thiruvananthapuram, midhulasoman86 @gmail.com

Dr. Somanathan Nair, K. P. Head, Dept. of Library & Information Science, Mahatma Gandhi University, Kottayam. 686560 somanathan_kp@yahoo.com

Dr. Sudhier, K. G. Assistant Professor, Dept. of Library & Information Science, University of Kerala, Thiruvananthapuram. 695034, kgsudhier@gmail.com

Swain, Dillip K. Assistant Librarian, KIIT University, Bhubaneswar, Orissa, swaindk_69@yahoo.co.in

Dr. Swaroop Rani, B. S. Associate Professor, Dept. of Library & Information Science, Sc. Bishop Heber College, Trichy. sinishree_b@yahoo.co.in

Varghese, M. Lecturer (Sel. Gr.), Dept. of Library & Information Science, University of Kerala, Thiruvananthapuram. 695034. emvarghese@teacher.com

Dr. Vijayakumar, A. Librarian, D. B. College, Sasthamcotta. Kollam. dbc_vijay@yahoo.co.in

Dr. Vijayakumar, K. P. Reader & Hon. Director, Centre for Information Literacy Studies, DLIS, University of Kerala Thiruvananthapuram. 695 034, kpvijayakumar@teacher. com

Vimal Kumar, V. Assistant Librarian, Asian School of Business Technopark, Thiruvananthapuram. 695581, vimal0212@ gmail.com

Index

Author Index

Anas, K 153
Aswath, Lalitha 81

Balaraman, S 519
Baradol, A K 189, 512

Chakrabarthy, Susmitha 197
Chandrakumar, V 411
Chaukimath, Puttaraj A 253
Chitra, S 213
Chudamani, K S 107, 363

Geetha, V 31
Gopakumar, V 189
Gopikuttan, A 489

Harinarayana, N S 409
Hima, P R 489

Jalaja, V 227
Jalajakumari, C 179
Johnson, Sofiya 135

Kabir,S Humayoon xi, 339, 507
Kalra, H P S 379
Kaula, P N 511
Khan, Khaiser Muneebulla 95
Koganuramath, Muttayya M 253
Koneru, Indira 161
Koovakkai, Dineshan 385
Kumbar, Mallinath 179

Leelakrishnan, P 516
Lone, Fayaz Ahamed 273

Manjula, K 363
Mohanakumar, T 39
Musthafa, Mohammed 143

Nagarathna, H C 107
Nair, Achutsankar S 1
Nair, K P Somanathan 69, 517
Natarajan, M 123
Nikesh, N 397
Noushadali, P M 143

Panda, KC 291
Parameswaran, M 443
Prasad, K N 471
Prasad, N N 409

Radhakrishnan, N 135
Rajani, R 339
Ramachandran, Puthusseri 521
Ramakrishnan, J 317
Ramesh Babu, B 317
Ramesha 57
Ramina, M 397
Reena, K K 69

Satija, M P 455
Singh, K P 455
Singh, Khushpreet 245
Soman, V S Midhula 301
Sudhier, K G xi, 351,507
Swain, Dillip K 291
Swaroop Rani, B S 31

Talawar, V G vii

Varghese, M 301
Vijayakumar, A 227
Vijayakumar, K P 13
Vimal Kumar, V 213

Keyword Index

AACR-2 414
Academic library services 81
Acquisition section 16
Adobe e-book reader 108
Adobe Photoshop 139
Alexandria 1
American National Standards Institute (ANSI) 443
American Standard Code for Information Interchange (ASCII) 192, 197, 198, 200, 248
Anglo American Cataloguing Rules 412
Animated Narrative Vignette (ANV) 139
ANOVA 43, 50, 51, 73
APPM 416
Artificial intelligence (AI) 102, 126
Arts and science colleges 31
Ask-a-service 307
Association of College and Research Libraries (ACRL) 168
ATM Technology 261

Bibliographic Information Exchange 449
Bibliographic Standards 443
Bibliometric analysis 339
BioMed Central 200, 202
Bit Torrent 139
Blog 143, 250
Boolean Searching 275
British Museum 6
British National Institute (BSI) 443
BSO 468
Budapest Open Access Initiative (BOAI) 192, 197, 198, 200
Bulletin board 156
Bureau of Indian Standards (BIS) 443

CAD 141
CD-ROM search 26
Center for Bioinformatics 5
Chat Reference 307
Chicago Style Manual 444
Checkout books 108
Chi-squre test 36, 37, 73
CILIP 163
Circulation 19
Classification 2, 455, 456, 457, 458, 459, 462, 469
Clay tablets 1
Cochin University of Science and Technology (CUSAT) 1, 508, 514, 519
Coefficient of correlation 75
Cognition 40
Collaborative reference 309
College libraries 39
Common Communication Format (CCF) 443, 448
Common Wealth of Learning 154
Computer conferencing 104
Computer literacy 182
Concept mapping 97
Content Management System (CMS) 107
Copyright 471, 473, 474
Corporate memory 97
Critical reviews 24
Cross tables 43
CSIR 92
Current Awareness Service (CAS) 24
Cybrarians 82

D Space 195
D Space Archives 206
Data gathering 86
Data mining 97, 102, 126
Data warehousing 102, 126
DBMS 102
Democracy 2

Depository collection 28
Descriptive statistics 43
Dewey Decimal Classification System (DDC) 2
Digital 254
Information culture 253, 271
Library initiative 107
Literacy 183
Object Identifier (DOI) 435
Reference service 302, 301
Rights Management Technology 108
Scriptorium 414, 417, 427
Digitisation 2
DNA 9
DOAJ 202
Documentation section 24
Dublin Core 414, 436

E- Portfolio 129
Books 107, 108
Commerce 107
Learning Nordic study 136
Mail 103, 25
Resources 109
Thesis and Dissertation (ETD) 147
Zine 147
EAMMS 414, 417
Ebrary 111
Educational re-designing 136
Electronic Copyright Management System (ECMS) 484
Database 146
Journals 245, 246, 247
Publishing 102, 143, 144, 145, 146, 148, 149
Resources 291, 292
Empowering 37 168
Encarta Online Dictionary 144
Euclid 6
European Conference on Educational Research 136
Expert systems 102, 105
Explicit knowledge 96, 99, 125
Extranet 102, 107

F-test 43, 50, 51,52
Face book 139, 148,388
Faculty Improvement Programme (FIP) 27
Field Searching 283
File Transfer Protocol (FTP) 250
Flickr 139
Friendster 139
Full-text searches 108

Genus- Specius Relation 460
Geometry 6
Google Search 111, 137, 285
Gopher 250
Groupware 102

H-index 369
Half life 349
Hepatitis 319
Hi5 390
Higher education 135
Hitchikr 139
Human resources 39, 40
Hyper linking 86
Hyper Text Markup Language (HTML) 146, 415
Hypertext systems 103

IASLIC 510
IATLIS 510
ICAR 92
ICMR 92
ICT 62, 69, 81, 92, 99, 135, 136, 137, 138, 139, 140, 141, 162, 163
IEEE Journals 146
IFLA 483
ILA 510
Image format 248
Implicit knowledge 99
Independent variables 48, 74
Indexing periodicals 25

Indian Institute of Science (IISc) 107, 351, 357,359
Indian manuscripts 411
Indian National Science Academy (INSA) 149
INDIMARC 448
Infonet service 26
Information economics 97
Information Fatigue Syndrome (IFS) 165
Information Literacy (IL) 137, 180
Information portals 259, 260
Information systems 64
Information Technology (IT) 9, 25
Instant messaging (IM) 139
Institutional Repository 189, 190, 192, 193
Integrated Library Management Softwares (ILMS) 109
Intellectual Property Right (IPR) 471
International Serial Data System (ISDS) 451
Internet 102, 126
Internet literacy 182
Internet search 25
Intranet 86, 87, 89, 90, 102, 107, 126
Invisible web search tools 285
ISBD 443, 444, 445
ISBN 450, 449
ISO-2709 443, 449
ISSN 451
iTunes 147

Job involvement 31, 32,34,35, 36,37
Job satisfaction 39, 40, 45,49,50,51, 54,55
Joint stoke company 6
JULIET 205

Kannur University 14, 15
KEEP toolkit 129
Kerala Agricultural University 7,15, 21, 24
Kerala Index 25
Kerala studies section 27
Kerala University Library 6
Knowledge Classification 464
  Creation 85
  Engineer 97
  Management (KM) 83, 84, 87,88, 9295, 96, 97, 98, 99, 101, 102, 104, 105, 123, 124, 125, 126, 127, 128, 130,131
  Management tools 81, 90, 91, 123, 125, 126, 127, 128,
  Managers 85
  Mapping 97
  Organisation 86
  Presentation 97
  Professionals 85
  Sharing 86
  Synthesis 86

LAN 25
Learning Management System (LMS) 174
Librarianship 95
Library and Information Science (LIS) 95
  Periodicals 489
Library Classification 465
  Fine 6
  Literacy 182
  Professionals 69
  Websites 109
LIBSYS 109
LimeWire 139
Listserv 250
Live chats 139

Machine Readable Catalogue (MARC) 412, 413
Maharaja Swathi Thirunal 5
Mahatma Gandhi University 7
MARC 414, 417

Mean scores 48, 49, 50, 51, 52
Meta-computing applications 107
Metadata 411
Standards 411, 414, 433, 435
Term Thesaurus 441
Metasearch engines 284
MetCafe 139
Metcalfe's law 148
MLA Style Manual 443
Morpheus 139
MS Access 86
MS Excel 86, 87
MS Word 86, 87, 248
Multimedia 107, 108
Multipurpose Internet Mail Extension (MIME) 415
MySpace 139, 387

NAAC 68
National Institute of Interdisciplinary Research in Science and Technology (NIIST) 185
National Institute of Technology 15, 206
National University of Advanced Legal Studies (NUALS) 14
Nested searching 276
Network literacy 183
NISCAIR 149, 451

Occupational Stress (OS) 69, 71,73, 74, 75
Online counseling 156
Online search 25
Online social networks 385, 386
OPAC 127
Open Access (OA) 189
Archiving 194
Journals 199
Publishing 193
Open Citation Project 206
Open e-book reader 108
Open Society Institute 197, 200, 201
Open Software Foundation 197
OpenDOAR 205
OSILIP 72

Pearson's Product Moment Coefficient of Correlation 73
Persistent Uniform Resource Locator (PURL) 435
Personal portals 127
Phrase searching 276
PloS 199
Podcast 137, 176
Podcatchers 147
Portable Document Format (PDF) 248
Product-based approach 60
Proximity Searching 276
Public library society 6
Public tagging 2
PubMed Central 205
Push and pull technologies 102

Quality 58, 69
Improvement 57, 64
Information Service 67
Management strategies 66
Management System (QMS) 57, 61
Work Life (QWL) 69, 70, 71, 73, 7475, 76
Queen Victoria 9
QWLSLP 72

Re-print collection 25
Reader-centric libraries 2
Ready reference 22
Reference Database 146
Queries 22
Section 22
Service 22
Video 309
Referral services 65
Resource Description Framework (RDF) 415
RFID 263

ROMEO 205
RSS feeds 139

Scheffe test 43, 52, 73
SciDevNet 205
Scientometrics 317, 367
SCONUL 166, 167, 168
Search engines 283
  Strategy 274
  Techniques 275
  Tools 283
Selective Dissemination of Information (SDI) 24
Self-archiving 199
Semi-demographic 32
Senate House Campus 9
Seven Pillars Model of Information Literacy 167
Shared screen editing 104
SHERPA 204
Simple random sampling 32
Skyrock 390
Smart Boards 139
Social networks 386
  Tools 137, 138, 139, 143
SPARC 194, 202
Sree Chithira Tirunal Institute of Medical Sciences and Technology 15
Sree Sankara University of Sanskrit 14
Sri Chithira Thirunal Balarama Varma 14
Standard Generalised Markup Language (SGML) 249, 146
State-of-the-art report 24
Statistical Package for Social Science (SPSS) 43
Stratified sampling 42
Subject directories 284
Supernet 9

Tacit knowledge 86, 96, 99, 125
Technology experts 84
Technical processing 18
Teleconferencing 156
Text Encoding Initiative 414, 419, 427
Text-based search 2
Thesauri 109
Total Quality Management (TQM) 57, 60, 61
Transcendent approach 59
Travancore University Library 3
Trend reports 24
Truncation 283
Twitter 143, 148

UKMARC 447, 448
Uniform Resource Locator(URL) 435
UNIMARC 447, 448
Union catalogue 28
UNISIST/ PGI 451
Universal Bibliographic Control 189
University of Calicut 15
University of Kerala 14
University of Madras 14
User satisfaction 65
User study 182
USMARC 447, 448

Video conferencing 139, 156
Virtual book shelf 108
Virtual social networks 139

Web 2.0 127, 143
Web 2.0 tools 176
Web 3.0 143
Web browsers 109
  Content management 107, 108
  Forms 306
  Portals 107
  Publishing 107
  Search tips 288

Searching 273
OPAC 109
Zine 147
Wikipedia 144
Wikis 138
Winamp 147
Windows NT 139
WIPO 483
World Cat 111
World Wide Web (WWW) 250

Yahoo 137
Yellow pages 127
YouTube 1, 139

Z-test 43, 48, 49, 50
Zoto 139
Zune 147